GRAFFITI IN ANTIQUITY

The graffiti that survive from the ancient world of the Mediterranean offer us an extraordinary insight into the everyday life – both public and private – of the time. Whether cut, painted, inked or traced in charcoal, graffiti were used to address topics as diverse as religion, magic, myth, politics, sport, commerce and sexuality.

Graffiti in Antiquity examines 3,000 years of history, drawing chiefly on sources from Egyptian, Greek and Roman cultures. The men and women of these cultures – both free and enslaved – used graffiti to comment on their own lives and to champion, satirize and protest against issues of the day.

The sources are carefully presented within their specific historical, cultural and archaeological contexts, but the purpose of the study is to explore how these sources can construct a broader picture of social identity and interaction. *Graffiti in Antiquity* offers readers a new way of understanding the lives of ordinary people in the ancient world.

Peter Keegan is Senior Lecturer in Roman History at Macquarie University, Sydney. He is author of *Gender, Social Identity, and Cultural Practices in Private Latin Inscriptions.*

GRAFFITI IN ANTIQUITY

Peter Keegan

LONDON AND NEW YORK

First published 2014
by Routledge
2 Park Square, Milton Park, Abingdon, Oxon OX14 4RN

and by Routledge
711 Third Avenue, New York, NY 10017

Routledge is an imprint of the Taylor & Francis Group, an informa business

© 2014 Peter Keegan

The right of Peter Keegan to be identified as the author of this title has been asserted in accordance with sections 77 and 78 of the Copyright, Designs and Patents Act 1988.
All rights reserved. No part of this book may be reprinted or reproduced or utilised in any form or by any electronic, mechanical, or other means, now known or hereafter invented, including photocopying and recording, or in any information storage or retrieval system, without permission in writing from the publishers.

Trademark notice: Product or corporate names may be trademarks or registered trademarks, and are used only for identification and explanation without intent to infringe.

British Library Cataloguing in Publication Data
A catalogue record for this book is available from the British Library

Library of Congress Cataloguing in Publication Data
A catalog record for this title has been applied for

ISBN: 978-1-84465-607-3 (hbk)

Typeset in Warnock Pro and Myriad Pro by Kate Williams, Swansea

CONTENTS

Abbreviations	vii
Acknowledgements	ix
Preface	xi
Introduction: Modern approaches to ancient graffiti	1

I. TECHNIQUES

1. Methods, types, contexts	16

II. TRADITIONS

2. History	27
3. Literature	46
4. Art and architecture	67

III. BELIEFS

5. Religion	86
6. Magic	114
7. Mythology	139

IV. LIFESTYLES

8. Politics	158
9. Sport	184
10. Commerce	218
11. Sexuality	243

CONTENTS

Conclusion	276
Appendix: Where to find ancient graffiti	289
Notes	299
Ancient references	315
Bibliography	319
Index	327

ABBREVIATIONS

AE	*L'Année Epigraphique: revue des publications épigraphiques relatives a l'antiquité romaine.* 1888–. Paris: Presses Universitaires de France.
CEG	Hansen, P. A. (ed.). 1983–9. *Carmina Epigraphica Graeca*, 2 vols. Berlin: De Gruyter.
CIG	Boeckh, A., J. Franz, E. Curtius & A. Kirchhoff (eds). 1828–77. *Corpus Inscriptionum Graecarum*, 4 vols. Berlin: Subsidia Epigraphica.
CIL	*Corpus Inscriptionum Latinarum: Consilio et Auctoritate Academiae Litterarum Regiae Borussicae Editum.* 1863–1974. Berlin: Berlin-Brandenburg Academy of Sciences and Humanities.
CLE	Buecheler, F. 1897–1926. *Carmina Latina Epigraphica.* Leipzig: Teubner.
Graf. Pal.	Solin, H. & M. Itkonen-Kaila. 1966. *Graffiti del Palatino I: Paedagogium.* Helsinki: Akateeminen Kirjakauppa.
IG	*Inscriptiones Graecae.* 1903–. Berlin: Berlin-Brandenburg Academy of Sciences and Humanities.
ILS	Dessau, H. 1892–1916. *Inscriptiones Latinae Selectae*, 3 vols. Berlin: Berolini.
LSJ⁹	Liddell, H. G., R. Scott & H. S. Jones (eds) 1996. *Greek–English Lexicon*, 9th edn. Oxford: Oxford University Press.
NSc	*Notizie degli scavi di antichità.* 1884–1929. Rome: Accademia nazionale dei Lincei.
PGM	Preisendanz, K. A. Henrichs. 1974. *Papyri Graecae Magicae: Die Griechischen Zauberpapyri*, 2 vols. Stuttgart: Teubner.
PIR²	Petersen, L. & W. Eck (eds) 2006. *Prosopographia Imperii Romani*, 2nd edn. Berlin: De Gruyter.
RIB	Collingwood, R. G. & R. P. Wright 1965. *The Roman Inscriptions of Britain.* Oxford: Clarendon Press.
SEG	*Supplementum Epigraphicum Graecum.* 1923–. Leiden: Brill.
Uley	Tomlin, R. S. O. 1993. "The Inscribed Lead Tablets". In A. Woodward & P. Leach (eds), *The Uley Shrines: Excavation of a Ritual Complex on West Hill, Uley, Gloucestershire, 1977–79*, 113–26. London: English Heritage.

ACKNOWLEDGEMENTS

The purpose of this volume is to give a general introduction to the non-official mark-making practices of the ancient world – graffiti in antiquity – in their physical and cultural setting. It covers the period from the invention of recorded human communication (prehistory) to the end of the post-classical period (late antiquity). This survey is built upon a socio-historical narrative, for which a broadly chronological structure and a particular focus on the major cultural entities of the Mediterranean (Egypt, Greece, Rome) seemed appropriate – especially given the sheer length of the period described and the scale of the changes in question. I hope, however, that the manner in which I have written, and my choice and presentation of illustrations, have resulted in a broadly integrated and balanced picture in which thematic interpretation is at least as prominent as historical description.

For the same reason – the length and variety of the period and the diversity of ancient cultures covered – my sole authorship may at first suggest that elements of the volume's range will lack that sense of immediacy that comes from direct acquaintance with the latest research. However, on two counts I hope that this is not true. First, while I have tried constantly to write for a mythical general reader, I have indicated areas of specialist controversy and made my position clear. Second, my own research interests – ancient epigraphic practices across antiquity; theoretical perspectives on ancient literary and sub-literary discourse; sexuality, gender and body history in pre-modern societies – should mean that this book is not biased in favour of the familiar (or at least not as much as you might expect), but rather of the peripheral periods and cultural facets of antiquity.

I have learned much from this study of ancient graffiti about the many thought-worlds that existed in our past, and also acknowledge with pleasure the collaboration of the editorial team at Acumen Publishing in the UK, especially Tristan Palmer, whose suggestions have much influenced the design of the book, and Katharine Green, whose advice in relation to the choice

ix

ACKNOWLEDGEMENTS

and presentation of illustrations was gratefully received. Scholars, too, have helped me, directly or otherwise, in a variety of ways, notably Jennifer Baird, Rebecca Benefiel, John Bodel, Angelos Chaniotis, Sandra Joshel, Martin Langner, Ray Laurence, Kristina Milner, Henrik Mouritsen, Claire Taylor, Antonio Varone, Andrew Wallace-Hadrill and many others who may not always have been aware of the purpose of the enquiries addressed to them by an author who has, in the course of writing, become more sharply aware how little he himself knows.

Thanks to a wonderful collocation of private generosity and institutional support – the inaugural Macquarie University/British School at Rome (Bill and Janet) Gale Scholarship (2005–6), a Macquarie University Research Fellowship (2005–8), and a Macquarie University Early Career Grant (2010–11) – I have been privileged to study the epigraphic culture of the ancient Mediterranean world *in situ* or through access to material and documentary collections belonging to some of the great museums and research institutions of the modern age. Without these invaluable contributions, and not forgetting the invaluable expertise and insight of my colleagues in the Department of Ancient History at Macquarie University – whose knowledge and understanding of official and non-official mark-making practices range across the welter of conceptual frontiers encompassed in this volume – *Graffiti in Antiquity* would not possess an iota of the geographical, historical and socio-cultural richness that I hope you will find as exciting and stimulating to explore as I have to describe and evaluate.

Peter Keegan
Sydney, Australia

PREFACE

Giving praise to [the god] Amun, kissing the ground before the lord of the gods on his festival, (on) the first month of Shomu, when he appears on the day of ferrying over to the valley of [the pharaoh] Nebhepetre [Montuhotep]. (Written) by the *wab*-priest of Amun, Neferabed.[1]   (*c.*1973–1795 BCE)

Mantiklos dedicated me out of a tithe to the Far-Shooter with the silver bow. May you, Phoebus, give (him) a pleasing return gift.
(*CEG* 326, *c.*700–675 BCE)

Indeed, in the time of the proscriptions, the following words appeared on [the emperor Augustus'] statue: "My father dealt in silver, I deal in Corinthian." (Suetonius, *Augustus* 70.2; 41–40 BCE)

When [the emperor] Trajan ... had drawn near ... where the barbarians were encamped, a large mushroom was brought to him on which was written in Latin characters a message to the effect that the [Dacian tribe called] Buri and other allies advised Trajan to turn back.   (Cassius Dio, *Roman History* 68.8.1; 101 CE)

The renowned English playwright William Shakespeare tells us – through the voice of one of his most famous literary creations, Macbeth – that life is "a tale told by an idiot, full of sound and fury signifying nothing".[2] Life in the ancient Mediterranean – the world of antiquity comprising the context for the present study – was as far removed from this conception of human existence as the character of Macbeth from historical reality. The words and images produced in ancient times – for our purposes, the period stretching from the third millennium BCE to the sixth century CE – possessed a variety of meanings, expressed a spectrum of emotional and intellectual

xi

PREFACE

understanding, and displayed a repertoire of forms and functions beyond the narrative.

The focus of this book is on one of the most visible (then) but least studied (now) methods of communicating thoughts and feelings in antiquity, graffiti – specifically, any idea displayed in informal contexts, written or drawn on static or portable surfaces by and for people living in urban and rural spaces of the ancient world. The survival into the modern age of non-official texts and images cut, scratched, painted, inked or otherwise marked on durable materials like clay, stone and metal – and even more ephemeral physical fabrics like wood, cloth, papyrus and other organic substances – is a remarkable gift, privileging the modern historian of ancient societies with access to a perspective that is often outside the traditional worldview of other extant literary, documentary and material sources.

Graffiti are the reason why, for example, we are able to see through the eyes (and feel something of the excitement) of one of the lesser religious functionaries of New Kingdom Egypt – the *wab*-priest, Neferabad – as he looked down from high above the temple of the pharaoh Montuhotep II, watching the sacred image of the Theban god Amun transported in a festival barque from the temple precinct of Karnak to a shrine on the western bank of the river Nile. It is only because of a non-official marking that we can understand how it was that a certain Mantiklos, living in archaic Greek Thebes, recited (for the first time outside its normal expression in epic literature) the recognized formula of mutual gift-giving – "I give to you so you give to me" – between mortal and god (in this case, Apollo), inscribed on the thigh of a bronze *Kouros* (statue of a male youth).

The ancients themselves recognized the importance of graffiti as a source of information about the world in which they lived. Writing in the early imperial period under Roman rule, the historical biographer Suetonius records a message scratched on a statue of the first Roman emperor, Augustus, by a disgruntled citizen. The author of this acerbic observation drew a telling comparison between the manner in which his father earned his living – the commercial sale of silverware – and Augustus' source of wealth – causing men to be entered in the lists of proscribed citizens (persons identified as enemies of the state) because of his fondness for (their) Corinthian vases. Another Roman historian, writing in the later third century CE – Cassius Dio – reports an encounter between the emperor Trajan and the Buri (a Dacian tribe at war with Rome) which reflects precisely how widespread had become the habit of inscribing messages on *any* surface – in this instance, a mushroom of all things.

THE SHAPE OF WHAT FOLLOWS

Taking the extraordinary repository of non-official writing and drawing as a starting point, *Graffiti in Antiquity* proposes to contextualize these precious messages from the past as both textual and material artefacts, as the domain of the social historian, literary critic and archaeologist. By looking at the margins of socio-cultural discourse in specific times and places in relation to historical and socio-linguistic analysis of under-examined verbal and non-verbal sources of evidence, this book aims to:

- establish the spatial and temporal parameters encompassing the limits of antiquity and the contexts within which non-official inscriptions made their mark (Introduction);
- provide an entry-point into arguments about the uses of literacy and cultural practices in the ancient world (Part I: Techniques);
- show how the study of graffiti allows us to test current theories about ancient cultural traditions in comparative socio-historical terms (Part II: Traditions);
- examine a series of contextualized studies of patterns of human activity offering evidence for interdependent discussion of related cultural phenomena and data (Part III: Beliefs); and
- explore how men and women represented perceptions of political, social and economic power circulating in the ancient world (Part IV: Lifestyles).

Ancient graffiti comprise a great variety of types. Differing in form and content, they divide into four main categories: (1) texts; (2) drawings and geometrical figures; (3) numbers and dates; and (4) simple series of down strokes. The quantitative breakdown of these types immediately demonstrates the significance of studying this material. More than a quarter of the total comprises non-textual graffiti. Given the modern emphasis on written communications, this may seem surprising. Editors have often dismissed such graffiti as less historically important. However, they *must* be considered as vital elements in the corpus, reflecting similar social practices to those producing textual graffiti. Thus, the primary historical value of studying ancient graffiti lies as much in the fact that collectively they represent a very specific cultural practice as in the insights they may provide into the minds and thoughts of individual men and women. It is natural, then, to ask both how ancient graffiti use contemporary modes of writing and drawing (their use of language, metre, style and visual representation) and how they are embedded in their particular physical environment (civic buildings, domestic residences, public spaces, natural settings) and socio-cultural contexts (i.e. the values, attitudes, beliefs and assumptions that influence the ways people in the ancient Mediterranean world use language, images and signs) (Chapter 1).

Once we are more familiar with the cultural practices which produced graffiti, then it will be possible to explore how these practices expressed traditions integral to our understanding of life and the communication of ideas in antiquity – history, literature, art and architecture.

PREFACE

Some people see history as the study of the past, but it is more about why and how the past has meaning in the present. Reflecting on the processes of change, and the activities and experiences of people in past times and places, of how men, women and children have made their worlds and may do so in the future, enables us to see contemporary issues in a broader context. It makes sense to look at some of the events, places and people recorded in ancient graffiti, and how ancient graffitists understood and represented these historical traces in their own right and in relation to the minutiae of their daily lives, each other and themselves (Chapter 2).

Of course, regardless of one's gender, social status, civic position or economic condition, the first and foremost requirement for writing text (as opposed to drawing images) as graffiti was to be functionally literate, or to be able to copy from a "script" written by someone who was functionally or scribally literate. While literacy experts do not agree about how to define literacy, and there are many possible interpretations of the word, it is important to recognize the existence of a continuum of literacy levels (from functional to scribal) and the fact that what ultimately matters is the ability to grasp the meaning(s) of a text in a specific context (often in relation to a picture or symbol) and develop critical judgment.[3] It will be important, therefore, to explore the ways in which graffiti reflect this broad spectrum of ancient literacy − literary quotations; popular aphorisms; religious dedications; word games; market inventories; alphabets; and so on − and how graffiti reveal different uses of literacy in varying times and places (Chapter 3).

Like the informal textual messages marked into the urban and rural fabric of antiquity, graffiti drawings are common throughout antiquity − preserved from prehistoric times to the end of the post-classical world. Interestingly, ancient graffitists, as well as being well-travelled and prolific, seem to have some respect for ancient art and architecture. They generally avoided defacing hieroglyphic reliefs, wall paintings, mosaics and most graffiti is found on columns and walls. Examining the relationship between graffiti, art and architecture in the ancient world, and evaluating the epigraphic evidence for artistic and architectural depictions will reveal important components of ancient graffiti to which little attention has been previously devoted (Chapter 4).

Building on this overview of traditions that were key to communicating ideas about self and society in antiquity, there is good reason to test the usefulness of graffiti as a transmitter of such ideas. In this regard, exploring how non-official messages reflect one of humanity's most ancient and enduring concepts − the notion of a level of existence beyond the perceived; that is, a supernatural realm outside ordinary human experience − makes sense. To this end, although there was in the past − as today − a blurring of boundaries in relation to how this idea could be expressed, it seems appropriate to consider three particular categories of belief and practice pertaining to the supernatural − religion, magic and mythology.

xiv

PREFACE

Though many persons in antiquity remained close to their place of birth for much of their lives, inhabitants of the ancient world *could* travel wherever they wanted and almost always met the gods they knew. Prayer and sacrifice, libations, processions and votive gifts were the elements of cult that made up the impressive festivals of ancient cities or were performed, alone or in combination, by individuals on their own behalf. Altar, temple and image were markers of space where cult took place. These ritual and architectural forms were almost ubiquitous elements of religion – and all who lived in the ancient world could recognize them and understand their basic message. Graffiti preserving references to, and images of, religions of the ancient Mediterranean world – Egyptian, Assyrian and Babylonian; Phoenician and Carthaginian; Jewish, Greek, Etruscan and Roman – reveal how those who participated in this experience communicated their beliefs and shared their understanding of a world other than their own (Chapter 5).

Magic, one of the by-products – or possibly a forerunner – of this religious experience, is something that today's world has consigned to the world of fantasy literature, popular entertainment, and belief systems like feng shui, shamanism and Wicca. In stark contrast to this modern view, men and women in the ancient world often turned to magic to achieve personal goals. Magical rites were seen as a route for direct access to the gods, for material gains as well as spiritual satisfaction. From the sixth century BCE to late antiquity, literary, documentary and material evidence confirms a pervasive belief in the efficacy of magic. Exploring testimony in ancient graffiti for magical beliefs and practices – Egyptian necromancy, Greek spells and Roman curses – touches on a facet of everyday social belief and cultural practice removed from the consensus worldview of the present age (Chapter 6).

A common facet of *all* perspectives on life as human beings – ancient *and* modern – understand it, mythology is a vital cultural narrative. People tell myths of themselves in order to communicate key ideas about their own culture. By means of myths, people explore and explain creation and composition of the natural world and the divine world, their own origins as an identifiable group, and the features of their everyday lives and social interactions, especially the occasions of conflict (within the family, in the city, between nations) and of uncertainty (death and the afterlife). Determining the extent to which ancient graffiti act as a fundamental mode of communication in the discourse of myth-making and myth-telling should illuminate further still what the ancients actually believed about themselves (Chapter 7).

Leaving the world of supernatural belief, it will be important for us to ground our perceptions of ancient knowledge and understanding in the historical world of human action and social relationships. Although there is a plethora of topics offering potential for insight into the *real* world of antiquity, our attention should turn toward those facets of ancient society which best reflect moments when men and women expended the greatest energy across time and space. In this regard, four areas take precedence, all in one

xv

PREFACE

way or another expressions of humanity's competitive nature, and in consequence profoundly represented in the residue of ancient graffiti: politics, sport, commerce and sexuality.

Scholars for many years have studied closely how government in the ancient world was conducted, how governmental decisions were arrived at, and what forms accompanying ideology took. While politics today may seem the dusty domain of lawmakers and pundits, in the classical era virtually no aspect of life was beyond its reach. Political life was not limited to acts of a legislature, magistrates and the courts but routinely included the activities of social clubs, the patronage system, and expression through literature, art and architecture. Exploring references in literature to the use and contents of political graffiti in public contexts – and thereby the ways in which graffiti record informal individual and group responses to the formalized processes and institutional arrangements of political power in the ancient world – will articulate the multiple layers of the ancient political landscape (Chapter 8).

Like politics, the history of sport in the ancient world can be traced from prehistoric to post-classical times: the ancient Near East; Classical and Hellenistic Greece; the Roman Empire; and Silk Road cultures. Archery, athletics, ball games, board games, combat sports, chariot racing, beast fights, gladiators, rowing, swimming – sport in its many forms find expression in ancient graffiti. Outlining the competitions, games and recreations recorded in informal comments and drawings will help to address issues that constitute an integral part of sport across continents and cultures: class, conflict, eroticism, gender, professionalism, violence (Chapter 9).

In the same way that much of the modern world is built on a foundation (however unstable) of exchange in commodities and currencies, commercial activity in antiquity was one of the means by which various peoples have at different times undertaken to supply their needs. In the urban context, if we allow the sort of vigour to the ancient economy that Tenney Frank or Rostovtzeff or the school of Wilhelmina Jashemski always argued for, then it is worth asking not what proportion of the population were using graffiti, but for what purposes they did so.[4] With this in mind, it will repay our attention to examine how graffiti reveal images of vigorous economic systems in cities of the ancient world (Chapter 10).

Perhaps most familiar to a modern audience, graffiti have the common reputation of dealing overwhelmingly with sexual and scatalogical topics. The graffiti of ancient times seem to be rich in obscenities, sexual insults and lewd solicitations. But the literary sources reveal that people in antiquity understood and represented affective, reproductive and socio-cultural acts and relationships differently from men and women today. Placing graffiti with sexual themes firmly in their original contexts, then, should provide an opportunity for closer analysis of these ideas and images and offer insight into the unfamiliar territories of ancient sexuality and categories of gender (Chapter 11).

xvi

All in all, the time is right to bring the study of ancient graffiti and their context together. This book will take epigraphic research on ancient history and culture in a direction that encourages a broader view of the evidence. Looking at graffiti from a representative social context will demonstrate the cultural significance that men and women placed in "the desire to fix their place within history, society, and the cosmos".[5] By showing how men and women in the ancient world used graffiti to define their personal and collective identities, this book will introduce a new way of reading socio-cultural relationships among people living in the ancient world. By addressing questions about ancient culture through a study of graffiti, it will provide an exciting thematic study of how men and women represented their social identity in the ancient world.

INTRODUCTION

MODERN APPROACHES TO ANCIENT GRAFFITI

Graffiti is a form of communication that is both personal and free of the everyday social restraints that normally prevent people from giving uninhibited reign to their thoughts. As such, these sometimes crude inscriptions offer some intriguing insights into the people who author them and into the society in which these people belong.   (A. J. Peden, *The Graffiti of Pharaonic Egypt*)[1]

Figure I.1 Graffito of Pyrrhus (*CIL* IV.1852), inscribed on a wall panel from the Basilica at Pompeii, Italy (Archaeological Museum of Naples/MAN 18.4684).

GRAFFITI IN ANTIQUITY

Gl.1   "Farewell, Chius, my companion. I, Pyrrhus, am desolate since
I heard you were dead. And so, farewell."   (*CIL* IV.1852)

Pyrrhus scratched this message on one of the plastered and painted brick walls inside the Basilica at Pompeii (Figure I.1). The Basilica was an important public place of legal and commercial business in ancient times, and Pompeii was a large coastal town in the region of Campania in southern Italy. Pyrrhus' emotional valediction to his partner or colleague (Latin *conlega*) is one of almost 200 graffiti inscribed in the Basilica that survived the volcanic eruption which destroyed Roman Pompeii in 79 CE.

Pyrrhus is the Latinized version of the Greek name Pyrros, which means "flame-coloured" or "red"; and Chius is the Latinized version of the Greek name Chios, which is also the name of a Greek island. Without doubt, we are dealing here with two men of Greek heritage, one at least with a degree of education that supported not only writing in the Latin language but composing (or copying) the second and third lines of his farewell in the form of a *senarius*, a distinctively Roman prosody type comprising six metrical feet.[2] Here, we can also address the question of how to access and understand the emotions of a culture other than our own (both in geo-social space and historical time). Lexical equivalences, such as dictionaries provide, offer only the crudest aid: to know (say) that *moleste fero* can be glossed in English either as "I take it ill" (i.e. "it annoys me") or "I lament", depending on context, only highlights the disjunction between how modern English speakers divide up their emotional universe and how ancient Latin speakers did. In *this* context, it is fascinating to note that another Basilica graffito refers to Pyrrhus' deceased companion in decidedly different terms:

Gl.2   "Chios, I hope that your piles rub again so that they burn
more than they burned (before)."   (*CIL* IV.1820)

The composer/inscriber of this excoriating indictment uses the Greek form of the name Chius (Greek Chios) (Figure I.2). The medical condition to which the graffito refers is recognizably a type of haemorrhoidal disease. Today, most varieties of this anorectal disorder will respond to conservative measures as long as the patient complies with the prescribed regimen. In the ancient world, however, it is more than likely that acute complications could well have resulted in management by cauterization, ligation or surgical excision – or, if untreated, especially in the case of persons outside the elite social classes, death. Pyrrhus' plaintive leave-taking may well reflect the end-point of Chius' oesophageal discomfort.

Individually and/or as a paired cluster, we can focus on the dynamic processes each of these graffiti displays. Specifically, we can identify and decipher the "script" – that is, a specific sequence of perception, evaluation and response – through which the data of life are processed; or, in other words,

Figure I.2 Graffito to Chios (*CIL* IV.1820), inscribed on a wall panel from the Basilica at Pompeii, Italy (Archaeological Museum of Naples/MAN 5.4696).

a set of moves and motives that a person who expresses a fact, an idea or a feeling enacts in inscribed form. The approach is cognitive rather than lexical, asking what each graffito *does*, and how it *works* socially and psychologically, rather than simply asking what it *is* (a question that would tend to yield lexical equivalents). Thus, in the first message, we share one man's reaction to the death of another – limited, naturally, due to the nature of the medium; but an expression of grief that, while reflecting the manner in which lamentation was codified, lies outside the usual range of acceptable ancient genres and contexts within which such a feeling would be produced (literary texts, funerary inscriptions). So, too, the graffito indicates two fundamental facets of the ancient world in the first century CE: that persons of mixed origins live together in settlements designated as strictly mono-cultural – in this case, persons of Greek descent living in a Roman colony; and that persons of indeterminate (but probably sub-elite) social status could read and write at a level of education beyond the purely functional. Usefully, the second message confirms the cultural diversity and literacy of this particular urban community, albeit an undefined proportion of Pompeii at this point in our study. We can also begin to scratch the surface of the threats to physical well-being, if not mortality, faced by persons living at this time; not to mention the manner in which ordinary people, if pressed or predisposed, resort to insult – something we might expect of the graffitist in the modern world, but more often than not in the rhetorical arenas of public discourse in any age.

Moreover, in relation to the issue of reception, we should always ask ourselves to whom these messages were written and what we might learn about the process of consumption of meaning, and the nature of the consumers, in ancient contexts.

These graffiti comprise only two of the hundreds of thousands of informal texts and images spanning millennia of historical time – a patchwork of fragmentary conversations in a variety of languages spread across the Mediterranean world that survives into the present. Cut, painted, inked or traced in charcoal on the durable surfaces of antiquity (stone, brick, clay), graffiti like Pyrrhus' lament and the incivility levelled at Chios open our modern eyes to a layer of lived experience in the ancient world unavailable from other approaches to history – the world of ordinary men and women, speaking their minds and their hearts, as best they can, to their family, their friends and their contemporaries.

This book hopes to provide a gateway to reading these thoughts and feelings as cultural documents of their time and introduce ways in which these graffiti help us to understand broader social and cultural patterns in the ancient world.

WHAT ARE GRAFFITI?

The modern age views graffiti in a very particular way: as "writings or drawings scribbled, scratched, or sprayed illicitly on a wall or other surface in a public place".[3] This definition encompasses a broad range of texts – single letters, letter combinations, single words, phrases, sentences – and graphic representations – pictures, diagrams, identifying artist(s) signatures ("tags", "throw-ups", "stencils", "stickers"). It also outlines the variety of stylistic choices available to the graffitist – writing or drawing hastily and carelessly on something, scoring or marking something with a sharp or pointed object, applying a coloured liquid preparation to something – and on what the writing or drawing will be seen – a man-made vertical or other exterior layer of some object or structure. What is interesting about this definition, and which marks our twenty-first-century perspective on graffiti as different from premodern conceptions, is the fact that the act of writing or drawing comprising the production of graffiti is seen as illegal and confined to public spaces.

Evidence from the ancient world demonstrates that the legal status of graffiti depended, as it does today, on the permission of the owner of the property on which persons write or draw. According to recent legislation in countries which have enacted laws against graffiti,[4] it is an offence to mark property in such a way that it can be seen by the public unless the owner has given permission. What the surviving evidence tells us is that the degree to which permission to mark property was granted in the ancient world was clearly determined on a broader definition of consent. Graffiti in antiquity can be found on every available public surface: not only the walls of civic buildings (arenas, baths, brothels, latrines, shops, temples, theatres, tombs) and associated infrastructure (altars, arches, gates, towers, water fountains), but columns, doorposts, floors, lintels and stepping stones. Moreover, writing and drawing are not confined to the substantial remains of the ancient urban fabric. Graffiti are marked on objects made from clay – pots, tiles, bricks, votive offerings, and the discarded fragments of the preparation and production process (*ostraca*) – as well as metal (lamps, mirrors, shields, strigils, swords, knives), stone (burial urns, mosaic *tesserae*, sarcophagi, sling-bullets, statues) and, if we are lucky enough to find it preserved, wood (agricultural and gardening tools, furniture, writing frames).

This plethora of extant evidence confirms the fact that writing and drawing graffiti in antiquity are widespread, commonplace and highly visible acts. We know that property owners in the ancient world *did* express their desire to restrict or debar the marking of certain surfaces. There are a variety of inscribed messages on particular public or private buildings refusing consent to do so. For example, at Pompeii, in the years prior to the eruption of 79 CE, we find the following prohibition:

GI.3   "If someone writes something here, may he rot and his name
        be pronounced no more."   (*CIL* IV.7521)

Similarly at Rome, on the cusp of the second century CE, the refurbisher of a portico of a temple (located just outside the Porta Portuensis and dedicated to Sol) asks the general public to refrain from marking the sun-god's sacred building:

GI.4   "Gaius Iulius Anicetus, at the behest of Sol, requests that no
        one inscribe or scribble on the walls or *triclia* [covered, porti-
        coed chamber]."   (*CIL* VI.52)

However, the fact that writing and drawing on a multitude of surfaces survived in so many contexts and in such numbers across the ancient Mediterranean indicates strongly that these warnings did not constitute a widespread ban on graffiti.

In the legal codes of modern nations, moreover, marking or defacing property with texts or images is a more serious offence if the graffiti is likely to offend a reasonable person. Political comments are an exception to this if they, too, are reasonable. It is clear that the criteria by which persons in antiquity took offence or judged political commentary as fair and sensible were at variance from today's conventions. A statistically significant proportion of ancient graffiti were marked on surfaces in contexts that would not, at least according to contemporary understanding, be regarded as public: namely, the interiors of structures on privately owned land or segregated work spaces.[5] Of the almost 11,000 graffiti surviving at Pompeii, at least half were made on the exterior *and* interior surfaces of occupied or used areas like houses, shops, bakeries, brothels, fulleries and gladiator quarters. In many instances, these graffiti were marked in full view of the persons who lived and worked in or visited these spaces. This tolerance for graffiti in domestic or occupational contexts is not confined to urban Pompeii. Whether the exterior or interior surfaces of temples and tombs in pharaonic and Graeco-Roman Egypt; the cave dedications, cemetery *ostraca*, domestic buildings, pottery, religious architecture and sanctuaries in archaic Pithekousai, classical Athens, Roman Ephesus and late antique Aphrodisias; or the fortifications, houses, sanctuaries and shops of Seleucid, Parthian and Roman Dura-Europos – tolerance towards graffiti in public *and* private contexts is a pan-Mediterranean phenomenon across all chronological, geo-political and socio-cultural boundaries in antiquity.

In many countries today it is an offence to carry tools that could be used to mark graffiti in particular areas without a good reason, such as needing to carry these tools because of work. This includes spray paint, gouging tool or even a marker pen. This legal prohibition did not apply in the ancient world, primarily since persons in antiquity produced and consumed meaning in very different ways to the means and methods of communicating ideas today. First, it is important to recognize the relationship between words and images in ancient urban, suburban and regional built environments.[6] Second, it is difficult – some would have it, impossible – to know how much men and women contributed to or took meaning from the epigraphic landscape.[7] What we can say is that, if we define literacy as the ability to figure out and transmit a short message at a "functional" or "craft" rather than "scribal" level, questions of practice, availability and transfer across households become less significant in the production of reliable quantitative interpretations. In fact, the impressively large numbers of male and female slave and ex-slave epitaphs[8] – as well as the significant phenomena of political pamphleteering, electoral posters (*programmata*), advertising posters and, of special interest to this study, graffiti – tend to support the contention that levels of male and female literacy are not as much of an issue *sui generis* (as purely quantitative ratios).

For instance, a major source of information relating to the study of graffiti in the Roman cities of the Vesuvian region[9] comprises 10,916 Latin (some Greek, and a very few Oscan) texts incised with a metal tool, painted or written on walls, pottery, metal objects and waxed tablets. Of these, there are 3,348 texts painted on the exterior walls of buildings; 4,664 inscriptions (including alphabets and stonemasons' marks) on exterior or interior spatial surfaces, incised with a metal tool (*stylus* or *graphium*) or written with ink, charcoal or chalk; and 2,242 items similarly incised or written on large earthenware vessels conforming to a variety of types: mainly large two-handled containers for liquids (Latin *amphorae*), as well as water pots (*hydriae*), and

INTRODUCTION

jugs or pitchers (*urcei*). As these inscriptions are listed according to location by street (*CIL* IV: I) or by region, city block and doorway (*regio, insula* and *ianua*: *CIL* IV: II–III.2), the collection provides a template of the inscribing habit with which to overlay the variety of other social and cultural features associated with Pompeii specifically and the other preserved cities of Roman Campania more generally. It also confirms that modern prohibitions on carrying implements used in making graffiti were not applied in any regulated manner to persons living or working in the Vesuvian cities of Roman Italy.

Most interesting of all is the sharp divide between ancient and modern views on graffiti as representing anti-social behaviour (ASB). In legislative terms, anything that causes "harassment, alarm or distress to one or more persons not of the same household" may be considered as ASB.[10] By any measure, this is a vague definition that can include *any* unwanted activity.[11] Informed by notions of normative conduct and incivility, graffiti are understood as ASB in relation to the cumulative impact on individuals or groups of action viewed as annoying or offensive, especially if repeated and perceived as specifically targeted.[12] In sum, graffiti in modern communities are deemed to conform to the definition of ASB because of the environmental impact, the correspondence to minor criminal vandalism and, in consequence, the effect on the quality of life of those who see the practice as ASB.

In contrast, graffiti in antiquity are the result of strictly social patterns of behaviour. Almost all ancient markings were originally located outside or within spaces used or viewed by people other than those responsible for setting them up – domestic, industrial and mercantile spaces; communal latrines, purpose-built brothels, theatrical and arena enclosures; commercial, legal and political meeting places; individual, family or group tombs in town cemeteries, burial plots that were part of larger family estates beside major roads, communal tombs set aside for household *familia* and members of burial collectives; cult sanctuaries, neighbourhood shrines, state temples. This means that the persons writing and drawing on fixed or portable surfaces in these locations – remember: finished objects made of various materials or the discarded remnants of the production process form a significant sub-group of the surviving record of graffiti – intended that others would read messages set up as part of a broader social context. At the very least, they would have been aware of the likelihood of some kind of viewership for their texts or graphic images, and so composed (or, far less likely, commissioned) their markings accordingly. Aware of the contexts within which these graffiti were placed, modern historians of ancient society are well situated to interpret the cultural conventions *and* differences expressed through private epigraphic practices. The idea that the practice of marking graffiti on civic or private property constitutes ASB must be viewed as a distinctively modern perspective.

Unlike considerable critical study in non-classical scholarship on the importance of graffiti,[13] few serious attempts have been made to grasp the

7

nature of graffiti and show ways in which it may help us to understand broader social and cultural patterns. Most serious engagement with non-literary material – that is, material that does not belong in the traditional canons of ancient classical and post-classical literature – has been carried out by philologists interested in the development of local forms of language. The cause of this relative neglect probably lies in the particular approach to the material, which prevailed for most of the last century. A strong feature of this movement was the particular emphasis on surviving traces of the ancient world as human documents; in other words, on places where modern people could connect directly with their ancient ancestors. However, while extensive archaeological reconstructions represent a significant step forward in the preservation of finds and structures and constitute an invaluable legacy, these advances were not matched in the field of epigraphy, and no more so than in the sub-field of informal inscriptions like graffiti. Here the idea of capturing the essence of life in the ancient world and connecting with ancient men and women led to a largely anecdotal approach which often descended into pure speculation.

Consequently, interpretative treatment of graffiti as a source for knowledge about social and cultural information exists only in brief, or in isolation in general studies of ancient literacy or surveys of ancient epigraphic practice.[14] Take, for example, graffiti found in the Vesuvian cities of Pompeii and Herculaneum. Some scholars who have studied graffiti as a source for popular culture in Pompeii see the inscriptions as isolated texts and so do not consider the ways in which a graffito might have been responding to its immediate material environment.[15] On the other hand, archaeologists and historians, whose interests lie in the material aspects of ancient social life, often are not interested in considering literary issues like representation and reader response.[16] Aside from a collection of conference papers looking explicitly at ancient graffiti in context[17] and a recent edited volume dealing with manifestations of written space in the Latin West,[18] the *only* attempts to integrate both aspects remain a seven-page study comparing the graffiti from Herculaneum and Pompeii with a view to identifying differences in the social make-up of the two towns,[19] and an important (unpublished) study of informal inscriptions found in an elite Pompeian residence (House of Menander: I.10.4, 14–16).[20] This phenomenon applies across the ancient world.[21]

As a form of written and/or graphic communication invariably free of the usual social restraints limiting more polished artistic and literary works, the phenomenon of graffiti offers a striking opportunity to explore ancient culture through a pattern of human activity and the symbolic structures that gave that activity meaning. This chapter will provide an overview of the Mediterranean world in the pharaonic and Graeco-Roman period of antiquity (geography, chronology, cultural setting) and a clear outline of the range, number, time period and locations of ancient graffiti in that world.

INTRODUCTION

THE ANCIENT MEDITERRANEAN (3100 BCE TO 600 CE)

Already we have experienced a taste of the historical breadth this book will incorporate; perhaps it would be just as well, before entering into any further discussion, to provide an overview of the chronology and cultural diversity which makes up "the ancient world".

First, for "world", substitute "Mediterranean". While it is regrettable, a book like this, which seeks to treat so many time periods in any depth at all, is restricted in the scope of its perspective on the ancient world. Consequently, we will focus our attention on the extraordinarily rich variety of peoples and cultures that flourished around the basin of the "sea between lands", the Mediterranean. In essence, the book traces a social and historical path through the cultural centres of a predominantly Western world. This is not to say that the margins of such a sprawling megalopolitan world are not included; simply, that the book will reflect the limitations of a ten-chapter introduction to a vast topic. Nonetheless, each chapter's parameters should allow the curious and intrepid among you to expand those horizons, to seek out points of entry into the equally valid and culturally heterogeneous worlds of African, Eurasian and Oceanic prehistory and ancient history.

Second, it would have been easy to deliberately compress the boundaries of this book into a more easily digestible survey of one or two historically particular cultural groups; for instance, the so-called "classical" age of fifth- and fourth-century BCE Athens, or the similarly resonant "Augustan" age which marks the fulcrum balancing the modern chronologies of before and after the year "dot", that is, the BC and AD of a Christianized world, or the coincident BCE and CE of a secularized one (where CE is the abbreviation for "Common Era"). This would have been an easier path to follow, certainly, but not necessarily as rewarding, or revealing, as the one chosen. Given the fact that the "history" of humankind can be measured from its beginnings over three million years ago, and that for more than 99 per cent of that huge span of time the study of past material culture is our only significant source of information, it seems appropriate to begin our overview of "the ancient world" with an introduction to modern research into the technological and cultural processes comprising the practice of graffiti. Chapter 1, therefore, will give us an insight into the questions raised by archaeologists and cultural anthropologists regarding the reconstruction of the means and methods of the people responsible for the material remains of graffiti. We are clearly interested in having a clear picture of how people lived, and how they exploited their environment. But we also seek to understand why they lived that way: why they had those patterns of behaviour, and how their life-ways and material culture came to take the form they did. In other words, by explaining change through an interest in the processes of that change, the modern student of social history can move forward, formulating questions about our human past rather than simply piecing together a static jigsaw of technological, organic and environmental artefacts.

9

Figure I.3 Deir el-Medina, west bank of Nile, Upper Egypt (1551–1050 BCE) (photo by Steve F-E-Cameron, CC-BY 3.0, http://creativecommons.org/licenses/by/3.0, via Wikimedia Commons).

From the "long past" of a "world history" – extending from the pre-historic epochs (i.e. prior to the development of written communication) to the Neolithic world – we travel to the Africa of ancient Egypt, and "history" in its narrow sense, meaning the study of the past using written evidence in sympathy with the finds of archaeologists. Characterized by cycles of stability known as "kingdoms" and stages of fragmentation and chaos referred to as "intermediate periods", we will traverse the dynastic periods of archaic, Old, Middle and New Kingdom Egypt, which cover a time-span stretching from the last years of the third millennium to the late eleventh century BCE (3010–1090 BCE). Situated in a small secluded valley in the shadow of the Theban hills, one of the major sites providing evidence for the practice of graffiti (on *ostraca* bearing a wealth of sub- and non-literary marks) is Deir el-Medina (Figure I.3) – a village inhabited by the community of workmen involved in the construction and decoration of the royal tombs in both the Valley of the Kings and the Valley of the Queens. Together with their wives and families the workmen occupied the neatly constructed houses of mud brick and stone for some 450 years during Egypt's New Kingdom. It is also important to note that Egypt gradually becomes a part of the wider geo-political world of the Mediterranean from the turn of the first millennium BCE on. During this time period the Sudanese, Assyrians, Persians and then the Greeks take turns ruling Egypt. Alexander the Great's conquest toward the end of the fourth

INTRODUCTION

century BCE leaves a new dynasty – the Ptolemies – in control; until finally, Rome takes Egypt and the death of Cleopatra ends the reign of the pharaohs. Looking at examples of graffiti produced in pharaonic and later Egypt will provide fragmentary glimpses of a distinctive worldview, garnered from a representative selection of epigraphic and documentary sources across the centuries.

GI.5   "When King Psammetichos came to Elephantine this was written by those who, with Psammetichos son of Theokles, sailed and came above Kirkis, as far as the river permitted; Potasimto commanded the non-native speakers, and Amasis the Egyptians; Archon son of Amoibichos wrote us and Pelekos son of Oudamos."[22]   (*SEG* 51.2201)

At first glance, the Homeric and archaic ages of mainland European Greece – immortalized in the mythological narratives of the Trojan and Theban epic cycles – might seem far more than a sea-voyage distant (in intellectual and social terms at least) from the Afro-asiatic civilization of pharaonic Egypt. But it will be as well to keep the Egyptian standpoint on the position of graffiti and the boundaries of ephemeral discourse in mind when we encounter the Greek world of the Dark Age bards. The eighth-century BCE Bronze Age world of the Homeric poets casts an enormous shadow over the so-called "classical" Greek civilization that followed. But there is a thread of scholarship – regarded with equal fervour by philologists, ancient historians and archaeologists alike as either theoretically audacious or empirically misguided – which focusses on Greek cultural borrowings from Egypt and Levantine Asia in the second millennium BCE. To be more precise, in the thousand years from 2100 to 1100 BCE, this historiographical revision of Greek cultural heritage proposes a scheme in which there seems to have been more or less continuous Near Eastern influence on the Aegean over this period, its intensity varying considerably at different times. Even in the study of religion and art of the archaic period, the near-eastern element has recently been stressed, though this too is a controversial topic. Regardless of the continuing debate in academic circles over the tenure of this hypothesis – over its claims for Egyptian colonies in Boeotian Thebes and mainland Athens, its historicist claims for an Egyptian conquest of the Argolid and the Phoenician foundation of Thebes, and its support for ancient traditions of colonization predating the rise of Hellenic culture – the world of pre-classical Greece deserves a fresh reading with respect to observable trends in the transmission of sociocultural ideologies through marked surfaces. The oral-literate universes of epic and instructive poetry (e.g. the *Iliad* and *Odyssey* ascribed to Homer, and the *Theogony*, the *Catalogue of Women* and the *Work and Days* of his contemporary Hesiod) provide a way into the *mentalité* of this fascinating age. So, too, graffiti like those found on Thera – an island community under the

11

influence of Sparta and its Doric culture, including the fertility rituals associated with Apollo Carneios (the ram-god) to which the graffiti refer – open modern eyes to a world at once familiar and very different. Similarly, texts on the legs of the colossal statues of Ramesses II at his funerary complex at Abu Simbel, inscribed by Greek soldiers serving with the Egyptian king Psammetichos II (594–589 BCE), confirm Greek contact with Egypt during the archaic and classical periods, exemplify the manner in which Egyptian and Greek cultures exerted an influence on each other, and point out the permeability of graffiti as a means of cultural expression in the ancient world. This, of course, should not suggest that all systems of cultural exchange in antiquity corresponded to the same conceptual template; nor that the modern student of ancient graffiti should apply a standardized approach to recognizing and dealing with the product of graffiti practices.

There exists a wealth of literary, archaeological *and* epigraphic evidence which helps us to reconstruct socio-cultural images of men and women in the period spanning the end of the lyric age to the intensely studied classical age of fifth and fourth centuries BCE Greece. Encompassing the evolution of Greek society from a plethora of small self-governing communities (a pattern dictated largely by geography) to rival city-states (notably Athens, Sparta, Corinth and Thebes), and spanning coinage, colonization and classical art, architecture, literature, and philosophy (not to mention the political variations of aristocracy, tyranny and democracy), this survey of graffiti – including those written in the many dialects of the Greek language and the associated graphic images, signs and marks of Greek-speaking persons – will illuminate evidence for mainstream and non-canonical "explanations" for the positions, roles, thoughts and feelings of men and women living and working on the mainland, as well as the island communities and colonial settlements of Greek origin. Among other ideas, it will focus on such concepts as the categorization of male and female and the construction of the social identities and realities of Greek-speaking individuals and groups in the archaic and classical ages. For example, informal inscriptions, incised or painted, appear on over 3,000 pieces of pottery, lamps and miscellaneous clay found in the excavations of the Athenian *agora* – including alphabets, names, numbers, marks denoting ownership of property, commercial notations, lists and messages. Evidence such as this should help to clarify a number of issues which continue to render the study of classical Greece absorbing and problematic: domestic and public space; marriage and citizenship; homoerotic attachment and heterosexist interpretation; reproduction and the continuity of generations.

This intensive look at classical Greece brings us to the period known as the Hellenistic Age, that which extended between Alexander the Great and the victory of Octavian (later Augustus) at Actium, conventionally from around 336 BCE to (a little after) 31 BCE. During this time, Greek culture was dominant throughout the Mediterranean, thus the name Hellenistic, which is derived from the Greek "Hellas" which means Greece. After Alexander's death, his

INTRODUCTION

empire was split up into smaller kingdoms, created by people known as the Diadochoi – the Successors of Alexander. The major kingdoms were the Ptolemies in Egypt, the Seleucids in Syria and the Antigonids in Macedonia. Numerous battles were fought to establish these kingdoms, but they eventually lasted for several hundred years. During the Hellenistic Age, many advances in philosophy, science, literature and art were made. As the Romans began to gain power throughout the Mediterranean, the kingdoms of the Hellenistic Age began to fall, and eventually were swallowed by the Roman Empire.

Gl.6   "[Someone] from Argilios dedicates [this vessel]."

As we have already noted in relation to Egypt, late twentieth- and early twenty-first-century scholarship has reacted against the simple picture of this period which derives in large part from the nineteenth-century historian J. G. Droysen's definition of *Hellenismus*.[23] Arguably, in the Droysenian and post-Droysen view of the ancient world, the diffusion of Greek culture through the Mediterranean basin in the post-Alexander period neglects non-Greek (especially Semitic) contributions to Greek achievements. Keeping this recurrent re-examination of cultural "givens" in mind, graffiti allow modern eyes to look at the ways in which highly traditional Greek forms of discourse – from philosophical and medical treatises to the sub-literary and visual media of the times – were used to negotiate a relationship with non-Greek culture in the Hellenistic period. Evidence from locations as diverse as Punta Planka (Croatia), Jebel Khalid (northern Syria), Maresha (Israel), Berenike and El-Kanais (Egypt), or Argilos (Greece) speak to the widespread dissemination of many and various cultural ideas across the Hellenistic Mediterranean world. Graffiti such as these display the retention or reinvention of local cultural forms, going right through the history of post-classical Europe, Asia Minor and Africa, impacting enormously on our understanding and interpretation of indigenous and Graeco-Macedonian views.

Gl.7   "Hieron, a Puteolan [inhabitant of Puteoli, a city on the Campanian coast, north of the Bay of Naples], painted [this]."

Gl.8   "Victor was here with Attine."

Gl.9   "Africanus is dying, a rustic boy writes. You learn who grieves for Africanus."

Gl.10   "Alexamenos worships god (or, Alexamenos, worship (your) god)."

At Rome, too, the acceptance or rejection of cultural Hellenism remained an issue, even after the possibility of Greek or Macedonian military or

13

GRAFFITI IN ANTIQUITY

Figure I.4 Alexamenos graffito, Palatine *paedagogium*, Rome (second/third century CE).

political victories over Rome had evaporated. To be precise, whether we speak of Archaic Rome (traditionally dated to 753 BCE), or of the early Republic, the "conflict of the orders" and the conquest of Italy (up until the mid-third century BCE), or of the wars of conquest against the Carthaginians and the Macedonians (concluding with the brutal destruction of Corinth in 146 BCE), or of the social conflict and political breakdown of the last years of the Republic (the so-called "Roman Revolution" of the last century BCE), or of the foundation of imperial rule from Augustus to the Antonines (31 BCE to 191 CE), or of the High Empire and the rise of Christianity from Septimius Severus to Constantine (193–337 CE), or of the division of the Graeco-Roman world into East and West, of the replacement of the imperial office by the kings of Italy, and the rise of the Byzantine world since the foundation of Constantinople (which takes us to the rule of Justinian in the mid-sixth century CE) – no matter what period of Rome's "thousand-year reign" we choose to interrogate, the evidence available to us offers a picture of a vigorous independent community developing its own hellenizing culture. Whether graffiti from Ostia, Pompeii, or from the city of Rome itself, modern viewers can discern ordinary persons taking a full and direct part in the circulation of ideas that transformed the ancient Mediterranean. The spread of this cultural *koine* through contacts, exchange and competition among Greek, orientalizing and native Italic social units could not help but disseminate the kinds of discourse already considered.

The remainder of this book will seek to identify key areas of intersection regarding ancient graffiti among the manifold dynasties of the pre-classical Egyptian world and the later Mediterranean-wide diffusion of verbal and non-verbal discourse across the Graeco-Roman cultural continuum.

CHAPTER 1

METHODS, TYPES, CONTEXTS

GRAFFITI: CULTURAL MARKS AND ARTEFACTS

One of the enduring images many Sydneysiders associate with the 1999 New Years' Eve millennium celebration is that of the word "Eternity" appearing in large illuminated letters on the Harbour Bridge. This word – also seen by over four billion people worldwide at the end of the opening ceremony of the Sydney Olympic Games in September of 2000 – represents a significant instance of how a single practitioner of *graffiti* writing can "speak" to a vast number of the simple and the sophisticated alike about a variety of historical, social and cultural issues.

The graffitist in question, Arthur Stace, chalked "Eternity" almost half a million times in handsome copperplate cursive writing on footpaths across greater metropolitan Sydney over a period of thirty-five years from 1932 to 1967. For most of this time, Stace's identity as author of the unvarying graffito remained unknown, unlike the widespread notoriety of his textual remainder. Though a ward of the state – a barely literate petty criminal and alcoholic whose sisters were compelled to prostitution and whose brothers died as derelicts – Stace was responsible for inscribing a message at once inspiring, cryptic and confounding to men and women of differing social identities across the developing urban landscape of twentieth-century Sydney.

In relation to the study of ancient graffiti (whether writing and/or drawing), what is important to note about the example of "Eternity" and the person responsible for its inscription is how historical, cultural and sociological contexts can combine to inform an audience – at once historically contemporary with *and* distant from the writer and the writing – about the individual, society and a plethora of perspectives on the wider world. In this sense, graffiti can be described and evaluated as both textual and figurative remainders *and* cultural artefacts. When studying antiquity, the usefulness of graffiti as part of the urban fabric or the inhabited countryside of the ancient world cannot be undervalued.

COMMUNICATION IN PREHISTORY AND ANTIQUITY

To situate the phenomenon of graffiti in antiquity and its relationship to the expression in the ancient world of information, ideas and feelings, it is important to consider briefly the history of pre-modern communication. This history dates back to those periods of time prior to the invention of writing and comprises significant changes in communication technologies (media and appropriate inscription tools) evolving in tandem with shifts in political and economic systems, and, by extension, systems of power.[1] As we understand it, communication can range from very subtle processes of exchange (e.g. auditory means, such as speaking or singing, and non-verbal, physical means, such as body language, sign language, paralanguage, touch or eye contact) to full conversations and mass communication. Human communication was revolutionized with speech, evolving from earlier pre-linguistic systems used by our primate ancestors, and either genetically coded or learned through social interaction.[2] Symbols were developed about 30,000 years ago, and writing about 7,000 years ago.[3] On a much shorter scale, of course, there have been major developments in the field of telecommunication in the past few centuries.[4]

While the origins of speech are unknown and subject to considerable debate and speculation, spoken discourse eventually resulted in the creation of new forms of communications, improving both the range at which people could communicate and the longevity of the information. All of those inventions were based on the key idea of the symbol: i.e. a conventional representation of a concept. Underlying the conceptual basis of communication are the processes involved in the transmission of information, thoughts or emotions, governed by three levels of semiotic rules:

- syntactic (formal properties of signs and symbols);
- pragmatic (concerned with the relations between signs/expressions and their users); and
- semantic (study of relationships between signs and symbols and what they represent).

To this list of visual sign processes we can add the sensory level of sound: specifically, the grapho-phonemic dimension, relating to heard sounds, both individual letters and letter combinations.[5]

Given this elementary semiosis (or study of signs and sign processes) of the levels of discourse, it should be clear that communication is a kind of social interaction where at least two interacting agents share a common set of signs and a common set of semiotic rules. In a simplistic model, information is sent from a sender or encoder to a receiver or decoder. In a slightly more complex form, feedback links a sender to a receiver. This requires that a symbolic activity takes place, sometimes (but not always) through the medium of a language. Communication development is the development of processes enabling one to understand what others say – or sign, or write, or see, or hear, or otherwise sense – to translate sounds and symbols into meaning and to learn the syntax of the language.[6]

The oldest known symbols created for the purpose of communication through time are cave paintings, a form of rock art, dating to the Upper Paleolithic or Late Stone Age (40,000–10,000 years ago). Just as the small child first learns to draw before it masters more complex forms of communication, so humanity's first attempts at passing information through time took the form of paintings. The oldest known cave paintings to date can be found in the Chauvet Cave, located in France and dating to around 30,000 BCE.[7]

As the original art is approximately 31,000 years old – probably Aurignacian[8] – we cannot automatically discern the nature of the images painted on the walls of this cave. That pre-modern images are not susceptible to easy interpretation will not cause surprise; however, the potential for alternative explanations should alert us to the differences in the perspectives and purposes of those composing and marking their ideas on available surfaces. For instance, consider a painting in the Chauvet Cave of a group of horses – a calmly walking horse; a second in an aggressive posture with its ears flattened backwards; a third in a relaxed posture, perhaps sleeping, with its ears up and oriented forward; a fourth, alert, its open mouth suggesting vocalization or snorting, possibly a pony. Given that it would be unusual for individual horses in proximity to display such behavioural diversity, the painting may not represent a realistic picture of the animals. Instead of a scene painted in perspective, the image of four horses may be some kind of aetiological study, that is, the representation of a single horse expressing different behaviours – showing, from left to right, calmness, aggression, sleep and grazing – or life-phases – various stages in the chronological development of the animal.[9]

This is precisely why the study of pre-modern graffiti – in this instance, prehistoric parietal art – requires some understanding of historical context and, where possible, patterns of social behaviour and cultural practice. In the case of the Chauvet horses, our modern logic of representation and our aesthetic sensibility may determine that we construe the painted images as a perspective drawing of a single moment in time. Why, though, should we assume that the original artist applied the convention of perspective and attempted to approximate a representation of visual depth to a painting on a two-dimensional surface? The development of a system of representation incorporating perspective cannot be identified until the fifth century BCE, many millennia after the Chauvet paintings.[10] Similarly, why should we adopt twenty-first-century judgements of images like these? In other words, the

18

overarching system of shared norms for viewing and drawing meaning from known images should not dictate that the viewer interpret the images of horses as part of a composite representation of factual or imagined reality fixed in time. As we have seen, this may not be the case.

Another assumption – integral to the study of pre-modern graffiti – which prehistoric markings reveal as contested is the significance of position. According to contemporary norms of representation and reception, the twenty-first-century viewer would usually prioritize as intended for consideration images and texts marked at eye level on the vertical surfaces of structures or objects. Markings in other locations – higher from or lower to the ground (on walls, columns, doors, or other vertical architectural or geological surfaces) or to the rim or base of portable objects; on the roof or floor of natural or human-made interior or exterior spaces – may be regarded as less important in a representational or aesthetic sense, as intended for a smaller viewership, or even as first attempts or drafts not meant for wider consumption.

How, then, should we understand what may be the oldest lifelike drawings of human faces, carved on the *floor* of a cave at La Marche in the Lussac-les-Chateaux area of France? The Le Marche cave system was discovered in 1937 by French scientist Leon Pencard. During subsequent excavation (1937–42), researchers found over 1,500 limestone slabs carefully placed on the floor, into which images were etched, including lions, bears, antelope, horses and 155 lifelike human figures. Even more suggestive is a series of pits which appears to have been arranged in the shape of the Pleiades star cluster – cosmic marks which have been identified in drawings on the walls of many Neolithic caves in several European locations.[11] Based on this reading of the surviving evidence, there is reason to suggest that Cro-Magnon people created the first calendar approximately 15,000 years ago.[12] In other words, it is possible that, contrary to modern expectations, prehistoric graffiti artists used the floor of the La Marche cave (and other cave systems, unknowingly erased during excavation) as the surface of choice for marking ideas more sophisticated that those painted on its walls. The fact that the images of animals found on the walls of the Chauvet and Lascaux caves (30,000 and 17,000 BCE respectively) are far more fully formed than those of human beings (in the main, depicted as stick figures) requires precisely the adjustment of perception that should define analysis and interpretation of *all* pre-modern graffiti.[13]

The next development in the history of marked surfaces relates to the practice of engraving images by striking the rock with a tool (percussion) or scratching or scraping the surface (abrasion). Also known as petroglyphs (Greek *petros*, "stone"; *petra*, "rock"; *glyphē*, "carving"), these images constitute graphic representations of physical objects (pictograms) or ideas (ideograms). Twenty thousand years elapse before cave paintings are joined by the first petroglyphs, which can be dated to around 10,000 BCE.[14] Like other forms of graffiti, these engraved images are a global phenomenon, found on rock surfaces on every inhabited continent.[15] For example, no one knows exactly how many individual petroglyphs litter the surfaces of stones on the islands of the Dampier archipelago in Western Australia, but estimates suggest more than one million.[16]

Far more recently, the first carvings on the monumental rock surfaces of a historical site in western Utah called Newspaper Rock – in the Navajo language, *Tse' Hone*, or "rock that tells a story" – were made around 2,000 years ago. A large panel of sandstone displaying the engraved images is liberally decorated with figures which can be variously interpreted as human, animal, astronomical and historical. Left by people from the local Archaic, Anasazi, Fremont, Navajo, Anglo and Pueblo cultures, these petroglyphs provide a glimpse into the life and world of the people who farmed the Puerco River Valley 650–2,000 years ago.[17]

Whether their messages were painted or engraved, the prehistoric artists and inscribers clearly intended their markings to convey meaning to a viewing audience. More often than not, the viewing community may have been confined intentionally to a known group of individuals cognizant of the significance adhering to the images. Occasionally, particular cave paintings or petroglyph clusters will have communicated equally effectively to individuals belonging to groups outside the targeted community, even if the modes of communication and cultural practices were different.

It is possible that people of these times used other forms of communication, often for mnemonic purposes – specially arranged stones, symbols carved in wood or earth, quipu (the enigmatic Inca knotted strings encoding data and instructions), tattoos (used to signify important life-way transitions, such as coming of age, tribal associations, social affiliations, and cultural information, including criminal conviction and slavery) – but little other than the most durable carved stones has survived to modern times and we can only speculate about their existence based on our observation of still existing "hunter–gatherer" cultures such as those of Africa or Oceania.

In response to the demands of communication across a broad range of cultural requisites – customs, laws, institutions, interpersonal relations – certain pre-modern societies developed a variety of familiar painted and engraved symbols into the component elements of logographic writing systems. Eventually, ancient Sumerian, Egyptian and Chinese civilizations began to use such representational, pictorial drawings as a basis for the wedge-shaped cuneiform script (Latin *cuneus*, "wedge") and, to some extent, hieroglyphic writing (Egyptian: *medu-netjer*, "god's words"; Greek: *hieroglyphikos*, "sacred carving"), which uses drawings also as phonetic letters (spelling a word as it sounds) or determinatives (a symbol to which no sound is attached, but which provides a clue to the meaning of a word) (Figure 1.1).

The intrinsic connection between drawing and writing is further shown by linguistics. In late third-millennium/early second-millennium Egypt and eighth-century BCE Greece, the concepts and words for drawing and writing were one and the same (Egyptian: *s-sh*, Greek: *graphein*).[18] This linguistic

METHODS, TYPES, CONTEXTS

Figure 1.1 Reproduction of Egyptian hieroglyphics in cursive script on papyrus: "Weighing of the Heart" spell (Book of Coming Forth by Day), Tomb of Ani (Dynasty XVIII), Thebes, Egypt (Papyrus Collection and Papyrus Museum, Vienna; photo by Manfred Werner (Tsui), CC BY-SA 3.0, http://creativecommons.org/licenses/by-sa/3.0, via Wikimedia Commons).

association integrated sketching, painting and scratching marks or figures, or otherwise inscribing shapes of one kind or another. Here we are finally in touch with the chronological period that forms the basis for our study of graffiti in antiquity.

GRAFFITI IN THE CONTEXT OF THE ANCIENT MEDITERRANEAN

As we have already seen, writing and drawing graffiti were not exclusively the prerogative of the inhabitants of a single cultural group or historical period in antiquity. The practice was a significant and widespread feature of the ancient Mediterranean world across an extensive historical period. Modern scholarship catalogues instances of graffiti in such diverse places and times as the villages, cities, tombs and temples of pharaonic, Ptolemaic and Roman Egypt, the meeting places of archaic, classical, Hellenistic and Roman Athens, the desert caves and cliff-faces of ancient Palestine and the Sinai, and the walls of buildings on the Palatine in imperial Rome.[19]

The subject matter of graffiti is just as wide-ranging as that found in any of these places or times. It can be as prosaic as partial or complete alphabetic

21

lists (referred to as *abecedaria*) or numerical notations (either acrophonic[20] or alphabetic); these may be written from left to right, in reverse, upside down, or in some combination of one or more of these. There can be messages, urging some action or accompanying and/or explaining a variety of different objects, persons or ideas; or sometimes inventories, listing items, amounts or other things in some kind of relation to each other. Names can be identified, often with an associated expression of admiration or distaste. Occasionally, graffiti notations can be identified as relating to commercial or taxation interests (the capacity, weight or contents of containers; the date of material produced, sold and/or delivered; probable prices); sometimes, the purpose is less clear.

Often, graffiti can be explicitly sexual in nature. For example, two erotic love-making scenes near a sixteen-line graffito[21] may be found penned along the walls of a small cave high above the funerary temple of the eighteenth Dynasty queen Hatshepsut at Deir el-Bahri. It is possible that these scenes depict Hatshepsut and her court favourite, the High Steward Senenmut, "engaged in a manner of sexual activity which is interpreted as a visual form of political satire by the artists".[22] In another historical context entirely, a variety of sexual insults has been identified in the Athenian *agora*, including texts using verbs to describe sexual proficiency and relationships, pledges of love, names of men admired or insulted in other texts, and even the picture and pet name of the male sexual organ.[23]

Either in isolation or as part of a larger figurative and textual representation, graffiti-drawings – as opposed to sketched or painted texts or images (Italian: *dipinti*) – are found in all regions of the ancient Mediterranean. The phenomenon of drawing graffiti was common throughout antiquity. These can be pictures depicting ornaments and symbols, heads or busts, single figures (especially gladiators), single animals, ships and copied monuments or objects. Mythological and historical portrayals are rare; similarly uncommon are descriptions of occupation, craft skills and erotic scenes, apart from numerous *phalli*.[24]

Something of this extraordinary variety of ancient graffiti will be explored in the chapters which follow.

PREREQUISITES AND ASSUMED KNOWLEDGE FOR WRITING AND DRAWING GRAFFITI IN ANTIQUITY

Regardless of one's gender, social status, civic position or economic condition, the first and foremost requirement for writing text as graffiti was to be functionally literate, or to be able to copy from a "script" written by someone who was functionally or scribally literate.

It is important to note the degree of uncertainty permeating modern discussions of literacy and orality in the ancient world. Literacy experts do not

METHODS, TYPES, CONTEXTS

agree about how to define literacy, and there are many possible interpretations of the word. Specialists in the field agree that the number of people who could read and write in antiquity is hard to determine.[25] Even so, given the lack of concrete information as to men and women's ability and propensity to read and write in pre-modern societies, many commentators on this problem[26] adopt an asymmetrical approach to questions of probability. Similarly, definitions of literacy differ depending on whether literacy is conceived of as narrow or broad, absolute or relative, fixed or dynamic, singular or multiple, autonomous or contextually specific. For the purposes of this book, literacy in antiquity relates to the predominant language spoken and written by local populations (indigenous or migrant). In this context, *functional* literacy is determined by immediate, practical needs, and *scribal* literacy refers to the reading and writing of literary works.[27]

The next requirement was to possess the necessary tools and materials for writing text and/or drawing images. These included:

- a cutting device of some kind: either the *stylus* or the *graphium*,[28] or some other kind of incising tool made from reed, stone, ivory or metal;
- a painting applicator: the *penicillus* or painter's brush; and
- an available assortment of pigments for painting, charcoal for writing, or inks for tracing.

That each of these marking implements and aids to communication possesses a lengthy record of use confirms formal and informal writing and drawing on static and portable surfaces as a phenomenon displaying remarkable continuity across historical time and socio-cultural space. As we have seen, cave art was a widespread practice in prehistoric France, but also in Africa, the Americas, Asia, Spain and Oceania. Discovered in caves and rock shelters and covering thirty millennia (between about 40,000 and 10,000 years ago), the content of this parietal art in the main represents a congeries of animals – plant forms are rare and human figures are relatively few. While the purpose of this extraordinary achievement is difficult to ascertain, the methods used to create the images are identifiable and develop over time. The pigments in cave paintings were made from dirt or charcoal mixed with saliva or animal fat. The porous nature of the rock surfaces and the binding quality of the organic mixing agents combined to provide a perfect medium for preserving the images. Preparing the surfaces by smoothing or abrading, the artists creating the images covered large areas with their fingertips or wads of plant material, produced drawn or linear marks with sticks, and blended areas of colour with feathers. Brushes made from horsehair or the chewed tips of leaves were used to apply paint and create outlines, and blowing paint through hollow bones yielded a fine-grained distribution of pigment. Calcium carbonate, chalk, charcoal, gypsum, oxides rich in clay (e.g. haematite, limonite, malachite), were formed into natural crayon sticks or

GRAFFITI IN ANTIQUITY

ground into pigments which were then liquefied into paste using animal fat, blood, bone marrow, soluble egg protein (albumen), urine, vegetable extracts and water.

While at first sight simplistic, dark, exposed surfaces of rock such as sandstone and basalt – as opposed to the light-coloured, protected surfaces in caves – served as an effective basis for petroglyphs – abstract as well as representational human, anthropomorphic supernatural, animal and plant figures as well as designs such as spirals, circles and stars. Known as *pecking*, the petroglyph artists incised their images by striking off mineral flakes with a hard stone, sometimes creating a preliminary outline of the figure. Different pecking techniques created different styles. Incising or scratching with a sharp tool was also done. Incised designs are often more expressive and detailed than pecked designs.

By the third millennium BCE, the peoples inhabiting Babylonia, Egypt and China adapted the form of the pictographic signs comprising their complex systems of communication – more than 700 in the earliest known examples – to being written with a rectangular-ended stylus made out of a reed. Cuneiform, the most widely preserved script of the ancient Near East, and the pictographic script of Chinese Wu Di culture, were impressed on clay, scratched on metal or carved in stone. In the first millennium BCE alphabetic scripts became widespread. These were written in ink – made from burnt bones, tar, pitch or graphite – with a brush on papyrus or parchment or occasionally on broken pieces of pottery. A pictorial hieroglyphic script was used by the Hittites and their successors in the Levant and Anatolia for monumental royal inscriptions.

FINAL THOUGHTS

Whether these signs and images – and, eventually, texts of one kind or another – were intended to stand the test of time or regarded by artist and viewer alike as ephemeral observations only, it should be clear by now that the practice of writing and drawing messages comprised a trans-historical phenomenon spanning thousands of years, a broad chronological and geographical ambit and a spectrum of techniques, implements and materials. By the time we encounter the world of pre-classical and classical antiquity (1000–800 BCE and thereafter), the tools and materials used by people living in the ancient Mediterranean for marking surfaces possess a considerable history of use and reflect their indebtedness to Egyptian and Near Eastern traditions. This continuity of marking practice continues into the period when Rome ruled a good deal of the coastal Mediterranean world (31–27 BCE and thereafter). For example, evidence for communication using petroglyphs, often regarded as used exclusively by prehistoric peoples, can be found in the deserts of first-century CE Jordan; and, famously, the walls of Roman Pompeii

24

Figure 1.2 Woman holding stylus and writing tablet, man holding a scroll (known as "the baker Terentius and his wife" or "Paquius Proculus and his wife"), VII 2.6, Pompeii, Italy (Archaeological Museum of Naples/MAN 9068; http://commons.wikimedia.org/wiki/File:Terentius_Neo_e_la_Moglie.jpg, photo by Olivierw, via Wikimedia Commons).

reveal the extent to which men *and* women participated in literate exchange (Figure 1.2) and the ways in which they shared ideas with each other – methods which find expression in later times as well.

In addition to these enduring methodologies of writing and drawing, one needed to locate an appropriate incising or painting surface (e.g. a wall, a doorway, a paving stone, a tombstone, even a piece of pottery). Naturally enough, the final requirements for participating in the practice of graffiti-writing and drawing were to have the time, the interest or motivation, the ability and the opportunity to "make one's mark". The following chapters will chart the extent to which graffiti in antiquity incorporated the learned, inherited or re-invented approaches of prehistory – based on incision or the application of pigments – and the manifold purposes underpinning the marking habit.

CHAPTER 2

HISTORY

When [the emperor Nero] had aroused the hatred of all, there was no form of insult to which he was not subjected. A curl was placed on the head of his statue with the inscription in Greek: "Now there is a real contest and you must at last surrender." To the neck of another statue a sack was tied and with it the words: "I have done what I could, but you have earned the sack [in which parricides were put]." People wrote on the columns that he had stirred up even the Gauls by his singing. (Suetonius, *Nero* 45.2)

DEFINITIONS OF HISTORY

History is often shaped by the stories of kings and religious and military leaders, and much of what we know about the past derives from official sources like military records and governmental decrees. But what did the people who lived in antiquity understand by the term? Did "history" mean the same thing to someone who lived in pharaonic Egypt or classical Greece or imperial Rome as it does to us living in the twenty-first century? The short answer to the second question is "no". An answer to the first question is less straightforward. The reason is this: a person from the ancient past thought about themselves, their family and friends, their acquaintances at work and leisure, and the wider world in relation to notions of time and space very different from our own.

Egypt

If we use a modern concept of history, Egyptians – in fact, all ancient Near Eastern peoples – did not write history at all. It is clear, however, that the Egyptians were intensely interested in the origin of the universe, in their gods, in life after death, and in making and preserving records of their past as a nation. Their kings carefully recorded what may be called the facts of public history and private individuals took great pains to preserve those facts of personal history which would reflect credit upon them. According to the modern view of making history, no Egyptian "historical" text *describes* the past, *explains* a rationale, or *infers* a cause and effect. At best, events are imbued with the concept of theodicy, by which individuals are punished for not having acted favourably toward the gods.

Therefore, any analysis of historical sources in ancient Egypt faces a major problem: linear sequences of fact receive no attention. The actors, pharaohs or officials, embed their vision of the world – peaceful stability over the country across eternity[1] – within and throughout their texts. In fact, it is in the scale of time represented by eternity that ancient Egyptians placed their own events: if a particular series of facts is part of it, eternity will see the same series happen sometime in the future.

These very different conceptualizations of history and historical time may help to explain the unusual juxtaposition of texts and images discovered recently at Gebel Tjauti, a site in the region of the high desert plateau west of ancient Thebes.[2] Over one hundred written and pictorial graffiti, dating from the protodynastic period (*c*.3200–3000 BCE) to the New Kingdom (*c*.1550– 1070 BCE), have been recorded at this point along the Alamat Tal road (one of the main routes connecting pharaonic Thebes to the southern oases).[3] Near the road construction stela of the Coptite nomarch who administered this area of the Upper Egyptian desert (Tjauti, after whom the site is named; cf. Chapter 10), a section of rock bordering the road is inscribed with symbols representing the rulers of Egypt – the large falcon and cartouche of Pepy (Dynasty VI), a small but finely incised falcon of about Dynasty XI, the official inscription of the nomarch Tjauti (Dynasty IX, or later), and Middle Kingdom ink inscriptions referring to the king travelling on the Alamat Tal Road – as well as a variety of seemingly unrelated images and texts – for example, an undated depiction of a Canaanite god, Resheph, carrying a spear and shield in one hand, a large and peculiar mace in the other, surrounded by speared desert game; and an astronomical observation associated with the rising of the star Sothis, herald of the inundation of the Nile river (Dynasty XI).

Of particular interest is a scene which appears to depict the defeat of the Naqada region by Abydos at the dawn of pharaonic history (the so-called Dynasty 0). The scene comprises images and text:

G2.1   A stork lifts up a snake, followed by the hieroglyphic sign-group for "victory", and an armed man leads a bound captive on a rope. A falcon above the head of one of the figures identifies the ruler – the earliest attestation of the use of the Horus title without the *serekh* (a rectangular enclosure representing the façade of a palace, used to distinguish a royal name).

HISTORY

The juxtaposition of this tableau of a proto-dynastic military expedition – predating the famous Narmer palette by almost a hundred years – and the numerous other inscribed and inked signs, symbols and images captures perfectly the Egyptian idea of history: a continuity of existence incorporating the natural world and human action, united under the rule of the divine (gods and kings). The Gebel Tjauti graffiti trace the interventions of the Egyptian state (royal and military) in conjunction with the life of the all-encompassing desert (land and sky) – a history of the use of the Alamat Tal road *and* pharaonic rule across almost two millennia.

Greece

Not all cultures in the ancient Mediterranean subscribed to the Egyptian view of history. To the ancient Greeks, history (ἱστορία) referred to an enquiry or investigation; in particular, the knowledge arising from the discovery, collection, organization and presentation of information acquired by observation, fact-finding, analysis and review.

At first glance, of course, this may appear very similar to modern ideas about historical study. It all depends, though, on the type of writer and the categories of evidence to which we apply this definition. Herodotus, for example, living in the fifth century BCE, wrote a work called *Histories* – an "investigation" of the origins of the military conflict between the Greeks and the Persians over the period 490–479 BCE. His sources included prose writers like Hecataeus of Miletus (fl. *c*.500 BCE: *Genealogy* or *Histories* and *Circuit of the Earth*), Dionysius of Miletus (early fifth century: *Persica*), Xanthus of Lydia (*Lydiaca*), Charon of Lampsacus, Hellanicus of Lesbos (a local history of Athens, *Customs of the Barbarians, Lydian Matters, Egyptian Matters, Persian Matters*). Poetic sources include Aeschylus' *Persians* and Phrynicus' *Fall of Miletus*, Mimnermus' history of Smyrna, Xenophanes' *Foundation of Colophon*, Semonides of Amorgos' early history of the Samians, Panyassis' *Ionian History*, and Simonides' *Seabattle of Salamis, Seabattle of Artemisium* and *Battle of Plataea*. Herodotus' main sources related to his own autopsy, oral inquiry, analogous conjecture and rational analysis. In brief, Herodotus relied on oral tradition and written records, both transmitted in the main through intermediaries. These sources comprised bureaucratic data, specialist documentation or testimony, elite family tradition and religious documents or commentary. Any decision about the reliability of Herodotus as a historical source in his own right will be governed by the relative proportions of his narrative which can be categorized as chronicle, poetry, performative script, mediated or direct testimony.

The fact that various themes can be discerned in Herodotus' narrative (e.g. the instability of human fortune) suggests a conscious construction of historical materials. This should not, however, imply a preponderance of fictive invention over factual reporting. What it does require of modern readers is

29

GRAFFITI IN ANTIQUITY

an awareness of the framework within which Herodotus constructed his narrative. We should also ask ourselves if our definitions of "fiction" apply in the same way to the composition of history in the ancient world of chroniclers and logographers as to modern historical writing. Certainly the line between fact and fiction is blurred in a context in which extracts from a work in progress are performed or delivered in recitation to audiences on the Greek mainland and throughout the Greek-speaking Mediterranean world.

As you can see, Herodotus the historian is a difficult quantity to determine – unless, of course, we make very sure that we apply an appropriate definition of "history" to what Herodotus did with his narrative. Such a definition will take into account the social and cultural contexts within which Herodotus composed and communicated his version of history, the types of sources he cites and which we can infer from his chronicle of events and personalities, and the manner in which he organized the content and thematic focus of his narrative.

But what do ancient inscriptions from columns, stones, tombs, floors and mosaics tell us about the life of the common men and women of antiquity? A third-century BCE wall painting exemplifies how the ancient mind recorded the quotidian details of everyday existence – those things which the inhabitants of particular places found important or interesting or attractive. Excavated in 1982, the ruins of an early Hellenistic sanctuary in the ancient city of Nymphaeum – near the modern village of Eltigen (Geroyevskoye), 17 km south of the city of Kerch – revealed fragments of polychrome stucco with images of people, animals and ships. The original painting covered two perpendicular walls forming the inner corner of the building. One of the panels displays the representation of a large ship drawn using the so-called sgraffito technique; that is, the image was incised in the upper layer of stucco. The depiction provides numerous fascinating details:

G2.2   two rams, a meander-shaped waterline, two decks supported
by hippocampi (fantastic creatures with the upper torso of a
horse and the lower extremities a composite of marine animal
features), a stern decorated with scaly patterns and representations of the sea gods, an inscription ISIS on the bow, and
so on. Interestingly, Isis was the goddess most venerated in
Ptolemaic Egypt. To the right of the ship, there is another,
much smaller vessel, drawn in the same technique but very
schematically. Its outline is blackened.

The panel may depict a battle scene, since the rams of both vessels are directed toward each other. A preliminary drawing, incised in thin lines, is also visible above the larger ship. Interestingly, the outlines of the ships must have been incised into the yellow band of the wall panel prior to the stucco drying. We can infer from this information that the representations belonged to the general original design of the fresco.

HISTORY

Underneath the ship composition is a band displaying a floral pattern. Below this stylized design, the wall is covered with a large number of small graffiti, including:

G2.3   images of animals, horsemen, archers, buildings, signs and inscriptions, both horizontal and vertical, some of them framed. Among the inscriptions there are names of gods, dates and verses, and the name of the ruler Perisades II (ruler of the Bosporan kingdom, *c*.283–245 BCE). The most numerous drawings are those of all sorts of ships.

The location of Nymphaeum (occupying a coastal plateau on the Cimmerian Bosporus), the presence of a good harbour and fertile plains (marking the site as part of the network of Black Sea grain trade), and the purpose of the sanctuary in which the plaster with polychrome paintings was found (connected with the gods-protectors of navigation) – all this explains the content and purpose of the sgraffito fresco and accompanying graffiti. Just as the Gebel Tjauti inscriptions spoke to the Egyptian view of history, so the sanctuary graffiti of Nymphaeum illuminate the history of the site and the beliefs, preoccupations and livelihood of its inhabitants.

Thucydides was another Greek writer of history during the fifth century BCE. What we make of his work – and how it informs our understanding of graffiti-history – will depend, certainly, on whether we regard it as a unity or, like the Gebel Tjauti or Nymphaeum graffiti, as a collection of disparate items welded together at some point or points in time coterminous and later than the events described. How, in practical terms, does our interpretation of his composition – as a unity or not, comprising individual statements, extended passages, and even book-length excurses – affect our reading of graffiti? Let's take, as a test case, this excerpt from Book 1 of his *History of the Peloponnesian War*:

With reference to the speeches in this history, some were delivered before the war began, others while it was going on; some I heard myself, others I got from various quarters; it was in all cases difficult to carry them word for word in one's memory, so my habit has been to make the speakers say what was in my opinion demanded of them by the various occasions, of course adhering as closely as possible to the general sense of what they really said.
        (Thucydides, *History of the Peloponnesian War* 1.22.1)

Before considering the historiographical significance of this statement, how should we imagine Thucydides composed and integrated his many speeches into the framework of his larger narrative? Did he undertake his reconstruction of what individual historical figures said (as heard by Thucydides or

31

transmitted to him by others who had heard): at the time the speech was delivered (or passed on); when Thucydides embarked on the final composition of his narrative; at various times after delivery or transmission? How might our choice in this single instance affect our reading of the received tradition? It depends, does it not, on the extent to which Thucydides' memory permitted accurate recording of what he heard (personally or from a second party); whether or not Thucydides kept notes; the extent to which these notes formed the basis of a single period of composition or of various writing drafts and revisions? In other words, before we even begin to come to terms with what, precisely, Thucydides meant by "the general sense of what [the speakers] really said", we must, at least for argument's sake, adopt a particular position with respect to the idea of unity or not.

This, of course, applies to the next section of Book 1:

> And with reference to the narrative of events, far from permitting myself to derive it from the first source that came to hand, I did not even trust my own impressions, but it rests partly on what I saw myself, partly on what others saw for me, the accuracy of the report being always tried by the most severe and detailed tests possible. (Thucydides, *History of the Peloponnesian War* 1.22.2)

When, precisely, do we imagine Thucydides conducted his "severe and detailed tests"? At, or more correctly, soon after the time during which the events described took place; at some other time more or less removed from the events; once the collection of information relating to a particular historical period in the narrative had reached a conclusion; at various times, denoting a series of verifications and critical reviews of the information collected? Again, our response to this question will determine our perspective on the narrative more generally.

And, in a way, this is what is required of us whenever we encounter an ancient text. How, for example, would the writers of the following messages – marked on potsherds (broken pieces of used or discarded pottery) found in the Agora of Athens – see themselves, their correspondents and their actions in relation to the life of the city and its place in the history of sixth to second-century BCE Greece?

G2.4   "Thamneus, put the saw under the threshold of the garden
       gate."   (Sixth century BCE)

G2.5   "Boy, bring other new couches for Phalanthos."
                                             (Early fifth century BCE)

G2.6   "Sosineos sent a bundle to Glaukos in town."
                                              (Late fifth century BCE)

HISTORY

G2.7   "Eumelis, come as quickly as you can. Arkesimos."
(Mid-fifth century BCE)

G2.8   "Return the stamnos to Philippa's brother Philip."
(Mid-fifth century BCE)

G2.9   "A stamnos for our good brother Hieronymos from his brothers."   (Mid-second century BCE)

Graffiti like these can be found scattered throughout the urban centres of antiquity. Incised, inked or painted on potsherds – the "scrap paper" of the ancient world – the composers of such notes urge others to do something (G2.4, 5, 7, 8) or label an object for delivery to a family member, friend, neighbour or customer (G2.6, 9). In doing so, they inscribe a personal history that supplements and fleshes out the broad sweep of the official histories of the city: a patchwork of memory traces that stitches together the canonical narratives of mythical foundation, legislative reform and geopolitical conflict into the social fabric of Athens.

Herodotus and Thucydides may well have delivered parts of their work in the Agora, and possibly Sosineos, Glaukos, Eumelis, Arkesimos or Philip may have been fortunate enough to hear the historians' selected excerpts. Given the low levels of education, it is less likely that any of those writers or their correspondents (living in the fifth century or thereafter) would have read Herodotus' *Histories* or Thucydides' *History of the Peloponnesian War* (in part or full); and, knowing what we do about the gender restrictions applying to the exposure of women to the public gaze in fifth-century Athens, it is highly unlikely that Philippa will have been permitted to listen to the declamation of either historian. Nevertheless, all of the named individuals would have had a clear idea about the nature of graffiti in relation to the life of the city and its quotidian history: the daily ebb and flow of social exchange almost always overlooked in the official record but integral to the urban fabric.

Rome

Like the Greeks, Romans understood history as the composition of literature rather than the product of learned investigation. Only in the political, social and intellectual contexts of ancient Rome can we begin to fathom the nature of historical thought as expressed in the works of writers like Sallust, Livy, Tacitus, Dio and Ammianus Marcellinus. Time and time again, it is the city of Rome itself which attracts the attention of writer and reader – its legendary foundation, its tumultuous political and social upheavals, its military conquests, and its pivotal historical figures. And it is precisely at this point – the intersection of history and the urban fabric – that graffiti provides the

33

touchstone by which the specific details of life in the ancient city can be identified and compared with the wider web of history.

Livy's *Ab Urbe Condita* – "From the Foundation of the City", a title based on the work's first sentence – was widely regarded in antiquity as *the* history of Rome. Much read and widely used, Livy wrote a Roman history that extended from earliest times to his own day, tracing a series of volatile turning points that saw the transformation of a city subjugated under foreign rule (Etruscan monarchy) to the hub of a Mediterranean empire under the rule of one man (Octavian Augustus). Although only Books 1–10 and 21–45 of the original 142 books survive, these and the abridgements (*Epitomae*) and summaries (*Periochae*) of the missing volumes reflect Livy's view of history. Livy may have lacked personal experience of military and political affairs – he was born outside the social and economic circumstances of the ruling class which usually produced writers of history – but he still managed to imbue his year-by-year (annalistic) narrative with the key values of traditional Roman society: the edifying example of a strict moral code, the social function of religion and cult, the virtues of the soldier and statesman.

Graffiti provide a similar perspective on turning points in history; namely, from the social periphery of the marginalized or excluded outsider looking toward the elite Roman centre. In 91 BCE the so-called Social War between Rome and its discontented Italian allies broke out, and traces of its intensity are still visible within the walls of ancient Pompeii, where Roman bullets and ballista bolts are lodged alongside World War II shrapnel. A series of inscriptions in Oscan, painted on the stone surfaces of walls at street corners, are thought to refer in some way to military operations relating to individual urban districts, giving the location of mustering points in case of an emergency.

These scrawlings were discovered under a few layers of plaster and are known as *eituns* inscriptions, a word which may refer to "soldiers on guard duty" or "mobilization point".[4] They may record instructions to the town's defenders, telling them to:

G2.10   "Go by this route between the 12th Tower and the Salt Gate, where Maras Atrius, son of Vibius, gives instructions."

G2.11   "Go by this route between the houses of Marcus Castricius and Maras Spurius, son of Lucius, where Vibius Sexembrius, son of Lucius, gives instructions."

or to:

G2.12   "Fight where Matrius, son of Vibius, is in charge."

G2.13   "Go by this route so that the public buildings between the middle of the street and the towers to the left of the Urblana

HISTORY

> Gate. On this street, left of the Urblana Gate and the Mefira
> Tower, Lucius Popidius, son of Lucius, and Maras Purellius,
> son of Maras, give instructions."

In addition to telling the citizens of the various sections of the city where they were to mobilize in times of attack, we also learn about the original names for parts of the city (G2.10, 13) or for the owners of private houses (G2.11). The Salt Gate is the original name for the Herculaneum Gate. These notices specifically refer to the towers in the city walls, numbered I–XII in anti-clockwise sequence. Opposition to Sulla within the town appears to have been well organized (G2.12, 13).

In the aftermath of the war, Italian settlements were integrated more tightly into the civic fabric of Rome. Pompeii was refounded as a Roman colony for army veterans, its name changed to Colonia Cornelia Veneria Pompeiana, signifying its status as a settlement for veterans who had fought under Dictator Lucius Cornelius Sulla, whose divine patron was Venus. Its Oscan chief magistrate was replaced by magistrates called by Latin names, like the *duoviri*, the "two men" designated to govern town business. Latin overtook Oscan as the language of public records in stone.

Historical events were also recorded by casual scrawlers. Within the entrance of one house is:

G2.14   a picture of two men, fighting on foot; two mounted men, one
        bearing a lance, and a figure with the head of a horse, playing
        a trumpet.

The painted images and accompanying text were discovered incidentally after plaster on the W. wall of the vestibule was dislodged during excavations in the 1920s.[5] One of the men (the rider to the right, closest to the trumpet player) is named "Spartacus" in Oscan ("Spartaks"). Spartacus – a Thracian by birth who may even have once served as an auxiliary in the Roman army before being sold into slavery – led a slave revolt against Rome which was certainly the most famous and arguably the largest, originating at Capua during 73 BCE in the gladiator school of Lentulus Batiatus, and eventually encompassing southern Italy, resulting in the defeat of nine Roman armies over a period of two years.

According to the historical tradition, at one point in time during the course of the revolt Spartacus and his rebels camped nearby on the slopes of Vesuvius.[6] One householder at least may have wanted to commemorate the event. Of course, it is also possible that the wall painting records the death of Spartacus. Ancient sources report that Spartacus was killed in the heat of battle between his gladiator army and two Roman legions under the command of the generals Crassus and Lucullus. Attempting to reach Crassus, he was severely wounded, but continued to wield his spear and shield until the

Romans swarmed over him and a small contingent of bodyguards. The problem with this interpretation is that the sources also tell us that, prior to this final battle, Spartacus commanded that his horse should be brought to him, drew his sword, and stabbed the animal to show his men that there would be no further retreat – only victory or death. This does not correspond with the painted image of *two* riders on horseback, armed with round shields: from left to right, one rider pursues the other, the former ("Phil...ians", according to the text in Oscan above the painted figure) wounding the latter ("Spartaks") with a long lance. A second theory hypothesizes that the wall painting pre-dates the Spartacus slave revolt and depicts a gladiatorial spectacle in the Pompeian amphitheatre. It is known that the name Spartacus was common among Thracian slaves.[7]

Whether "reliable" literary records or fragmentary documentary or epigraphic evidence, *all* historical sources from Roman antiquity – indeed, antiquity in general – tell more than one story. The fact that a partially preserved wall painting discovered accidentally during the excavation of a small house close to the amphitheatre in ancient Pompeii *might* tell us something about the renowned leader of a slave rebellion that shook the foundations of Roman power is at once tantalizing; yet – in the way of the nature of history as Livy and his contemporaries understood it – interpretation of the surviving images and text remains ultimately inconclusive. Graffiti in antiquity, therefore, act in very similar ways to traditional historical sources derived from the ancient past. No matter what this fresco and its associated writing depicts, and whether it complicates or confirms our knowledge of historical events at this time, the marking of this residential entrance serves to enhance our appreciation of what it meant to live in first-century BCE/CE Pompeii; and, incidentally, to supplement our awareness of the way in which graffiti helped to preserve the memory of a community's history – be it of gladiators in general or a rebel leader in particular.

It is possible to discern this difference between the description of events and interpretation of the same in Tacitus, a historian writing in Latin about the first century CE in works such as *Annals* (dealing with the years 14–68 CE) and *Histories* (covering the period from the downfall of the emperor Nero to the death of Domitian, i.e. 69–96 CE). Tacitus avers in the prefaces to both works that he will strive for emotional dissociation and historical balance in his treatment of early imperial personalities and events – he states categorically that he will neither be bitter or partial (*Annals* 1.1.3; *Histories* 1.1). But he is not successful in keeping these subjective perspectives at a distance from his historical narrative. While Tacitus is aware of the difference between objective and subjective history, and is at pains to delineate his history as the former, he is ready to indulge in the latter. The saving grace of Tacitus' annalistic account of the Julio-Claudian and Flavian periods is his willingness to integrate the factual record with his self-aware, retrospective revision of past events in light of his contemporary socio-political context. The job

HISTORY

of the modern reader, of course, is at one and the same time clear-cut and problematic, dependent on how much of the past we can reconstruct from other sources.

In Book 14 of the *Annals*, after recounting the death of the emperor Nero's mother, Agrippina the Younger, in 59 CE, Tacitus explores the nature of the emperor Nero (the instigator of Agrippina's murder) and his rule by way of a series of events in the city of Rome and Italy. The epigraph at the beginning of this chapter provides evidence for non-official expressions of dissatisfaction with Nero's rule in the city of Rome. One of the events that Tacitus records relates to a tumultuous episode of civic unrest in Pompeii:

> About this time [59 CE] there was a serious fight between the inhabitants of two Roman settlements, Nuceria and Pompeii. It arose out of a trifling incident at a gladiatorial show ... During an exchange of taunts – characteristic of these disorderly country towns – abuse led to stone-throwing, and then swords were drawn. The people of Pompeii, where the show was held, came off best. Many wounded and mutilated Nucerians were taken to the capital. Many bereavements, too, were suffered by parents and children. The emperor instructed the senate to investigate the affair. The senate passed it to the consuls. When they reported back, the senate debarred Pompeii from holding any similar gathering for ten years. Illegal associations in the town were dissolved; and the sponsor of the show and his fellow-instigators of the disorders were exiled.   (Tacitus, *Annals* 14.17)

While it may at first appear so, it is improbable that the conflict between the Nucerians and the Pompeians was incited only by the games that day. During the so-called Social War (91–88 BCE), a century and a half earlier, Rome's Italian allies had fought to acquire the benefits of citizenship. Pompeii joined the revolt but fell to Sulla, who settled a colony of legionary veterans there. According to two identical inscriptions, located over the main entrances to the amphitheatre, around 70 BCE the arena was dedicated in perpetuity to the colonists of Pompeii (*colonies locum in perpetuom deder(unt)*) and for the honour of the colony (*coloniai honoris caussa*).[8] In effect, C. Quinctius Valgus and M. Porcius, local magistrates named in the inscriptions and responsible also for the construction of the Covered Theatre at Pompeii, financed the building of the amphitheatre for the benefit of Pompeii's new colonists, both because of its association with the Roman military and as a monumental reminder of their dominance over the local Samnite population. We know that Nuceria had not rebelled against Rome and subsequently was awarded territory confiscated from a neighbouring town that had been destroyed during the fighting. Less than two years before the riot, Tacitus (*Annals* 13.31) informs us that Nero settled a veteran colony at Nuceria,

37

which no doubt provoked old enmities, especially if Pompeii contested the assignation of land to Nuceria.

Famously, a wall painting in a private house celebrates this event (Figure 2.1). Located in the peristyle of the so-called House of Anicetus (I.3.23), the fresco depicts a pivotal moment of the episode. Clusters of individuals are shown fighting in the arena itself, across the raised areas encircling the arena, on the exterior walls, and into the surrounding streets. Underlying the riot's savage nature, itinerant vendors operating temporary stalls outside the building and casual pedestrians are caught up in the heat of the disturbance. If the scene is studied closely, it is possible to read two painted acclamations, one in Greek, the other in Latin, bearing the names of a local magistrate, Decimus Lucretius Satrius Valens, and the emperor Nero.[9] Valens may have interceded with Nero to reopen the amphitheatre after the Roman senate's decision to revoke the city's permit to conduct gladiatorial shows in the wake of the riot.

Less famously, the riot may also be commemorated in a graffito image and accompanying text, both now lost. On the façade of the House of the Dioscuri (VI.9.6):

G2.15 A picture sketched in chalk once showed, to the left, what appears to be a prisoner, bound at the wrists, dragged away by a rope tied around his neck. To the right of the same image, the artist depicted a gladiator descending a flight of stairs, holding a palm of victory above his head.

Underneath someone had scratched the following words:

G2.16 "Campanians, you perished together with the Nucerians in victory."[10]

Figure 2.1 Wall painting of riot in amphitheatre, rear wall of peristyle, I.3.23 (Casa di Anicetus), Pompeii, Italy (Archaeological Museum of Naples/MAN 112222; photo by U.D.F., via Wikimedia Commons).

HISTORY

In other words, it may well have been the case that the inhabitants of Pompeii could claim victory over the Nucerians in the aftermath of the riot; but the decision of the senate to prohibit gladiatorial combat for ten years must have struck the city's prestige, not to mention its local economy, as serious a blow as the passing defeat of their belligerent neighbours.

It is highly unlikely, however, that the amphitheatre was closed for the entire decade prescribed by the senatorial edict. A number of painted inscriptions (*dipinti*) scattered across Pompeii advertise beast hunts (*venationes*) and athletic competitions. In addition to Satrius Valens, Poppaea, the second wife of Nero, whose mother's family lived in Pompeii, may have interceded for the amphitheatre's reopening. In 62 CE, a devastating earthquake struck Pompeii (*Annals*, 15.22), a precursor to the eruption of Vesuvius in 79 CE, and, once the amphitheatre had been repaired, it may have been opened as a gesture of consolation to the populace.

Roman historical writers, whether writing in Latin or in Greek, had little freedom to decide what to write about and how to organize their material. For those who aspired to write full-dress Roman history the choice was largely made by the tradition in which they worked. They could, if they wished, write a monograph, normally on a war – like Sallust on the Jugurthine War, or Appian on the Mithridatic or Civil Wars. Alternatively, they would follow the majority of their predecessors in writing annalistically, and in that case their subject matter was clearly defined as the deeds of the Roman people, at home and at war (*domi militiae*), arranged by consular years. The aspiring annalistic historian had merely to decide which of the two main branches of that tradition he should join – whether, like Livy, say, to take as his subject the whole history of the Roman people from the origins to their own time, or, like Tacitus, to confine himself to a limited period of relatively recent history.

Cassius Dio's *Roman History* falls into the former category. Originally composed in Greek and comprising 80 books, Dio's monumental work covered the period from the legendary landing of Aeneas in Italy to the reign of Alexander Severus (222–35 CE). As should be clear by now, it is quite typical of ancient historians *not* to name their sources, and Dio is no exception. We can say, however, that a lot of the narrative detail in Dio is confirmed by other literary sources – Suetonius, Tacitus, Cluvius Rufus,[11] and so on – or by inscriptions.

This is what Dio himself has to say about the obstacles facing him as an author wishing to provide authentic and reliable information about his subject:

> The government was thus transformed then for the better and for the greater safeguard of the people, for under the republic it was quite impossible for them to be protected. But subsequent events cannot be reported like earlier ones. Previously, it is clear, issues were brought before the senate and the citizen body even if they

39

GRAFFITI IN ANTIQUITY

took place far away. In consequence, everybody learned about them and many noted them down as a result, even if the accounts of some were seriously tainted by fear or favour, partisanship or hostility, a truthful picture of the issues was to some degree manifested in others who wrote of them and also in the public records. But from this time on most things started to become secret and concealed, and though some things might happen to be published they are not trusted, as being incapable of confirmation: for there is a suspicion that everything is said and done in accordance with the wishes of the powerful and their henchmen. Consequently many things that did not happen are spread about and many things that incontestably did happen are not known and virtually everything is broadcast differently from the way it happened.

(Cassius Dio, *Roman History* 53.19.1–4)

Book 44 of Dio's history deals coincidentally with the year 44 BCE, the fifth year of Julius Caesar's dictatorship and the year of one of the most famous political assassinations in world history, much less antiquity.[12] In the wake of widespread rumour that Caesar sought kingship – anathema to the republican ideal of popular sovereignty – Dio reports that various individuals

not only privately approached Marcus Brutus and such other persons as were proud-spirited and attempted to persuade them, but also tried to incite them to action publicly. Making the most of his having the same name as the great Brutus who overthrew the Tarquins [Rome's pre-republican Etruscan kings], they [the common people, or *hoi polloi*] scattered many pamphlets, declaring that he was not truly that man's descendant; for the older Brutus had put to death both his sons, the only ones he had, when they were mere lads, and left no offspring whatever. Nevertheless, the majority pretended to accept such a relationship, in order that Brutus, as a kinsman of that famous man, might be induced to perform deeds as great. They kept continually calling upon him, shouting out "Brutus, Brutus!" and adding further "We need a Brutus". Finally on the statue of the early Brutus they wrote "Would that you were living!" and upon the tribunal of the living Brutus (for he was *praetor* at the time and this is the name given to the seat on which the *praetor* sits in judgment) "Brutus, you are sleeping" and "You are not Brutus".

(Cassius Dio, *Roman History* 44.12.1–3)

Dio refers here to three graffiti:

G2.17   "Would that you were living!"

40

HISTORY

G2.18 "Brutus, you are sleeping."

G2.19 "You are not Brutus."

Naturally enough, these graffiti no longer survive in the urban fabric of the city of Rome. Only in the literary record do we learn about the "pamphlets" (which we might understand as documents distributed to the populace or affixed to surfaces used for the purpose) and the statue base and praetorial tribunal (a raised platform on which was set the curule chair, Brutus' magisterial seat of office) on which the messages were originally written.

What is fascinating about this historical episode – situated in the popular political landscape of republican Rome – is that Dio incorporates the practice of graffiti writing and its subject matter as historical evidence for the political temperature of the city. In the face of a perceived threat to the Roman constitutional system (what the Romans referred to as the *res publica*, from which our term "republic" springs), the people – and the Greek term Dio employs (*hoi polloi*) identifies this collective as the non-elite of the city – agitate for a political response from a person they see as the heir (in name and position) to Brutus, the legendary defender of Rome from the extremities of monarchical rule and first consul of the then neonate republic.

Later on, to portray what he saw as a yawning gap between the epitome of republican leadership and the worst of a new breed of imperial ruler, Dio provides another equally poignant reference to popular engagement with events of historical currency – and, in relation to matters of state, in the early imperial period, profound significance. Inscribed, so Dio informs us, on the base of a statue of Agrippina the Younger – wife, mother and sister of emperors in the Julio-Claudian period – was the following message:

G2.20 "I, I am ashamed of you; but you, do you not blush?"
           (Cassius Dio, *Roman History* 61.16.2a)

According to the narrative tradition, Agrippina's son, the emperor Nero, had recently set in train his mother's murder (59 CE). Adopting the voice of the recently deceased Agrippina, the admonishing graffito reveals – at least as Dio would wish us to understand – both the depths to which the 22-year-old emperor would sink in seeking freedom from the controlling personality of his mother and the extent to which the population of Rome was aware of his complicity in her death. Calling for some recognition on the part of Nero – as well, we might expect, as his coterie of supporters – of the shame which he – and, by extension, the institution of imperial leadership – had incurred, the anonymous inscriber constructs *another* kind of history, incised on the civic space of the city of Rome. It is little wonder that Dio cited the spare but chilling message. Reporting how this graffito channelled popular outrage by dint of ventriloquizing the dead Augusta (empress), Dio captures perfectly

41

GRAFFITI IN ANTIQUITY

the synergy between formal historical discourse and expressions of popular sentiment in response to signal episodes in Rome's story.

If we return briefly to the Brutus graffito, we can see that the third-century CE historian is not alone in his record of this polemic campaign on the surfaces of the city. Two biographers of famous Roman leaders – Suetonius, writing in Latin (*Twelve Caesars*), and Plutarch, in Greek (*Parallel Lives*) – and a historian of the seismic internecine conflicts marking the transition from republic to empire – Appian, in Greek (*Civil Wars*) – also report the use of graffiti as a tool of popular agitation.[13] In other words, it is very clear that ancient recorders of personalities and events like Suetonius, Appian, Plutarch and Dio recognized the importance of graffiti as an integral element of popular discourse and a corroborating register of evidence for episodes of historical significance.

In another context, Suetonius records a fascinating vignette distilling the fundamental relationship between non-official inscribing practices across civic spaces and the voicing of popular commentary on historical episodes relating to civic leadership. In the last years of the first century CE, the degree to which the emperor Domitian's building programme bordered on self-aggrandizement as opposed to renewal of the urban fabric reached its zenith. In response to the multiplication of arches erected in his name – "he erected so many and such huge vaulted passage-ways and arches in the various regions of the city, adorned with chariots and triumphal emblems" – Suetonius tells us that:

G2.21 "On one of [the arches] someone wrote in Greek: 'It is enough.'"
(Suetonius, *Domitian* 13.7)

Knowing that the Greek word used by the inscriber (*arcei*) mirrored in sound and form the plural form of the Latin word for "arch" (*arci*) allows us to appreciate the playfulness of the Roman mind, even in matters regarded as seriously detrimental to the nature of the *res publica*. As importantly, it should be clear that non-official markings like this depend on the viewer's recognition of language, spatial context and current events to generate meaning. In this regard, the historical moment was very much in the eye of the beholder: on the one hand, those city-dwellers living under the rule of Domitian, who found the plethora of monumental edifices in his name above and beyond the just due of a single man, albeit emperor of the Roman world; on the other, Suetonius' readership, familiar with non-official epigraphic practice in their own age and consequently well aware of the historical – and psychological – point the biographer was making about a ruler with a mixed popular reception, to say the least.

This inherent connection between graffiti in antiquity and the historical record is confirmed in the pages of Ammianus Marcellinus, regarded as the last major Roman historian. Writing in Latin during the fourth century CE, Ammianus' history, *Rerum gestarum libri* ("The Chronicles of Events")

42

HISTORY

comprised 31 books, covering a period of three and a half centuries, which began where Tacitus' *Histories* ended (the accession of Nerva) and extended to the death of Valens in 378 CE. Like his predecessors, Ammianus' work must be viewed in light of the precarious historiographical balance between objective reality and literary invention: what was – to modern eyes – an odd amalgam of artistry, moralizing, contemporary perspective and accuracy to observed and recorded detail.

In Book 19 of his thirty-one volume history, Ammianus records the following intervention in local Egyptian affairs by the then Roman emperor Constantinus II:

> There is a town called Abydum [Abydos] in the most remote corner of the Egyptian Thebais, where an oracle of the god, known in that region by the name of Besa [Bes], had formerly enjoyed some celebrity for its prophecies, and had sacred rites performed at it with all the ceremonies anciently in use in the neighbouring districts. Some used to go themselves to consult this oracle, some to send by others documents containing their wishes, and with prayers couched in explicit language inquired the will of the deities; and the paper or parchment on which their wants were written, after the answer had been given, was sometimes left in the temple. Some of these were spitefully sent to the emperor, and he, narrow minded as he was, though often deaf to other matters of serious consequence, had, as the proverb says, a soft place in his ear for this kind of information; and being of a suspicious and petty temper, became full of gall and fury; and immediately ordered Paulus to repair with all speed to the East, giving him authority, as to a chief of great eminence and experience, to try all the causes as he pleased.
> (Ammianus Marcellinus, *History* 19.12)

Erected in the early years of Dynasty XIX (1290–1279 BCE), the monument known as the Memnonion of Seti I at Abydos housed the oracle to which Ammianus refers. The oracle – relating to a broad spectrum of human concerns, including marriage, health, women's fertility and agricultural matters – is a direct answer (spoken, written or provided through another means) from a deity to a question posed by an individual of any class from the later New Kingdom into the Roman period. The oracle in this instance is of the god Bes, protector of households, mothers, children and childbirth. Graffiti on the walls of the building confirm the practice outlined in the testimony of Ammianus. Inscribed during the fourth century CE, at least 28 graffiti refer explicitly to Bes. One of the graffiti lends credence to the historian's account that Constantinus II took offence at people asking the oracle about the imperial succession. Dating from the last quarter of the fourth century CE to the first decade of the fifth, the graffito comprises:

43

GRAFFITI IN ANTIQUITY

G2.22   A horoscope (giving a birth date of 21–22 September 353
        CE), a name (Artemidorus), and a prayer ("may I not be wiped
        out").

Given the nature of the monument as a pilgrimage site (for this phenomenon, see Chapter 5), the nature of the graffito makes perfect sense; and the
inferred period during which its inscription took place supports Ammianus'
account. It may even be the case that this graffito was one of the last vestiges
of the oracle's operation, since the historian goes on to describe the fact that
the emperor's notary Paul acts on Constantinus II's order to close the Abydos
shrine.

One last example of historical graffiti should suffice. In Book 1 of his fragmentary *Histories*, the imperial historian *par excellence*, Tacitus, refers in
passing to a certain Titus Suedius Clemens – a *primipilaris* (leading military post) in the punitive expedition against the province of Gallia Narbon-
ensis in 69 CE.[14] Tacitus describes Clemens as a man who "used his office to
gain popularity, being as reckless toward maintaining discipline as he was
eager to fight".[15] In point of fact, Clemens appears to have been responsible
for allowing his troops to loot Ventimiglia – ancient Albium Intemelium, on
the north-western borders of Roman Italy. Albium Intemelium was at that
time occupied by partisans loyal to Vitellius, with whom Otho was in conflict
to determine who should hold imperial authority.

Clearly a survivor, mention of Clemens next surfaces in an inscription
carved into the right foot of the famous statue of Memnon. While the significance of the so-called Colossi of Memnon will be canvassed in more detail
in the next chapter (Chapter 3), it is sufficient in this context to note that T.
Suedius Clemens, who identifies himself in the inscription as an officer of the
emperor Titus, recorded the following message:

G2.23   "(Titus) Suedius Clemens, prefect of the camps. I heard
        Memnon ... on 12 November in year two of the emperor Titus
        [=79 CE]."   (*CIL* III.33)

Ammianus' notice of imperial indignation from the fourth century CE,
and Tacitus' less-than-complimentary observations regarding T. Suedius
Clemens, both reflected through the filter of graffiti in Roman Egypt, brings
us full circle – returning us in space, if not time, to the starting point of this
chapter – and completes our introduction to the historical usefulness of
informal markings in image and text. Here I think that we come to the crux
of graffiti's attraction as a source of historical information and of the surviving literary record as a point for comparison in regard to the evolution of
inscribing and historiographical practices over time. As an intellectual discipline, a particular way of thinking about the past (not better or worse, but
peculiar to itself), the tradition of history that finds expression in the works

HISTORY

of Herodotus, Thucydides, Livy, Tacitus, Dio and Ammianus Marcellinus has an essential ingredient that separates it from other traditional approaches to the past. History's defining characteristic is not record-keeping or list-making, though it shares its interest in the past with these pursuits (not to mention using them as source material). What distinguishes history's attitude to the past is the overarching goal of rational explanation. History is about explaining the past, not just recording it.

FINAL THOUGHTS

As the exemplary catalogue of graffiti in this chapter demonstrates (G2.1–23), written and pictorial markings offer the possibility of writing history about people living in ancient times which does not depend solely on the views of the cultural elites surviving in the European manuscript tradition and in formal epigraphic contexts. Examining these words and images – displayed on natural surfaces along well-travelled trading routes, walls and architectural elements of private homes and public buildings, useable fragments of discarded pottery – provides a means of assessing the manner by which and the degree to which ordinary men and women absorbed and exchanged information about history, culture and language. Regardless of who the persons marking surfaces were – soldiers travelling the high desert road near protodynastic Thebes, traders and customers conducting business in the Agora of classical Athens, non-elite political dissidents living in late republican Rome during the months prior to the murder of Julius Caesar, indigenous and immigrant residents of pre-eruption Pompeii, or pilgrims in search of the oracle of Bes in later imperial Abydos – the chronological specificity, social diversity and cultural heterogeneity of the persons who composed these messages reinforce the dynamic current of observational discourse coinciding with, confirming and elaborating on the historical preoccupations of the extant narrative tradition. Graffiti in antiquity comprise a historical wellspring rich in subject matter, reflecting how ancient writers and readers understood the times in which they lived and decided how best to communicate what they saw as important in their lives.

CHAPTER 3

LITERATURE

Narciss[us] writes: "Whoever you are, forget the Greeks, lost here, already." (*CIL* IV.1841; cf. Virgil, *Aeneid* 2.148)

What is harder than rock, what softer than the wave? Yet hard rock is hollowed out by soft water.
(*CIL* IV.1895; cf. Ovid, *Art of Love* 1.475–6)

I advise you, if you are anxious to be read about, look for some intoxicated poet of the dark archway who writes verses with rough charcoal or crumbling chalk which people read while they shit. (Martial, *Epigrams* 12.61.7–11)

GRAFFITI AND LITERACY

While literacy may be defined in a variety of ways, most experts in the field would agree that the term implies as a consequence or condition the ability to read and write. In any social context based on economic exchange, this literal meaning should be expanded to include an understanding of rudimentary mathematics. However, despite what appears to be a straightforward meaning, literacy in the ancient world remains a slippery quantity. In no small measure, this elusiveness is the result of nineteenth and twentieth-century attitudes, which applied low literacy estimates to pre-modern populations on the basis of the absence of mass education in the Western world. Before this, the common outlook was that most people in antiquity (and pre-Reformation medieval societies) could not read or write. Conventional wisdom, therefore, tells us that a limited and privileged elite possessed knowledge of reading and writing. Literacy, then, proved a useful instrument in the creation of kingdoms, nation-states and empires, grounded in the skills of administration and record-keeping. Given the evidence of the verse-inscriptions in the epigraph to this chapter – both found in the Basilica at Pompeii, both drawing heavily on finely crafted literary products of their day, both representing a plethora of graffiti texts that display knowledge and understanding of reading and writing – and the Roman poet Martial's satirical observation, this view requires testing.

Egypt

In ancient Egypt levels of literacy were statistically insignificant. According to available evidence, specialists give estimates of 1–5 per cent of the population.[1] Of course, as we have already seen, such generalizations conceal regional variations and differences between urban and rural populations. For example, in 1889 Flinders Petrie acquired around eighty separate groups of fragmentary papyri dating to the late Middle Kingdom (*c.*1800 BCE). Found at Lahun, a village of workers and their families associated with the pyramid of Senusret II, these thousands of fragments represent a fraction of the written output of a town of perhaps 5,000 inhabitants across a period of perhaps five decades. Although few findspots were recorded, the papyri seem to reflect levels of literacy in both the palatial town houses of the elite, and the smaller houses covering most of the site.[2] The estimate of literacy for this urban population may need to be revised upwards to around 15 per cent.

The so-called "Letters to the Dead" – letters written on linen, pottery bowls and papyrus to relatives who had recently died – from a man (Qau) to his parents and a woman (Hu) to her husband present the earliest evidence (the late Old Kingdom, *c.*2686–2181 BCE) for daily writing in the provinces of Upper Egypt.[3]

Similarly, a broken-off piece of stone (*ostracon*) found at Deir el-Medina – a walled village for the builders and decorators of the New Kingdom tombs in the Valley of the Kings – records work attendance over a period of 280 days during Year 40 in the reign of Ramesses II (1239 BCE). Accompanying the list of 40 names, which are arranged in columns of hieratic script (simplified cursive hieroglyphic writing) on the right-hand edge of each side, are dates written in black in a horizontal line. Above these dates, written in red ink, are reasons for absences from work, such as illness, the death of relatives, purifications (perhaps in association with the birth of children), home renovations, festival attendance and even intoxication.[4]

Without these chance survivals, the archaeological record of literacy in ancient Egypt might begin with substantially later and more formal writing (i.e. hieroglyphic inscription). It is in this respect that the ephemeral markings of graffiti come into their own as indicators of ancient literacy.

In the desert west of the Nile, along the main road between Luxor and Farshût, several texts carved in cliffs of limestone provide evidence for the

47

origins of alphabetic writing. Written in a Semitic script exhibiting Egyptian influence, the two inscriptions, incised into the soft stone at some point over the course of a century (*c.*1900–1800 BCE), reflect the first attempts at experimenting with the alphabet (i.e. individual symbols corresponding to single sounds) in a cultural context within which hieroglyphic scripts like ancient Egyptian consisted of hundreds of pictographs or idea pictures (see Introduction). What these texts denote is twofold: (1) historically, it would appear that people familiar with Semitic script were living far from their homeland in the region now known as Syria–Palestine; and (2) as it is unlikely that the people responsible for inscribing these texts belonged to elite Semitic society, we can infer that the idea of using alphabetic script arose in the minds of ordinary individuals – at least here in the place known today as Wâdi el-Hôl. Whoever these Semitic speakers were, their graffiti show that they were capable of simplifying the complex system of pictographic script, adapting the formal symbols used by religious, military and political officials into an alphabetic form far more user-friendly and accessible to ordinary men and women without need of official mediation.

Recent epigraphic surveys of the road between Thebes and Abydos suggest that Wâdi el-Hôl marked an important caravan stop used from the Predynastic period until early Islamic times. Frequented by soldiers, civilian travellers and couriers, the late Middle Kingdom alphabetic markings comprise two of a number of graffiti reflecting a broad spectrum of literacy and persons capable of writing and reading messages about holidays, pilgrimages to participate in religious events, worship of the goddess Hathor, not to mention numerous signatures of soldiers active in the Western Desert.

The practice of marking surfaces extends into the New Kingdom period, demonstrating how ancient Egyptians continued to express their interests, actions and accomplishments informally, in the expectation that others would be able to read their messages and share in their experiences or observations. Preserved on a number of fragmentary limestone blocks which once formed part of the wall of the upper sanctuary of the sun-temple of Userkaf, several graffiti record the reasons for the writers' sojourns to this Dynasty V mortuary temple and pyramid complex at Abû Sîr.[5]

Writing in hieratic with black ink during the reign of Thutmosis III (*c.*1479–1424 BCE), one of the visitors composed the following message:

G3.1 "[Year, month, day, under the Majesty of the King of Upper and] Lower Egypt, Menkheperre – light, prosperity, health [LPH] – Son of Re, Tuthmosis III – LPH – Neferkheperu – LPH – may he live for ever and [ever]! [The Scribe ..., son of the Scribe (?) ... came] to see the temple of the King of Upper and Lower Egypt, the deceased Sahure. He found it as though heaven [were within it, Re shining in it (?)]. [Then he said: 'May heaven rain fresh myrrh], may it drip incense upon the

roof of the temple of the deceased Sahure ... fresh (?). May I
then offer it to the deceased Sahure[.]'"

The unknown writer may appear to wax lyrical at the sight of Sahure's
"temple", but it should be clear that he – and the self-identification as "son"
confirms the gender of the graffitist – is not simply a tourist in the necropolis at Abû Sîr. Part of the burial landscape of Memphis to the south of Giza
and north of Saqqara, it is thought that Abû Sîr once comprised 14 royal
pyramids in addition to a number of smaller pyramids, temples and mastaba
tombs. The necropolis, therefore, was a site of historical and religious significance: a destination for pilgrims and incidental travellers eager to experience by association some vestige of past dynastic glory and to participate
in the continuity of care, nurture and protection integral to pharaonic rule.
A second graffito – composed by the scribe Amenemhat and dating to the
reigns of Amenophis II (1424–1398 BCE) or Thutmosis IV (1398–1388 BCE) –
confirms the attraction of the sun-temple within its mortuary setting:

G3.2   "Year 2, 3, Akhet 7, under the Majesty [of] the King of Upper
and Lower Egypt, ... LPH. Amenemhat, [son of the Scribe
(?)], Anath-manata, came to see the temple of the Majesty
of the King of Upper and Lower Egypt, the deceased Sahure.
He found it extremely pleasing. It appeared to him as great
as heaven when the moon is bright. Then he said, 'How fair is
[the temple of the *ka*] of the Majesty of the King of Upper and
Lower Egypt, the deceased Sahure. [Let?] oxen, fowl and bread
[be offered to ... (?)].'"

There is a good deal to learn from these two graffiti. Both writers insert
chronological markers ("year, month, day"), forms of address ("the Majesty
of the King of Upper and Lower Egypt", name and filiation of writer) and
expressions ("light, prosperity, wealth") which correspond to inclusions
in formal epigraphic texts and letters on papyrus. Amenemhat and the
unnamed scribe communicate their record of facts (observation of Sahure's
sun-temple), the feelings which the encounter evoked (awe and wonder), and
the actions which followed (offerings to the pharaoh's *ka*, the spiritual double
of the now-divine king and the receptacle of his power). The likelihood that
both men were scribes – persons who knew how to read and write, using
both hieroglyphic and hieratic scripts to copy out documents – explains the
"official" nature of the graffiti. Yet it is still possible to discern the conversational tone and epistolary form of their messages: "This is who I am, this
is what I saw and did, this is when it happened, and this is how I felt." Both
men clearly want to share their thoughts and feelings with others, and, in the
process, to memorialize their experience for posterity.

GRAFFITI IN ANTIQUITY

Most of the New Kingdom sources for literary texts comprise *ostraca* (polished limestone chips or pottery sherds) from the village of Deir el-Medina (Chapter 4). These graffiti consist in the main of:

- painted or inked figural drawings – ranging from small jottings to accomplished sketches;
- non-literary or "documentary" exercises – drafts of administrative documents, letters, notes and records of transactions, deliveries, appointments, and the like; and
- literary texts – didactic treatises like *The Instruction of a Man for his Son*, *The Instruction for Merikare*, *The Instruction of Hordedef*, and *The Instruction of Amenemhat I*; and narrative works like *The Story of Sinuhe* and *The Story of Khonsemheb and the Ghost*.

The wide range of written materials and forms found on a multiplicity of *ostraca* in the tombs and waste fills of Deir el-Medina – a village of artists, draughtsmen and builders who worked on the royal tombs of New Kingdom Thebes – reflects a heterogeneity of purposes illustrating both the social contexts for the use and expression of literate practices and the propensity in certain Egyptian communities for a spectrum of literacies. Some texts may be identified as the products of activities associated with education – exercises for scribal students. Others may have been copied or composed with a view to the transmission of practical information, cultural edification or aesthetic pleasure – ranging from the equivalent of "laundry lists" to epistolary compositions, catalogues of moral conduct and works of fiction. Yet other graphic or textual expressions may have performed a ritual function – votive or magical, dependent on the context in which the *ostracon* was placed (private domestic space or tomb) as well as the symbolic and linguistic content (Chapters 5 and 6). Taken together, the survival of thousands of such *ostraca* – due in large part to the durability of the materials used and the marginal location of the site outside the path of transforming physical degradation – allows us to appreciate the possibilities for transmitting and consuming verbal and non-verbal texts in pharaonic Egypt. In this respect, comparing the alphabetic graffiti found at Wâdi el-Hôl with the hieratic texts from Abû Sîr and Deir el-Medina demonstrates precisely the spectrum of literacies – across a range from functional to scribal – existing in ancient Egypt, and how such markings flesh out the history and culture of particular places and times.

Greece

Historical research, therefore, shows that literacy was often transmitted and practised outside the contexts which the modern world categorizes as institutionalized education.[6] Across time and geography, literacy should be

50

LITERATURE

viewed primarily as a cultural phenomenon, encountered and experienced in a variety of settings beyond what we know as formal schooling. Three centuries after the arrival of alphabetic writing in Greece (the archaic period, eighth to sixth centuries BCE), classical Greeks living in the fifth to fourth centuries BCE left a substantial body of literature, and the city-states (*poleis*) used documents, inscriptions and archives for the purposes of government, the law, administration and religion.

However, in much the same way as ancient Egyptian graffiti exhibit the mixture of spoken and written language – whether the transformation of sound and symbol marking the change from pictograph to alphabet at Wâdi el-Hôl or the scribal exchange of ideas at Abû Sîr – graffiti produced in classical Greece reflect the relationship which existed between literacy and the long-standing oral tradition in ancient Greek society. This nexus is important to bear in mind when attempting to construe the form and function of ancient Greek – indeed, ancient Mediterranean – graffiti, simply because the culture of communication in antiquity did not rest on the firm sub-structure of carefully planned and revised written texts which characterizes the modern age. A good deal of ancient discourse constituted "word of mouth": ideas communicated, composed, and transmitted without writing. For example, Homeric epic poetry – the famous evocation of heroic and legendary action in the *Iliad* and *Odyssey* – is regarded as the archetypal expression of the archaic Greek oral tradition, composed originally in performance, spoken or sung, using a repertoire of set pieces, formulae and established themes.[7] But we should also take into account, *inter alia*, memorials to the dead (dirges, laments, eulogies), official discourse (proclamations of law, court proceedings) and cultural activity (theatrical performance, public recitation, philosophical dialogue). In other words, the transmission of knowledge and understanding in an oral culture like archaic and classical Greece was experienced immediately and deeply socialized. To the extent that the advent of alphabetic script acted on this cultural tradition, writing was used primarily in the service of the spoken word, deriving its significance from pre-existing oral customs and practices.[8]

Graffiti incised during the archaic period provide a perspective on ancient Greek literacy that reflects a greater degree of social diversity than the evidence of formal inscriptions might otherwise lead us to expect. Alphabets (*abecedaria*), signatures by writers and other graffiti on pottery sherds from the sanctuary of Zeus (identified by several sherds with inscribed dedications) on Mount Hymettos, indicate that from the start of the seventh century BCE (and on into the later sixth century) inhabitants of regional Attika were carving letters and texts of various kinds, and felt sufficient satisfaction in the act to dedicate their efforts. Of the 172 graffiti discovered at the sanctuary which can be deciphered, the majority are inscriptions bearing epithets of gods (notably, of course, Zeus, but other deities as well) and heroes (e.g. Herakles), fragmentary alphabets, personal names (and associated observations) and toponyms, miscellaneous letters (individual and grouped), and various

51

GRAFFITI IN ANTIQUITY

symbols (e.g. a five-pointed star). Here are a few examples of the extant body of evidence:[9]

G3.3   "Androg[...], son of D[...], made [i.e. wrote or performed] ... [a dedication] ... to Zeus [and/or Apollo?] Anax." (*c.*600 BCE)

G3.4   "[A dedication to] Zeus the Sign-giver." (Seventh century BCE)

G3.5   "[A dedication to] Gaia."

G3.6   "[Someone] set this up."

G3.7   "I am the property of Zeus. [Someone] wrote me."

G3.8   "[Line 1:] ABCEDE ... | [Line 2:] ABCEDEF ..."

G3.9   "Drink this up."

G3.10 "I am [the cup] of [De]isitheos."

G3.11 "Philai[i]des takes it up the arse." (650–625 BCE)

These inscriptions acknowledge a variety of cultural attitudes and practices. It is natural to find texts which express religious sentiment within the context of a mountain sanctuary. It makes sense, too, that a number of dedications feature the name of Zeus, supreme deity of the Greek pantheon, who ruled from Mount Olympus and controlled the weather. What is interesting about these graffiti is the collocation of ideas they embody. Anax (G3.3) is the ceremonial epithet of the god, reflecting his authority over the universe. Zeus, however, receives the title on rare occasions. On the other hand, Homer and other classical literature associate the title more frequently with Apollo, who was also worshipped on Mount Hymettos.[10] The relationship between Zeus and meteorological phenomena like the flash of lightning is expressed neatly in the epithet Semios (G3.4), that is, Zeus the Sign-giver, or Zeus of the weather signs. It is especially fitting that this conceptualization is formulated in writing. In a similar fashion, reference to the Earth goddess, Gaia (G3.5), falls into place as soon as the provincial setting of the sanctuary is taken into consideration. The economy of Attika in the eighth and seventh centuries BCE was based on an agricultural way of life: ensuring the continued productivity of the soil would have been foremost in the minds of rural Athenians.

In these ways, the Hymettos graffiti confirm the social and spiritual value of piety in archaic Greek society. The writers of these dedications composed their messages both as indicators of personal *and* public devotion. In this regard, the fragmentary text commemorating the act of "setting up" something (G3.6) may at first sight appear inconsequential. However, in the sixth century BCE, dedications referred to in this way are common on the Athenian Acropolis, and relate to objects "set up" in honour of particular deities. This much earlier reference to the practice follows (at least partially) the same formula: the name of the dedicator (in this case, due to the fragmentary nature of the vessel on which the text was inscribed, lost), followed by the verb "set up" (*anetheke*), after which would appear the name of the deity in the dative case. The object dedicated to the unnamed deity (most probably Zeus) remains unknown. Given the proximity of so many pottery vessels, the author may refer to the surface on which the dedication is written, and could include the text as part of the offering. While this is speculative, the very Greek notion of reciprocal exchange between divine and human beings is neatly captured in this "setting up" inscription (*anathem*). More certain is the attribution of object and text as "property of Zeus" (G3.7), foregrounding the vessel (its ownership and donation) and the dedication (the act of writing and the message) as integral components in the ritual offering.

The remaining graffiti represent cultural practices essential to the proper performance of worship at the sanctuary, and an unexpectedly vituperative message far more in keeping with earthly matters. The two incomplete *abecedaria* (G3.8) may attest to a pedagogical context: the first line, inscribed in what seems a more practiced hand than the letters in Line 2, could represent the alphabetic script of a person providing instruction in the art of writing to someone with less experience. The inclusion of *digamma* (F), a letter that had no phonetic value in the Attic dialect and fell out of use during the sixth century BCE, indicates a person who is copying the alphabet as provided. This failure to recognize the superfluity of the *digamma* adduces the teacher-pupil relationship. A desire on the part of the writer of the second *abecedarium* to participate more fully in votive practice at the Hymettos sanctuary explains the presence (and, possibly, purpose) of the graffito in this context. So, too, the writer of the imperative to "drink this up" (G3.9) may well have intended this as a reference to the ritual action of drinking from one's own cup (in this instance, a type of vessel known as a *skyphos*) before dedicating it to the god (again, most likely Zeus). The cup of [De]isitheos (G3.10) would, according to this view, fit the same ritual pattern.

The last inscription in the sample catalogue of Hymettos graffiti appears, initially at least, decidedly out of place. Variously translated, the word used in G3.11 which follows the name P[hil]ai(i)des (Greek *katapugon*) is a derogatory word for a sexual partner who is penetrated anally. Frequently attested as a term of abuse, whoever wrote *katapugon* on the one-handled cup found in the sanctuary may have meant to cast aspersions on the subject of the graffito in more general terms. In this regard, *katapugon* encapsulates the use of the extended middle finger, a gesture which may be rendered succinctly as "Up yours!"; or, more explicitly, it is possible to translate the message along the lines of "P[hil]ai(i)des is sexually obsessive". However the graffito is read, the underlying sentiment of derision, playing on insult and obscenity, would have been clear to anyone reading this text.[11] That the inscription sits outside the categories of message found in the sanctuary goes without saying. But it could well be that the inscribing individual wished to invoke vituperation on the unfortunate P[hil]ai(i)des within a context potent enough to ensure an appropriate response, either from the commemorating community of fellow dedicators, from the subject of their dedication (Zeus or Apollo), or from P[hil]ai(i)des himself. Much more will be said on this subject in Chapter 11.

In sum, then, these markings should not be seen simply as early evidence for the use of alphabetic script: morphology (letter forms) shows that the Hymettos graffiti belong to an early stage in the history of writing in Attika. Like the Wâdi el-Hôl texts, the Hymettos graffiti denote a formative stage in the development of writing: the moment in time when individuals – in this case, Attic citizens (i.e. Athenians) situated in a rural context – expressed in tangible and lasting form ideas which until recently in their history were confined to oral discourse or personal memory. Just as important in assessing the value of these inscriptions is the likelihood that their survival represents the prevalence of literacy in seventh-century BCE Attika; or, to put it another way, it is *more* likely that the Hymettos graffiti denote a widespread ability to read and write than that they comprise an isolated and incidental find, divorced from what would otherwise be a radically illiterate provincial context.

Greek graffiti reflecting these facets of the ancient literacy spectrum can be found in any number of locations and times. If we return briefly to Egypt, but move forward in time to the Hellenistic (or Ptolemaic) period (332–31 BCE), a variety of surfaces in and near the small rock temple of Seti I at El Kanais (east of Edfu in the Wadi Mia) displays a record of graffiti inscribed by Greek travellers, incised in relation to earlier Egyptian markings, later Roman messages, as well as post-classical and early modern writings.[12] Like Wâdi el-Hôl, the El Kanais site was used as a way-station for military traffic and workers associated with mining operations. The facility of the site for such a purpose was the reason why Seti I (*c.*1294–1279 BCE) originally constructed the small temple: to mark the digging of a well to service one of the major routes between the Nile Valley and his gold-mining operations in the eastern desert. An inscription on the walls of the shrine records the sinking of the well shaft and the pharaonic foundation of the temple.[13] Another inscription, recorded on a pillar in the temple a millennium after Seti I's foundation, describes the place as the "Paneion", reflecting the identification of iconography associated with the Egyptian god Amen-Re (namely, the attributes of the ithyphallic god of fertility, Min) which corresponded to the Greek god of wild places, Pan.

In relation to this cultural appropriation, Greek textual graffiti are directed for the most part to Pan – bearing the epithets Euodoi ("of the good road"), Euargos ("of the good hunt"), Epekoos ("who listens in prayer"), or Soter ("Saviour") – and comprise expressions of thanksgiving for safe return from distant places, acts of adoration in relation to the dangers of desert travel,

LITERATURE

and a miscellany of personal signatures. Two of the 92 extant graffiti warrant special attention:

G3.12   "Pan of the good road, Zenodotos son of Glaukos has given you this [ornament? Altar?], having come back from the land of the Sabaeans [modern Yemen]."

G3.13   "[I dedicate] this to Pan of the good hunt who listens to prayer, who has saved me from the land of the Troglodytes [an epithet for the African inhabitants of the Red Sea], having suffered greatly in redoubled hardships, and from the sacred land which produces myrrh and from among the Koloboi. You saved us when we went off course on the Red Sea, and you sent a breeze to our ships when they were rolling on the ocean, whistling in shrill breaths in the reeds, until you your-self brought us to the port of Ptolemais, steering us with your hands, most skilful from the hunt. Now, friend, save the city which Alexander first founded in Egypt, the most famous of cities. I proclaim your power, friend Pan, having come back safely from Ptolemais [?] ..."

More will be said later with respect to what these graffiti tell us about the belief system of Greeks inscribing thanks-offerings (Chapter 5) and the purpose of their travels (Chapter 10). What stands out about the inscriptions of Zenodotos and the unnamed dedicator is the nuanced sophistication of form in service to votive function. The elevated tone, clarity of language choice, and use of literary Greek mark these graffiti as the eloquent prayers of educated Ptolemaic Greeks. While a larger number of the El Kanais inscriptions offer only brief, highly stylized formulae, along the line of the Hymettos graffiti, it is fascinating to observe, once again, how a particular socio-cultural context preserves such a mixture of writing styles (formal epigraphy, non-official cursive inscriptions), language use (hieroglyphic, demotic, Greek, Latin, Arabic), and social location (royalty, the scribal class, soldiers, miners, commercial travellers) across more than 3,000 years.

The site *par excellence* which demonstrates this illuminating aggregation of literate practices, including a large corpus of Greek graffiti, is also located in Egypt – though, as you will see, the inscriptions vary in one significant detail from what we have considered so far. Standing in ruins today, the so-called Colossi of Memnon – at 17 meters in height, the monumentality of these landmarks is self-evident – once flanked the entrance gate of the mortuary temple of Amenhotep III (1388–1350 BCE). Cut from two enormous blocks of granite, shipped to the site on the West Bank of Luxor from quarries near Cairo, these statues were carved on site to represent the Dynasty XVIII pharaoh. The northern statue represents Amenhotep with

55

his mother Mutmwaya; the southern statue depicts the pharaoh and his wife Tye. Amenhotep's memory, however, faded with time, and the colossal figures came to be associated with Memnon, a mythological hero, son of the Goddess of Dawn (Eos). King of the Ethiopians, he appears briefly in a lost version of the story of the Trojan War, coming to Troy's aid and slain by Achilles. Following Herodotus in the tradition of a Classical author writing about Egypt, this is how the Greek geographer Strabo (64 BCE to c.24 CE) describes the Colossi during his visit to Thebes and the tombs in the Valley of the Kings in 27 BCE:

> Here are two colossi, which are near one another and are each made of a single stone; one of them is preserved, but the upper parts of the other, from the seat up, fell when an earthquake took place, so it is said. It is believed that once each day a noise, as of a slight blow, emanates from the part of the latter that remains on the throne and its base; and I too, when I was present at the places with Aelius Gallus [Roman Prefect of Egypt, 26–24 BCE] and his crowd of associates, both friends and soldiers, heard the noise at about the first hour [i.e. sunrise], but whether it came from the base or from the colossus, or whether the noise was made on purpose by one of the men who were standing all round and near to the base, I am unable positively to assert; for on account of the uncertainty of the cause I am induced to believe anything rather than that the sound issued from stones thus fixed.
>
> (Strabo, *Geography* 17.1.46)

Strabo was the first to comment on the phenomenon of the "singing stones" associated with the Colossi of Memnon. Rightly sceptical about the "singing statue" – modern science informs us that an earthquake in 27 BCE split the statue in such a way that sudden changes in humidity and temperature at dawn set up a sympathetic vibration in the stone – Strabo's account nonetheless explains the attraction of the Colossi for an ancient audience. Drawn to the site in the belief that they would overhear Memnon in conversation with his grief-stricken mother, the statue emitting the sharp cracking sound – reminiscent, so we are told, of the snapping of the string of a musical instrument or the clashing of a metal cymbal – attests to the popularity of the experience. Hundreds of graffiti (in Greek and Latin) cover the statue's legs and record the observations of visitors in brief or at great length.[14] They range in date from the reign of Tiberius (14–38 CE) to 205 CE, six years after the emperor Septimius Severus ordered the statue to be repaired, rendering Memnon mute.

G3.14   "Dionysia's worship. Many a time will she hear."

(September 122 CE)

56

LITERATURE

G3.15 "I heard the wonderful Memnon along with my wife ... and my children ... 11 Choiak, 15th year of Hadrian."

(7 December 130 CE)

G3.16 "I, Caecilia Trebulla, wrote after hearing Memnon here. Cambyses smashed me, this stone, made as a likeness of an Eastern king. My voice of old was a lament, groaning for Memnon's suffering, which Cambyses stole. Today I cry sounds inarticulate and unintelligible, remains of my former fate."

(130 CE)

G3.17 "When the August Hadrian heard Memnon. By Julia Balbilla. Memnon the Egyptian, I learnt, when warmed by the rays of the sun, speaks from Theban stone. When he saw Hadrian, the king of all, before the rays of the sun he greeted him – as far as he was able. But when the Titan driving through the heavens with his steeds of white brought into shadow the second measure of hours, like ringing bronze Memnon again sent out his voice sharp-toned; he sent out his greeting and for a third time a mighty roar. The Emperor Hadrian then himself bid welcome to Memnon and left on stone for generations to come this inscription recounting all that he saw and all that he had heard. It was clear to me that the gods love him."

G3.18 "I saw and I wondered."

In the same way that people today would visit a sacred site, many Greeks travelled to see the Colossi and hear the hero Memnon's voice emanating from the northern statue. However, the nature of the statue – which presented itself to those onlookers with a mind to leave their mark as a potential surface for inscribing their observations and experiences – will have prevented the travellers *themselves* from commemorating their visit. Granite is a notoriously hard stone to carve; only skilled stonecutters possessed the tools and the skills to incise texts with any hope of clarity or lasting success. As such, while it is abundantly clear that the messages preserved on the leg of the northern Colossus were composed by those people who visited the site, the fact that the graffiti are carefully carved confirms the hands of professional intermediaries (Latin *ordinatores*) as the instruments used to inscribe the various prosaic and poetic reflections.

Though we read the Memnon graffiti at (at least) one remove from the original writers, the standard of Greek composition indicates that the men – and, notably, women – responsible for these texts were literate, in some cases, well-educated, and in a few instances will have belonged (as the chronology and content of the inscriptions confirm) to the elite echelons of imperial

Roman society. What this tells us is very different from the Hymettos and El Kanais graffiti. The messages of Dionysia, Caecilia Trebulla, Julia Balbilla, the unknown husband (and the many other texts carved into the granite) mark a transition-point between non-official, often ephemeral graffiti – written in charcoal, scratched with a stick or stylus, or painted with a brush – and monumental lapidary epigraphy inscribed in formal public spaces with a view to permanent memorialization.

It is likely, for example, that, instead of representing spontaneous expressions incised at the moment of inspiration or impulse to write – which is often the case in regard to less crafted, cursive graffiti – the composers of the Memnon inscriptions will have had time between their experience of the "singing statue" and their enunciation of what they observed and felt. Dionysia's brief epigram (G3.14), for instance, is written in a quantitative measure known as iambic trimetre, used in ancient Greek (and Latin) dramatic and comic poetry – namely, dialogue in verse spoken by characters on stage. The theatrical associations reflect Dionysia's social condition and education, the former also indicated by her possible links with other travellers responsible for three prose inscriptions on the statue. It is only just possible that she formulated her short, pithy verse on the spot. But Dionysia will not have been able to inscribe it; she will instead have sought (and paid) a local stonecutter to render her poetic thought in more permanent fashion.

This applies in equal measure to the inscriptions composed by Caecilia Trebulla (G3.16) and Julia Balbilla (G3.17). Otherwise unknown, Caecilia Trebulla composed three epigrams – two, including the quoted example, written in the first person, and the third adopting the persona of Memnon himself. While she proudly inserts her name at the beginning of each verse, in the view of modern scholars of post-Classical Greek her poetic aspirations should be regarded as modest. Nevertheless, however technically limited her ability, it is important to note that, like Dionysia and Julia Balbilla, Caecilia Trebulla's reflections represent respectable poetry in Greek composed by a woman. Her verses – and that of her fellow female poets inscribed on the leg of "Memnon's" statue – comprise almost 6 per cent of the literary works written by women in the ancient world that survive to this day.

Similarly imperfect in a technical sense, Julia Balbilla's poem (G3.17) – one of four Memnon inscriptions by the same woman – is composed in an Aeolic dialect affiliated with the poetry of Sappho. This artificial inclusion also lends her verses a Homeric quality, showing Balbilla's engagement with a literary tradition that attests to her erudition and ambition. The final section of the poem strongly implies that the emperor Hadrian commissioned her to write the verse, commemorating the occasion of his visit in the company of his wife Sabina and attendant courtiers, and confirming Balbilla's literary status, at least in the eyes of her august patrons.

Rome

From what has gone before, it should be clear that we need to see literacy in the ancient world in terms other than those on which modern definitions are based. In light of recent studies, it might be better to imagine a spectrum of "literacies" – economic, literary, military, political, religious, and so on – operating within a variety of contexts across historical time.[15] This revised understanding helps us to make sense of the different approaches to reading and writing we have encountered in ancient Egyptian and Greek settings. It is also extremely useful in clarifying the ways in which the Roman world conceived of literacy processes and products.

For people living under Roman rule in Italy and the wider Mediterranean, the ability to read and write and the purposes to which this capacity was put does not encompass a single approach. Like their Egyptian and Greek counterparts, Roman readers and writers employed a range of strategies, dependent on the reasons for acquiring a particular level of literacy and the extent to which reading and writing proved useful (in relation to the satisfaction of daily needs, familial responsibilities or occupational requirements), beneficial (with respect to improving one's social condition, standing for civic office or acquiring information) or enjoyable (in other words, for aesthetic, intellectual or leisure purposes). This range of literacies manifests itself in relation to the different types of writing, located in a broad cross-section of private and public contexts:

- altars (cult temples, domestic shrines, rural sanctuaries, tomb precincts);
- arena advertisements (Latin *munera gladiatoria*) and theatre tokens (Latin *tesserae*)
- citizenship and military discharge certificates (Latin *diplomata*, awarded to private individuals and veteran soldiers);
- electoral notices (Latin *programmata*);
- monumental lapidary epigraphy (civic architecture, market places, cemeteries);
- milestones (along the network of roads crisscrossing the Roman landscape);
- manufactured objects (armour, weapons; bricks, mosaics, water-pipes, tiles; containers; decorative items in bone, ivory, glass, metal, pottery, stone and wood; domestic utensils; weights and measures); *and*, of course,
- graffiti.

As a test of the applicability and adequacy of this revised definition of literacy in antiquity, and confirmation of the widespread nature of the practices of reading and writing, consider one of the better-known graffiti at Pompeii:

GRAFFITI IN ANTIQUITY

G3.19 "I am amazed, O wall, that you have not fallen in ruins, you who support the tediousness of so many writers."
(*CIL* IV.1904, 1906, 2461, 2487)

This graffito is scratched by different writers (*scriptores*) into the surfaces of three buildings at widely separated locations in the city: the Basilica (twice), the Large Theatre and the Amphitheatre. As we saw earlier (Introduction), the Basilica at Pompeii (Figure 3.1) – identified by misspelt graffiti on the plastered interior of the building (*bassilica*) – played a significant role in the civil and commercial life of the city: the administration of justice; the conduct of business meetings; the management of legal affairs.

The Large Theatre, built into a natural hollow in the hillside adjacent to the ancient Triangular Forum, was a centre of entertainment at Pompeii. During the pre-colonial period it was used for gladiatorial matches, spectacles of various kinds and plays. When the building was transformed in the early years of the first century CE, it catered to an audience of around 5,000 people, there to enjoy tragedy and comedy performed in Greek, Latin or the local Oscan language.

The Amphitheatre – referred to in the dedicatory inscription of the building as a *spectacula*[16] – was a place for spectators to congregate and watch. The gladiatorial games and blood sports that took place in its arena were extremely popular (Chapter 9).

Figure 3.1 Basilica (VIII.1), Pompeii, Italy (photo by Mboesch, CC BY-SA 3.0, http://creativecommons.org/licenses/by-sa/3.0, via Wikimedia Commons).

LITERATURE

Individually or as part of a cluster of representative civic elements, these buildings constitute precisely that nexus of spatial locations within the fabric of Pompeii which served as incubators of popular oral and literate discourse. If we conceptualize urban space in relation to the symbolic language of graffiti markings, it is possible to trace a variety of alternative pedestrian journeys through Pompeii, using the inscribed instances of the *admiror* message as a guide. Traversing the city, the pedestrian would encounter a potential constellation of incidental social performances: the rapid-fire calculus of conspicuous consumption adhering to the market-place economy; the cut and thrust of philosophical, legal and commercial rhetoric; improvised and crafted poetic compositions, dramatic performances and public readings; ball-games, dicing and table-games; song, dance and instrumental music; lullabies, nursery rhymes and folktales; funerary laments and the rituals of beast-hunt and gladiatorial combat. It should be clear how closely this speculative tour of ancient Pompeii and its extra-mural precincts follows the catalogue of reading and writing contexts listed above. Moreover, it is important to note how naturally attestations of civic epigraphy and graffiti practices intersect in a flexible matrix of daily cultural diffusion.

Likewise, the relationship between this discursive sensory network and the quotidian opportunities for "memorialization" on offer to the traveller in Pompeii is readily apparent. Following Horsfall's idea that a music-orientated, memory-based oral culture might have co-existed in the Roman world with the stiffer but more familiar world of Virgil, Tacitus and their readers, the *admiror* inscription neatly encapsulates the various levels by which a pedestrian might participate in the cultural streetscape of Pompeii.[17] Whether or not the viewer recognizes the elegant simplicity of the inscribed elegiac verse, or on a technical level notices the metrical error in *admiror* (scanned with a short "i", usually long), is not as important as the possibility that the writer anticipated the message would be read and remembered. On one level, the composer attests to the prevalence of spontaneous inscriptions in the city; on another, the irony of participating in the same process is a supple and durable pleasure for the thoughtful passerby. Anticipating Juvenal's complaint[18] that the recitation of stale themes in wealthy patrons' colonnades threaten to crack their marble columns with a surfeit of rhetoric, the graffito displays both the right combination of generic imitation and creative variation, and the right blend of poetic pleasure and moral usefulness, appreciated by consumers of Roman literary and popular culture. That the tedium of others cannot really be alleviated by the recitation of an epigraphic convention is a stale joke along with all the others.

Reflecting this intersection of movement and inscription in the urban fabric of the ancient world, Plutarch refers to a series of parietal graffiti written in the city of Rome at least 50 years, and more likely over a century after the inhabitants of Pompeii took a liking to the sentiments expressed by the composer of the *admiror* inscription.

61

GRAFFITI IN ANTIQUITY

G3.20   "Most of all, the energy and ambition [of Tiberius Gracchus]
         was fired by the People, calling upon him through writings
         upon porticoes, walls [Greek *toichoi*] and monuments [Greek
         mnemata] to recover the public land for the poor."
                            (Plutarch, *Tiberius Gracchus* 8.7)

Tiberius Sempronius Gracchus came from the heart of the Roman nobility. Yet, despite his place in the aristocratic order of Roman society, he came up with a radical plan that the state could implement to deal with the many problems it faced at the time (133 BCE). This plan involved redistributing land to landless peasantry, in large part, the urban poor. Where, though, was the land that Tiberius Gracchus needed to implement his planned redistribution? The land he had in mind was the public land (*ager publicus*). In this respect, two of the most radical things that any society can do in terms of government intervention is (1) to cancel debt, which of course sends shockwaves through the property-owning classes, and (2) to redistribute property. It is very important to note here that Gracchus was not proposing to take private property away from anyone. No private property was involved in his proposal. Instead, he put forward the idea that his planned redistribution would draw on the public land in Italy. However, the owners of large ranches (*latifundia*) had been occupying the *ager publicus* for generations, never contemplating in their wildest dreams that it would be taken away from them. They did not own the public land, however; they were squatters.

We will explore the political significance of references like this later (Chapter 8). However, it should be clear that the authors of the graffiti in support of Tiberius Gracchus' radical initiative displayed their messages on a variety of highly visible architectural features across the city of Rome. What Plutarch describes as "writings" (*grammata*) appear on the covered walkways or porticoes (*stoai*), commonly for public use, often surrounding the marketplaces of large cities like Rome. Open at the entrance, and usually having columns on one side and the wall of a building on the other, these porticoes were heavily frequented by the urban population and offered any number of surfaces suited to the marking and reception of messages. So, too, the walls and monuments mentioned in the passage (*toichoi, mnemata*) afford similar vantage points for producing and consuming information. In relation to the issue of literacy, Plutarch's record of what appears to be an outbreak of politicized action in late republican Rome registers an important fact: it was the "People" (*autos ho Demos*) who made their mark. Whether they reflect a genuinely popular outpouring of support or an organized campaign orchestrated by a group in favour of Gracchus' proposition, the graffiti of 133 BCE point to a broader constituency of writers and readers than the literary record at first suggests.[19] But how would these graffiti have appeared to pedestrian onlookers as they moved through the urban fabric of Rome? If we return for a moment to Pompeii, it is possible to discern something of the diffusive

62

LITERATURE

physicality of graffiti in the urban landscape, and suggest a way in which those who could read and write were able to make sense of the sometimes elaborate collocation of markings covering the walls, porticoes, monuments and other surfaces of the ancient city. The ease by which a viewer, literate (and numerate) at either a functional or scribal level, could detect a related pattern of texts among the accumulation of ephemeral inscriptions in any given spatial context, and thereby interpret naturally the record of particular exchanges, can be seen in the *CIL* IV transcription of Latin graffiti inscribed on the exterior wall of a small house with stairway (VI.2.9–10) (G3.21–3; Figures 3.2–4).

G3.21 *CIL* IV.1333: Bilius. 1333a: Iun[iae] Primae. 1334: verna Vernionis | Secundus | Secundus. 1335: Antonius Rustio s[alutem]. 1336: Phospor tuis | choreis. 1337: Phosphor tuis c[h]ore[i]s. 1338: Restituta tuis choreis. 1339: memor. 1339a: Accia. 1340: Iulius Quintus. 1341: Restituta tuis chore[is]. 1342: veteri. 1343: Quintinus. 1343a: tecum | pia.

G3.22 *CIL* IV.1345: Severus | Severus. 1346: C. Vinif. 1347: felices homines va[le] | felices. 1348: Sabinus | de quinq[ue]. 1349: Pompeianus. 1350: Pompeianus. 1352: Successus. 1352a: mil. mod. 1352b: Elene. 1352c: Nyptae | [Vat]ile.

G3.23 *CIL* IV.1353: cum Lub. 1353a: quibus nomini. 1353b: Anti[-----] et Successus Amphia[rtes?] 1353c: tuis | cum. 1353d: commun[----]. 1354: bonum Faustum Felix. 1355: Successtus. 1356: Primigeni felixs et [------]. 1357: Primigni es Felex. 1358: rixa. 1359: Vestalis. 1360: Kinnamos. 1361: Xantus. 1362: Psyce. 1363b: Ampliatus | Marcus. 1363c: Myrtale. 1364. Nomina Nychi | genice | Th[-]e[-]ice | Dotice Patagricae | Onomastice Onogricae | Phyrrice | Byxantice | Cretice | Dymastice | Gymnice | Chizecae. 1365: Hermes | Hostis | Bena.

Leaving this cluster of graffiti untranslated not only enables easy identification of individual texts in the related transcriptions. It is more readily apparent how a person able to read the Latin language at a functional level – someone, that is, with a knowledge of the Latin alphabet, of common nomenclature, and basic grammatical structure; as well as familiar with the local community – could participate in the exchange of information and ideas on the wall of this ordinary dwelling in Pompeii. Single names and commemorative dedications comprise the bulk of the graffiti at VI.2.9–10, representing a bulletin board of individuals living and working in – or passing through – the neighbourhood (known in modern terms as Region VI) and an abbreviated record of activity and interests. Certain individuals appear to refer to

63

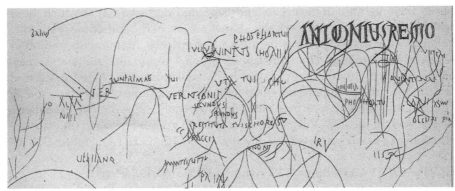

Figure 3.2 Transcription of graffiti, exterior wall of VI.2.9–10 (= *CIL* IV.1333–1344), Pompeii, Italy (*CIL* IV.Tab. II.1).

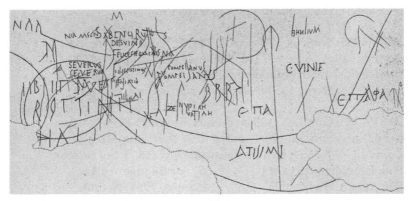

Figure 3.3 Transcription of graffiti, exterior wall of VI.2.9–10 (= *CIL* IV.1345–1352c), Pompeii, Italy (*CIL* IV.Tab. II.2).

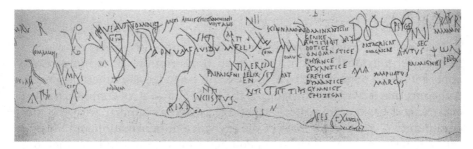

Figure 3.4 Transcription of graffiti, exterior wall of VI.2.9–10 (= *CIL* IV.1353–1365), Pompeii, Italy (*CIL* IV.Tab. II.3).

elements of musical dance and ritual devotion ("dance in a ring", "pious": *tuis choreis pia*) (G3.21); others exchange words of encouragement ("Be fruitful": *felices*) or (to us) inscrutable messages ("Sabinus, concerning [the] five", *Sabinus de quinq(ue)*) (G3.22); and one assiduous person inscribed a vertical catalogue bisecting the surrounding texts, a list of distinctive names for an otherwise unknown purpose (G3.23).

Here, it is important to reinforce, when considering the modern remainder of graffiti almost two thousand years old, how legible and memorable the original marks of letters, words, statements and sketches inscribed, painted, inked or outlined in charcoal would have been to a contemporary viewer. Following a pathway of related messages would not have been nearly as difficult to an individual used to doing so, especially for a participant in the ongoing process of meaning production through ephemeral inscription. Importantly, the proximity of a public cistern (*castellum aquae*) and drinking fountain, directly opposite the entrance to VI.2.9–10, helps to explain the number and variety of graffiti on the exterior wall. It also provides a natural context for memorializing particular aspects of individual and shared social experience in a neighbourhood of the city used to regular, diverse pedestrian traffic along the Via Consulare through the Herculaneum Gate.

Figure 3.5 Entrance, Roman *cryptoporticus* in the *Horti Sallustiani*, Villa Ludovisi, Rome.

A brief examination of the graffiti in the Roman *cryptoporticus* of the late antique *Horti Sallustiani* – that is, the partially subterranean corridor supporting a covered passageway in the so-called Gardens of Sallust[20] – confirms the widespread nature of literacies delineated by socio-cultural context in antiquity. Enlarged and embellished over the centuries since the foundation at the end of the republican period (first century BCE) of the gardens – originally part of the estate of the dictator Julius Caesar; acquired after his death by the historian and orator Gaius Sallustius Crispus (Sallust) – the *Horti Sallustiani* saw the inclusion during the third and early fourth centuries CE of a long, partially open, frescoed structure which ran through the estate (Figure 3.5). The only part of this structure which is visible today comprises a series of wall paintings and a number of graffiti, located on two walls of the *cryptoporticus* and an ancillary room, which cover the frescoes.

Consisting of literal texts, some Christian monograms and a Jewish *menorah*, the graffiti can be dated to the period corresponding to between some point in time after the beginning of the third century CE and the invasion of Rome by the Goths in 410 CE. While it is impossible to determine with any degree of accuracy the nature of historical circumstances under which graffiti were inscribed over the paintings on the walls of the main communicating corridor and one of the associated rooms, the mixture of complete words and letter-groups in a variety of cursive types, and of Christian and Jewish symbols, once again emphasizes the use and reception of text and image displayed on public surfaces susceptible to inscription with a variety of literate audiences in mind.

FINAL THOUGHTS

Like the texts reported in Plutarch, and the *admiror* and Region VI inscriptions from Pompeii – not to mention the Egyptian and Greek material explored earlier in this chapter – the *Horti Sallustiani* graffiti display a clear relationship between acts of graffiti practice and contexts conducive to textual and visual literacy. As Hillier and Hanson observe, "space ... creates the special relation between function and social meaning in buildings ... [and] through the ways in which buildings ... create and order space, we are able to recognize society".[21] While at no point inferring a literal relationship between specific types of building or civic space and graffiti practices in the ancient world, it would seem that the material traces of messages – the writing and imagery painted, marked and inscribed on the visible surfaces of the urban fabric and preserved for us as *graphio inscripta* – allow modern eyes and minds to identify, connect and reconstruct facets of past lives. Situated within their spatial contexts, the extant remains of graffiti help us to reconstitute social and cultural meanings known by and shared among a spectrum of heterogeneous ancient communities.

CHAPTER 4

ART AND ARCHITECTURE

In tribute, a gift donated by Marcus Martiannus Pulcher, most honourable of men, pro-praetorian legate of the emperors, who restored this temple of Isis, collapsed in old age and in ruins.

(*RIB* 2503.118)

ANCIENT ART AND ARCHITECTURE IN CONTEXT

Recognizing art may at first appear to be a straightforward exercise. As the expression or application of human creative skill and imagination, art can be identified typically in a visual form such as painting or sculpture. Of course, this distillation of what art *is* implies more than objects produced by the artist – a statue, a portrait in relief, a piece of decorated pottery. Dance, music and literature are also forms of art. Moreover, as with all forms of communication, art is not only produced; it is also consumed. In its most general sense, what we in the twenty-first century call art can include anything that is pleasing to the senses – the *aesthetic* of the artistic enterprise – and has been created by a person or group of people – the process of *creativity* embodied in the imagination and technical skill of the artist – for other persons or groups of people – the *reception* of information and ideas. This set of principles – aesthetic, creativity, reception – underlies and guides any work of art, whether modern or ancient.

Our definition of art also implies a practical dimension. Because paintings and sculptures are pleasing to look at, they often are used to decorate spaces that would otherwise be plain and drab. Artisans, the craftspeople who create useful objects such as pottery, furniture and tools, often decorate their products to make them unique and more attractive. It is in this regard that art also features in the design of construction of buildings and other elements of civic and domestic infrastructure. In the simplest of terms, this is what architecture is all about. Scratched into a piece of pottery from third-century CE Roman Britain, the graffito in the epigraph to this chapter neatly captures this relationship between art, architecture and non-official inscriptions in the ancient world.

Since antiquity and through to the present age, architecture and the pictorial arts have not been rigidly separated but interrelated – the one informing the other, and establishing patterns of creation and reception. Moreover, in the aesthetic and built fabric of every human society, art forms part of a complex structure of beliefs and rituals, moral and social codes, magic or science, myth or history. In some ways, art exists at some point between scholarly or scientific knowledge and magical or mythological thought, between what is perceived and what is believed, and also between human capabilities and human aspirations. As a medium of communication it is very similar to language. Like the words we speak or write, art makes statements that can give someone facts or information, or advise people about questions of morality or interpreting social codes of behaviour. But, like the vocabulary of myth, it can establish something unfamiliar about the physical world, or capture moments in time and render them permanent. Within any social group – the smallest association of human beings in a rural village or urban neighbourhood; the largest cultural collective or geopolitical empire – art and architecture draw motifs, themes or subjects from a common stock. The manner of representation and fabrication is limited by what materials and tools are on hand, by the particular abilities passed on from one generation to the next, and by the ways in which aesthetic, creativity and reception are usually done.

It is within this context that graffiti in antiquity reflect aspects of ancient art and architecture. Whether Egypt or Greece or Rome, the production of any artefact – building, sculpture or painting – is dependent on both manual skill and technical knowledge. Pottery vessels, baskets, textiles, statues, frescoes, temples: all of these demand coordination of form and function with skill in handling and control in executing ideas, drawn together in such a way that guarantees durability. What graffiti can provide in relation to this process of creation is the teasing out of concepts, the representation of those steps between the idea in the maker's mind and the skill needed to express it and give it form. In the same way that graffiti can shed light on past history and the uses of language in antiquity, the non-official markings of artisans and craftspeople, architects and builders, and the people who commemorated what and who they saw, provide us with a window on methods of construction, carving and painting in the ancient world – structure and style, function and form – and on the ideas and activities associated with the varied contexts of ancient art and architecture.

Egypt

As we have already seen (Chapter 1), hunters and herders inscribed, pecked or engraved an extensive repertory of images on rock surfaces in prehistoric

ART AND ARCHITECTURE

times. From the beginning of the fourth millennium BCE, the rock surfaces of the Egyptian deserts, particularly the eastern desert, provided a similarly attractive location for distilling memories, expressing ideas or passing time. These rock drawings encompass the period of change from the emergence of civilization in the Near East – hunting and gathering, seasonal movements of people with livestock – to the development of state-ordered, stratified societies – characterized by a settled way of life, the domestication of plants and animals, and the control of people and territory under a central hierarchy. As a result, they reveal a great deal about hunting, ritual, dance, costume and the way of life of the desert people who produced them and the fauna with which they shared their lives. From Egypt through Palestine and Syria into Mesopotamia, rock graffiti trace the radical social reorientation of these Neolithic and Bronze Age societies by way of the organic synthesis of human and animal imagery into pictographic symbols.

In Egypt, the greatest density of drawings engraved into rock surfaces can be found in the southern regions, extending down into Nubia. While this area today is rather desolate, during the period in which pictorial graffiti were scratched into the rock the Egyptian climate would have supported a cross-section of human and animal life. Centred on the Wâdi Hammâmât and its tributaries, the great eastern desert wadi (valley) system displays a rich array of sophisticated images exhibiting considerable artistic proficiency.[1] These drawings were scratched into the regular, friable surfaces of freestanding rock outcrops and sheltered overhangs located along tracks that extend across the eastern desert. They comprise a range of thematic interests – people, animals, boats – and a variety of skill sets – the rough scribblings of unskilled travellers, images reflecting originality of thought and execution, and representations of significant artistic quality.

One of the better-known sites among the 15 valleys of the eastern Egyptian desert is Wadi Abu Markab el-Kes (also called Wadi Abu Wasil). First identified by Hans Winkler in the early twentieth century (1936–8), the Abu Markab rock drawings, spread out along the valley at 26 separate locations, include an image of two tall human figures, holding bows across their chests, and three smaller companions, all standing in a high-prowed boat. The boat is attached by a rope to another figure, situated to the right, wearing an elaborate headdress, standing in a second, smaller boat. While the meaning of this image remains uncertain, the superhuman dimensions of the larger figures – depicted wearing what appear to be body-length robes and a pair of plumes or feathers in their hair – may indicate their identity as individuals of political or religious authority ("chiefs"), important socio-cultural status ("warriors"), or divine beings. Certainly their size – in comparison with the smaller figures that we might identify as their human companions – suggests the representation of a hierarchy of power-relations. The enigmatic figure, also wearing double plumes, that stands to one side, holding the rope attached to the boat, must remain unidentified, although its dimensions

69

imply another category of human being, related perhaps to the smaller figures in the boat.

Other images crowd around this larger vignette. For instance, it is possible to discern another high-prowed boat engraved above, bearing a standing figure with a double plume; and, further to the right of the figure joined to the larger boat by rope, is a depiction of a plumed figure (a hunter?) in the act of killing (as part of a ritual act?) a tethered animal (most likely a bovid) with a bow and arrow.

The Abu Markab boat graffito described above is not an isolated example. Winkler (and others) found a number of drawings depicting high-prowed boats and mysterious standing figures of varying heights. In the same wadi, predynastic images comprise a range of boat motifs – a boat carrying a figure with raised arms, dragged by five other figures; a boat with a single sail; a boat with a covering of some kind stretched in a semi-circle from bow to stern – and subject matter related to hunting and pastoralism – a scene of an ostrich hunt; a drawing of figures in boats in pursuit of large-horned animals; a vignette of cattle controlled by humans.

The rock drawings of the valleys of southern Egypt east of the Nile are not limited to scenes which focus on the daily life and beliefs of the people indigenous to predynastic desert contexts. North of the Wâdi Hammâmât, at the seventeenth site examined by Winkler in the years before World War II (Wadi el-Atwani), a graffito engraved amid a cluster of animal figures represents what appears at first sight to be a crude amalgam of wavy lines and spirals; if not a doodle scratched idly by someone sheltering under the rock, then surely nothing more than a simple design. Comparison with modern survey maps of the region reveals something much more interesting: a top-down cartographical diagram corresponding closely with the modern geography of Wadi el-Atwani; in all likelihood, therefore, an aerial view of the predynastic hunting grounds associated with the area.

Since the original discovery, other "maps" have been identified, reflecting a widespread hunter-gatherer society occupying Egypt's eastern desert that was profoundly familiar with regional geography. One modern study interprets the aggregation of graffiti pictures at various sites as focal points of a series of interrelated killing zones: "regarded as spiritual places, regularly visited by generations of hunters."[2]

In the same geographical region of southern Egypt, but engraved closer to the beginning of the pharaonic period, we can discern the evolution of a common graffiti motif into something more familiar to scholars of Egyptian religious iconography. Among a small cluster of drawings located in a valley due west of Luxor, dating to Naqada II (c.3600–3200 BCE) or later, an ithyphallic figure (that is, a figure depicted with an erect penis) is shown, standing on a boat very similar to those we have already encountered – depicted with oars and an almost vertical prow and stern. The figure wears a headdress of two feathers (or, possibly, sticks). At Wâdi Hammâmât, an ithyphallic

ART AND ARCHITECTURE

figure with the same kind of headdress appears to be holding a defeated enemy by the hair. Another drawing – situated between Kom Ombo and Edfu in a rocky gorge 65 km north of Aswan, where the cliffs bordering the Nile narrow (Gebel Silsela) – shows a mummiform figure (i.e. drawn with legs connected) with erect penis, a streamer of some kind falling from the back of his head and holding a bow and a stick. Comparing the style and execution of these figures to the iconographic representations of Egyptian gods, the resemblance to that of one of the foremost deities throughout dynastic history – Min, the ithyphallic god of fertility and regeneration, associated with the perpetuation of agricultural prosperity and the renewal of the powers of kingship – is quite clear.

While any explicit association between these representations of Min and the earlier rock drawings of plumed figures is incidental, we can see how graffiti like these help us to obtain a picture of the historical development, changes and interrelationships of various aspects of artistic form and function. In this instance, it is possible to identify the manner in which ancient graffiti artists expressed ideas intrinsic to their thought-world at the cusp of the transitional period between predynastic transhumant and dynastic subsistence society – the connections between the acquisition or production of food (from hunting and gathering to settled pastoralism and agriculture), the reproduction of society (symbolized as agricultural and human fecundity) and cult iconography (the divine attributes of the god Min).

Much of what we know about pharaonic Egypt – including its art and architecture – derives from royal inscriptions, from the tombs of the rulers, and from the monuments of officials. However, in one particular village, home to the men who built the tombs of the pharaohs in the Valley of the Kings, it is possible to reconstruct something of the lives of these ancient Egyptians from official records, literary texts, private letters *and* simple drawings. Egyptologists use the Arabic name for the site, Deir el-Medina ("monastery of the town").

In the late New Kingdom (*c.*1550–1069 BCE), the decoration of a royal tomb – which took the form of a series of corridors and chambers cut into the desert valley west of Thebes – required a full-time team of draughtsmen, carpenters and their suppliers. The administrators and draughtsmen of the Deir el-Medina community were literate. Given that these men comprised a highly specialized group of royal craftsmen and architects working on the most important building project in Egypt, they did not belong to the working class: they were well-educated, accomplished in their respective occupations and, as such, possessed a sophisticated literacy level across a spectrum of visual and written fields. In relation to our previous discussion of reading and writing in the ancient world (Chapter 3), it is interesting to note that this comparatively high level of literacy includes the women of the village, who were responsible for all aspects of household management in the absence of the men working in the tombs.

71

Importantly for the purposes of this chapter, the workmen of Deir el-Medina often used a convenient writing and drawing material present in abundance in the desert and generated as a by-product of tomb building: limestone chips and pottery sherds (*ostraca*). The archaeologists Schiaparelli, Moeller and Bruyère discovered thousands of *ostraca* in the rubbish heaps of the village, and the Czech scholar Jaroslav Černý transcribed a large proportion.[3] Together with the numerous papyri from the site, these *ostraca* represent the largest group of daily records surviving from ancient Egypt.

The figured *ostraca* or pictorial sherds provide unparalleled evidence of the artistic manner in which the workmen made known their thoughts and feelings. Some exhibit preliminary sketches or fully developed drafts of scenes to be incorporated into the decorative repertoire of the royal tombs – profiles of funerary deities (e.g. Osiris, lord of the underworld); portraits of pharaohs wearing royal regalia (e.g. the white crown of Upper Egypt; the crook and flail, insignia of rule); other details of kingship (e.g. the falcon's head, representing Horus; the cobra or *uraeus*); and individual motifs associated with tomb paintings (e.g. profiles of royal officials; animal images appropriate in hunting, offering or funerary scenes).

Less frequently the *ostraca* represent copies of tomb paintings. Illustrating either a historical or mythological scene, one of the discarded limestone flakes depicts a young woman sitting beneath an enclosure covered with vines nursing an infant. The composition of the scene and the various inclusions reflect both the skill of the artist and the traditional nature of the painted image. We can note, for example, that, while the woman appears to be naked, she is nonetheless elaborately outfitted with wig, jewellery, sandals and belt; and she is attended by a female servant, whose earring and partially shaven hairstyle identify her as a Nubian slave. It is highly unlikely, then, that the woman suckling her child was an ordinary villager.

Sketched in rust-red, another of these limestone flakes shows a standing scribe wearing a knee-length kilt. The arms of the scribe are raised to present a papyrus scroll and possibly a writing palette. Behind him the artist has drawn an offering table. Clearly the individual who produced this graffito has provided us with a novel image of an Egyptian scribe with the tools of his profession. The pictographic symbol which completes the scene – the hieroglyphic sign for "scribe" (*sesh*), written in an expert script – confirms the nature of the artist's calling. It is worth noting that scribes are traditionally depicted in official sculpture and formal painted scenes in a seated position, with legs crossed, holding writing equipment. The Deir el-Medina scribe who has left behind his self-portrait with autograph wanted to portray himself in a manner perhaps more in keeping with the reality of his daily activity or possibly as he would have preferred himself to be seen.

Unlike the official art in the tombs and the temples, the Deir el-Medina *ostraca* provide an uncommon insight into the creative process of these skilled workers and the rich variety of ideas underlying their professional output.

72

ART AND ARCHITECTURE

Given the wealth of evidence available to us, it is easy enough to imagine these men – the so-called "servants in the Great Place" occupied in dressing tomb masonry, carving funerary texts and images, and painting traditional scenes of offering, thanksgiving and divine transformation – sourcing a limestone flake in a moment of leisure, drawing a picture, and afterwards throwing away what was always intended as nothing more than the impermanent expression of a passing thought. What makes these graffiti drawings so valuable is the fact that the subject matter and designs represent the personal choice of the artist. As a result, the figured *ostraca* of Deir el-Medina often preserve themes and motifs outside the traditional canon of state-sanctioned art. In a similar vein, the pictorial sherds of the off-duty workmen also display personal stylistic modes free to a large extent from the limiting conventions associated with the production of official religious art.

Greece

Pictorial graffiti found in the Athenian Agora date from the late eighth to early seventh century BCE until the late Roman period (after the fourth century CE). The fact that the informal marking of surfaces within a circumscribed urban setting is recorded across such an extensive chronological period confirms the trans-historical nature of the phenomenon and illustrates its usefulness as a means of examining concepts springing from a specific cultural context. Incised with a fine-pointed tool on the interior or exterior surfaces of a variety of pottery vessels – drinking cups, vases for mixing wine and water; decorative stands, lamps; containers for oil and grain; bowls, pots and plates – the drawings depict a range of designs, occasionally with associated text. Due to the fragmentary nature of the surviving evidence, it is impossible to establish any verifiable motivation behind the production of these graffiti. Nonetheless, like the Deir el-Medina sketches, the Athenian graffiti would most likely reflect the work of resident Greek artists and potters and their apprentices.

Engraved using the same implements that decorated the objects commissioned in their workshops, the drawings comprise (in no particular order):

- Human anatomy – a bearded head wearing a wreath, dating to the Classical period; the act of sodomy, similarly from the second quarter of the fifth century BCE; a late Roman head with helmet.
- The world of Greek mythology – a sixth-century BCE ithyphallic satyr (one of the male companions of the god Pan and Dionysus, with the pointed ears, legs and short horns of a goat); a creature of some kind with a head and wings, from the fourth century CE.
- A late fifth-century BCE drawing of a pygmy, evoking unfamiliar lands outside conventional Greek experience.

73

- Certain figures representing traditional religious or magical attributes – a late fifth-century BCE swastika; an early fourth-century BCE phallus.
- Architectural elements – a late fourth to early third-century BCE herm (a squared stone pillar with a carved head at the apex, typically that of the messenger of the gods, Hermes); a first-century CE bucranium (the skull of an ox adorned with floral wreaths or garlands).
- A miscellany of animal images, rounding off the catalogue of figural graffiti – a fish, dating to the first half of the sixth century BCE; a crane, to the left of the fighting pygmy; a late Roman dolphin.

These non-official drawings from the Athenian Agora are incised on surfaces which once featured other, more formally painted or engraved images. Another collection of pictorial graffiti, located within a specifically Greek context in the ancient Mediterranean, is situated in a space that did not primarily serve this function. Aphrodisias – a city in Caria (a region in southwest Turkey) only sporadically attested in literary sources – has produced an impressive quantity of information, primarily from a wealth of epigraphic evidence stretching across eight centuries of ancient history (first century BCE to seventh century CE).[4]

As a major urban centre in the Roman province of Asia Minor (the Anatolian peninsula), the city features a variety of civic spaces offering opportunities for the display of formal epigraphy *and* non-official graffiti: two municipal precincts – the North and South Agora – and a number of public buildings – a large temple (dedicated originally to Aphrodite, converted into a Christian cathedral *c.*500 CE); a basilica (one of the best preserved buildings of its type); an imperial cult centre (the Sebasteion, dedicated to Aphrodite and the Roman emperors); a stadium (used for Greek-style athletic festivals and Roman-style gladiatorial games and wild animal hunts); a theatre (comprising an auditorium and elaborate three-storied marble stage building, one of the oldest in Asia Minor); a bath complex (dedicated to the emperor Hadrian in the early second century CE); and a Bouleuterion (the equivalent of a council house or town hall). It is to the last of the buildings listed here that our attention will turn.

Constructed in the late second or early third century CE, the Bouleuterion at Aphrodisias was intended as a meeting place for the city council (*boule*) (Figure 4.1). It served this purpose for over three centuries, until converted in the fifth century into a *palaestra* ("wrestling place") hosting non-political activities like public recitations, performances of various kinds, and a range of competitive displays.[5] Built centrally on axis with the North Agora, the Bouleuterion was an important building connected to one of the city's pre-eminent spaces housing both civic and religious functions. Like other buildings of its type in the imperial East, it displayed Aphrodisias' power and organization as a community, embodying the city's regional character under Roman rule. A number of pictorial graffiti carved into the seats of the semicircular auditorium – a shape favoured in the eastern provinces – reflects the

ART AND ARCHITECTURE

Figure 4.1 Bouleuterion, Aphrodisias, Turkey.

building's use as a multi-functional complex, echoing in some respects its formal role as a tangible expression of Hellenistic–Roman identity.

Three drawings were scratched into the plaster of a corridor wall located behind the stage structure which fronts the auditorium of the building. All three exhibit elements of the human form: (1) a figure wearing a long robe; (2) a half-profile of a head; and (3) the head and shoulders of a man wearing a short tunic. The sketch of the robed figure may represent a speaker delivering a lecture or a glimpse of a festival or ritual performance. The fact that the garment worn by the person depicted in the sketch is carefully shaded along all its edges with a series of closely drawn parallel lines could well reflect the status or prominence of the individual. If close attention is paid to the outline of the figure, it is clear that the left hand, extending down, holds a horizontal object, from which two lines, ending in circular marks, hang. While it is not possible to determine with any accuracy what this object represents, given the context of the space in which the graffito appears it could indicate something used by the figure in the course of speaking or participating in a civic activity; possibly a scroll, or a ritual instrument of some kind.

The other two sketches provide no specific detail, other than suggesting that the easternmost recess of the backstage corridor was used as a canvas for idle doodling or transmitting information about what was seen or done in this place.

The use of the Bouleuterion corridor wall as a site for artistic expression is confirmed by another small cluster of pictures in close proximity to the

75

figural graffiti above. Two complete images and a partial sketch depict the same design: a man riding a horse. One of the complete drawings and the partial outline constitute a view of a man on a horse, holding a long pole, advancing to his left. Both pictures are drawn without particular skill or elegance. The second complete image is far more carefully rendered. It, too, depicts a rider, wearing a long tunic. He holds in his right hand the reins of a horse, shown with its front legs together, jumping forward to the left; in his left hand, he holds a long pole. The sudden movement of the horse is accentuated by the manner in which the horse's legs are shown in a moment of suspension when all four feet are off the ground, and the rider's knee digs into his mount's flank. Whatever the artist may have intended this image to represent, the fact that the horseman is meant to be observed is suggested neatly by the way in which the rider's head turns to look directly at the viewer, framed by the fringe of hair gathered on either side of his face.

An astonishing archaeological find in two rooms of a small stoa north of the Bouleuterion suggests a dynamic intersection of artistic form and function between official and non-official artistic expression at Aphrodisias. Together with the open area immediately south of the stoa, the rooms excavated in 1964 revealed what appears to have been a sculptor's workshop. Reflecting a lively sculptural (and commercial) tradition that flourished in the city from the first to the sixth centuries CE, the excavations discovered stone working tools, unfinished statuary and marbles that had been used to test or demonstrate tools. The workshop and associated open-air space yielded unfinished portrait sculptures and numerous large- and small-scale mythological statues and fragments, including a bichrome statuette of Europa and the bull, a full-scale statue of a satyr holding the infant Dionysus, and a statuette of Aphrodite cradled in the arms of a portrait of a priest (both now headless).

That we find pictorial graffiti depicting portraits of standing and equestrian figures in a context spatially adjacent to a workshop specializing in the design and manufacture of portrait sculpture and ideal works is a fascinating juxtaposition of art and architecture. Reflecting cultural relationships between the production and display of sculpture and other artistic forms in antiquity, the graffiti images of Aphrodisias' Bouleuterion provide a fuller understanding of the ways in which the creative expression of ordinary individuals took inspiration from the established artistic vocabulary and – with varying degrees of success – regenerated or modified conventional pictorial principles. Just as the adaptive architectural contexts housing both sculptor's workshop and pictorial graffiti underwrite the city's accommodation of Roman rule in relation to a Hellenistic community, the cluster of human and animal drawings scratched in the wall plaster of the Bouleuterion corridor represent an amalgam of change at one level while continuity is maintained at another.

76

ART AND ARCHITECTURE

Rome

Whether informal engravings cut into surfaces susceptible to incision with a sharp instrument, or painted, pictorial graffiti depicting designs or objects comprise a significant proportion of non-official markings in the Roman world. Like their counterparts in ancient Egypt (eastern desert, Deir el-Medina) and Greece (Athenian Agora, Aphrodisias), Roman non-verbal graffiti are found on a wide variety of surfaces (clay pots, stuccoed walls, exposed bedrock, flagstone paving, stone seats, as well as non-durable materials like wood and leather) across a broad geographical sweep (encompassing coastal and inland Mediterranean sites) and chronological duration (from the regal period to late antiquity). These graffiti images appear without explanation or accompanying a written text.

At the end of the seventh century BCE the process of urban formation giving rise to the cities of Latium – the region of central western Italy where Rome was founded – was almost complete and the use of the alphabet, to be adopted by the Latin language, appears in several epigraphic contexts. Of course these are rare and exceptional, and attest to private uses of writing, probably practised only by a narrow circle of people. Inscribed texts and pictorial engravings appear to be used in connection with offering gifts to the living or the deceased. In this sense, like the graffiti incised on the pottery found in the Athenian Agora, these proto-Roman texts and images constitute a transition-point between the formal epigraphy of civic spaces and the informal markings of private individuals.

The written texts are mostly formed from the name of the recipient or the donor. In this context, it is worth noting an Etruscan inscription engraved on a small globular flask with a narrow neck (an *aryballos*).[6] Made from bucchero – black ceramic ware characteristic of the Etruscans prior to Rome's archaic period (580–490 BCE) – the *aryballos* comes from a chamber tomb, unfortunately collapsed and plundered by illegal excavations, in the territory of Veii near Volusia. The text, inscribed around the widening neck of the flask, gives the names of the donor (Venel Setiu) and of the person intended as the destination of the gift (Thancuil Kanzina). Texts like this, carved to claim ownership of an object, usually consist of a noun in the nominative (the subject of the statement) or genitive (indicating possession). Likewise the offer of a gift to the divine was characterized usually by the name of the god or goddess in the genitive to emphasize the consecration of the property.

The text inscribed on the Veii *aryballos* is useful in clarifying the purpose for which the object was originally produced. However, examination of the flask below the writing reveals two pictorial incisions: depictions of a horse and a boat. Far less codified than the plethora of geometric symbols characterizing pre-Etruscan pottery decoration, these seventh-century BCE images of a horse and a boat reflect an artistic repertoire that could be "read" (i.e. recognized and interpreted) more easily, communicating more effectively across

77

cultural frontiers. On one level, these pictures act as ornamental additions to object and text, serving to embellish the donative flask and thereby making it more attractive to the identified recipient of the gift. From a perspective of cultural exchange, the motifs encapsulate and reinforce certain connotations of status and power (e.g. horsemanship and luxurious decoration) in contemporary use by privileged groups in Latium and Etruria specifically, but more generally in the eastern Mediterranean (Greeks, Phoenicians). According to both "readings" of the Veii flask, pictorial markings may have been appreciated by a contemporary audience as decoration *and* communication. In the latter sense, close critical analysis of images like these highlights a need to incorporate contrasting forms of symbolism and cognition when coming to grips with the meaning of figural graffiti.

Dating from the foundation of the Roman colony in 80 BCE until its catastrophic destruction in 79 CE, graffiti drawings (with and without textual messages) comprise a significant quantum of non-official markings on the surfaces of ancient Pompeii. While a variety of locations provides evidence for the artistic tendencies of the local population and the city's many visitors, one cluster of graffiti attests to the wide-ranging interests of the people who frequented this particular space. On the north and south walls of the long, narrow corridor running from the Via Stabia behind the Odeon or Covered Theatre to the east entrance of the Large Theatre, *CIL* IV records 57 graffiti. Recent autopsy of the surviving plaster which covers the lower sections of the corridor walls shows that a number of inscriptions remain in situ: *inter alia*, a horse, a donkey, at least two ships, an anchor, two gladiators, an ithyphallic Priapus (a minor fertility deity), architectural fragments, including perhaps a tower, as well as numerical marks and a few recognizable text-types. Given the diversity of motifs, some of these images will be discussed in later chapters dealing with religion and mythology, sport, commerce and sexuality. However, as a pastiche of pictorial designs and writing, the graffiti found here in Pompeii's theatrical precinct reflect the way in which art and architecture inform community knowledge and practice.

Founded at some point during the later seventh to early sixth century BCE by the Osci (a central Italian tribal people) on what was an important mainland junction (linking Cumae, Nola and Stabiae), Pompeii had already been used as a safe port by Greek and Phoenician sailors. Occupied successively by Etruscans, Greeks, Samnites (another central Italian people) and finally Roman colonists, its fertile and well-drained volcanic soil and mild climate made Pompeii an agricultural nexus, and her port and geographic position gave her easy access to markets near and far. The city's history reflects this agricultural, commercial and multi-cultural heritage – a complex network of traditions that finds expression in graffiti like those in the Odeon corridor.

We know, for instance, that wheeled traffic in Pompeii was organized into an efficient system governed by the rule of right-side driving, the imposition of congestion-relieving detours, and by alternating series of one-way streets.[7]

78

ART AND ARCHITECTURE

However, while the city's transportation economy relied for the most part on mules and porters, these means of transport did not make the same physical impact as wheel ruts and worn street features. Comparison with two frescoes in one of the city's numerous inns (VI.10.1) – both depicting scenes of a cart delivering wine, with the mules resting unharnessed beside the covered vehicle – indicates the commonplace nature of this commercial practice.[8] The drawing of a mule on the Odeon corridor wall is valuable evidence for the visibility of this method of conveyance.

Similarly the drawing of a boat attests to the proximity of the city to the Italian coastline and its nature as a busy, commercial city. Archaeological evidence indicates that Pompeii enjoyed considerable trade with many places in the Roman empire. The port of the city, at the mouth of the Sarnus river, also served the towns in the interior and the villas in the surrounding countryside. The geographer Strabo informs us that Pompeii acted as the port for Nuceria and Nola.[9] Their products would be brought to Pompeii, and if intended for export to other parts of the Mediterranean would be transferred to seagoing vessels. More will be said about this later (Chapter 10). However, the cross-hatched outline of a boat with figured prow confirms the importance of maritime trade to Pompeii's economy. The corridor drawing may be compared with the impressive and elegant graffito of a cargo ship named "Europa" (Figure 4.2)

Figure 4.2 Graffito of the ship "Europa", north wall, peristyle, I.15.3 (Casa della Nave Europa), Pompeii, Italy.

79

– incised carefully on the north wall of a peristyle courtyard in a private home close to the Amphitheatre (I.15.3) – or another detailed image of a sailing vessel (Figure 4.3) – scratched into the wall of the Forum Baths (VII.6.18).

The architectural elements featured in a few of the Odeon graffiti – now very faded and extremely difficult to photograph – may shine a light on the

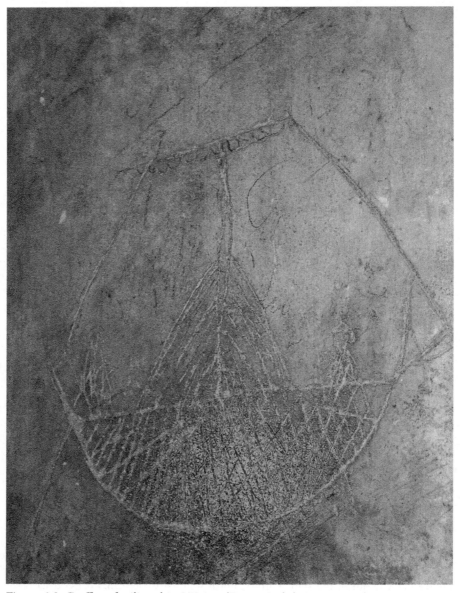

Figure 4.3 Graffito of sailing ship, VII.6.18 (Forum Baths), Pompeii, Italy.

ART AND ARCHITECTURE

period of reconstruction throughout the city in the aftermath of a severe earthquake in 62 CE. The Roman philosopher and statesman Lucius Annaeus Seneca provides a contemporary account of this event, telling his first-century audience that "Pompeii, a busy town in Campania, ha[d] subsided under an earthquake".[10] An inscription referring to the reconstruction of the temple of Isis confirms the severity of the incident.[11] From Seneca and other sources it is clear that Pompeii and Herculaneum were located at the earthquake's epicentre; but other sites, including Nuceria and Naples, were also affected. In Pompeii itself, the Vesuvius and Herculaneum Gates fell, and aqueducts and other elements of the city's hydraulic system – including residential plumbing – were broken. A sculptured relief on the household shrine (Latin *lararium*) in the home of the banker L. Caecilius Iucundus vividly portrays the collapse of the temple of Jupiter Optimus Maximus, a ceremonial arch and various statues in the Forum. A second relief in the same house depicts the collapse of the Vesuvius Gate. In relation to the previous discussion, it is interesting to note that two mules and a cart are shown lifted into the air by the force of the tremor. That the architectural elements scratched into the Odeon corridor wall preserve a record of the building activity that characterized the last years of Pompeii makes perfect sense. Drawings such as these provide further indication of how pictorial graffiti transmitted essential information about ancient urban life – in this case, the explicit intersection of art and architecture as part of a vibrant socio-cultural canvas displayed in a highly frequented public space.

As noted above, pictorial graffiti can be found in urban contexts across the Roman world. Built on a larger scale than Pompeii – a small Italian city in relative terms – Ostia, Rome's port city, evolved from its original strategic function as a defensive outpost at the mouth of the river Tiber into a city of imperial officials and international traders living and working alongside local freedmen and artisans in a major trading centre at the heart of the Roman empire. Closely associated with Portus – the maritime harbour to the north of Ostia, established by the emperor Claudius in the mid-first century CE, enlarged by Trajan, and subsequently modified during the third and fourth centuries CE – the river port of Ostia supplied imperial Rome with foodstuffs and materials from across the empire and acted as both a point of export for supplies and products from the Tiber Valley to the north of Rome and a major hub for the redistribution of goods from ports outside Italy. As a consequence, Ostia acted as a major conduit for people visiting Rome from around the Mediterranean.

Understanding the urban geography of this large site would have been as complex a task in the ancient world as it is for those who study such spaces today. How, precisely, did the residents of Ostia and its variable transient population find their way through the city? An intriguing graffito – to all intents and purposes nothing more than a series of unrelated intersecting lines – suggests that the variable pedestrian and vehicular network governing

81

GRAFFITI IN ANTIQUITY

movement and traffic made it necessary for someone to map out a section of Ostia's web of streets and buildings. Resembling a street plan of a section of the north-west region of the city (Region I) – stretching from the Via della Foce (also known as the Via Laurentina) to the Via Epagathiana – the heterogeneous and differentiated pattern of lines incised into the plaster of an exterior wall marks the attempt of a person familiar with this area of the city to reconstruct (more than likely for someone new to Ostia) a passage through the town which gave ready access to the principal buildings in the neighbourhood. If this "reading" of the graffito is correct, then the person responsible for this map has left us with a practical reminder of the variable social practices that distinguished this part of Region I – from the sacred precinct of republican temples that border the Via della Foce to the large storehouses of grain to the east (the Horrea Apagathiana et Epaphroditiana and Piccolo Mercato) – and an indication of the difficulties faced by newcomers when confronted with the Ostian streetscape.

Another graffito drawing confirms the highly developed commercial foundation of the city (Chapter 11). A number of the buildings in Ostia which stored grain (*horrea*) can be identified by referring to the presence of large storage jars (*amphorae*). In a house dating from the first quarter of the second century CE, a sketch of an *amphora* can (with some difficulty) be identified. Following the lead provided already from our earlier study of such contexts as Deir el-Medina and the Bouleuterion at Aphrodisias, it is fascinating to observe that many large, buried jars (*dolia defossa*) have been discovered in a building adjacent to the house with the *amphora* graffito. Interpreting pictorial graffiti like this in light of the spatial context is logical and potentially very useful. We know from the elder Pliny[12] that it was usual in temperate climates to store wine in such sunken jars. These *dolia defossa*[13] could be used for the storage of liquids such as wine and oil, and solids like grain, fruit or ham.[14] In Ostia four deposits of *dolia defossa* have so far been discovered.[15]

The depiction of an *amphora* in a space adjacent to a *dolia* storehouse sets up what appears at first sight a puzzling juxtaposition of storage options. Again, however, contextual analysis provides a plausible explanation for the seemingly inappropriate image. If, as is highly likely, the context in which the graffito is drawn – the House of Annius (III.14.4) – originally had a commercial function, then the collocation of *amphorae* and *dolia* is perfectly reasonable. In this sense, representations of objects like the Annius *amphora* reflect their constitution as part of a socio-cultural process – the commercial activities of storage and exchange – informed by the reality of physical urban space.

An elegant engraving of a human face within a stylized boat's stern offers a final reflection on the association of artistic expression and social frameworks in Ostia. The outlook of the face is enigmatic: either staring directly out at the viewer or looking down and to the left. Comparison with a wall painting at Ostia elicits a striking similarity between the composition and placement of

82

ART AND ARCHITECTURE

the face in the graffito drawing and the figurehead on the "Isis Giminiana" – a large boat unloading its cargo into smaller barges for transport to storehouses in the city – depicted on a wall painting in a tomb (possibly Tomb 31) located south of Ostia in the Porta Laurentina necropolis. Once again, a pictorial graffito reflects the critical role Ostia played in Rome's rise, as goods flowed into the port for transport to the rest of the Italian peninsula. Just as importantly, of course, this carefully incised detail suggests a direct engagement between the graffiti artist and the prevailing cultural representation of life in the imperial harbor city – a reciprocal relationship reflected in the similar ways in which a commissioned wall painting and non-official engraving participate in a shared vocabulary of design (composition, perspective, detail) and motif (subject matter, idea, theme).

Two final examples of the manner in which graffiti in antiquity captured aspects of art and architecture will complete this introduction to the range of ancient images drawn and painted informally in non-official contexts. The first relates to a single image, sketched conceptually (according to what the mind knows); the second, to a spectrum of representations drawn and painted perceptually (according to what the eye sees at a particular moment).

Returning briefly to ancient Pompeii, the first example relates to a single large graffito, one of over 300 located in the House of Menander (I.10.4), including 41 drawings and figures. Given the state in which this very large residential block was preserved, it would appear more than likely that parts of the building were undergoing renovation prior to the eruption which buried the city. As a consequence, a number of wall surfaces had yet to receive the final coats of plaster required before artisans moved in to apply the decorative programme of painting and figured stucco commissioned by the owners. The remains of an architectural plan etched onto an unplastered wall in I.10.4 demonstrates how graffiti provide conceptual images which record the salient characteristics of a subject – in this case, the building work taking place in this section of the Menander residential block – by taking it apart and reassembling it so that all important features are captured. This way of viewing the world creates an explicit link between informal markings like this and the historical minutiae of daily life.

The humble Menander plan may be compared with contemporaneous etchings carved into surfaces like the unfinished inner walls of the temple of Apollo at Didyma (in modern Turkey) and on the paving in front of the monumental Mausoleum of Augustus in the city of Rome. Used as a drawing board, the paved surface outside the Mausoleum was inscribed with a set of building plans incised one over another in no perceptible pattern. Two of the inscriptions in question have been identified as preliminary architectural outlines for a specific monument – templates used as a design for assembling a pediment and inverted Corinthian capital for the monumental portico of the Pantheon. The size of the drawings – the pediment measures 18 m and the upper moulding of the capital is 2.8 m – indicates that the scale used by the

83

drafting artist was 1:1. These "blueprints" served the same conceptual function as the Menander plans. The Roman workmen most probably used them to construct the architectural elements they describe, measuring the blocks of marble required directly against the lines chiselled into the pavement.[16]

While the incised plans of the Pantheon's porch cannot be characterized as official inscriptions, they clearly represent the working out of practical architectural questions in relation to the form and function of what would be one of the crowning achievements of the emperor Hadrian's imperial building programme. In this regard, it is possible to delineate the Pantheon graffiti as another point of transition between the ephemeral sketches of ordinary Roman citizens – like the renovation plans of the workmen in pre-eruption Pompeii – and formal lapidary epigraphy – notably, the massive third-century CE marble map of ancient Rome produced under the emperor Septimius Severus.

The second example pertains to a trend in graffiti drawings of the past which stretches from Palaeolithic times to late antiquity. The depiction of animals represents a significant focus in the production of ancient art. We have already seen the kinds of images depicted in pigment on the cave walls of prehistoric Europe – figural renderings of bears, deer, horses and mammoths – and noted in passing other animal images in ancient Egyptian, Greek and Roman contexts – cattle in Wadi Abu Markab; the falcon and cobra at Deir el-Medina; cranes, dolphins and fish in the Athenian Agora; a horse at Veii; mules at Pompeii. The artistic expression of animals in pictorial graffiti across antiquity points to the perceptual nature of ancient representation. For instance, in the same house at Roman Pompeii where the building plans were found, numerous animal images are displayed in a variety of domestic contexts – including ducks floating on water (painted on the E. wall of the main atrium); a dolphin (on a mosaic at the entrance of Room 46, a smaller atrium); a dog chasing a fawn (painted on the inside of the peristyle balustrade).

The manner in which these formally commissioned images depict animals find informal expression in a fascinating array of graffiti drawings throughout the Vesuvian city. This variety may be illustrated by reference to a single domestic context. Beneath a Second Style wall painting from the House of the Cryptoporticus (I.6.2), residents or visitors scratched numerous graffiti – including three scenes with animals (a deer and a horse; an oryx; and a bear), which, like the peristyle painting in I.10.4, likely capture the memory of one of the many animal hunts (*venationes*) advertised as part of the entertainment in the city's amphitheatre.

FINAL THOUGHTS

Perceptual images such as these may be viewed as attempts to record the truth of visual appearances, though in practice they are invariably affected by

ART AND ARCHITECTURE

what the artists concerned know about not only the physical characteristics of a particular animal subject but also the ways in which it has previously been depicted. In this sense, over and beyond the conceptual reality that lies behind certain image-making (the Wadi el-Atwani hunting ground graffiti, the Menander plans, the Pantheon inscriptions), graffiti art in antiquity may also acquire a symbolic or referential role, addressing broader socio-cultural issues like agriculture and domestication, control over the wild forces of nature, associations of the divine, referencing human power and ideology.

CHAPTER 5

RELIGION

> Close by is an ancient and venerable temple. There the god
> Clitumnus stands ... clothed in the *praetexta* [the toga worn by
> Roman youth]. The oracles which are delivered there indicate not
> only the presence but the prophetic power of the god. Several
> shrines are scattered about the neighbourhood, each containing
> an image of the god ... some also contain fountains ... and along
> the banks of the river are a number of villas ... In a word there is
> nothing with which you will not be delighted. For you may even
> indulge your propensity for study and may read many inscrip-
> tions written by different persons on every pillar and every wall,
> in honour of the fountain and the god. Many you will applaud;
> some you will laugh at ... Farewell.   (Pliny, *Letters* 8.8)

RELIGION AND CULTURE

Trying to define exactly what is meant by the term "religion" – whether in
a modern sense or in relation to the world of antiquity – is complicated.
Religion is often understood in relation to a number of different concepts
and practices. For many people, it goes without saying that religion involves
attending a place of worship (church, synagogue, temple or similar space),
reading and contemplating the meaning of certain sacred texts, possessing
a belief system, carrying out certain actions performed in relation to prescribed ritual, and/or living one's life in a certain way. Of course, while it
can – and often does – fulfil some or all of these criteria, religion very often
embodies considerably more. When examined according to a cross-cultural
perspective – in different contexts and societies across historical time and
geopolitical space – religion may be seen to impact on all levels of life, at
both the individual and social level.

RELIGION

Following on from this basic premise, it makes sense to examine ephemeral religious expression in graffiti of the ancient world from a cultural standpoint. Naturally, religion can be understood as a concept and practice apart from culture. But, in terms of the ways in which people interact – in any age – such a differentiation seems to be an artificial distinction, separating the reality of individual and popular knowledge and experience of religion from the everyday world of action and reaction. Though problematic in its own right, if we define "culture" as the way of life of a group of people – the behaviours, beliefs, skills and values acquired and transmitted from one generation to the next – then the culture in (and by) which a person lives will be influenced (to a greater or lesser extent) by the predominant religion (or religions) of that person's society. In a reciprocal sense, the religion that a person practices will be influenced by factors of cultural context and location. Written in the early second century CE, the letter cited in the epigraph to this chapter identifies the extent to which non-official inscriptions may be situated within the spatio-cultural environment of ancient religious practice.

Across the modern world, religious plurality offers a range of gods and goddesses, customs and convictions. Many cultures comprise a spectrum of religious experiences, making up a diversity of traditions based to varying degrees on the major religious systems – Christianity, Judaism, Islam, Hinduism and Buddhism – as well as a welter of newly constituted regional variations like Scientology and Wicca. What is striking about religion in antiquity in comparison with the current age is the similar diversity of religious beliefs and practices and comparable range of cultural influences which people experienced on a plethora of intellectual and emotional levels. As long as we recognize this essential fact – that religious experience pervaded all facets of life in antiquity – then it should be easier to understand the ways in which people in the ancient Mediterranean represented religion in graffiti.

Egypt

Religion influenced life across all strata of Egyptian society. From natural forces like the rise and fall of the river Nile and the passage of the sun, to death, healing, childbirth and prosperity – all were inseparable from the gods. Throughout Egypt's history beliefs and practices were constantly changing, though the themes of fertility, rebirth, death and resurrection generally remained constant. The ancient Egyptians had a tendency to merge new beliefs with the old ones rather than simply replace them. This tendency has made it difficult for modern scholars to fully understand the ancient beliefs and, although much is known, there is still much that remains a mystery.

In simple terms, however, religious beliefs and practices in ancient Egypt – like those expressed by many cultures in antiquity – conformed to the tenets of polytheism. Ancient Egyptian religion recognized a multitude of gods and invested power in an astonishing array of cult objects. It possessed neither a central dogma nor a single holy text, professed a variety of complementary *and* contradictory truths, and did not attempt to solve the ultimate problems of existence by way of a single, coherent theory. Of course, certain symbols and objects held greater value than others; and in such cases the relationship between the object and its symbolic significance developed a correspondingly important place in the religious experience and expression of popular Egyptian culture. For instance, the insignia of royalty in ancient Egypt came to be charged with the superhuman power of kingship. As a result, the symbol of the throne took on something of the "real" significance of royal power, becoming in essence an objectification of that power – something more, that is, than a metaphorical expression of the bond between king and throne. In this sense, then, when the name of the goddess Isis is written as if it means "throne", then the ancient Egyptian view of the relationship between object and deity is perfectly expressed.

For the most part, Egyptian kings were portrayed as the living image of the most respected god, the distillation of everything that was perfect in heaven and on earth. In this sense, even prior to Egypt's official socio-political unification (as Upper and Lower Egypt), the pharaoh was understood as unequivocally divine – a god himself; son of various deities – *and* undeniably human – offspring of man and woman; part of the natural *and* civilized world. His role, therefore, as an intermediary between humanity and the gods was always of primary significance. Various graffiti evoke this paradoxical conception of royal monarchy and what it meant for the people who accepted such an ideology as representative of the order of things

Engraved at Saqqara, on the stone floor of two chambers opening into the pyramid-tomb of Djedkare Isesi (a Dynasty V pharaoh who ruled *c.*2405–2367 BCE), is a small cluster of partially hieratic graffiti texts. These inscriptions record the names and titles of certain individuals who performed duties associated with the temple in late Dynasty V or early Dynasty VI (*c.*2405–2335 BCE).[1] It is possible that these persons incised – into the paving stones of what was regarded as a sacred space – details of identity and profession to draw some advantage from the inherent godliness of the dead king, perhaps also in association with offerings for the deceased ruler.

Similarly, a few people living during the later Middle Kingdom – most likely Dynasty XII (1976–1793 BCE) – scored a small number of hieratic graffiti into the exterior surface of the funerary temple serving a pyramid originally constructed almost thirteen centuries earlier. Located at Meidûm, approximately eight kilometres south of Saqqara, the structure in question represented the earliest known attempt to build a "true" pyramid, and was most probably built under the Dynasty IV pharaoh Sneferu (2639–2604 BCE). Like the Djedkare Isesi graffiti, the texts incised on this funerary monument display the personal names of the inscribers. Though no corroborating textual evidence survives, the fact that these graffiti appear on a surface which

RELIGION

formed part of a religious context – where the deceased king could receive worship and offerings after his death in order to ensure his continued well-being in the afterlife – strongly suggests that the inscribers were either visitors on pilgrimage to the site or members of a resident priesthood serving the cult of the divine Sneferu.

Scratched on several rock surfaces some distance from the historic Upper Egyptian town site of El-Kâb – 80 km south of Luxor, on the east bank of the Nile at the mouth of Wadi Hillal – is a large cluster of hieroglyphic and hieratic graffiti. Comparing this relatively large number of non-official texts – which date for the most part to Dynasty VI (2347–2216 BCE) – with information discovered in the Old Kingdom rock tombs constructed nearby reveals that they preserve the name and titles of some of the local priesthood attached to the main temple of the goddess Nekhbet at El-Kâb. As the vulture-goddess upholding the pharaoh's rule in Upper Egypt, Nekhbet was originally an early pre-dynastic local goddess known to have been favoured by the rulers of southern Egypt. Their capital (Nekhen or Hierakonpolis) was on the opposite bank of the Nile to Nekheb (modern El-Kâb).

Why these religious officials chose to memorialize their presence with graffiti texts on the Wadi Hillal sandstone remains unclear. On a very basic level, it could be that the isolated rocks provided opportune surfaces on which the priests could mark their autographs for posterity while acting as functionaries in a desert temple not far away which was also part of their responsibility. It is also possible that we see attested here an expression of the intimate relationship between inscribing one's name and occupation and the significance of place. The proximity of these markers of personal and social identity to a smaller, ancillary temple space – all in relation to the broader context of the desert landscape – may reflect a desire on the part of the inscribing priests to situate themselves physically and symbolically within the environment from which Nekhbet's divine power was born.

As we have previously seen (Chapter 4), the New Kingdom community of Deir el-Medina – scribes and draftsmen – provided skilled workmen for the elaborate tombs of the Ramesside rulers carved out of the rock in the Wadi Biban el-Muluk (now known as the Valley of the Kings). In view of the religious associations we have noted between certain types of graffiti text and the proximity of pharaonic power, it is fascinating to find that a good number of the ordinary village craftsmen, guardians, doorkeepers and workmen (as well as the skilled artisans) scrawled their names and titles (e.g. Qenhirkhopshef, "scribe of the tomb"; Huy, "scribe in the place of truth"; Amennakhte, "draughtsman"), occasional prayers, and even figural graffiti of gods and goddesses on numerous rock faces. As a focal point for religious expression, the context of a rock face within the valley cemetery set aside for New Kingdom royalty must have seemed both logical and convenient to the villagers inscribing these texts and images on the way to and from their artistic duties.

89

GRAFFITI IN ANTIQUITY

In addition to the symbolic function of ancient Egyptian graffiti, there is evidence for the descriptive expression of religious ideology and practice. Incised on a wall in the first court of the Luxor temple constructed under Ramesses II (1279–1213 BCE), a graffito drawing with associated hieroglyphic text portrays Piankh, the (deceased) high priest of Amun, standing in front of a figure of the god. Four of the late official's sons stand behind him: Pinudjem I, the new high priest of Amun; Heqanufer, second prophet – the high priest was first prophet – of Amun; Heqamaat; and Ankhefenmut. The text reads:

G5.1   "Adoration to Amun-Re, foremost of [Karnak,] for the *ka*-spirit of [the first prophet] of Amun-Re, king of the gods, who judges the Two Lands, the leader, Piankh, made by his son who causes his name to live, the overseer of the city and vizier, the first prophet of Amun-Re, king of the gods, the great general of the entire land, the leader, Pinudjem, together with his son, the second prophet of Amun, Heqanufer, the justi-fied, together with his son, the *setem*-priest in Medinet Habu, Heqamaat, the justified, together with his son, the overseer of cattle, the great steward of Amun and the prophet of Mut, Ankhefenmut, the justified."[2]

Given his status and nature, the pharaoh acted *ex officio* as the high priest of every god's cult. However, since the number of Egyptian gods requiring a religious functionary to act as the primary conduit between humanity and the divine was considerable, the king traditionally named other individuals as his representative in the role of high priest. Serving as the high priest of Amun – Amun was the chief of all Egypt's gods – was equivalent in many ways to being Anglican Archbishop of Canterbury, Ecumenical Patriarch of Constantinople, Pontiff of the Roman Catholic Church or Dalai Lama. The Luxor forecourt graffito, therefore, provides us with a snapshot of the rarefied religious (and political) landscape of Egypt in the aftermath of Dynasty XIX (the Third Intermediate Period), the quasi-dynastic nature of priestly succession, and a startling representation – outside the usual funerary context – of how Egyptian belief mirrored temporal relationships of power and influence.

A second scene with accompanying text in the same location confirms the usefulness of non-official inscriptions as a barometer of religious sentiment and the degree to which state cult and dynastic politics intersected in New Kingdom Egypt. The graffito portrays the high priest Pinudjem I with three female children: Maatkare, the God's wife – effectively, high priestess – of Amun; Henttawy; and Nudjemmut. The graffito drawing shows Pinudjem I and his daughters worshipping images of Amun, Mut and Khonsu, the Theban triad to which the Luxor temple was dedicated. The inscriber of this graffito scene provided precise explanatory labels for each of the divine and human figures.

90

RELIGION

G5.2 Amun, for example, is described as the "great god", "foremost of Karnak"; to him should be given "all valour and all victory", "all life, stability, dominion and health". Mut is styled as "mistress of all the gods", and Khonsu (child of Amun and Mut) as "resident in Karnak".

The status and nature of the Theban triad are expressed in terms familiar from official hieroglyphic inscriptions. In addition, Pinudjem I and his daughters are accorded significant prestige;

G5.3 Pinudjem is "hereditary prince and superior of the Two Lands, first prophet of Amun"; Maatkare is "bodily daughter of the king, his beloved, the god's wife of Amun and lady of the Two Lands"; and Henttawy and Nudjemmut are, respectively, "chantress of Amun-Re" and "chief of the musical troupe of Amun".

What this informal captioned scene and the related Piankh graffito capture qualify our understanding of religious graffiti in Egypt – and graffiti in antiquity more generally. All textual and figural markings transmit matters regarded as important enough by the inscriber(s) to share with a particular but often broader audience. However, dependent on the identity of the inscriber, the location of the inscription, the choice of script and the content of the composition, graffiti will serve a multiplicity of functions. In the case of these highly charged inscriptions, the message is crystal clear. On the wall of one of the most sacred precincts of Amun, a hieroglyphic record memorializes the intimate relationship which the deceased Piankh, his son Pinudjem I, and their dependants shared with the Theban triad, and the roles which this priestly dynasty performed in maintaining right relations between Egypt and the gods. Embedded in traditional religious phraseology, Pinudjem I's informal commemorative scenes borrow the epithets, embellishments and even elements of the titulature of pharaonic status to which he and his successors clearly aspired – and which we know they eventually acquired. In these declarations of religious belief, political status and personal desire, we can discern not only that transition point between official and non-official graffiti but a neat illustration of the ways in which graffiti like these represent variegated attitudes and beliefs, intents and purposes – dependent, as always, on context, form and function.

To conclude our brief look at how graffiti can capture religious experiences in ancient Egypt, consider the phenomenon of pilgrimage. Dating to the pharaonic age, we have already noted (in discussion relating to G2.22, G3.1 and G3.2) various non-official declarations, made by travellers in what they clearly regarded as sacred places. These encounters may have been casual (lacking, in other words, a particular reason for the marking individual's presence in the temple or tomb) or intentional (namely, for the purpose of visiting the sites in question). Inscriptions marked by the latter category of visitor can be observed in Egyptian religious contexts during the Graeco-Roman period as well – and graffiti messages constitute the bulk of the surviving evidence.

Deriving from the Greek term *prokunesis* (worship of a deity), the inscriptions which conform to the intentional type and purpose noted above are technically known as *proskunemata* (prayers of praise, or acts of adoration, for the benefit of the dedicator and/or other nominated persons). Whether a person visited a sacred place in Graeco-Roman Egypt to consult an oracle, to ask for protection or healing, to sacrifice or pay homage to a deity, or even to express what might be regarded as a theological point of view, the medium of discourse regularly took the form of non-official texts and/or images displayed on the built surfaces of sacred structures or associated spaces. Although there are too many to cite in any detail, it is sufficient to note that the graffiti left by visitors in Egyptian sanctuaries and tombs during the Hellenistic and Roman periods survive from the sixth century BCE until late antiquity in contexts like the Memnonion and Osireion at Abydos, the Ptolemaic–Roman temple of the Nubian god Mandoulis (equated to Graeco-Roman Apollo) at Talmis (modern Kalabsha), the mortuary temple of Hatshepsut at Deir el Bahari, the temple of Isis on the island of Philae, even the royal tombs in the Valley of the Kings.[3]

Composed mainly in Greek (in a variety of dialects), Latin and Demotic Egyptian[4] (with a smattering of other languages like Aramaic, Carian, Coptic and Phoenician), the pilgrimage-graffiti range from brief, direct and unembellished – often, simply a declaration of "falling down and worshipping" (*proskunema*), sometimes accompanied by the word for, or a drawing of, feet (symbolizing the presence of the pilgrim), followed by a name – to extensive, allusive and stylistically sophisticated. Here are a few examples of this fascinating and wide-ranging phenomenon:

G5.4   "Philokles, son of Hierokles, from Troizen, I arrived making adoration to Serapis."[5]

G5.5   "I Spartakos, son of Phaidros, have come to Abydos; save me, Osiris!"[6]

G5.6   "Here slept and saw dreams Harpokras of holy Panias, a priest, dear descendant of Kopreias the priest, for Besas whose voice is all. And his gratitude is not small."[7]

G5.7   "... Isis of Philae and the Abaton, the great goddess, the beautiful noble lady, the beautiful refreshment of this year, giver of wealth, the mistress of heaven, of earth (and of) the underworld."[8]

RELIGION

G5.8   "The year I was high priest I went to Philae ... on the fourth of
        Thoth, the birth of Isis, there being a beautiful festival that we
        celebrated in the presence of the great mistress of the whole
        country, Isis, the great goddess, upon the court ..."[9]

G5.9   "At all times I celebrate you, son of Leto, Pythian Apollo, |
        Guide of the immortals and Paean of the golden lyre. | For I
        have come before your gates. Give me, | Lord, great successes
        in the army. | For if you give me them, I will give you libations,
        | Such as those due to a great god and to Isis the queen. | I will
        always make libations to both for these successes. | To find out
        the name of the one who wrote this, | Count two times two
        hundred and twenty-one. | Act of dedication for the one who
        wrote it | And for the one who recognizes it today | For the
        god Mandoulis."[10]

The first three graffiti (G5.4–6) comprise a few only of the very many graffiti
which were marked all over what was originally the mortuary temple of the
New Kingdom pharaoh Seti I, and which evolved over time into a cult centre
of Osiris (sixth to third centuries BCE) and Serapis (second century BCE to
second/third centuries CE), and then an oracle of Bes (later Roman period).
These inscriptions reflect something of the kind of visitor and range of purposes which brought so many pilgrims to Abydos: the pious worshipper
(G5.4), the seeker of healing from illness (G5.5), and the oracular dreamer
desiring knowledge (G5.6).

The pair of graffiti that follow (G5.7–8) reflect something of the long history of multi-ethnic pilgrimage to the smaller of two islands (Philae) located
just to the north of the First Cataract. Travelling from Egypt, North Africa,
Crete, Greece and Asia Minor to worship the goddess of the island (Isis), visitors, pilgrims and priestly officials alike left the traces of their devotion: for
example, an elaborate epithet of Isis in demotic (G5.7); and reference to a visit
(by the high priest from the Graeco-Roman temple of Dakka in lower Nubia)
to the Birth Festival of Isis (G5.8).

The final inscription (G5.9) was painted in red on the eastern portico of
the temple of Mandoulis-Apollo at Talmis, a town on the western bank of the
Nile south of Philae. It is one of two graffiti written (ostensibly at least) by a
Roman soldier called Paccius Maximus – a decurion living in the first century
CE. Composed in Greek using a combination of hexametre and pentametre
verse, and ending in five prose lines, the painted graffito takes the form of an
acrostic: read vertically, the first letter of the first word in the opening seven
lines spells the author's forename (P-A-K-K-I-O-S). The fact that Greek numbers correspond to letters of the alphabet explains the underlying purpose
of the riddle posed at the beginning of the section in prose: M (40)-A (1)-X
(60)-I (10)-M (40)-O (70)-S (200) = (2 × 200) + 21 = 421 (ll. 8–9).

93

Given that other acrostic inscriptions have been found here, written in a hand which suggests that the same person marked them on the walls of the temple, it is possible, of course, that a professional prayer-writer or priest in residence was responsible for all the literary inscriptions that survive at Talmis or that the individual in question acted as the scribe for the individuals named in the inscriptions (including Paccius Maximus). Nonetheless, in view of our previous discussion regarding a spectrum of literacies in antiquity (Chapter 3), it is also within the realms of likelihood that inscriptions like G5.9 reflect more than one scribal hand and dedicatory voice seeking to express religious sentiment within a self-consciously sophisticated literary form.

Greece

In the same way that religion in ancient Egypt consisted of many different and connected elements, ancient Greek beliefs and practices were extraordinarily complex. Similarly polytheistic in nature, Greek religion encompassed a plethora of gods and goddesses, demi-gods and divine entities worshipped across almost two millennia in hundreds of formally constituted city-states and a spread of civic and local contexts. The Greeks in antiquity believed in many gods, each of whom had control over different aspects of the world and of human behaviour. Some gods, like Zeus and Poseidon, exerted power over natural elements like storms and the sea. Other gods, such as Ares and Artemis, held sway over areas of human activity, like war and hunting. The Greeks also sometimes worshipped heroes like Theseus – mythical humans conceived as coming into divine power after they died. We will touch on this aspect of Greek culture in the next chapter.

Like ancient Egypt, Greek society was fundamentally different from our own, and the concepts that we use to represent current religious phenomena are unsuited to drawing out what the Greeks regarded as divine. Likewise, the function of religion will differ in a society such as ours, in which communal life is largely secularized, and in one where religion was comprehensively interwoven with all areas of public and social interaction. In this regard, religion and the ritual life of the community were central to belief and practice in ancient Greece. Sports, politics, entertainment and war all incorporated religious rituals of one kind or another. Every important event in the lives of individuals, groups, even whole cities, included rituals.

Essential to the ritual life of all persons living in archaic and classical Greece (eighth – fourth centuries BCE) – and those whose heritage and language identified them as Greek in the post-classical, Hellenistic and Graeco-Roman epoch (third century BCE to late antiquity) – was the manner in which the gods were honoured. This occurred in a variety of ways, dependent on the fundamental notion that, in order to acquire something, first something

RELIGION

had to be given. According to this view, if the gods were provided with the things they liked, they would be grateful and return the favour. This exchange sometimes constituted nothing more than offering a cake or incense; on other occasions, gifts holding greater significance – statues or personal items – were required. Whatever the gift – a trinket; the sacrifice of an animal; a procession; athletic or dramatic competition; or the dedication of a temple and cult statue – the altar served to receive offerings to the gods. Since giving offerings was a fundamental form of worship for the Greeks, the altar was the essential physical component of cult ritual in ancient Greek society.

Familiar to us from our earlier discussion of literacy in the ancient Greek world (Chapter 3), graffiti practice has been located in proximity to a site of religious ritual near the summit of Mount Hymettos in eastern Attika. Definitely identified as a sanctuary of Zeus, the site comprises structural foundations for three small buildings, enclosure walls with simple open-air altars, and the remains of what might have been a stone-lined storage pit for votive offerings. It was probably established originally and used subsequently by people living on the western side of the mountain, residents of the Athenian plain. Inscribed on the outer and, in some cases, inner surfaces of Phaleron cups and sub-geometric *skyphoi* (dating to the late eighth and seventh centuries BCE), the Hymettos graffiti – preserved as part of a large, undifferentiated mass of pottery in the "votive pit" or in the area of the altar close by – offer a glimpse of archaic Greek religious belief and practice within a context integral to the expression of archaic ritual activity in relation to the life of the local community.

In addition to the texts already considered (G3.3–7), surviving pottery fragments preserve the following graffiti:

G5.10   "[A dedication to] Zeus Semios [the Sign-giver]."

G5.11   "[…]deia [dedicates this to] Herakles."

G5.12   "Phaidim[os]"; "Autome[dos]"; "[Hero]dotos"; "[Lam]ptreo[s]";
         "[A]ntil[okos]."

G5.13   109 fragments, comprising single-letter inscriptions, letter-
         pairs and composite groups; written in retrograde or left-to-
         right; incised on one or two lines.

A number of the Hymettos graffiti consist of dedications of the type "To Zeus Semios", "[Someone] dedicated [this, or 'me'] to Zeus", or "I am the property of Zeus [Semios]" (G3.3, 4, 7; G5.3). While dedications of this kind are common in votive deposits across the ancient Greek world, the designation of Zeus "Sign-giver" (G5.10) – in other words, Zeus in control of weather signs (Greek *sēmata*) – is not only a unique (to date) attestation of this

95

GRAFFITI IN ANTIQUITY

epithet: it also prefigures the widespread literary practice (in epic poetry, cult hymnody and the like) whereby the names of deities come to be inextricably linked with descriptive epithets characterizing both their nature and their significance in cult ritual. In this particular instance, the dedicatory name + epithet is a wonderfully evocative illustration of the manner in which the local population both understood and sought to interact with the divine in relation to the natural world. Such a collocation of identity and nature is a visible marker of Greek polytheism, which suggests why Zeus Semios is not the *only* divine being whose intervention was sought at the shrine (e.g. Gaia is referred to in G3.5, or the hero and demi-god Herakles in G5.11).

It is intriguing to note that some of the Hymettos graffiti were incised on unglazed sherds, which means that the pottery was already broken when the inscriber picked up the fragment and scratched the dedication. What this tells us is interesting, both in relation to the nature of the religious expression captured by this act, and as an addendum to our consideration of literacy in archaic Attika. Given the significance of the ritual transaction, it seems unlikely that a single, broken potsherd would be regarded as a suitable gift to dedicate to the weather god. However, given the novelty and prestige which use of alphabetic writing must have represented – to the farmers and herdsmen who habitually visited Zeus' sanctuary and to those Athenians who discerned the meaning of cloud formations over Hymettos as indicators of divine favour or displeasure – it makes sense that worshippers at the shrine would express their dedication in a manner which embodied this very new and highly visible kind of cultural capital. Therefore, whether writing one's name (G3.6, 7, 10; G5.12) or incising letters of the alphabet (G3.8; G5.13), it may not necessarily have been the identity of the dedicator or the content of the message *per se* which made the incised potsherd important; rather, it was the fact that the pottery fragment displayed writing – *any* written text, in fact – which constituted the gift to the god.

In this regard, a graffito on fired clay from the first decades of Greek alphabetic writing – a verse incised on the so-called "Dipylon Jug" (Athens, *c.*740 BCE)[11] – indicates how writing invested ritual acts with this newfound sense of dedicatory permanence and symbolic potency. Inscribed on a late Geometric *oenochoe* (wine jug), the text is written in retrograde (right-to-left) and consists of one hexameter line (which is perfectly legible) followed by twelve signs (quite unintelligible, though interpreted by some as an *abecedarium*). It reads:

G5.14   "Of all the dancers, he who performs most gracefully here and now, this [jug] is his."

The language of the graffito is closely associated with epic (hexameter) poetry, attested by the use of the expressions *orchēstōn* ("dancers"), *atalōtata* ("most gracefully") and *paizēi* ("performs"). That said, it may seem, at least

96

initially, that this verse does not capture the sense of dedication inherent in the Hymettos graffiti. After all, the inscription omits any reference to a god or goddess, and the vocabulary lacks any religious resonance. Nonetheless it has been suggested that the performative nature of the graffito – in relation to the vessel on which it is incised – holds the key to the jug's ritual significance.[12] Thinking through the contexts associated with ritual in the Greek world, it seems appropriate to list occasions associated with religious festivals of one kind or another; namely, competitive events involving dance. This relationship finds additional support when one takes account of the find-spot of the inscribed vessel: Athens, in walking distance of the Theatre of Dionysus (site of festival dancing contests). Contextualizing the "Dipylon Jug" in this way – as an object which was part of a competitive festival event – allows us to see the ritual significance underlying the language of rhythmic movement performed to musical accompaniment. Of course, the addition of incoherent alphabetic signs after the original retrograde verse, which points to another writer, is problematic; but only as long as we seek to decipher the meaning of the script. Like the Hymettos graffiti, the incision of an *abecedarium* may represent another way of dedicating something in a ritual context. Transmitted in this case by means of a graphic *stoichos* (row of letters) or alphabetic series, the ability to write – on its own or in conjunction with the accomplished literary verse of the original inscriber – acts both as the medium by which the ritual gift is offered, and the gift itself.

Far removed from archaic Attika in time and space, Dura-Europos – a Hellenistic (Seleucid) foundation situated on the left bank of the Euphrates, subsequently ruled by Parthians and Romans – displays a range of informal inscriptions serving as a fascinating corollary to the earliest attestations of religious expression in ancient Greek graffiti. Like Pompeii, Dura-Europos is well known for the large amount of material testifying to daily life, including the architectural remains of small sanctuaries and private houses, as well as the artistic and documentary evidence of wall paintings, reliefs and legal documents – *and* the epigraphic residue of sub-literary and pictorial graffiti. Established originally as a caravan city at the intersection of widely used trade routes along and across the Euphrates (303 BCE), it served as a frontier fortress under Arsacid Parthian rule; captured by the Romans, the city was eventually abandoned after a Sassanian siege (second century BCE to 256/7 CE). Over the course of its history, the city acquired a multicultural population which communicated in a broad cross-section of Mediterranean languages (Greek, Latin, Aramaic, Hebrew, Syriac, Hatrian, Palmyrenean, Middle Persian and Safaitic Pahlavi). After its abandonment in the third century CE, Dura-Europos was rediscovered only in the late nineteenth century (1885).

While Greek remained the official language of Dura-Europos throughout much of its history, the architectural fabric of the city belies its cultural diversity as an outpost of the Parthian and Roman East. With the exception of the city walls and the typically Greek (Hippodamian) civic plan, much of the architectonic fabric of Dura-Europos reflected local cultural features. These distinctively indigenous influences impacted not only on the monumental structures of the city but just as pervasively in relation to its religious character. Next to deities of Greek origin such as Zeus, Artemis and Apollo – introduced by the founding Macedonian settlers – many Semitic and Arabic deities are represented, including Palmyrene cults (Bel, Iarhibol, Aglibol, Arsu), local village cults (Aphlad, Azzanathkona) and Aramaic cults (Artagatis, Adonis, Baalshamin).

A number of graffiti and related inscriptions dating from the Roman period attests to this multi-cultural exchange of religious beliefs and practices. Found on or near the main gate of the city, the so-called Palmyrene gate, the graffiti refer to the "good fortune" associated with the goddess Tyche.[13] Two examples – of the more than 200 graffiti found on the gate; cut and painted red – reflect something of the tenor of the city's relationship with Tyche.

G5.15   "I give thanks to Tyche of Dura."

G5.16   "Zebainas (dedicates this) to Tyche."

There are various sides to *tychē* ("fortune") – the good and the bad, the divine and the profane – in the thought world of ancient Greece.[14] In Greek literature of the fifth and fourth centuries BCE, *tychē* had often been held accountable, as an indifferent, worldly force, for the profound immorality, wickedness

Figure 5.1 Palmyrene Gate, Dura-Europos (photo by Heretiq, CC BY-SA 2.5, http://creativecommons.org/licenses/by-sa/2.5, via Wikimedia Commons).

RELIGION

and depravity manifest in people's actions, but especially death. While this view continued into the fourth century, there was a growing inclination to ascribe to *tychē* obligation for some favourable activities once more frequently assigned to the gods. Establishment of the state cult of Agathe Tyche ("Good Fortune") in the later fourth century (*c.*335/4 BCE) marked the culmination of this trend. By the time Dura-Europos was founded – the middle of the Hellenistic age – popular Greek religion of the period gave responsibility to the Olympian gods for what was good in life. When *tychē* was conceived of as beneficial Agathe Tyche, she too became a deity.

The examples cited above form part of the variety of dedications to Tyche associated with the lower storey of the Palmyrene Gate (Figure 5.1). In fact, the number of altars, reliefs and inscriptions found in the gate demonstrate that it was regarded as a suitable location for religious dedications. For example, a shallow recess cut into a chamber in the gate's northern tower contained a shrine; and a thin, rectangular piece of wood discovered in the same room – on which was painted an image of the goddess personifying victory (Nike) – probably formed one of the panels of a small shrine. That this shrine was dedicated to Tyche – who is often associated with Victory – is further indicated by the dedication in the gate's central passageway of an altar bearing a Palmyrene inscription to the Gad. The term *gad* is an Aramaic word meaning "luck" or "good fortune" and can refer to a divine being, most commonly the tutelary god or goddess of the city. Inscriptions on three altars found in the gate – dedicated in Greek (Tyche of Dura), Palmyrene (*gad*) and Latin (*genius* of Dura) – reflect both the fixation on the cult of Fortune in this part of the city and adduce the growing conflation of religious ideas under Roman rule.

Both Tyche graffiti are written in neat, monumental Greek script, incised respectively into one of the stones forming the north-east section of the northern wall (G5.15) and the lintel of the entrance to the southern tower (G5.16). They participate in a community of religious practice centred on the main gate of the city. Indeed, it is this concentration of inscriptions referring to Tyche at this location that provides a clue to the identity of the worshipping population. During the period in which these inscriptions were cut, a detachment of the Roman garrison guarded the Palmyrene gate and a section of the desert road which led through the gate into the city. The accumulation of various inscriptions on the walls – and of inscribed votive monuments inside and outside the southern tower of the gate – points to the fact that the cult of the Tyche of Dura was closely associated with the Roman army. It is also more than likely that – in addition to the shrine adduced in the northeast room of the northern tower (above) – there was a sanctuary of the Tyche of Dura somewhere in or near the southern tower.

It is probable, therefore, that the dedicants in the graffiti cited above – Zebainas (G5.16) and the anonymous "I" (G5.15), whose name may have been given in the first lines of the inscription, which were painted and have now

99

GRAFFITI IN ANTIQUITY

disappeared completely – were soldiers in Roman service. In this regard, it is interesting to note that the only surviving image of the Tyche of Dura similarly occupies a military context. A wall painting in the so-called Temple of the Palmyran Gods – located in an angle of the city wall in the far north-west corner of the city; comprising an altar and a group of 16 frescoes associated with cult worship – depicts a certain Julius Terentius taking part in a ritual of bloodless sacrifice. Terentius, tribune of the Palmyran cohort (a cohort of mounted archers stationed on the Euphrates in the third century CE), burns incense in offering to the cult statues of three Palmyran gods dressed in military costume – Yarhibol, Aglibol and Arsu (upper left) – and to the *gads* of Palmyra and Dura (lower left). Both *gads* are represented as goddesses. An inscription identifies the goddess seated next to the tribune as Tyche.

Another type of graffiti – constituting approximately 12 per cent of the non-official textual inscriptions at Dura – provides further evidence in relation to the nature of popular religious expression in the city.

G5.17 "May Aurelius Antoninus, *beneficiarius* of the tribune, be remembered."

G5.18 "May Aurelius Th[e]ma[ll]as [= Taimarsû], *beneficiarius* of the tribune, be remembered."

Both of these prayers were composed by soldiers of the garrison attached to the Palmyrene gate. Antoninus and Th[e]ma[ll]as self-identify as *beneficiarii*. A *beneficiarius* was a soldier who, through the favour of his commander, was exempt from menial offices like throwing up entrenchments, procuring wood and water, foraging or digging latrines. Both of the inscribers, therefore, were privileged soldiers. A curious feature of the first inscription (G5.17) is the fact that the message was originally carved in monumental letters and included the beginning of a traditional expression used to indicate the date. However, in the vacant space following the word that initiates the dating formula is painted in red an inscription of two lines in small characters. This small inscription practically repeats with some modifications that carved in monumental letters. Immediately below the double inscription of Aurelius Antoninus, a second man smeared the space with stucco and painted in tiny black letters his message (G5.18). The name of this soldier is frequently found in Syrian inscriptions and corresponds to the Palmyrene name Taimarsû.

Like the Tyche graffiti, these inscriptions represent a religious practice shared by a community of like-minded individuals living and working in the neighbourhood of the Palmyrene gate. The fact that this inscribing practice was commonplace and widely embraced is strongly suggested by the abbreviated nature of the key term in the formula. The transcription of Aurelius Antoninus' first message shows that he truncated the word *mnesthe* ("may [Antoninus] be remembered"), writing only the first two letters in a

100

distinctively arranged monogram (the larger letter N superimposed over a smaller M). As this abbreviation can be found in a number of examples of this type of graffiti, it seems clear that the formula was well known and used frequently. Technically, *mnesthe* may be understood as a substandard but commonplace spelling for *mnestheiē*, optative aorist passive of *mimneskesthai*, "to be reminded, to remember", a verb with middle and passive voice in Greek. Given the context and the explicit purpose, it is logical to interpret *mnesthe* as "to be remembered", passive of "to remember". The importance of this technical discussion lies in the relationship between the unconventional (passive) Greek usage and the cultural context of Dura-Europos. It is possible that the phrase itself may be the translation of a shortened form of a typical Semitic blessing formula, the full form of which is "may [so-and-so] be remembered before the god [so-and-so]". Both the shorter and the longer versions are found on inscriptions by Semitic peoples such as Phoenicians, Hebrews, Nabataeans and Syrians.[15] The use of this passive form with passive meaning in devotional formulas is likely to be at the root of its use in this particular type of graffiti.

Whether we refer to the rural graffiti of archaic Attika or the military messages inscribed on the surfaces of Roman Dura-Europos, one thing is clear. Writing – popular, informal; scribal or sub-literary – in and of itself identifies a number of non-official textual markings as religious communication. Taken in context with spatial location, social convention and cultural practice, the expression of Greek religion in graffiti across antiquity is characterized by the physical act (scratching, chipping, hammering, or incising and painting), the durable presence (as votive sherd or visible message in stone) and the recognizable statement (dedication, thanksgiving, commemoration).

Rome

What any study of religion in antiquity uncovers very quickly is the fact that it is not a separate society on its own, with its own people engaged in an organized undertaking, its own mechanisms of influence and management, infrastructure, ideology and fellowship: it is simply part of the way the broader society in question works. In the modern age, we think of religion as a set of beliefs attached to a particular lifestyle. It is possible to contest that definition, but it is a useful way of thinking about religion in contemporary terms. So religion in the modern sense can be defined as a *dogma* or a set of beliefs, and a way of life that flows out of or derives its purpose or direction from those beliefs. For the Romans, *religio* – the Latin word – was nothing like that. *Religio*, like "ligature", relates to the things that bind a person, things that ask one to be dutiful. *Religio* for the Romans is about mutual obligation, about cultic performance or ritual practice; it is all about tradition. So it is as much about *doing* things as *believing* things. There is belief, belief in gods, in lots of gods, in some gods who are more powerful than other gods, but essentially, for the Romans, *religio* was about practice, cultic practice performed according to traditional rules or laws. These rules were often very local, so the Romans could assimilate the kind of cultic practice that was inherent to a place that they appropriated through conquest or bequest, provided of course that the local practice wasn't too much about *dogma*. If a person living under Roman rule visited a particular city, he or she would follow the *religio* of that particular city: the person would conform to local practices – sacrifice to the local gods, participate in the local feasts. The important point to take from this is that for the Romans *religio* was about *orthopraxis*, about *doing* the right thing according to local tradition, not as much about *orthodoxy*, that is *believing* the right thing.

Any threat to that kind of structure was regarded by the Romans as a kind of *superstitio*, from which our modern English cognate "superstition" derives. Again, the modern and ancient words do not mean the same thing. So in the ancient world a *superstitio* was a lot more concrete in terms of its beliefs. If a system came along that suggested that one ought believe a certain thing, and that system conflicted with Roman *orthopraxy*, that way of doing things according to traditional rules, then it was an unauthorized belief, a *superstitio*, a belief that conflicted with the Roman ideal of dutiful adherence.

This allows us to begin to anticipate how Judaism and Christianity – and, though outside our present frame of reference, eventually Islam – fit into this specifically Roman pattern of responses to *religio* in the ancient Mediterranean, given how each derives so firmly from a characteristic set of beliefs. By the same token, even though both Judaism and Christianity present with a clear *dogma* and consequently come into conflict with the Roman view on *religio* and local cultic practice, the Roman response to Jews and Christians is significantly different, and we need to think carefully about why that was the case. What, precisely, was it about Judaism and Christianity that attracted such different responses from the Roman authorities?

In this regard, what is it about Judaism and Christianity that attracts the attention of the Roman authorities? After all, the religion of the Greeks and Romans in the period before the "invention" of Christianity provides the background against which these monotheistic religions first arose, and it deeply influences their development. Fundamentally, it is an issue of visibility. On the one hand, Roman *orthopraxy* dictated a certain structure that overlaid the annual rhythms of social activity in those parts of the Mediterranean under Roman rule. Each locality would refer to a sanctioned calendar of civic activities. If the local tradition required that a particular element of *religio* listed on the calendar required dutiful action, then persons would refer to the calendar's directives, participate in the appropriate practice, most likely a sacrifice or libation of some kind. In other words, people under Roman rule were required to behave in a particular way.

Under the terms of this structural pattern, what is it that the Jews and Christians are doing that makes them stand out? Here, visibility is clearly a

RELIGION

key issue. For the Jews, male circumcision is certainly a practice that draws attention to their belief system. When Romans bathed in public, they bathed naked, and so they were able to distinguish Jewish men without difficulty. Jews also had what looked to the Romans like particular cultic practices; for instance, eating habits based on dietary regulations. Public meals were a feature of Roman civic life, and formed a part of most calendars of public action. Jewish dietary regulations naturally conflicted in significant ways with the performance of this important social practice.

Similarly, the Christians' refusal to eat meat and worship idols increased the level of their visibility as a believing community under Roman patterns of *religio* and *orthopraxy*. There were, therefore, some practices to whose performance the Romans expected dutiful adherence with which Christians could not comply because of their set of beliefs. It is this failure of compliance which presents the Roman authorities with a problem. When one looks at Pliny's correspondence with the emperor Trajan over the refusal of Christians to comply with expected patterns of Roman public behaviour[16] or, later, the periods of Christian persecution, it is easy enough to pick up on this issue of visibility deriving from conflicting action (or inaction) based on *dogma*.

As the preceding sections of this chapter have shown, it will be possible only to touch briefly on a few of the ways that graffiti reflect attitudes and actions characteristic of Roman religion. What will become clear soon enough are the cultural continuities underpinning the world of Roman antiquity: a world of religious communities, representing a concentration of devotion and obligation – at times affiliated with, at times quite separate from the political institutions of the state; a world offering a spectrum of religious options, choices which might have an effect on who a person is or understands himself or herself to be – on one's self-concept, that is, the individual perception of identity; on his or her aspirations; and the notion of where he or she fits in the world.

Religion played an important role in the life of Pompeii from the sixth century BCE until the city's destruction in 79 CE. Reference to a modern map of the archaeological site will show a range of temples tracing the religious history of the city: e.g. temple precincts next to, near and in the Forum (the imperial cult; Augustan Fortune; Jupiter, Juno, Minerva). Religious experiences in the city were not confined, however, to traditional Roman cults. Pompeii drew on a variety of foreign influences from Greece and Egypt, represented in evidence for worship of deities such as Asclepius, Ceres, Isis, Neptune and Pompeian Venus. The following selection of graffiti texts reflects this diversity of belief and practice and shines further light on the relationship between religion and culture in the ancient world.

G5.19 "Popidius Natalis, his client, with the worshippers of Isis, call
for Cuspius Pansa as aedile."   (*CIL* IV.1011 = *ILS* 6419f)

Painted on the wall opposite the entrance to the small temple of Isis (V.7.28), this public notice refers to a group of people identified as "worshippers" of the Egyptian goddess (G5.19). Messages urging Roman citizens to vote for the election of local officials flanked the major thoroughfares of the city. These electoral posters (*programmata*) were painted on the whitewashed facades of shops and private residences across Pompeii. We will look at this unique phenomenon more closely later (Chapter 9). What is interesting in the present context is the fact that no separation of state and religion existed as far as Pompeii was concerned. Popidius Natalis belonged to a family with known connections to the temple of Isis, possibly in relation to the reconstruction of the temple precinct after the earthquake of 62 CE; and Cuspius Pansa is known to have been involved (with his father) in the related reorganization of the city. This broader context helps to explain why others affiliated to Isis would support Pansa's candidature for one of the highest political offices in Pompeii (*duumvir*). That a foreign cult was so visibly entrenched in the political and cultural life of the city reflects both the diversity of religious practice in Pompeii and how profoundly religion was embedded in everyday thought and action. Moreover, within the broader context of polytheism, it is fascinating to note that the citizens voting with Popidius Natalis are represented in relation to their cult affiliation. While it is common in Pompeii's painted and incised graffiti for cliques to be identified according to occupation or activity, adopting a collective identity based on worship of a single deity is striking.

G5.20   "May you, girl, thrive, and may you have the goodwill of Pompeian Venus."   (*CIL* IV.4007 = *CLE* 233)

G5.21   "Methe, slave of Cominia, from Atella, loves Chrestus. May Pompeian Venus be dear to both of them and may they always live in harmony."   (*CIL* IV.2457)

Sentimental allusions to Pompeii's divine protector, Venus, are preserved in an anonymous wish (G5.20) and an explicit declaration of love (G5.21). Venus occupied an important intellectual and emotional space in the minds and hearts of Pompeians. The goddess acted in the capacity of tutelary deity, serving as the city's guardian and patron. She also formed an essential element in Pompeii's political and social identity – the Latin name of the city after its foundation as a Roman colony was Pompeiana Colonia Cornelia *Veneria*. The first graffito was scratched on the white plaster of a peristyle column in a small house close to the Amphitheatre (I.3.30).

Expressing the hope that Venus will look kindly on the subject of the wish-statement – identified as *pupa* ("girl"), a Latin word connoting a close friendship or more intimate relationship – may seem peculiar in the context of a peristyle garden. However, this small residence did not possess an *atrium*, and so the peristyle performed a number of functions usually reserved for

104

separate spaces within a private home. In this instance, a *lararium* was situated in the western wall of the peristyle. This shrine to the household's guardian spirits (*lares*) comprised an arched niche decorated with painted flowers. The niche was bordered on either side by a painted *lar* holding instruments used in ritual offerings (a *rhyton* and *situla*); below, a serpent was depicted moving towards the altar. Praying that someone regarded with affection might do well in life, and that Venus would look after that special person's journey toward prosperity, is not odd in itself: writing such a prayer on a column within a space used for private ritual would have seemed a perfectly natural extension both of the garden's function in this particular home and a coincidental doubling of the protective blessings of Venus *and* the household spirits.

The second graffito referring to Pompeian Venus (G5.21) is located in the theatre district. It is written in a single line on the southern wall of the corridor behind the Large Theatre, the space which also displays a number of figural inscriptions (Chapter 4). Composed, it would seem, by a female slave in service to another woman, the message is a proclamation of love, simply stated and indelibly authentic. Chrestus – whose single name indicates that he, like Methe, is a slave – is evidently cared for deeply. Once again, invoking Venus' name, with a view to securing a lasting relationship based on harmonious devotion, seems eminently sensible.

It is worth noting that these two statements reflect the social spread of Pompeians devoted to Venus and deliberate choice of setting for display. The first graffito aspires to metrical verse, betraying a composer with a level of education, and the socio-religious context in which it was scratched implies a visitor or resident of freed or free status. The second inscription is prosaic, direct, and evidently the product of a servile composer, addressed to a fellow slave; but it appears on a wall which also displays a number of erotic messages – highly relevant to Venus' divine duty of care – that adopt modes of expression closely modelled on formal epigraphic and literary genres (Chapter 11).

G5.22 "May god always make Felix Aufidius felicitous." (*CIL* IV.6815)

G5.23 "He who disdains life will easily despise god." (*CIL* IV.5370)

These two graffiti capture something of the nature of popular religious expression in Roman Pompeii. Whoever composed the first inscription (G5.22) – it may be the product of an anonymous well-wisher or written in the third person by the potential beneficiary of the statement (Felix Aufidius) – the "god" whose power to bestow happiness is sought is not specified. The source of divine intervention, like the message, is ephemeral, associated with Aufudius' desired state of being rather than any specific entity. The manner in which this inscription is expressed may correspond to usage of the term *feliciter* in many Pompeian graffiti ("congratulations", "blessings", "long life");

105

or, in certain particular instances (as a divine abstraction). In either case, the context in which the graffito appears was undoubtedly a hub of social exchange – on the wall running between a private home and a small shop (VI.16.4–5); near a water fountain-and-tower on the corner of the Via del Vesuvio. Highly visible and on display to a potentially large readership of regular shoppers and passing traffic, the message embeds religious sentiment in traditional urban networks of social movement and cultural communication.

Scratched on a column between the atrium and peristyle of a small house in Region IX, the second graffito (G5.23) affords a glimpse into a more philosophical understanding of the relationship between humanity and the divine. Like the Aufidius prayer, this message draws out the intimate connection between lived reality and the supernatural world. Of course, it may not represent the belief system of the inscriber as much as an aphorism which appealed enough to the sensibilities of the writer to share with a wider audience. Other sentiments can be found repeated at various locations in the city; and, in a few cases, other parts of Italy, and even overseas. This graffito could fit equally well into the latter category. The absence of additional versions elsewhere in Pompeii may be simply due to an accident of survival. Regardless, it is the idea underlying the statement which identifies what must have been a popular religious perspective here and elsewhere in the Roman world: the divine as a pervasive aspect of human existence; and disbelief in this "reality" as a rejection of life and all it has to offer.

G5.24   "The gods' days: of Kronos, of the Sun, of the Moon, of Ares, of Hermes, of Zeus, of Aphrodite."   (*CIL* IV.5202)

This notion of the divine as inextricably linked to the working out of daily human life is eloquently expressed in a graffito listing the days of the week (G5.24). Written in Greek, the inscribed catalogue records, one below the other, each day in relation to the celestial object, visible to the naked eye, with which it was associated. In the order provided by the composer of this list, we can read: Kronos (Saturn), Helios (Sol, the Sun), Selene (Luna, the Moon), Ares (Mars), Hermes (Mercury), Zeus (Jupiter) and Aphrodite (Venus). Similar lists written in Latin give the Roman equivalents for the astronomical objects (provided, where necessary, next to the equivalent in English, above). Tracing the sequence of days within a heptagon, around which the planets are listed in their celestial sequence, makes apparent the relationship as understood in first-century CE Pompeii.

It is possible that this graffito reflects the degree of general knowledge possessed by the inhabitants of Pompeii in relation to what they could see in the Campanian sky during the day and at night, and how the movement of these objects might have corresponded in various ways to the passage of time as they understood it. The astrological significance of the named objects/gods certainly predates the emperor Constantine's official incorporation

RELIGION

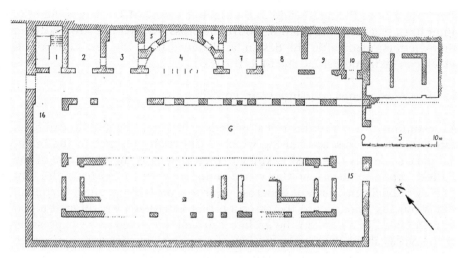

Figure 5.2 Plan of the Palatine Paedagogium. Rome, Italy (redrawn based on Solin & Itkonen-Kaila 1966: fig. 1).

of a seven-day week into the Julian calendar during the fourth century CE, and more than likely can be traced to Pythagorean notions – the so-called "harmony of the spheres" – circulated by Greeks in southern Italy. What is very clear, however, is that the activities of the Roman colony conformed to a seven-day weekly cycle – a cycle constituted in terms of the belief that certain deities exerted an influence over the heavens or in some way could be identified with objects visible in the day or night skies. The Greek and Latin graffiti testifying to this cycle adduce the close relationship between commonly held ideas about the divine and the quotidian social and economic life of the city.

Moving to the city of Rome during the imperial period (first to fifth centuries CE), it is interesting to note a graffito – confronting to many Christians in the modern age – which marks out another perspective on religious expression in the Roman world. The inscription, which attests directly to a Christian presence on the Palatine hill, seat of imperial power from the late first century CE on, is well-known as the Alexamenos graffito (Figure I.4, p. 14).

Discovered in one of the rooms of a building which served as a training school for imperial guards and personal attendants, it comprises a drawing and textual caption inscribed on the south-east wall of a small room (Figure 5.2, no. 7). The pictorial aspect of the graffito depicts a crucified man, seen from the rear, with the head of a donkey, and dressed in a *colobium* (an item of servile clothing) without sleeves. The cross is in the form of a T. The transverse under the feet most likely represented a *suppedaneum*, a support for the crucified person projecting from the vertical shaft of the cross. Under the crucified figure, and to the left, is a youth, also in *colobium* and seen from behind, in an act of prayer, with his right hand extending towards the man on

107

GRAFFITI IN ANTIQUITY

the cross. Above the figure, and to the right, is a kind of Y – larger than the other lines that form the graffito. Above the cross, written in badly executed Greek letters, made after the design, as deduced from the vertical of the E which can be found behind the M, is the text:

G5.25   "Alexamenos, worship [your] god."[17]

As testimony from other historical periods is lacking, this graffito can been dated to the Severan age, during which a Christian presence in the imperial palace (*domus Caesaris*) is known. The drawing is therefore one of the earliest representations of the crucifixion. However, Christians did not employ publicly any form of the cross prior to Constantine. Since Tertullian and Minucius Felix record the assertion that Christians worshipped a god with the head of a donkey, the graffito can be interpreted as an expression of this view, albeit the representation of a punishment (crucifixion) which Alexamenos may well have observed during his lifetime.[18]

That we deal with a caricature is demonstrated by the rough aspect of the drawing and its shabby execution. The attitude of the praying youth's hands confirms this interpretation: Christians, and also non-Christians, worshipped with arms extended and raised, while here we see the left arm lowered and the right extended towards the figure on the cross with the fingers open and separate in the Roman manner (*iactare basia*).[19] If we allow for the probability that a young slave named Alexamenos worshipped the Christian god in the Palatine Paedagogium, then the person who scratched this inscription was most likely ridiculing the act of prayer itself. This interpretation is strengthened by another graffito found in a neighbouring building of the same complex, which reads:

G5.26   "Alexamenos, faithful."[20]

It is not too hard to formulate a credible link between the two inscriptions: a pagan sentry or doorkeeper in the imperial palace first sought to condemn a fellow guard by scratching on the wall, "Alexamenos is a Christian"; when this did not result in the desired effect, he sketched a caricature of Alexamenos as the worshipper of a crucified god. For major derisory effect, the crucified is shown from the rear and wears servile clothing. Intriguingly, text and image feed into a common figure of fun – the "ass-man" – and a well-established motif – crucifixion – depicted on stage in ancient mime.[21] As an effective parody of Christian practice in general, and an explicit belittling of one man's belief in the central tenet of that faith, the Alexamenos graffito is at once a representation and rejection of religious expression in the heart of imperial Rome.

The earliest evidence of Christian practice on any large scale is connected with the universal ancient impulse to care for the dead, demonstrated particularly in the catacombs of imperial Rome. The word "catacomb" originally

108

RELIGION

meant nothing more than "by the hollow". It is a description applied to one particular district of Rome, on the Via Appia near the Circus of Romulus – a complex of buildings erected by the emperor Maxentius in the early fourth century CE; dedicated to his deceased son, the "divine Romulus" – where, in the same century, the church of Saint Sebastian was built. Beneath the church there was a large cemetery in which the bodies of the apostles Peter and Paul were thought to have rested for a time, and the lasting reputation of this cemetery caused its name to be applied in a general way to any subterranean burial place in Rome – and, indeed, elsewhere in the Roman world, as, for instance, at Naples.

The Romans thought it appropriate that their dead should be disposed of beneath the earth, although, for reasons of convenience, this was often done after cremation. The Jews, however, objected to the practice of cremation, and preferred to place the bodies of their dead in *loculi* (recess) tombs – rock-cut tombs consisting of a shaft with steps leading down to a chamber with recesses hewn into each of the walls. The Christians, influenced by thoughts of resurrection or at any rate by a keen sense of the fellowship of believers in death as in life, adopted the Jewish custom, constructing large groups of burial chambers following the Jewish model, close by the cemeteries which, as the law directed, lay just outside the city boundaries and usually along the main roads.

Quite apart from the Jews, pagan practice furnished ample precedents for underground burials in the fashion of the catacombs. A number of Roman households and guilds saw to it that there were excavated *columbaria* ("dovecotes") – so called from the rows of openings like pigeon-holes in which urns, containing the ashes of the deceased, were stored. For example, the *columbarium* of the empress Livia contained as many as 3,000 urns.

Some of the catacombs were built on four levels connecting an enormous system of galleries and linking passages with steep, narrow steps. Bodies of the deceased were placed in niches – 41 to 61 cm high by 119 to 150 cm long – cut from the wall of soft tufa rock. The bodies were fully clothed, wrapped in linen and sprinkled with ointments to offset the decaying odour and sealed with a slab inscribed with the name of the deceased, date of death and a religious symbol. Although built in the main as a subterranean burial place for Christians,[22] several large catacombs in Rome and three smaller *hypogea* (underground chambers) were built for Jews also.[23] The Roman catacombs date from the end of the second to the early fifth century CE; the Jewish catacombs predate Christian burials by about 100 years.

The majority of graffiti marked in these explicitly religious contexts were pilgrims who wished to leave a record of their visit, a prayer, or an invocation. Jerome – a noted Christian historian, theologian, and priest of the fourth/fifth century – was the first to recount how as a student he would go on Sundays to visit the tombs of the apostles and the martyrs together with his study companions: "We would enter the galleries dug into the bowels of the earth … Rare lights coming from above land attenuated the darkness a little … We

109

would proceed slowly, one step at a time, completely enveloped in darkness" (Jerome, *On Ezechiel* 40).

The Iberian poet, Prudentius, also recalls that in the early years of the fifth century, many pilgrims would come from around Rome and even from the surrounding regions to venerate the tomb of the martyr Hippolytus (buried in the catacombs on the Via Tiburtina), and refers to the "countless martyrs' tombs" in Rome.[24]

Carved in haste, sometimes without being completed, the visitors' graffiti display a range of script types, from the classical capitals of formal epigraphic texts to the disjointed italics of non-official cursive writing. A large cluster of informal inscriptions – the so-called Memoria Apostolorum ("Apostolic Memorial") – is located in the Saint Sebastian archaeological complex (cited above). More than 600 graffiti, written in Latin and Greek, request the intercession of Peter and Paul or recall ritual meals eaten in their honour:

G5.27 "Paul and Peter, intercede for Victor."

G5.28 "Peter and Paul, remember us."

The devotional nature of these textual markings is self-evident. They are among the strongest evidence in support of the theory – advanced by some scholars – of the partial and temporary translation of the apostolic relics from their original sites on the Appian Way in the years of persecution under the emperor Valerian.[25] Unlike many of the inscriptions in the catacombs, these graffiti can be assigned to a well-defined chronological period: between the second half of the third century CE and the first decades of the fourth century, when the construction of the Constantinian basilica, in the same area but at a higher level, put an end to that custom followed previously by the faithful for rites in honour of the Apostles, thereby sealing all that belonged to that phase of its construction.

In the nearby catacombs of Saint Callistus, two graffiti enabled Giovanni Battista de Rossi, excavating in the second half of the nineteenth century, to identify the crypt of the martyrs Calocerus and Parthenius, whose names were expressly mentioned. In the same cemetery, at the foot of the stairs leading to the Crypt of the Popes, there are many other graffiti, inscribed by persons who visited that place where many pontiffs were buried, some of them martyrs. Among others, we can read the names of foreign priests who celebrated a liturgical rite there, such as the priest Felicio, who described himself as "sinner". Not far from here, other inscriptions scratched on the corridor walls invoke Sixtus II, deceased members of the Christian community renowned for their devotion, and elements of Christian ideology associated with the witness of deceased martyrs:

G5.29 "Saint Sixtus, remember in your prayers Aurelius Repentinus."

RELIGION

G5.30 "Holy Souls, remember Marcian, Successus, Severus and all our brothers."

G5.31 "Jerusalem, city and ornament of the martyrs of God."

In the cemetery of Marcellinus and Peter, along the ancient Via Labicana, many graffiti document the devotion which the two eponymous martyrs received for many centuries:

G5.32 "Marcellinus and Peter, intercede for Gallicanus the Christian."

G5.33 "Leo, may you always live in God with all your family."

G5.34 "Lord, preserve Calendion [for eternity] in your holy name."

G5.35 "O Lord of the holy martyrs and Saint Helen, save your servants John and Thomas, monks of the monastery [dedicated] to the saint."

Regarding this last prayer, it should be noted that the ruins of the mausoleum of Constantine's mother (Helen) are preserved directly above the catacomb.

In underground Rome we can also read numerous graffiti of the faithful in the small basilica of the martyrs Felix and Adauctus in the cemetery of Commodilla on Via Ostiense. One deserves particular mention: it is so far the only inscribed text in Rome written in runes, the ancient Germanic alphabet (ẽà db a l d). It was evidently carved by a pilgrim who had come from Central Europe to visit Rome's many churches and tombs associated with Christian martyrs or saints (*martyria*).

In this regard, although the majority of these inscriptions were presumably written by foreigners, in only a few cases are their origins expressly indicated in the texts. However, they can sometimes be inferred from the nature of the names of the faithful. Thus in the crypt of the catacomb of the martyr Pamphilus, one discovers that a certain Paschal had come from Naples, but it is likely that the priests Grimoaldus and Gaidus (who also visited the cemetery of Commodilla) were of Lombard origin, while Madalger was very likely an African.

Outside Rome there are certainly other examples of graffiti in many shrines frequented by pilgrims from other regions of the ancient Christian world, from the Holy Land to the catacombs of Hadrumetum (modern Sousse in Tunisia), from the Euphrasian Basilica of Poret, Croatia, to Saint Michael on Mount Gargano in Apulia. The latter revealed, among other things, the presence of important figures of Lombard society. Indeed, it is thought that at this last site craftsmen were available who, upon payment, would etch artistic graffiti on the rock walls – very much like the local

Egyptian masons employed by Graeco-Roman visitors to the Colossi of Memnon.

To conclude this introduction to religious expression in ancient graffiti, it is interesting to note that Jewish catacombs at Rome display identical markings to the inscriptions found in the subterranean galleries set aside for Christian burials. Mourners have embellished the plethora of artistic motifs painted on the walls – and parts of the vaulted ceilings of the Jewish catacombs – with incised, hand-written messages. Interestingly, a statistical analysis of the graffiti tells us that the language of the Jewish community was predominantly Greek.[26]

G5.36 " ... in peace your sleep."

G5.37 "In peace lies Kuros."

G5.38 "Blessing [*menorah*] to all."

G5.39 Marking representing either an amphora or an oil flask.

Mostly epitaphs of one or two words, scratched on the brick or tufa closures of the *loculi* or the plaster to left or right or below, these graffiti resonate explicitly with the formal inscribed and painted epitaphs marking the final resting places of deceased members of imperial Rome's large Jewish population. The notion of death as "sleep" or "taking rest" (Greek *koimēsis*) pervades the catacomb inscriptions (G5.36, G5.37), identifying the interment of family, friends and fellow members of the synagogue community as a transitional phase – from temporal life to another plane of being – rather than a terminal separation from physical and spiritual existence.

In addition to the textual residue, a range of symbols similar to those carefully elaborated or crudely cut into the marble plaques and sarcophagi of the primary burials can be found – scrawled with paint, or roughly scratched on the closures of the graves. By far the most common is the *menorah* (the candelabrum used in Jewish worship) (G5.38). Other frequently displayed symbols are the *ethrog* and the *lulah*, both connected with the Sukkot festival (Feast of Booths or Tabernacles); the *shofar*, which is associated with Rosh Hashanah (the Jewish New Year); an oil flask, probably associated with the celebration of Chanukah (Hannukah, the Festival of Lights) (G5.39); and, less frequently, the ark for the Torah scrolls.

FINAL THOUGHTS

Whether inscribed in Egyptian, Greek or Roman contexts – Old Kingdom rock outcrops, Middle Kingdom pyramids, New Kingdom state temples, or

RELIGION

Ptolemaic and Graeco-Roman sites of pilgrimage (temples, sanctuaries and tombs); archaic mountain sanctuaries, imperial frontier cities; first-century CE Roman colonies, second- to fifth-century CE Christian and Jewish catacombs – graffiti in antiquity reflect the cultural interactions inherent in the expression of religious ideas and practices. Regardless of the framework on which these beliefs and customs were based – that is, oral, oral-literate or primarily scriptural modes of transmission – non-official texts and images help us to clarify the complexities, nuances, similarities and differences of knowing and understanding that characterized the network of religious traditions found in the ancient Mediterranean. Although geographically disparate, the informal religious markings of pharaonic Egypt, classical Greece, republican Rome and, eventually, the world under the wider Roman empire – stretching from the Rhine to the Euphrates; from Britain to Libya, Upper Egypt and the lands east of the Euphrates – provide us with an entry-point into the diversity and richness of ancient religions: their theological heterogeneity; their ritual dynamism; their manifold systems of communication; and their cultural complementarities and continuities.

CHAPTER 6

MAGIC

Cenacus complains to the god Mercury about Vitalinus and Natalinus his son concerning the draught animal which has been stolen from him, and asks the god Mercury that they may have neither health before/unless they return at once to me the draught animal which they have stolen, and to the god the devotion which he has demanded from them himself. *(Uley* 1)

To the holy god Mercury. I complain to you about those who are badly disposed towards me [and] who are acting badly over [?] ..., whether slave or free, whether male or female. Do not allow them to stand or sit, to drink or eat, or to buy off these provocations [?] unless with their own blood ... *(Uley* 76)

MAGIC IN ANTIQUITY: BELIEFS AND PRACTICES

It may at first seem surprising that many people in the ancient world professed belief in the reality of magic and its efficacy as a force for continuity or change, conservation or radical reform, restoration or retaliation – the power, that is, of influencing the course of human behaviour and historical events by using mysterious or supernatural forces. To a twenty-first-century readership (and, more broadly, a demographically and culturally diverse audience of technologically astute consumers of information), the vocabulary of magic is strangely familiar – sorcery; enchantment; witchcraft; spell; and so on. Yet, despite its "market recognition", magic as a practical adjunct to human cognition and action is widely regarded as the product of superstitious, premodern thinking. In the aftermath of the Reformation and Enlightenment, subsequent to the consolidation by conquest and exploitation of European control over so-called "primitive" Asian and African cultures, and within the broader geopolitical terrain of state formation and centralized power-structures, magic came to represent a way of thinking about new Western theories of cultural and religious evolution. In short, current views of magic must always be seen in relation to the rise of new mechanical views of the world and related notions of "natural" religion feeding the Enlightenment war against superstitition.

Magic in the ancient world, however, is not so easily classified. Indeed, as modern scholarship grudgingly admits, magic is a very elusive category.[1] No definition of the term has ever found widespread consensus, much less overarching agreement; and myriad efforts to disentangle it from religion on the one hand and science on the other have proved less than successful. The difficulty lies for the most part in the slippery valencies of applied meaning: in other words, what one society may quantify as "magic", another would tag as "religion", and another as "science". By choosing one label, we are implicitly supporting a particular intellectual position whenever conflicting definitions of magic compete with each other. Along the same lines, we are potentially liable to force our own epistemological categories upon societies in which these perspectives of knowledge and understanding would have made little sense.

Given these difficulties, this chapter will not attempt any rigorous defini-tion of ancient magic. Its purpose is far more moderate – to present some of the materials in the surviving corpus of textual and figural graffiti which might prove useful in any discussion of magic and its practitioners in the Mediterranean basin from the third millennia BCE to the seventh century CE. This extensive period saw the magical traditions of various different cul-tures come together to form an aggregated, international, even multicultural framework of magical praxis – with its own rituals, symbols and words of power. Of course, presenting the available evidence, and pointing to some of the interrelations between different types of evidence and to the possi-ble origins of some of the motifs and practices embedded in it, are only first steps on the road to understanding, but crucial steps nonetheless. Finally, studying expressions of ancient magic in graffiti can show us a good deal not only about ancient society, but about human nature and social structures in general, especially as they relate to the generation, accumulation and trans-mission of knowledge about powers outside the worlds of natural and human power. Magic, after all, is just another manifestation of the innate human desire for control – to control our natural environment, to control our social world, and eventually to control our own destiny. Incised on lead tablets and buried within the precinct of a Romano-British temple complex, the two curses quoted in the epigraph to this chapter – from Uley in Gloucestershire – give something of the flavour of that desire as it manifested itself in ancient expressions of magical belief. The techniques may have changed over the last fifteen centuries, but the goals remain the same.

Egypt

The Egyptians were famous in the ancient world for their knowledge of magic. In the early second century CE, Clement of Alexandria (a Greek theologian) referred to Egypt as the "mother of magicians". His sentiments were echoed by many others. For example, in the Old Testament, the pharaoh summons his magicians, who match Moses and Aaron in performing "the snake trick", changing their staves into serpents and water into blood.[2] Early opponents of Christianity in the Jewish tradition accused Jesus of having trained as a magician in Egypt and of working his miracles by means of magical tattoos acquired there.[3] A later writer (Arnobius) reports that Jesus had spent part of his youth in the homeland of magic, after his escape from Palestine, and learned magic in "the secret chambers of Egypt".[4] Under the emperor Nero, the physician Thessalus of Tralles found authentic magic in Egypt, where he is taught by Imouthes-Asclepius himself.[5] In his (apocryphal) autobiography, Cyprian (an orator turned bishop) tells about his ten years with the Isis priest of Memphis who taught him magic.[6] The first book of the *Alexander Romance*, a third-century CE Greek text, includes passages about the amazing magical powers of the last native-born ruler of Egypt (Nectanebo II).[7] The story of the sorcerer's apprentice, made famous by Walt Disney's dramatization of Dukas' music in *Fantasia*, was originally told by Lucian about an Egyptian magician (Pancrates) trained at Memphis.[8] A high proportion of the surviving stories written in ancient Egyptian also feature men and women who can work magic.

The evidence for ancient Egyptian magic spans about 4,500 years, from the end of the fourth millennium until the fifth century CE – amulets; spells written on papyrus or the walls of temples and tombs; literary texts; and sub-literary and non-verbal references, including graffiti.[9] The role of Isis, a major deity in Egyptian religion known as the one who is "great of magic", epitomizes the prominence of the concept by way of her ability to bring her husband Osiris back to life.

As an integral element in the world – as conceived by the Egyptians – "magic" (*heka*) constituted one of the five senses, or cognitive powers, by which Re, the sun god, participated in the first moments of creation. This power – representing the generative force which initially formulated the gods – was the first manifestation of Re. Although viewed originally as a power possessed by the gods, *heka* came to be seen as an innate sense in human beings which operated in the natural sphere through magical acts.

Essentially, "magic" comprised natural functions, like eating and breathing, energized by way of divine agency. Egyptians represented this magical relationship between humanity and the divine as four functions or senses: *sia* (innate intelligence – perception, understanding), *hu* (utterance – taste, authoritative speech), *maa* (sight – intuition, clairvoyance) and *sedjem* (hearing – listening, paying heed).[10] Importantly, while Western "magic" assimilated this native Egyptian terminology for magic as a category during the Coptic (Christian) period, examining the older Egyptian concept and its associated vocabulary, mythology and theology reveals fundamental distinctions between the range and meaning of "magic" within the two cultures. According to this emic perspective, it makes sense to evaluate the evidence for magical concepts and practices independently and in terms of the particular cultural context.

The earliest reference to Heka – divine personification of the concept "magic" – is on a wall of the funerary temple of the Dynasty V king Sahure (2498–2483 BCE), where Heka leads a procession of deities bearing offerings to the pharaoh. In terms of the human-divine nexus, burial stelae from the same period refer to physicians in two, related, ways: as "doctors" *and* "prophets of Heka". The first evidence providing a clearly defined explanation of the relationship between the "idea" of magic and how it was channelled via the gods can be found in what we would describe as a "spell": "The sky trembles, the earth quakes before [So-and-so]. The Magician is [So-and-so]. [So-and-so] possess magic" (Spell 472, Pyramid Texts).

Used as part of a longer incantation – that is, a series of words spoken to evoke a magical effect – this text is one of a series of ritual and magical spells inscribed on the walls of the inner chambers and corridors of Egyptian

Figure 6.1 Pyramid Texts: pyramid of Teti I, Dynasty VI (2345–2333 BCE), Saqqara, Egypt (photo by Chipdawes, via Wikimedia Commons).

pyramids at the end of the Old Kingdom (Figure 6.1). Known to scholarship as the Pyramid Texts, these inscriptions constitute the oldest body of Egyptian writings. Usually literary in form and language, they are also the oldest representatives of Egyptian literature. Designed to help the deceased king overcome the great crisis of physical death and achieve rebirth among the gods, a number of these texts seem to be versions of rituals used during the lifetime of the king, while others may have been adapted from everyday magic and were not royal in origin.While they do not conform strictly to the definition of graffiti (as informal or non-official messages), the Pyramid Texts are nonetheless essential primary sources for the history of ancient Egyptian thought and its relationship to the wider Mediterranean cultural landscape.

The excerpt from Spell 472 establishes clearly that, as far as ancient Egyptians were concerned, it was impossible to disentangle or separate – intellectually or materially – the god Heka and the concept *heka*. But how did this understanding of magic translate into the physical world of speech and action? In other words, how did ancient Egyptians "do" magic? Two other texts – belonging to a collection of funerary texts consisting of spells and magical formulas known as the Coffin Texts – provide the answer.

> I am he who Re ("the unique Lord") made ... when he put Hu ("the Word") upon his mouth ... the son of Him who gave birth to the universe ("the All") ... (Spell 261, Coffin Texts)

> His powers put fear into the gods who came into being after him, his myriad of spirit is within his mouth. It was Heka who came into being of himself, at seeing whom the gods rejoiced, and through the sweet savour of whom the gods live, who created the mountains and knit the firmament together.
> (Spell 648, Coffin Texts)

Combined with the Pyramid Texts (from which they were derived), the Coffin Texts were painted on the burial coffins of the First Intermediate period (*c.*2130–1938 BCE) and the Middle Kingdom (1938–*c.*1630 BCE). Used in the burials of wealthy officials, they were the primary sources of the Book of the Dead, a third series of mortuary spells placed in New Kingdom and Late period tombs to protect the deceased in the afterlife, especially in relation to the progress of individual souls through the realm of the dead.

The snippets from Spells 261 and 648 demonstrate that the Egyptian view of magic is linked to verbal utterance. For a person – king, priest, worker – living in pharaonic Egypt, magic resided in the word itself. Integral to the created order of things, this equivalence of magic and the spoken word lies at the heart of Egyptian magical practice. "Doing" magic, therefore, relied first and foremost on words and the power inherent in speech. Words – special words, based on a vocabulary, grammar and syntax which successive generations of

Figure 6.2 Thoth, Egyptian god of writing (by Jeff Dahl, CC-BY-SA-3.0-2.5-2.0-1.0, http://creativecommons.org/licenses/by-sa/3.0, via Wikimedia Commons).

magical practitioners developed into a substantial repertoire of spells – penetrated the *ka* ("vital essence") of any element in creation (divine, human, natural) and invested it with power. Importantly, unlike modern definitions of "magic" which require a supernatural component, magical activity in ancient Egypt was very much a part of the natural order. Moreover, the fact that references to *heka* – god *and* concept – can be found across two millennia in the official literary record distinguishes magic as an authentic category of Egyptian thought and its practice as a legitimate part of daily life.

The intrinsic association of magic and word is expressed clearly in the epithets assigned to Thoth, the god of writing (Figure 6.2), and therefore the deity who presided over the composition and inscription of official *and* non-official texts: "Lord of hieroglyphs", "great of magic", "wise of magic", "who first fashioned signs and wrote magic".[11] A fascinating declaration of the connection between speech, ritual and material components – the three essential elements of practical Egyptian magic – is preserved in a text which, when inscribed on everyday objects, was used as a talisman by the Egyptians.

G6.1 "I have spoken by means of your spell, I have recited by means of your magic, I have spoken by means of your statement, I have made spells by means of your spells, I have enchanted by means of your words which you created by means of this magic which is in your mouth."

GRAFFITI IN ANTIQUITY

Placed inside private homes and domestic gardens, and even buried in the ground, the inscribed object protected ordinary people and their property from the attacks of noxious beasts, reptiles and insects of every kind. The text is preserved on small rounded stelae mounted on convex bases – the so-called Cippi (small pillars) of Horus. Figures of the god Horus standing upon two crocodiles were carved in relief on the front of this class of object; on the side, back and base of the stelae were written a variety of magical texts. While the ideas suggested by the figures and the texts are extremely old, surviving examples date from no earlier than Dynasty XXVI, last dynasty of the Third Intermediate Period (760–656 BCE).

In relation to the magical qualities invested in objects used for personal protection, a bilingual (hieroglyphic and demotic) funerary text declares that:

G6.2   "If the amulet stays sound, then I am healthy; if it is undamaged, I am uninjured; if it is not struck, I am unwounded ... my limbs shall not become dried out."
                                                            (Spell 160, Book of the Dead)

First mentioned in Spell 106 of the Coffin Texts, and later described in Spells 159 and 160 of the Book of the Dead, the amulet referred to comprised a small column of feldspar, shaped in the round to resemble the papyrus plant – or, in the Late period, a plaque with a column or two incised or carved on it in raised relief – which was placed at the throat of the deceased. The magical protection described by the inscribed text on this type of (papyrus) amulet (G6.2) relates to the journey which the deceased was believed to experience prior to entering the Egyptian equivalent of paradise – the Field of Reeds, the Blessed Realm. Other kinds of inscribed amulets used as protective devices in ancient Egypt included objects crafted in the shape of natural creatures (bird, scarab, serpent), bodily parts (eye, heart, pectoral), or man-made objects (cord, pillar, potion).

Certain texts display a basic connection between magic and medicine, confirmed by the close equivalence of terminology for "magical potion" and "prescription". For instance, a hieroglyphic text describing how to treat a fractured skull provides details of the action required to care for the injury, followed by the statement "that which is said as magic over this prescription".[12] It is evident that medical intervention – no matter how effective – will only prove efficacious if the recommended magical spell was spoken over the treated body part (Figure 6.3). The same word, in demotic, appears repeatedly in the magical papyri:

G6.3   "A potion for laming human limbs."   (Papyrus Rollin I.1)

G6.4   "A remedy for a donkey's not moving."
                                                            (Papyrus BM 10588, col. 7/12)

120

MAGIC

Figure 6.3 Edwin Smith Papyrus (plates 6 and 7, on facial trauma), Second Intermediate Period (c.1600 BCE).[13]

G6.5 "A potion for causing a woman to love you."
(Papyrus BM 10588, col. 8/1)

It should be obvious that Egyptian magic could be generative (G6.2, G6.5) or destructive (G6.3, G6.4), and applied to the living (G6.3–5) and the dead (G6.2).

In the same way that graffiti reflect the close bond between religious power and the pharaoh (Chapter 5), it is interesting to note that certain informal texts corroborate the relationship between magical power and the king. A few very short graffiti texts – inscribed along the cliffs between Gudhi and Abû Simbel, and on rocks at Tôshka and Arminna East – preserve royal names and titles of Dynasty XI Nubian rulers very similar to those of Egyptian pharaohs on which the local rulers may have modelled themselves.

G6.6 "Heka-nefer."

Similarly, at Philae, the king is:

G6.7 "Effective/magical of spells, good of utterance, who pacifies the gods with his words."

121

At Kom Ombo, the text qualifying a scene in which the king officiates at an offering to the temple god describes him as:

G6.8   "Lord of magic."

Fragments of a vase found in Cairo – dating to Dynasty XIX or XX (between the thirteenth and ninth centuries BCE) – record the relationship between magic and the emotional life of Egyptians.

G6.9   "Brother: My sister's love is over there, on the other side, and
        the river in between. The waters are powerful in [their] season
        [i.e. at flood-time] ... A crocodile stands on the sandbank.
        [Yet] I have gone down to the water that I may wade across
        the flood. My heart is brave in the channel. The crocodile
        seems to me nothing but a mouse and the waves are like dry
        land. It is her love that makes me steadfast. Thus she makes
        for me a water spell. I can see my heart's beloved. There she is
        right in front of me."

Inscribed over an effaced copy of another literary text, this section of a longer poem in seven stanzas describes how a young girl's love acts as a magical spell to keep her suitor safe as he swims across a crocodile-infested river to meet her. In both poems there is a regular alternation of male and female speakers. It should be noted that the terms "brother" and "sister" are used through-out as terms of endearment, not as indications of kinship. Importantly, these texts should not be seen as spontaneous expressions of affection: their style, prosody and choice of words all bear the stamp of deliberate, literate art-istry. That said, the manner in which the composer of this verse describes the magical power of love is unqualified. Another poem, written on papyrus, demonstrates this association more explicitly still:

G6.10   "How well she knows to cast the noose, and yet not pay the
        cattle tax. She casts the noose on me with her hair. She cap-
        tures me with her eye; she curbs me with her necklace, she
        brands me with her seal ring."   (Papyrus Chester Beatty Ic)

In the same way that the young girl in the Cairo Vase poem casts a spell in order to protect her lover from the dangers of the natural world, the young man in this verse compares the power which the object of his affection wields over him in terms equivalent to techniques of magical practice.

To conclude this section, we should return briefly to that aspect of ancient Egyptian thought which is preserved in much of the surviving evidence: death and the journey to the afterlife.

122

MAGIC

G6.11   "To be spoken over an image of clay ... upon which the name
of a man has been placed, in the ground: Go, go my soul that
this man may see you. Stand before him wherever he may be.
Rise up before him in the form of [a spirit]."

(Spell 103, Coffin Texts)

Found in a funerary context – inscribed on three Middle Kingdom coffins
from Gebelein and Saqqara – this text was intended for use by the deceased,
specifically to permit one man's soul to appear to another. As the introduction to Spell 103 indicates, however, the text more than likely originated as
part of a magical ritual used by the living. In either case, the spell is designed
to transmit the soul of the intended recipient (*b3*, or *ba*) from the earth to
the netherworld; in other words, to become one of the damned (*mwt*). Unlike
many of the magical graffiti touched on to this point, this text formed part
of an execration ritual, uttered as a curse. In such a ritual, the image representing the person was bound, spat upon, trampled underfoot, struck with a
spear, cut with a knife, thrown in the fire, and spat on again.[14]

There is evidence in later Graeco-Roman Egyptian papyri for a range
of what might be described as "necromantic" magical spells like this: texts
designed to assist the magical practitioner to communicate with the dead,
especially in order to predict the future. Here is a single example, reflecting the framework of verbal utterance, ritual action and intended result
which we have seen as characteristic of magical formulations in pharaonic
Egypt.

G6.12   "Prescription for enchanting the vessel quickly so that the
gods come in and tell you an answer truthfully ... If you wish
to bring in a deceased spirit [*akh*]: you should put a [certain
kind of] stone and a glass [?] stone on the brazier. The spirit
comes in. You should put the heart of a hyena or a hare, [it is]
very good. If you wish to bring in a drowned man: you should
put [another kind of] stone on the brazier. If you wish to bring
in a dead man: you should put ass's dung and an amulet of
Nephthys [protective goddess of death] on the brazier. He
comes in. If you wish to send them all away: you should put
ape's dung on the brazier. They all go away to their place. And
you should recite their spell for dismissing them also."[15]

Speaking with the dead to discover hidden knowledge was, of course, only
one of the ways in which magic was used in a funerary context. Inscribed on
each side of the entrance to the tomb of Ramesses-Montuhirkhopshef (KV
19) is a hieratic graffito written in black ink. Each graffito contains magic
spells designed to assist the deceased, a son of the pharaoh Ramesses IX, on
his journey through the Underworld. These particular spells belong to the

123

Book of the Dead (mentioned above), a collection of almost 200 spells also known as the "Spell for Coming Forth by Day".

The scene depicted at the tomb entrance shows the Ramesside prince offering a small animal forelimb to Amon-Re, which he presents between two leaves. The inked graffito can be seen above the table of offerings. The fact that the quarrying of the tomb was abandoned after the start of the second corridor suggests that the graffiti were incorporated into the design of the funerary scenes shortly after Montuhirkhopshef's death, before more formal painted texts were included.

What, of course, is abundantly clear from these final texts is the quintessential relationship between the written word (graffito), its symbolic utterance in relation to an associated ritual action (offering) and the desired end (divine favour). Aimed at solving a specific problem – to summon the dead to provide an answer to a particular question; or to facilitate how the deceased soul will safely find his way to Aaru (the Field of Reeds where Egyptians believed the dead spent eternity) – the spells written in demotic on papyri dating to the Late Period or recorded in ink on the walls of a partially completed Dynasty XIX tomb reflect the diverse nature of magic in ancient Egypt. Whether associated with kingship and royal burial, the affairs of state officials, affective relations between men and women, control over the cycles (fertility) and dangers (wild animals) of the natural world, or the mysteries of death and the afterlife, magical texts and images on papyri, potsherds, coffins or tomb walls demonstrate the degree to which the world of *heka* finds expression in ancient Egyptian culture.

Greece

Much has been written on the conceptualization of magic and the techniques of magical practice in Greek antiquity.[16] Significant headway has been made in comprehending more clearly the manner in which spells written on a variety of durable or valued surfaces (lead, papyrus, pottery) were composed, what kinds of conceptual relationships were expressed in them, what symbolic markers were inscribed on magical amulets, and what categories of device were worn to guard against dangerous, destructive or evil powers.[17] The systems of knowledge and understanding that formed the basis for ritual practices of the more nuanced and erudite magical practitioners of the ancient Greek world have been studied, in particular what they owed to the philosophical perspectives of Platonism and its variant offshoots, Neo-Pythagoreanism and Gnosticism.[18] So, too, some attention has been paid to the men and women who were believed by their contemporaries to be expert in magic or who themselves professed expertise; as well as to the educated elite who made collections of magical lore or engaged in magical ritual.[19] Of course, trying to recapture something of the cultural texture of ancient Greek

124

MAGIC

society in relation to magical beliefs and practices will be limited by the fragmentary nature of the surviving evidence. Nonetheless, while there is a limit to how complete a picture can be drawn of life in any period of Greek antiquity, graffiti texts and images provide us with an opportunity to engage more closely with the nature of magic both as a category of thought and a way of dealing with the world.

At first sight, the following example of a retrograde verse graffito – found in an archaic cremation grave at Ischia (ancient Pithekoussai) and dated to between 735 and 720 BCE – contains magical elements of the Egyptian love poetry we considered earlier.[20] Written in the early Euboean form of the western Greek alphabet, the text reads:

G6.13 "I am Nestor's cup, good to drink from. Whoever drinks this cup empty, at once desire for beautiful-crowned Aphrodite [= sexual intercourse] will seize him."

It is very likely that the first line of this graffito alludes to the large drinking cup described in Homer's *Iliad*[21] that belongs to the legendary king of Pylos, Nestor, who may have been a namesake of the cup's owner. The two hexameters which follow, however, draw their vocabulary (*poterion*, "cup"; *tode*, "this") and composition (metrical verse) from the language of Greek magical practice. In particular, the inscription mimics the form of a conditional "curse": something done (in this instance, imbibing wine from the *kotyle* or drinking cup on which the text was inscribed) would precipitate a magical response (here, sexual desire). An aphrodisiac effect may not appear especially maleficent. Early Greek thought, however, regarded the seizure of mind and body with uncontrollable erotic feelings as undesirable. In short, the Nestor graffito represents a performative magical text, an incantation intended to evoke a sympathetic response when triggered by a designated action.

A roughly contemporary text – written in retrograde Greek on a *lekythos* (a narrow, cylindrical vessel used for storing oil) found in Magna Graecia (Cymi, in S. Italy) – provides a representative template for the type of magical curse on which the Nestor graffito was modelled.

G6.14 "I am the *lekythos* of Tataies: anyone who steals me will go blind."

A verse epigram – composed in iambic trimetre and incised on a *skyphos* (two-handled wine cup) and found at the ancient Eretrian settlement of Methone (in the region of Pieria) – appears to be an earlier example of the Tataies graffito.

G6.15 "I am the cup of Akesandros: [whoever takes me] will lose his sight [or money]."

125

GRAFFITI IN ANTIQUITY

These graffiti testify to the presence of magic in the ancient Greek world from the very earliest historical times – the beginning of alphabetic Greek writing in the eighth century BCE. What is interesting to note in this regard is the fact that magical practices were a commonplace feature of life in Greek antiquity, part of the cultural repertoire of men and women from all social strata. That the Nestor inscription was composed with considerable care and incised in a neat hand reflecting proficiency in the new language indicates a level of education beyond the purely functional. By the same token, other texts indicate a broad cross-section of participation in the belief systems and ritual activities associated with the Greek vocabulary of magic in antiquity.

In relation to the subject of the first graffito cited above (G6.13) – namely, love – Xenophon, a historian and essay-writer living on the Greek mainland during the Roman period, refers incidentally to the armoury of magical tools used to influence the course of affective relations in fourth-century CE Athens: love potions (*philtra*), incantations (*epōidai*) and *iunx* spells (*iugges*).[22] But love is only one aspect of ancient life over which magic was thought to exert control. For instance, a body of papyri from Graeco-Roman Egypt dating from the second century BCE to the fifth century CE – the so-called Greek magical papyri, found in the vicinity of ancient Thebes – contain a variety of magical spells and formulae, hymns and rituals. These magical texts derive in large part from earlier Egyptian ideas and ritual activities we have already touched on in this chapter and previously (Chapter 5). The following example reflects the scaffolding in late Hellenistic and Graeco-Roman magic of word, action and result identified earlier as integral to effective Egyptian magical practice.

G6.16　"Memory spell: Take hieratic papyrus and write the prescribed names with the myrrh ink of Hermes. Once you have written them as they are prescribed, wash them off into spring water from seven springs and drink the water on an empty stomach for seven days while the moon is in the east. But drink a sufficient amount."[23]

Four papyri, the so-called Demotic magical papyri – written in a combination of Greek and the form of the Egyptian language known as Demotic, and glossed in Old Coptic (Egyptian written in alphabetic Greek); also found at Thebes – confirm this continuity of religious and magical beliefs and practices. Reference to a text previously examined (the London Magical Papyrus) demonstrates the fundamental tenacity of these principles of thought and action in the evolution of magic in Graeco-Roman antiquity.

G6.17　"The ointment which you put on your eyes when you are about to inquire of the lamp in any lamp-divination: you take some flowers of the Greek bean; you find them in the place of

126

MAGIC

the garland-seller, otherwise said of the lupin-seller; you take
them fresh and put them in a *lok*-vessel of glass and stop its
mouth very well for twenty days in a secret dark place. After
twenty days, if you take it out and open it, you find a pair [?]
of testicles in it with a phallus. You leave it for forty days and
when you take it out and open it, you find that it has become
bloody; then you put it on a glass thing and put the glass thing
into a pottery thing in a place hidden at all times. When you
desire to make inquiry of the lamp with it at any time if you fill
your eyes with this blood aforesaid, and if you go in to pro-
nounce a spell over the lamp you see a figure of a god standing behind [?] the lamp, and he speaks with you concerning
the question which you wish; or you lie down and he comes to
you."[24]

Moreover, we know that these texts were collected in antiquity. According
to the Roman historian and biographer Suetonius, for instance, the emperor
Augustus ordered 2,000 magical scrolls to be burned in the year 13 BCE;
a little later, during the first century CE, a number of magical books were
burned in Ephesus.[25] Beyond these extant texts, however, we also possess
many other kinds of material: artefacts, symbols and inscriptions on gem-
stones, on *ostraca* and – as we have seen – pottery vessels, and on tablets of
gold, silver, lead, tin, and so on.

A significant category of non-official inscribed text pertaining to the
expression of Graeco-Roman magical ideas is the curse tablet or binding spell,
known in Greek by the collective term *katadesmoi* – literally, "things (made)
to tie up (or bind down)"; informally, "magic knots"); or, in Latin, *defixiones*
– literally, "things made to fix (fasten, or nail down)"; informally, "enchant-
ments". Written on broken pottery, precious or semi-precious stones, limestone, papyrus, wax, and, most frequently, small, thin sheets of lead or lead
alloy (lead and tin, or copper), these texts comprised messages intended to
have a harmful effect on the character, development, or behaviour of people
or animals.

Inscribed on both sides of a thick lead tablet, a fourth-century BCE binding
text from mainland Attika confirms the widespread preoccupation of Greeks
with matters of the heart.

G6.18   "[Side A] I bind Theodora in the presence of the one [female]
at Persephone's side and in the presence of those who are
unmarried. May she be unmarried and whenever she is about
to chat with Kallias and with Charias – whenever she is about
to discuss deeds and words and business ... words, whatever he indeed says. I bind Theodora to remain unmarried to
Charias and [I bind] Charias to forget Theodora, and [I bind]

127

Charias to forget ... Theodora and sex with Theodora. [Side B] [And just as] this corpse lies useless, [so] may all the words and deeds of Theodora be useless with regard to Charias and to the other people. I bind Theodora before Hermes of the underworld and before the unmarried and before Tethys. [I bind] everything, both [her] words and deeds towards Charias and toward other people, and [her] sex with Charias. And may Charias forget sex. May Charias forget the girl, Theodora, the very one whom he loves."[26]

This erotic binding spell of the later Classical period invokes a variety of deities and anonymous forces in support of the composer's desire for Theodora to terminate her relationship with Charias. Usually depicted in Greek vase painting as a woman holding two torches, Hekate is referred to as "the [one] female at Persephone's side". Goddess of magic, witchcraft, the night, moon, ghosts and necromancy, Hekate assisted Demeter in her search for Persephone, kidnapped by the god Pluto and taken to the underworld. Her spheres of influence mark Hekate as an ideal deity whose supernatural aid might be profitably sought – especially so as the tablet must have been deposited in a grave (confirmed by the observation on Side B of the tablet: "as this corpse lies useless"). While the individuals (or symbolic category) named "the unmarried" cannot be identified in the extant literary or documentary record, the quality by which this group is distinguished was most certainly apt to the desired outcome of the spell – and may possibly relate to a divine abstraction of the condition wished for Theodora. Certainly, appealing to Hermes – like Thoth, the equivalent Greek god of writing and magic – would have made perfect sense; and, though initially she might appear an unexpected deity to whom one would direct this petition, it was believed that Tethys – goddess of the sources of fresh water which nourished the earth – drew water from her husband Okeanos through subterranean aquifers, thus satisfying the appellant's criteria for divine aid in contact with potent forces of the underworld.

Originally rolled up and bisected with a nail, a second lead tablet – found in Patissia, a modern neighbourhood of Athens, dating no later than the second century BCE – identifies the competitive world of Hellenistic theatre as another of the areas of ancient Greek life subject to magical intervention.

G6.19   "[Side A] I bind Evandros with a leaden bond and ... Evandros the actor | [Side B] and all the ... of Evandros ... Asteas, son of Evandros the actor."[27]

Incised into one side of a soft lead sheet with a metal (most likely, bronze) stylus, the first-person introductory verb ("I bind") delineates the function of the text – literally, to tie or fasten the object of the invocation (Evandros)

MAGIC

– and the type of bond specified as the component effecting the desired end ("a leaden bond") indicates a magical ligature corresponding in efficacy to the material (heavy and cold) on which the text was written (lead). The profession of Evandros ("actor"), stated on one side and repeated on the other, situates the *katadesmos* as a binding spell directed most probably towards a theatrical rival of the person who composed – or commissioned, if a professional inscriber of magic was hired to mark the lead sheet – the text. Athens hosted a variety of annual dramatic festivals, at which participants competed against each other for the privilege to stage their plays and public acclaim as the production nominated as the winning entry over the course of a particular festival's period of agonistic performance. Any advantage, it would seem – even a magical one – was deemed a practical strategy in acquiring victory.

One of the most competitive spheres of life in any age relates to the determination of guilt or innocence in civil, criminal or political courts of justice. Discovered in a late fourth-century BCE grave just beyond Athens' city walls, three lead objects speak eloquently about the fundamental role legal and political disputes played in the Greek world. In particular, they identify the pivotal function of magic as a means by which persons expecting to participate in a lawsuit or public trial could prepare themselves emotionally against their accusers. Buried in the Kerameikos – the sprawling cemetery of classical Athens – excavators found two lead plates and a figurine. The figurine is a crudely modelled human figure with phallus; its arms, folded behind the back, suggest the intention to tie or bind them. The name Mnêsimachos is inscribed on the right leg of the figurine. The plates are elongated in shape, like saucers, forming the upper and lower half of a small coffin for the figurine. There is writing on one of the plates. These objects, along with the partially disturbed and mutilated remains of a human skeleton, were found precisely where they were originally located: the figurine, placed at the pelvis of the skeleton; the inscribed plate, just above. On the inscribed plate – in which there are two holes, probably intended for a nail – the text reads:

G6.20 "Barbutidês Xôphugos | Nikomachos Oinoklês | Mnêsimachos | Chamaios Teisônidês | Charisandros | Dêmoklês | and if there is anyone else with them | as an advocate or witness."[28]

Literary evidence reveals that certain individuals named in this curse graffito were prominent citizens in classical Athens – Nikomachos (*anagrapheus*, archivist and registrar of public documents); Charisandros (*prutanis*, official presiding over a variety of public events); Demokles (public figure). This would strongly suggest that *all* persons included in the inscription were significant players in the socio-political life of the city. That Mnêsimachos' name appears twice – on the figurine's leg and in the graffito – indicates that he was the primary target of the spell. Given that there survives an oration by the fourth-century orator Lysias against the Nikomachos named in the

129

GRAFFITI IN ANTIQUITY

inscription, evidence for a speech against a certain Mnêsimachos by the same orator adds historical support to the contention that magic was used in legal affairs in classical Athens.

A final graffito affords a view of the extent to which magical expression permeated the ancient Greek-speaking world. Found in the pit of a private house on the island of Delos, a text inscribed on a square lead tablet seeks retribution against those responsible for the theft of a necklace.

G6.21   "[Side A] Lord Gods Sukonaioi, K[...], Lady Goddess Syria Sukona ... punish, show your power and direct your anger at whoever took [and] stole the necklace, at those who had any knowledge of it, at those who took part in it, whether man or woman. [Side B] Lord Gods Sukonaioi ... Lady Goddess Syria ... Sukona, punish, show your power. I register [with the gods] whoever took [and] stole the necklace. I register those who had any knowledge of it and those who took part in it. I register him, his head, his soul, the sinews of the one who stole the necklace/bracelet, and of those who know anything about it and who took part in it. I register the genitals and private parts of the one who stole [it]; and of those who took [and] stole the necklace, the hands ... from head to feet ... toe-nails ... of those who took the necklace ... those who had any knowledge of it ... whether man or woman."[29]

From the fourth to the first century BCE, the Mediterranean saw a period of intense interaction, mobility and movement of peoples, primarily as a result of war, conquest and trade. During this time, Delos played a key role in trade between the eastern Mediterranean and the Italian peninsula, especially with regard to the slave trade. According to the formal epigraphical record, three main groups lived on the island: Greeks (Athenians in particular); Italians/Romans; and Syrians/Phoenicians. This melange of cultures – and the influences transmitted as a result of extended social interaction between the prevalent groups – is reflected in the composition and emphasis of the inscribed text.

Numerous infelicities of spelling and grammar suggest that the author of the Delos graffito either possessed a limited knowledge of the Greek language or may not have been a native Greek-speaker and writer. The latter speculation seems more likely, especially given the fact that the spell is addressed exclusively to Syrian gods and goddesses. For instance, the "Syrian Goddess" to which the first line of the graffito refers is almost certainly Atargatis, chief goddess of northern Syria. Known to ancient Greeks by the name Aphrodite Derceto,[30] and to the Romans as Dea Syria,[31] Atargatis is mentioned in other Delian inscriptions using a synthesis of these names – Deasura, or *suria theos*. The Graeco-Roman conflation of the goddess' name is also found in the graffito.

130

Reference to Atargatis in a graffito of this kind is perfectly understandable, since she was responsible for the protection and well-being of her people.

The form and function of this non-official text, therefore, reflects the transmission of linguistic and ritual elements of magical knowledge across boundaries in the ancient Mediterranean. While the transfer of language skills in this particular instance was not completely successful, the formulaic statements used draw closely on the distinctive expressions of Graeco-Roman *katesdesmoi*. Though clearly a secondary language, using Greek was obviously important to the composer of this text. Moreover, invoking fair and reasonable treatment of the offended party – the owner(s) of the stolen property – and revenge on the perpetrator(s) of the injury or wrong inflicted on the former – the theft of the necklace – reflect widespread magical practice in relation to the purpose and use of spells.

As this first-century BCE (or early first-century CE) inscription from Delos exemplifies, graffiti in Greek represent a significant category of magical expression in the world of antiquity. More than sculptures, architecture or literary works, non-official messages inscribed in Greek on durable clay, metal or other natural surfaces do not have the same boundaries of gender, literacy or class. This distinction from other preserved texts and material culture can help to give a more rounded view of ancient society, even if it is only a small piece of a greater puzzle.

Rome

Writing about events in the early years of imperial rule under the emperor Tiberius (19 CE), Tacitus recounts an extraordinary incident involving political rivalry, high treason and magical practices. Julius Caesar Germanicus, Tiberius' adopted son and heir, was travelling in the Roman province of Syria on the emperor's business, when he died in suspicious circumstances. Germanicus himself, according to the historian, believed that his political enemies – Gnaeus Calpurnius Piso, governor of Syria; and Piso's wife, Plancina – had poisoned him. However, a "forensic" examination of the house revealed evidence of what many thought had really killed him.

> Explorations of the floor and walls brought to light the remains of human bodies, spells, curse tablets, leaden tablets engraved with the name "Germanicus", charred and blood-smeared ashes and others of the implements of witchcraft by which it is believed that the living soul can be devoted to the powers of the underworld.
> (Tacitus, *Annals* 2.69)

As the evidence of Egyptian and Greek graffiti has already verified, this historical episode demonstrates the interaction between the worlds of real life (in this case, politics) and magic in antiquity. The extravagant nature of the gruesome discovery associated with Germanicus' terminal illness should not dissuade us from the depth of belief in the efficacy of magical spells and artefacts nor diminish our acceptance of the authenticity of magical practice in the Roman Mediterranean. A formal inscription from the later first century CE underlines the prevalence of magic in word and deed under Roman rule.

> For having saved the city, the city council, and the people of Tuder, L. Cancrius Primigenius, freedman of Clemens, member of the committee of six men in charge of the worship of the Augustans and the Flavians, the first to be honoured in this way by the order, has fulfilled his vow to Jupiter Optimus Maximus, because through his divine power he has brought to light and protected the names of the members of the city council, which, by the unspeakable crime of a worthless communal slave, had been attached to tombs so that a curse could be put upon them. Thus Jupiter freed the city and the citizens from the fear of danger.
>
> (*CIL* 11.4639)

Again we can see the connection between politics and magic, albeit, in this instance, on a smaller level than that involving a prince of the imperial Roman dynasty. Tuder (modern Todi) was a relatively small town in central Italy, located on the border with the territory of Rome's legendary kings, the Etruscans. What the inscription makes abundantly clear is that certain members of Tuder's *decurio* (town council) had been interdicted under a magical spell. From the preceding discussion on Greek *katadesmoi*, it is possible to read between the lines here: the unnamed slave – who must have held a grudge against the administrators of Tuder – will have inscribed the names of his intended victims on lead tablets, burying these in or near the local cemetery precinct. Only through the swift action of L. Cancrius Primigenius – setting up the inscription that contained a vow to the chief god of the Roman pantheon and the state – was the threat to the council avoided.

Politics was not the only sphere of human activity susceptible to magical influence. Like the graffito curse directed at the Hellenistic actor Evandros (G6.19), non-official magical texts from the Roman world target other contexts of organized competition.

G6.22   "I conjure you, daemon, whoever you may be, and order you, to torture and kill, from this hour, this day, this moment, the horses of the Green and the White teams; kill and smash the charioteers Clarus, Felix, Primulus, Romanus; do not leave a breath in them. In conjure you by him who has delivered you, at the time, the god of the sea and the air: Iao, Iasdao, Oorio, Aeia."[32]

MAGIC

Inscribed on a lead tablet from third-century CE Carthage in Roman North Africa, this graffito curse was found in a tomb close to the city. Chariot races in the circus were among the most popular of Roman spectator sports. This inscription identified four teams, distinguished by the colour of their uniforms: Reds, Whites, Greens and Blues. These colours represented "factions" which organized the financial, technical and professional side of the sport. Followed by emperors and ordinary Roman citizens alike, the intensity of emotion invested in the success or failure of particular drivers and their factions in the circus contests made it almost inevitable that some supporters would resort to seeking advantage in magic. The composer of the graffito was obviously a supporter of the Blues and Reds: the opposing teams' riders and horses are given over to the harmful attentions of an anonymous daemon. Interestingly, the spell is strengthened by invoking variant forms for the name of the Jewish deity Yahweh – Iao and Iasdao.

The majority of *defixiones* from Roman North Africa have been found in Carthage and appear to date, like this one, from the third century CE. Many others have been found in Hadrumetum (modern Sousse), a seaport lying 60 miles south of Carthage, and a few have been unearthed in other former Roman cities. Their texts are representative of the various types of binding spells that we have seen were commonly entrusted to lead tablets – business, justice, love, revenge and competitive activities like theatrical performances and sporting events. Of the 120 published tablets from North Africa, the majority involve athletic competition, especially chariot races (54) and gladiatorial contests (9); to a lesser extent, there are several tablets used for erotic magic (20) and spells meant to bind the tongues of opponents in legal proceedings (17); additionally, there are two that perhaps deal with competition in the workplace, and twenty miscellaneous or unidentifiable spells.

Like the Theodora graffito we considered earlier (G6.18), one of the most common uses for binding spells in the Roman world was erotic magic. As we have seen, such spells occur repeatedly in the corpus of magical papyri; and of the 1500 or so published curse tablets, a quarter are erotic in nature.[33] A graffito text incised on lead, found at Minturnae – an important port city south of Rome on the banks of the river Liris – displays the lengths to which ordinary people might be driven as a consequence of love.

G6.23   "Spirits of the underworld, I consecrate and hand over to you, if you have any power, Ticene of Carisius. Whatever she does, may it all turn out wrong. Spirits of the netherworld, I consecrate to you her limbs, her complexion, her figure, her head, her hair, her shadow, her brain, her forehead, her eyebrows, her mouth, her nose, her chin, her cheeks, her lips, her speech, her breath, her neck, her liver, her shoulders, her heart, her lungs, her intestines, her stomach, her arms, her fingers, her hands, her navel, her entrails, her thighs, her knees, her calves,

133

> her heels, her soles, her toes. Spirits of the netherworld, if I
> see her wasting away, I swear that I will be delighted to offer a
> sacrifice to you every year." (*CIL* X.8249)

Written in imperfect Latin – the text exhibits a variety of inaccuracies in spelling and grammar – this curse consigns the object of the spell (Ticene of Carisius) to the "care" of *manes/daimones* ("spirits of the underworld"). In revenge over a thwarted relationship, or perhaps in the aftermath of a failed love potion, the composer of this *defixio* magically transfers the bitterness of his (her?) emotional rejection to the infernal forces which the ancients believed inhabited the subterranean realm of existence between gods and humans. That the author "felt" Ticene's indifference or displeasure profoundly is embodied – literally – in the catalogue of anatomical parts on which the underworld spirits were invoked to inflict pain. The inclusion of Ticene's "shadow" indicates just how consumed with anger her rejected lover must have been.

Other types of graffiti similarly reflect the pervasive nature of magical belief and practice in ancient Rome. In the same way that some people used magic to influence others – for better or worse – others sought to protect themselves against the excesses of physical, emotional or spiritual control directed their way. In this regard, so-called apotropaic magic played an important part in the daily life of Roman society. The Greek word *apotropaios* ("apotropaic") is a descriptive term meaning "averting evil"; it derives from the Greek verbal root *apotrépein*, "to hinder, avert evil, or desist". Apotropaic ritual and its associated symbols, therefore, relate specifically to the notion of keeping out evil influences and were prophylactic against danger. One of the more familiar examples of this practice relates to the Old Testament episode concerning the smearing of lamb's blood on the door lintels of Jews living in Egypt at the festival of Passover to ward off the Angel of Death.[34] Likewise, Pliny the Elder refers to the practice of averting such forces by using "satyric images against envious charms".[35] Whatever Pliny meant by *saturica signa* – in all likelihood, statues of satyrs (rustic fertility spirits, akin in some ways to the spirits of the underworld, at least in relation to their supernatural power) – it is clear that the images in question were set up (often in gardens and on hearths) to act as protective magical objects.

One of the forces against which both Greeks and Romans most frequently protected themselves related to the power of *fascinum* ("fascination", "enchantment"). The ancients believed that some persons possessed the power of injuring others by their looks. Cited often in the literary record, this power was – and still is – known as the "evil eye" (*ophthalmos baskanos*).[36] Of the many amulets used as apotropaic protection against the evil eye, the most common appears to have been the phallus, which the Romans called by the name of the power it acted against (*fascinum*).

Graffiti at Pompeii often represent or refer to the symbol of the phallus. Of course, the meaning of particular markings will depend entirely on the context in which the images appear. However, the following examples represent the use of non-official texts and drawings as apotropaic signs.

G6.24   "Here lives [phallus] good fortune."   (*CIL* IV.1454)

Incised above an oven in a small bakery (VI.6.17), this inscribed text incorporates an explicit representation of a phallus in high relief. The commercial nature of the premises in which graffito and phallus image appears provides an explanation for the location in which the display has been mounted and also a rationale for its primary function as an apotropaic device. The bakery – comprising a bench, oven and three flour mills – formed part of a larger commercial and residential complex (VI.6.18–20), indicating that the fortunes of the family which resided there were firmly based on the success of the bread production facilities. Placing a message advertising the presence of good fortune, in association with a symbol well known as a device used to ward off its opposite, would have been a logical – indeed, necessary – inclusion in the functional design of a space important not just to the owners of the property but many living in the local neighbourhood as well.

Compare this with a graffito drawing on the northern corridor wall behind the Odeon or Small Theatre (Figure 6.4). The image scratched into the wall

Figure 6.4. Graffito of gladiator with oversized phallus, corridor behind VIII.7.20 (Odeon or Covered Theatre), Pompeii, Italy.

GRAFFITI IN ANTIQUITY

plaster depicts a gladiator with a phallus much larger than the rest of his body. At first sight, this sketch might appear nothing more than the boastful or arrogant declaration typical of male *braggadocio*. However, if we take into consideration the potent ritual symbolism associated with gladiatorial contests, then it is as likely that this image represented a visual expression of the artist's intention to protect the fighter against evil fortune in the arena.

G6.25 "Thyas does not want to love Fortunatus. [phallus] Farewell."

(*CIL* IV.4498)

Scratched into the red plaster of a large home's *tablinum* in Region VI, Thyas' message to the ironically named Fortunatus is explicit and direct. It may seem odd that a woman clearly unattracted to any kind of relationship – let alone a sexual liaison – with an undesired suitor would include in a message of rejection the image of a phallus. Given what we now know about the significance of the phallus as a magical sign, it seems more reasonable to infer that Thyas incised a phallus before saying goodbye to Fortunatus as a safeguard against further unwanted advances. In this instance, Thyas' use of the *fascinum* represents an adaptation of the apotropaic function of the symbol to avert Fortunatus' amorous glances. The subtext of her message would have been crystal clear, if deflating – especially in Roman Pompeii, part of a wider society in which power of any kind accrued to men far more than women.

Evil, of course, comes in many guises. For example, written on the wall of a narrow alley between two city blocks in the eastern precincts of the city (III.4–5), three messages address the unhygienic intrusions of passers-by who soiled the thoroughfare with excrement. Two of these graffiti are brief, to the point and iterate a verbatim sentiment – *cacator cave malum* ("Shitter, beware evil");[37] the third provides more specific detail:

G6.26 "Shitter, be on your guard against evil [*cave malum*], or else, if you disregard this, may you incur the wrath of Jupiter [*Iovem iratum*]." (*CIL* IV.7716)

Despite the prevalence of public latrines, the problem of inconsiderate individuals relieving themselves in this narrow byway just off Pompeii's main east–west thoroughfare (the Via dell'Abbondanza) was clearly entrenched in customary practice. The size of the graffito – 7.6 m long by 50 cm high – reflects the displeasure of house-owners in this part of the city towards inconsiderate neighbours or, far more likely, itinerant workers or transient visitors making their way to or from Pompeii's eastern gate (the Porta Sarno). What stands out here is the conflation of connotations relating to magic (*cave malum*) and religion (*Iovem iratum*) in what amounts to a variant of the conditional curse we have already encountered (G6.13–15). A graffito painted on a wall in the Baths of Titus in imperial Rome displays a similar

136

MAGIC

conflation of magic and religion in seeking to avert the unsanitary deposition of bodily waste:

G6.27 "Anyone who urinates or defecates here will incur the wrath of the twelve gods [*Dii Consentes* = Juno, Vesta, Minerva, Ceres, Diana, Venus, Mars, Mercury, Jupiter, Neptune, Vulcan, Apollo] and Diana and Jupiter Optimus Maximus."

(*CIL* VI.29848)

A final example of non-official text and image illustrates this transitional expression of magico-religious ideas, distilling in passing the intrinsic nature of such beliefs and practices in Roman antiquity. In the corridor leading to a public latrine (IX.7.21/2) is what appears to be a *lararium* wall painting of Isis Fortuna.

A terracotta support (*monopodium*), which may have formed part of a table, stood against the wall under the painting, suggesting the context of a public shrine (*compitum*). Isis-Fortuna – figurative syncretism of the protective Egyptian goddess Isis with Roman Fortuna, personifying the capricious and variable influence of the divine over human affairs – was venerated by the Romans until the end of antiquity. The painting depicts Fortuna's twin attributes, the rudder (symbolizing destiny) and the cornucopia (fertility). The serpents depicted on either side of the squatting man represent the spirit of this particular place (*genius loci*). That they appear to attack him under the watchful gaze of the assimilated goddess suggests, again, the indictment of the conditional curse: namely, the consequence of an action advised against. Here, the text written above the man – *cacator cave malu(m)* – confirms this interpretation. Caught in the act of disregarding the injunction of the accompanying inscription, the guardian of the place – marked by painting and text – would naturally be expected to watch over it and punish any who defiled it. Like the contexts in which the apotropaic magic of the phallus protected individuals against harm, this corridor was well defended against malefactors; like the retributive magic of the binding spell, graffito and image combined here to ensure justice meted out to those who offended against public order.

FINAL THOUGHTS

The ubiquity in the ancient Mediterranean of magical beliefs is reflected across a range of literary, documentary and material evidence. Given the widespread nature of graffiti texts and images as a staple form of communication, it follows that non-official inscriptions record examples of the ways in which the ancient mind formulated and articulated ideas pertaining to magic. Whether prophylactic or maledictory, traditional or transgressive, messages detailing the approach in antiquity to the personification, publication and practice of magic find expression in a wide variety of cultural contexts – in Egyptian society, from the burial places of the elite to the protective amulets of ordinary men and women; in the ancient Greek world, from the property of expatriate colonists to the magical papyri of the market-place; and in the Roman empire, from the curses of slaves, freed persons and freeborn citizens alike to the everyday spaces of human activity. Esoteric and scorned by the sceptical in the modern age, this spectrum of references to magic in the graffiti of antiquity denotes the commonplace nature of belief in a dimension of human existence outside the purely physical world and foregrounds the extent to which such knowledge and understanding permeated the cultural fabric of ancient society.

CHAPTER 7

MYTHOLOGY

I, Dioskorammon, looked upon this nonsense and found it bewildering! (Weeks, *Ramses II*)[1]

Eurypylos. Thóas. Mēriónēs. (*SEG* 33.821)

Plasma. Prometheus. Psyche. Hector. Achilles. (*SEG* 44.1395)

MYTHOLOGY IN ANTIQUITY

Ancient mythology in the twenty-first century is a source of tremendous fascination, though in almost all cases this curiosity relates to whatever religious or heroic legends are so foreign to modern experience that they cannot be believed to be true. If one seeks out a definition of the word "mythical", then it is likely that the result will favour a meaning tending toward "idealized, especially with reference to the past" or, more often than not, "fictitious". In other words, myth can be used as a term of metaphorical abuse, in the sense that it is used to denote something exaggerated or untrue. Clearly, Dioskorammon, a late antique visitor to the tomb of Ramesses VI in the Valley of the Kings, found this to be the case. Of course, the other graffiti in the epigraph to this chapter – painted on the inner side of the lid of an Apulian *lekanis* (330–320 BCE) or labelling mythological scenes on various walls of the so-called Tomb of Prometheus (Capitolias, Arabia) – reflect the pervasiveness of mythological narrative in the ancient Mediterranean. Many educated people consider myth as something outside the realm of the scholarly or rational; rather, it should be viewed in terms of its poetical, symbolic or even aesthetic elements. While the references to Eurypylos, Thóas and Mēriónēs (three heroes of the Trojan War) might be obscure to most today, in the ancient world such figures would have been recognized and their stories well-known, in story, song and performance. Even so, the graffiti labels on the fresco in the Capitolias tomb – identifying Prometheus (credited with the creation of humankind), a human being he has created (known simply as *plasma*) and Psyche, symbolizing the concepts of "soul" or "breath of life" – hint at the range of ideas beyond the world of epic heroism and scientific reason. This perspective, of course, will explain, in part at least, why, for example, the narratives comprising the early sections of the Old Testament – notably Genesis – are regularly excluded from standard studies of European mythology, even when the biblical tradition closely parallels myths from Persia, Babylonia, Egypt and Greece. In reality, of course, myths often lack these artistic or literary qualities; a significant number of mythological stories can best be described as pedestrian, practical and singularly lacking in beauty.

How should we understand mythology in the ancient world? It will perhaps make the most sense to avoid as much as is possible any attempt to incorporate extensive discussion of philosophical concepts or religious experience – to a large extent, we have already touched on these elements of ancient life (Chapter 5), at least as they apply to the explanatory usefulness of graffiti dealing with these ideas. Instead, considering myth in close association with the social complex of antiquity should repay our close attention. In this respect, the simplest conceptualization of mythology (ancient or modern) requires a consensus of two viewpoints: myth records and validates institutions; *and* myth speculates and solves problems. The first requires careful regard for the overt content or narrow allegorical interpretations of mythological ideas, symbols and stories; the second focuses explicitly on underlying historical, sociological and anthropological structures. In both instances, it is important to note that myth in the ancient world did not carry the negative connotations which modern definitions of the term entail – namely, comprising an enhanced or altered representation of reality; lacking historical validity or inherent truth.

If we combine these two perspectives – simplistically, the Anglo-American and European traditions – then myth in antiquity can be seen to have possessed two primary functions:

- To justify existing social systems and to account for traditional rites and customs.
- To answer fundamental questions about life and its meaning and the world.

Regardless of which function exerted more influence on the creative process of myth-making – and, at times, both will have operated simultaneously to establish a particular tale – the resulting myth tended to confer significant power on whichever deities were credited with the origin and care of particular customs, institutions, or ideas that formed part of the belief, ritual or customary practice in any given society. As a logical consequence, this will also have invested those who enacted and maintained these social, cultural and philosophical-religious artefacts. Very simply, myths added considerable value to the cultural capital of individuals and groups, thereby determining the levels of status and prestige associated with rituals, organizations and conceptual systems based on or explained by such myths.

Egypt

The character of Egyptian mythology is highly complex, and should always be examined in relation to its cultural and historical contexts. The conceptual framework underpinning this intricate system of ideas, literary narratives, linguistic signs and symbolic iconography formed an essential element of the pharaonic civilization that lived along the Nile valley for over three thousand years. Highly distinctive personalities and critical episodes from the mythological tradition pervade Egypt's creative expression through artistic imagination, architectural skill and literary composition. Myth grounded the rituals of state performed by Egypt's rulers and religious functionaries. Educated Egyptians regarded mythological knowledge and understanding as integral facets of defence against the many possible sources or harm or injury to be faced in the ebb and flow of daily life *and* the realm of the dead.

A brief case study will help to clarify our understanding of mythology in ancient Egypt and set the scene for considering the relationship between Egyptian myths and graffiti in antiquity. Certain rituals performed on the mummified body of a deceased person demonstrate clearly the twin functions of myth – institutional and conceptual – in Egyptian society. The "Opening of the Mouth" ceremony was a symbolic animation meant to restore the senses and faculties to the deceased so that they could both participate in the judgment process and also function properly – for example, eat, speak, and so on – in the afterlife. This allowed the *ba* (the unique character of an individual; the personality, or "soul") and the *ka* (the vital essence distinguishing the living from the dead) to unite.

Before the ritual started, the ground was ceremonially cleansed with water from four vessels representing the four corners of the Earth. Incense was burned, various gods were called on as witnesses, and a calf was slaughtered to celebrate the battle in which Horus avenged the death of his father Osiris. In the myth, the conspirators who aided Osiris' brother Set in dismembering Osiris' corpse, attempted to elude Horus by transforming into a miscellany of creatures, but Horus intercepted their escape and beheaded them. At the Opening of the Mouth ceremony, various other animals were ritually killed, including two bulls – one for the north (Lower Egypt) and one for the south (Upper Egypt) – gazelles and ducks. When the bull of the south was slaughtered, one of the legs was cut off and, along with the heart, offered to the mummy. The final part of the ritual was the ceremonial "opening of the mouth". It involved touching various cult objects to different parts of the body. Of primary importance, a priest took an implement shaped like a miniature adze (carpenter's tool) and touched it to the mummy's mouth. When the body of a head of state was involved, the ceremony was performed either by a high priest or by the heir to the deceased pharaoh. The purpose of the heir performing this ritual was as part of legitimizing his succession.

Associated with this ritual – which brought the spiritual and physical essence of the deceased to life – was the "Weighing of the Heart" ceremony. Logically, of course, this ceremony took place in the realm of the dead. The key idea explaining its purpose lay in the belief that the heart was a witness to the deeds of a person's life. As such, the heart "testified" on behalf of the deceased during the Weighing ceremony, which therefore formed part of a person's transition to the afterlife. The heart was symbolic of a person's *ka* and ensured the continuity of the person from the world of the living to the afterlife. As such, the physical heart was protected by spells and a scarab and – unlike the other major organs of the body (brain, lungs, liver, intestines) – left inside the corpse during mummification.

An analysis of another scene from the Book of the Dead, painted on the walls of many New Kingdom tombs, helps to explain the mythological facets of this "ceremony". In the illustrated scene, the only "real" characters are Ani and his wife (dressed in white garments, bottom left). By the scales is an array of mythical characters, including Anubis, Ammit, Thoth, Ani's *ba*, Fate, and so on. There are also 12 gods as part of the tribunal along the top. Some of these can be identified by their heads/headdress. These include: Horus (with falcon head), Isis, Nephthys, Sekhmet (lion head), Ma'at (with feather on her head), Osiris and Horus again (as the son of Ra). The role of Osiris was pivotal to the right judgement of the deceased. Osiris was the lord of death, rebirth and vegetation – this is why in many images, Osiris has green skin. He was also known as the Lord of the West – that is, where the sun sets – and this is why many funerary complexes, such as the Valley of the Kings, are on the west side of the Nile. The dead, like the Sun who "dies" in the west, hoped to be reborn again. Osiris also sat on the tribunal of judges. Because Osiris had already "died" and been "reborn" himself, he was the only god who had gone through what the dead hoped to achieve. The dead were often called "Osiris" in an attempt to emulate this process and be "reborn" as well in the afterlife. Being referred to as "Osiris" may also have helped the deceased to pass some of the tests and guardians during the transition to the afterlife.

Ma'at was symbolic of truth, justice and order. If this mythological abstraction could be distilled to its essential ingredients, it would be "balance". Everything in Egyptian culture was viewed though the lens of "balance" – hence the scales in the Weighing ceremony. As part of this ceremony, the so-called "Negative Confession" uttered by the deceased – a statement listing all the evil deeds he or she had avoided in life – was a means to bring

MYTHOLOGY

about Ma'at. Many of the declarations can be broken down into religious and social constructs. By declaring "what he has not done", the text also illustrated "what could be done". Clearly some of the things that the deceased declared he had not done – such as catching fish or removing cattle from their pasture – cannot be taken at face value; unless, that is, he had starved himself to death! As such, the Egyptians recognized that, in order to survive, they may have to do things that the gods may find abhorrent – an etiological explanation of why the world was the way it was. However, by "renouncing" these offences in the Negative Confession, the "sin" was effectively erased, thus bringing about Ma'at. If the gods before whom the deceased uttered the declaration were convinced, then they would declare him or her "true of voice" (*Maatkheru*) and permit the penitent to continue on the journey to the afterlife.

The Negative Confession also demonstrated piety and reverence of the gods and cult practices and other institutions of the state. Perhaps the biggest demonstration of Ma'at was the declaration that the name of the deceased had not reached the ears of the ruler. In other words, the deceased had not done anything overtly bad or criminal during his life. However, he also had not done anything overtly good in order to be recognized by the ruler either. Thus, what the Negative Confession tells us about Egyptian morality is the importance of this concept of balance and order within Egyptian society: everything had its place, and everything should be in its place.

A variety of graffiti dating to the New Kingdom corroborates the mythological narrative associated with Osiris and its relationship to pharaonic Egypt's ritual and commemorative tradition. Inscribed on one of the exterior walls of the Old Kingdom ruler Djoser's step pyramid – a context which we have already encountered (Chapter 4) – a graffito written by a visitor to the burial complex during Year 4 of Tutankhamun's reign (1328 BCE) states:

G7.1   "The scribe Tjay came to see the temple of the King of Upper and Lower Egypt, the deceased Djoser. He said, 'Let me come to the West of Memphis, O Osiris, may I serve your *ka* after a good (burial?) ... Osiris ... if you make it well ... reach a good old age like ...'"[2]

The state functionary, Tjay, a pilgrim to Djoser's pyramid, confirms Osiris' mythical role in ensuring safe passage for the spiritual essence of the ritually cleansed body (*ka*). Another graffito located at the Step Pyramid complex, dated to Year 10 (or thereabouts) in the reign of Ramesses II (*c*.1293 BCE), uses the formula intended to petition Osiris as god of the dead for divine intervention (ir nfr ir nfr). A significant number of New Kingdom visitors to the mortuary precincts of pharaonic burials – particularly at the Amun temple of Tuthmose II at Deir el-Bahri – incorporated into their commemorative graffiti this ritual prescription. Another graffito associated with

143

GRAFFITI IN ANTIQUITY

Djoser's Step Pyramid, dating to Year 47 of Ramesses II's reign (1256 BCE), situates Osiris in relation to his divine wife Isis and the deceased inhabitants of the burial precincts of Memphis (Ankhtawy).

G7.2   "Year 47, 2 *Peret* 25. There came the Treasury-Scribe
        Hednakhte, son of Sunero, his mother being Twosret, to stroll
        and to enjoy [himself] on the West of Memphis, together
        with his brother, Panakhte, the scribe of the vizier, saying, 'O
        [all] you gods, Lords of the West of Memphis, the Ennead
        [nine deities][3] at the head of the necropolis, Osiris, Isis, and
        the great glorified dead of the West of Ankhtawy [Memphis],
        grant a happy lifetime following your will and a good burial
        after a happy old age, to [be able to] see the West of Memphis
        as one greatly favoured like yourself.' [Written] by the
        Treasury-Scribe of the Lord of the Two Lands, Hednakhte,
        justified, and the Scribe Pankhte."[4]

It is interesting to note that the two important state officials mentioned in this graffito are also cited as responsible for jointly writing the message. While it might be logical to infer that the individual given priority in the subscript of the text (Hednakhte) was the actual inscriber, something would appear to have dictated that he include his brother in ascribing authorship. The content of the graffito provides the explanation for this epigraphic quirk. Both men belong to the educated class of state functionaries who administered economic and political affairs in New Kingdom Egypt. They will have been well-versed in the religious *and* mythological associations of the funerary context which was the object of their journey across the Nile. It is especially clear that they wished to acknowledge their explicit belief in the purpose of Djoser's pyramid complex: namely, as a site of religious pilgrimage; and as a physical embodiment of the mythology of resurrection and universal order. This underlying purpose of Hednakhte and Pankhte's visit is reflected in the references to the Ennead of Heliopolis – a group of nine deities very important in Egyptian creation myths – as well as to the deities integral to resurrection (Osiris and Isis) and the "great glorified dead of the West" (the timeless dynastic family of deceased pharaohs and important state officials). The worlds of politics and religion, of social condition and cultural belief, are subsumed within the mythological framework of this non-official inscription on the wall of the south temple in Djoser's Step Pyramid complex. The desires of the pilgrim brothers – a long, happy life (in positions of authority and prestige) and a good burial (implying successful rebirth into the afterlife) – follow closely the mythical script of the Book of the Dead, echoing the tales of Osiris, Set, Horus and Isis, and the mythical history of royal succession, resonating with the architectural fabric of Djoser's funerary precinct.

144

Also on the western side of the river Nile, inscribed on a section of the entrance to the ritual palace of the Dynasty XIX pharaoh Merneptah at Memphis, is a graffito of a seated woman with a child in her lap. This ephemeral drawing – sketched amid images of the king interacting with the gods and smiting Egypt's enemies – resembles the scene on a pottery sherd from Deir el-Medina depicting a woman seated in a birth garden decorated with vines (Chapter 4). In the case of the figure etched into the gateway jamb of Merneptah's palace, the female supporting the infant on her lap most likely represents the goddess Isis holding her child Horus. Marsh plants enclose the seated mother, while another figure appears to present her with a large lotus flower.

Depictions of Isis holding her son Horus were a popular subject in ancient Egypt. This same motif appears on tiny amulets, in statuary, and on walls of temples. The marsh elements surrounding the woman's seat (or, possibly, throne) may refer to the place known as "the papyrus thicket of the king of Lower Egypt" (Akh-bity) – part of the myth which recounts the story of the pregnant Isis hiding from her unborn child's uncle Set. Set had already killed Horus' father Osiris and sought to do the same to the infant Horus, his competition for Osiris' throne. To escape her husband's fate and protect Horus, Isis concealed herself and her child in the marshes of the Nile delta. While there, a poisonous creature bit the child and Isis employed her considerable magical powers to cure him.

A final example of graffiti that draws its inspiration from the mythological tradition of ancient Egypt can be found on a funerary stela (upright stone slab with inscribed text or relief figures) now on display in the Louvre.[5] Dating to the reign of the Dynasty XIII pharaoh Sobekhotep III Sekhemra Sewadjtawy (*c*.1725–1722 BCE) and likely set up at Abydos, the stela depicts two daughters of the king worshipping Min-Horus, a local variant of the ithyphallic deity assimilated with the son of Osiris. Across the surface of the commemorative stone, several individuals have scratched or incised figural graffiti of jackals – depicted as the nocturnal omnivore, in a standing posture, or with the head of the creature surmounting the symbol representing life (*ankh*). In view of the inscribing context, it is likely that these figures represent Wepwawet or Upuat ("Opener of Ways"). In Egyptian mythology, Wepwawet was first and foremost understood as the god of warfare and hunting. Like the small dog-like hunter of small prey on which the mythic tradition drew for inspiration, the animal-god was seen as the embodiment of the predatory spirit. By the Middle Kingdom, Wepwawet was also seen as the divine force which opened the ways to and through the underworld. Marked by unknown visitors to the site where the stela was originally set up, the common orientation of the jackal figures with the conceptual orientation of the official scene – aligned with the worshipping princesses facing Min-Horus – reflects the mythological connotations of the graffiti in relation to what clearly was an original funerary context.

Greece

For the ancient Greeks, the etymological understanding of myth (*muthos*) was extremely straightforward: a narrative, or something spoken, in a wide range of senses – a message or statement, a record or account of imaginary or real people and events, the content of a theatrical composition. For Plato, the first person known to have employed the term, *muthologia* referred to the transmission of stories. Our modern understanding of the term "mythology" is far more complicated, since it may denote either the study of myths, or their content, or a particular set of myths. The ambivalence of the modern term is unfortunate, since it tends to suggest that we are participating in a scientific study – the study of the mythology of ancient Greece, in other words, can be seen as the same as the study of the archaeology of ancient Greece. In actuality, most find Greek (or Egyptian or Roman) mythology interesting or informative because the stories provide amusement or enjoyment; or it supports our view of myth as an established tradition or system, when with most ancient cultures what we experience is a sporadic collection that may not form an organized method of communicating customs or beliefs at all. Although this is certainly true in the Egyptian context, in the case of Greek myths, we *do* possess something like a process of transmitting mythological ideas – but a method which was fixed comparatively late in the scheme of history (in relation to the likely age of the tradition as a whole) by people like Homer and Hesiod, the composers of tragic poetry performed on stage, the Hellenistic poets who created lists of mythological characters and events, and the cataloguers and epitomators (summarizers) of the Graeco-Roman world.

In light of this correlation between the evolution of mythological concepts and the oral-literate culture of ancient Greece, a brief case study drawn from the "pages" of the so-called "Orphic tradition" seems appropriate. According to mythic Greek history, Orpheus was the son of a Muse. The Muses (*mousai*) were goddesses associated with literary, scientific and artistic inspiration. Legend names Calliope (the eldest of the Muses, goddess of music, song and dance) as Orpheus' mother; some accounts identify his father as Apollo, but most Greeks will have known his sire as the Thracian river god Oiagros. Orpheus, so the tales tell us, could sing and play the lyre so beautifully that he could subdue the fiercest creatures and draw all natural things to him. Like Osiris, he knew the secrets of the underworld, where he journeyed in search of his wife, Eurydice, who had died prematurely of a snake bite – a deadly version of the fate almost suffered by the infant Horus. Although he employed his song to induce the deities of the underworld to permit him to guide his wife out of the infernal depths, he was unsuccessful in abiding by the divine warning (the law of Persephone) against looking back at her. After the second loss of his wife, he persistently avoided the company of women and was associated with the category of homosexual love, at least among the

Thracians. The most established tradition makes him the fatal victim of the Thracian women, who in a Bacchic frenzy murdered him either for rejecting them or for enticing away their husbands; alternatively, Dionysos (god of fertility and wine) may have sent his savage maenads (Dionysos' female worshippers) to punish Orpheus for worshipping Apollo. According to the most widely accepted version of the sacrificial murder (the *sparagmos*), the body of Orpheus – like Osiris' corpse – was completely dismembered, and his head and lyre were thrown into the river Hebros; his head miraculously continued to sing and the lyre to play as they floated to Lesbos. There the head was buried in the shrine of Dionysos, and the lyre was enshrined in the temple of Apollo. The head achieved renown as a giver of oracles until a jealous Apollo suppressed it.

Because of the close connection between Greek music and poetry (always sung), the ancient Greeks regarded Orpheus as a composer of metrical verse as well as skilled in musical expression and a minstrel, and even as the originator of alphabetic script and all fields of creative skill and imagination. He was the conduit of discourse about the gods and the beginning of existence – what the ancient Greeks referred to as a *theologos*. The esoteric nature of his musical prowess meant that people thought about Orpheus as the father of everything difficult or impossible to understand or explain and as the source of Greek ritual practice and sacred literature. It is here that written and graphic sources help to clarify aspects of the obscure cult associated with Orpheus. These include: gold leaves from Hipponion with verses offering esoteric knowledge (revelation), the Derveni Papyrus with a poem comprising theological and cosmological insights, supposedly from Orpheus himself; *and* graffiti from Olbia on the Black Sea.

G7.3   "Life – death – life | [zigzag symbol] | the truth | the Orphics."

Inscribed on a small piece of bone, this graffito is one of three cryptic textual and graphic messages that mark a transition between the literary tradition, ritual practice and the spoken word of myth. Found in a paved enclosure adjoining the *agora* of the ancient Greek colony of Olbia – a major harbour emporium on the Black Sea – all three inscribed objects speak to the existence of a group of individuals calling themselves *Orphikoi* ("the Orphics"). From the content of the graffiti – text *and* images – it would appear that the Orphics were in all likelihood a community of some kind, dating from the associated finds to the fifth century BCE, which drew on the narrative threads of life, death and resurrection embedded in the myth of Orpheus and Dionysus as inspiration for cult belief and ritual revolving – again, like the tales of Osiris, Isis, Horus and Set – around the hope of an afterlife.[6]

The emblematic sequence "life–death–life" is comparatively free of misinterpretation – the inevitability of death followed by the promise of being born again. The zigzag symbol, of course, could represent any of a number of possible meanings. Given the context and related detail, however, the most likely explanations relate to notions of recurring change, destruction or rebirth – all of which can be found in the mythic tradition of Orpheus' life and death. Declaring this mystery "the truth" (*alētheia*) is, naturally, tantamount to verifying the graffiti as ritual tokens of the Orphic community living on the shores of the Black Sea.

Similarly, in the sanctuary of the Kabeiroi near Boiotian Thebes there came to light – initially in 1887–1888 and again in 1955–562 lead and bronze statuettes of archaic date, most representing bulls; a mass of fragments of black-figured vases, dating about the end of the fifth or the beginning of the fourth century BCE; and several hundred votive graffiti, mostly on potsherds, dating to the archaic *and* classical periods – all of local technique and obviously having been used in a local cult. Like the Olbian graffiti, these Theban texts (and, occasionally, images) resonate with Dionysian myths – the associations of the bull and the symposium (drinking party) – but place their own local spin on the tradition. In this instance, Kabiros and Pais (very loosely, "Father" and "Son") – depicted elegantly and identified by textual superscripts on the remains of a painted *kantharos* (drinking cup) – represented for the Theban cult community the guardians of vines and the fertility of animals. Like the Hermettos graffiti naming Zeus, Hercules and Gaia (Chapter 5) and the bone plaques of Olbia, the Theban votives confirm the intrinsic relationship in ancient Greece between religious practice – like the messages on Mount Hermettos, votive offerings of some kind – and the variety of mythological traditions that formed Orpheus' abstruse and composite story.

A neatly ironic literary fragment points out the degree to which both the practice of graffiti writing was recognized in the ancient Greek world and its relationship to the expression of mythological thought. In one of his surviving *Epigrams*, the Hellenistic poet, critic and scholar Callimachus (310/305–240 BCE) wrote the following:

G7.4 "Momos [Mockery] himself used to write on the walls:
'Kronos is wise.'" (Callimachus, *Epigrams* fr. 393)

Kronos was the king of the Titans deposed by his rebellious son Zeus. It would seem that Momos – god of mockery, blame, ridicule, scorn, complaint and stinging criticism – was stirring up trouble with his contemptuous scribbling. By the same token, Callimachus, knowing very well that the mythic tradition recounted Momos' expulsion from Olympus for ridiculing the gods – and perhaps also familiar with the propensity for non-official inscriptions as a medium for depicting mythological ideas and personalities – employed the motif of the censorious graffito as a suitable illustration of the actions which precipitated Mockery's eventual downfall.

Pausanias, the second-century CE Greek traveller and geographer of the imperial Mediterranean world, confirms the usefulness – though not always

148

MYTHOLOGY

the necessity – of textual graffiti as a means of communicating mythical knowledge. According to his description of a cedar-wood chest belonging to Cypselus, the seventh-century BCE tyrant of Corinth:

G7.5   "There is a figure of a woman holding on her right arm a white child asleep, and on her left she has a black child like one who is asleep. Each has his feet turned different ways. The inscriptions declare, as one could infer without inscriptions, that the figures are Death and Sleep, with Night the nurse of both."
(Pausanias, *Description of Greece* 5.18.1)

The famous fourth-century BCE Greek philosopher, Plato, describes how epigraphic practice incorporated this process of weaving together historical legend and mythical figures.

G7.6   "Hipparkos [a well-known late sixth-century BCE Athenian statesman] ... proceeded, with the design of educating those of the countryside, to set up figures of Hermes for them along the roads in the midst of the city and every district town ... that his people ... should regard as wise the utterances of Hipparkhos ... There are two such inscriptions of his: on the left side of each Hermes there is one in which the god says that he stands in the midst of the city or township, while on the right he says: 'The memorial of Hipparkos: walk with just intent.' There are many other fine inscriptions ... this one in particular, on the Steiria road, in which he says 'The memorial of Hipparkhos: deceive not a friend.'"   (Plato, *Hipparchus* 228d)

The "figures of Hermes" (*hermai*) which Hipparkhos erected relate to the Greek (eventually Graeco-Roman) practice of erecting a square or rectangular pillar of stone, terracotta or bronze, surmounted by a bust of the god Hermes' head, usually bearded, on which male genitals may also be carved at the appropriate height (Figure 7.1). Recalling Hipparkhos' self-aggrandizing programme of sculptural advertisement, Plato provides a fascinating insight into a practice which used inscribed text and crafted image to fuse magic and myth – in this instance, in service to promoting a tyrant's personal reputation, cultural capital and socio-political prestige. Placed strategically in a variety of rural and urban locations, *hermai* performed an apotropaic function. Originally a phallic god, and eventually a guardian of merchants and travellers, Hermes was associated with fertility, luck, roads and borders. *Hermai*, then, acted as a form of protection from evil. Incised into archetypal bearers of magico-mythical significance, the "wise" texts identified by Plato reflect how official epigraphy modelled for informal inscribers a way of sharing similar knowledge to consumers of non-official script and drawing.

149

Figure 7.1 *Herma* of Demosthenes, Agora, Athens (*c*.280 BCE) (Glyptothek, Munich; photo by Bibi Saint-Pol, via Wikimedia Commons).

Although comparatively rare in relation to ornamental and symbolic drawings, unidentified heads, or images of gladiators, animals and ships, sketched figures and mythic episodes from Greek legend can still be found throughout the ancient Greek world: for example, a profile of the goddess Athena (or her Roman equivalent, Minerva), found in a terrace house at imperial Ephesus; a frontal depiction of Eros in flight, from the Temple of Azzanathkona in second/third-century CE Dura-Europos; or a full-length portrait of Tyche (or her Roman equivalent Fortuna) on a corridor wall of the Odeon in third/fourth-century CE Aphrodisias.

In conjunction with the text-only messages and composite textual and figural graffiti, these drawings – and informal depictions of other identifiable mythological personalities scattered across the Graeco-Roman Mediterranean (Aphrodite, Artemis, Dionysus, Hera, Herakles, Hermes, Nike, Pan) – reflect the breadth of the Greek pantheon of gods and goddesses (Olympian, Titan, primeval), as well as the variety of heroes and heroines, nature spirits and fabulous creatures, which together provided Greek men and women of all ages, classes and social groups moments of beauty and pleasure and helped them to understand their history and the world in which they lived. We need only refer in passing to the extraordinary cache of enigmatic graffiti – scratched on 26 *ostraca* (*amphorae* and black-glaze pottery sherds) found at Chersonesus on the Black Sea and dating to the fifth century BCE – which refer to male names with or without patronymics *and* to epithets of mytho-logical figures or deities.

G7.7   "Abas" (hero) "Dardanis and Herakles" (heroes) "Hippolyte"
       (Amazon warrior) "Priólas" (hero).   (*SEG* 30.965)

Rome

In the same way that Egyptian and Greek societies were shaped to an extent by legendary narratives of the historical past and tales of cosmological crea-tion, human evolution and the afterlife, mythology shaped many aspects of daily life in the Roman world. Epigraphic calendars of days and months and literary traces of annual festivals, processions and games tell us that Romans integrated the world of mythology deliberately and visibly into their indi-vidual beliefs and community practices. Many historians believe this was because tales of gods and heroes reflected people's needs in their everyday affairs. Importantly, Roman customs, rituals and holidays were born from the recognition of the relationship between mythology and the history of the city of Rome and its people.

Of course, it was never the case that the ancients (Egyptians, Greeks or Romans) were inclined to lay down principles declaring their myths as incon-trovertibly true. However, as we have already seen, writers of literature in antiquity often viewed myths as a source of knowledge about the past, and they almost never regarded myth as equivalent to a fabrication or lie. The Olbia graffiti testify, in fact, to the opposite – namely, casting the Orphic belief in a magico-mythical afterlife as "the truth". In what some literary his-torians consider the most complex exploration of myth surviving from the ancient world, the Roman poet Ovid (43 BCE to 17/18 CE) examines in his *Metamorphoses* a series of transformations from the origins of known space and time down to the deification of Julius Caesar. Mythical figures such as Herakles, Midas and Orpheus, quasi-historical individuals responsible for establishing institutions and settlements like Aeneas and Romulus, and the developing mythology of the Roman imperial family all constitute part of an ongoing story-telling tradition. In Ovid's poem, the freshly composed myths of imperial power are not explicitly or substantially unlike the older tales of gods and heroes. Another Roman poet, Lucretius (first century BCE) – a fol-lower of the Greek philosopher Epicurus – reworked inherited myths and fashioned new stories informed by philosophical views of knowledge.

GRAFFITI IN ANTIQUITY

What *is* controversial, however, is the question of *how* distinct Roman mythology was from the prevailing Greek accounts. Indeed, there is little in the ancient sources pointing to an established body of Roman literature – or, for that matter, traces of a long-standing oral tradition in the visual record – independent from the existing collection of Greek myths. That said, a repertoire of legends speaks to the great figures of early Roman "history" – individuals like Romulus, Camillus and Coriolanus. Though not "mythological" in any modern sense of the term, this spectrum of legendary tales – fused to the existing mytho-poetic narratives of the epic and cosmological tradition (Homer, Hesiod and Pindar); the classical dramatists (Aeschylus, Euripides, Sophocles); and the Hellenistic rhapsodists and mythographers (Apollodorus, Apollonius Rhodius, Aratus, Callimachus, Theocritus) – concerned the deeds of great men and integrated Rome's legendary history with the heroes of Greek mythology – Aeneas, Herakles, Diomedes, Hippolytus, Evander and Orestes.

Incised in the plaster of an exterior wall facing south onto the main E-W thoroughfare of early imperial Pompeii (the Via dell'Abbondanza) is a wonderfully evocative, deceptively clever graffito that epitomizes the relationship between mythology and specifically Roman ways of thinking.

G7.8   "I sing of fullers and a screech-owl, not arms and a man."

(*CIL* IV.9131)

One of the most common graffiti found at Pompeii is a transcript of the first words from the opening line of Virgil's *Aeneid*: "I sing of arms and a man" (*arma virumque cano*). These words – or, infrequently, other brief excerpts from the epic – appear over thirty times in a variety of public and private contexts across the colony. The *Aeneid* is a Latin epic poem in twelve books that relates the travels and experiences of Aeneas after the fall of Troy. As a character in Homer's *Iliad* (*c.* eighth century BCE), the hero Aeneas – a Trojan prince – was already known to Graeco-Roman legend and myth. Virgil took the disconnected tales of Aeneas' wanderings, his vague association with the foundation of Rome and a personage of no fixed characteristics other than a scrupulous piety, and fashioned this into a compelling founding myth or national epic that at once tied Rome to the legends of Troy, explained the Punic wars, glorified traditional Roman virtues and legitimized the Julio-Claudian dynasty (31/27 BCE to 68 CE) as descendants of the founders, heroes and gods of Rome and Troy.

The building on which *CIL* IV.9131 is inscribed was a workshop for laundering clothes (a *fullonica*), one of a number of such establishments that operated at Pompeii. Those who soaped, rinsed and finished clothes were known as fullers (*fullones*). Another statement painted on the same wall reveals the name of the person who managed the laundering operation. Supporting two candidates for election to magisterial positions on the local

152

council, this painted message identifies Fabius Ululitremulus as the individual most likely to have owned and operated the adjoining workshop.[7] In addition to the texts inscribed and painted on the fullery wall,[8] there were once two paintings bordering the entrance to the fullery.[9] To the left is a frontal portrait of the founder of the city of Rome, Romulus, wearing a soldier's garb. He is depicted carrying a spear in his left hand and resting the symbol of military triumph (*tropaion*) on his right shoulder. On the right the artist portrayed the hero Aeneas (the central standing figure), famously carrying his father Anchises on his back and leading his son Ascanius from the burning city of Troy.

What the graffito outside the *fullonica* of the wonderfully named owner of the property does with the best-known opening line of contemporary poetry in the Roman world is deliciously subversive. Playing with the mythological resonances of the figural paintings and their relationship to the crux of Virgil's epic composition, the reworked text foregrounds the priority of local personalities and issues – the fullery and its owner, whose name echoes the Latin word for "screech-owl" (*ulula*); serendipitously, the owl was also the symbol attributed to the goddess Minerva, patroness of Pompeii's fullers – over and beyond national ideology – Romulus and Aeneas, the *Aeneid*, and underlying imperial claims.

Mythology was an important element in many of the wall paintings in Pompeii, even in comparatively modest homes. The tales were well known from long association with what was still a significantly oral culture; but the depth of knowledge about the detail of the narrative tradition also foregrounds the relatively broad spectrum of literacy in Pompeian society. As one would expect, representations of Venus (Aphrodite) can be found throughout a town known officially as Cornelia Veneria Pompeianorum – a name which tied the founder of the Roman colony (P. Cornelius Sulla, nephew of the famous general and dictator) to Venus, the goddess he particularly venerated. Paintings on the exterior and interior walls of buildings depict her image and episodes from her life story in religious, apotropaic and mythological contexts: giving advice to Helen about seducing the Trojan prince Paris (in a small room west of the *atrium* in I.7.7); leaning seductively against Ares (Mars) after having convinced him to lay aside his arms (in the *tablinum* of VII.9.47); helping the hunter Adonis, wounded fatally with sympathetic love (in the garden of VI.7.18). Zeus, too, appears in his various guises – most frequently, a swan or bull; as, too, do the heroes of legend – Perseus, for example, engaged in freeing a bound Andromeda from the nefarious grasp of a sea monster (on a pilaster in the *peristyle* of VI.9.6); Theseus, honoured by the Athenians after killing the Minotaur (on the east wall of an *exedra* in VII.2.16) – and key episodes from Homer's saga of the Trojan War (in I.6.2, I.10.4, II.2.2) or Virgil's epic reworking (VII.1.25, IX.13.5).

Given the fact that this propensity for covering the walls with paintings cut across all levels of society in Pompeii – and the Roman world more generally

153

GRAFFITI IN ANTIQUITY

– it is interesting to note the relative paucity of informal drawings on mythological subject matter surviving in the material record. Perhaps it was precisely *because* of the trend towards pictorial decoration on nearly all the wall surfaces in Roman residential (and even occupational) spaces that only a few residents took the opportunity to sketch identifiable figures or scenes from the pages of established myth. Nevertheless, it is possible to discern in the extant record figural graffiti depicting mythological identities such as Athena (Minerva) (IX.8.6), Eros (Amor) (I.7.7), Dionysus (Bacchus) (I.7.7) and Herakles (Hercules) (VIII.7.20).

An extraordinary collocation of painted, incised and artefactual evidence displaying religious, magical and mythological symbolism can be found in a small home just off the Via di Nocera (II.1.12). According to an election notice painted on the southern side of the dwelling's entrance, this property most likely belonged to a certain Biria and her father Onomastus.[10] No longer *in situ*, scenes painted on pilasters to either side of the entrance depicted traditional figural compositions drawn from the mythological narrative record – frontal figures of Mercury and Bacchus; and Venus Anadyomene ("Venus rising from the sea") with a small naked Eros and a leaping dolphin. This traditional façade of electoral text and mythic image-making reflected the participation of the citizen occupants in Pompeii's political calendar and the customary religious beliefs of the Roman world. However, moving from the entrance corridor into the rear of the peristyle garden will have revealed to any visitor a small private shrine (*sacellum*) and altar dedicated, we now know, to the mystery cult of the Thracian god Sabazius. Sabazius was a Phrygian god whose orgiastic cult came to Athens as early as the fifth century BCE and who is well attested in the imperial period. Identified with Dionysus – and, in Asia Minor, with Zeus (Jupiter) – Sabazius was clearly worshipped in this otherwise unremarkable Roman house.

G7.9   "Cave (*antrum*)."[11]

What ties together the esoteric characteristics of Eastern ritual – denoted by a variety of cult objects found in storerooms to either side of the peristyle *sacellum* – and the Romanness of this quintessentially Pompeian dwelling – an atrium house in the amphitheatre precinct of the town renovated after the foundation of the Sullan colony – is a graffito etched on a wall of the sacred space (G7.9). Part of a repertoire of non-official inscriptions quoting lines from Virgil's *Aeneid*,[12] the word *antrum* refers explicitly to that section of the epic poem where the author describes the holy place of the Cumaean Sybil (priestess of Apollo). Here, the religious and mythological connotations of word, image and object are explicit and resonate profoundly with the superstitious and ceremonial life of the town – as son of Zeus and Cybele (Phrygian mother of the gods), worship of Sabazius satisfied the desire for mystical or specialized knowledge; of sufficient volume to accommodate a

MYTHOLOGY

relatively large number of Sabazius devotees, the garden would have hosted a vibrant ritual ceremony associated with the mysteries of the god.

This esoteric amalgam is characterized most explicitly by the so-called "Hand of Sabazius" – a metallic object depicting the Phrygian god of fertility resting in the open palm of a hand, surrounded by signs of renewal (pinecone, snake, bird, nursing mother), whose fingers form a gesture of blessing. Taken together, we can imagine – united under the sign of the prophetess of Apollo (*antrum*), the priestess known as the Sibyl who interpreted the oracular declarations of the protective god of song and music – Biria and Onomastus officiating over a cult community connected by a network of Roman and non-Roman magico-mythical ideas and beliefs.

To complete this brief overview of myth in antiquity, it is useful to consider a final sample of non-official inscriptions attesting to the quotidian interactions between ancient Romans and the ideas and practices associated with indigenous and imported mythologies. In the imperial period, a number of private spaces set aside for cult activity dedicated to the figure known as Mithras displays evidence for figural mosaics, painted scenes, formal epigraphy *and* ephemeral images and texts. Incorporating Indo-Iranian magical lore from polytheistic Persia (Mithra, Zoroaster) and mythological ideas from the Hellenized Greek Near East (Perseus, Nike, Dionysus), Mithras – invincible sun god – occupied the central focus of a mystery cult immensely popular in the Roman legions from late in the first century CE until around the turn of the fifth. Born from a cosmic egg, surrounded by the signs of the zodiac and epitomized as the slayer of bulls, ephemeral references to Mithras in the Graeco-Roman Mediterranean are numerous.

Like the cult activity associated with Sabazius, it is not so much from any literary canon that we in the modern age can draw together the threads of belief and myth associated with the cult of Mithras. Indeed, any Mithraic narrative or ritual instruction consists in the main of iconographical reliefs *and* the residue of formal and non-official epigraphy. The central theme of Mithraism was the killing of the bull (the *tauroctony*) (Figure 7.2). A young Mithras is conventionally depicted, heroically naked, holding the bull down while he drives a dagger into its neck, at the same time twisting up the creature's head by inserting his fingers into its nostrils. Simultaneously, he prevents the bull from getting up by pressing his left leg hard into its back. Though cryptic, the significance of the scene revolves around the idea of regeneration through sacrifice – the tail, ending in heads of wheat, connoting fecundity; the scorpion, attacking the bull's testicles, perhaps absorbing some of the animal's life-force; the snake, licking at the wound, likewise symbolizing the transition from this world to the afterlife.

G7.10 "Ulas [offering] | Babenus [offering] | Becton [wine offering] | Proclus [wine offering] | Ermes [offering] | Fortuninus [offering] | Maximus [wine offering]."

Figure 7.2 Mithras killing a bull (*tauroctony*) (*c.* second or third century CE) (Department of Greek, Etruscan and Roman antiquities, Louvre/MA 3441; photo by PHGCOM, CC BY-SA 3.0, http://creativecommons.org/licenses/by-sa/3.0, via Wikimedia Commons).

Incised into the base of a small shrine (*aedicula*) constituting the ritual focus of a two-room cult space in the House of Diana (I.3.3–4), the Ostia graffito (G7.10) represents a catalogue in two columns of persons (most likely, slaves) and votive offerings (notably, wine). The graffito is situated directly above a marble head of Dionysos, whose mysteries Roman Mithraism emulated to a marked degree. The constituency of dedicators identified in the tabulated list attests to wide-ranging participation in Mithraic cult. Here, the informal inscription of a Mithraic functionary provides form and function to the ceremonial activity – a register of cult devotion and offering practice.

Similarly, the walls of the sanctuary belonging to the *mithraeum* at Dura-Europos – used originally by Palmyrene archers of the earliest Roman-period garrison; later by a vexillation of *legiones IIII Scythica* and *XVI Flavia Firma* – were covered with graffiti written by worshippers, mainly military and cult

Figure 7.3 Sketch of a member of the Mithras cult community, Dura-Europos, Syria (Cumont 1934: fig. 9).

titles and names, suggesting that here Mithraism was an exclusively military cult. A carefully composed figural drawing – outlined in red on the right-hand side of the arched recess in the Dura *mithraeum* – depicts one of the initiates to the mystery cult (Figure 7.3). Dressed in Palmyrene costume, the newly invested member of the Mithraic community holds a staff in his right hand and a scroll in the other.

FINAL THOUGHTS

Mythology was an integral element of socio-cultural practice in antiquity. Whether the world was Egyptian, Greek, Roman, or a later imperial Graeco-Roman hybrid, myths attempted to explain the mysteries inherent in the origins of the universe, the earth and humanity. Like the genetic markers of DNA, themes of life and death etched the strands of mythical stories across multiple generations and vast geographical and conceptual distances. Essential to these tales were explanations of the causes of natural phenomena. Passed down orally – and eventually in written and graphic form – these narrative traditions underwent numerous transformations and reconstructions. As we have seen, in addition to the canonical literary and artistic record, graffiti provide a touchstone for measuring the extent to which attitudes and ideas in particular oral-literature communities derived inspiration and instruction from ancient mythology.

CHAPTER 8

POLITICS

Peisistratos. (*SEG* 39.42)

Therefore at night, beneath the inscription on the temple [of Concord], somebody carved this verse: "A work of mad discord produces a temple of Concord." (Plutarch, *Gaius Gracchus* 17)

At [the emperor] Nero's entrance into Rome they pulled down the statues of Agrippina. One statue they did not have time to remove, so they threw a cloth over it so that it would look veiled. Immediately somebody wrote and affixed to the statue: "I am embarrassed, and you are not ashamed." In many places one could read also this inscription: "Nero, Orestes, Alcmaeon – matricides." (Cassius Dio, *Roman History* 61/62.16.2a–b)

POLITICS IN THE ANCIENT WORLD

While at first it may seem an exaggeration, in many ways contemporary political systems and the philosophical, ethical and cultural traditions on which they are based – across geographical and ideological divides (East/ West, democracy/despotism, capitalist/communist, Christian/non-Christian, and so on) – can be traced back to ancient ways of thinking and acting. Whether we refer to the earliest literate civilizations (Egypt, Mesopotamia, Iran, Israel, India and China) or to the nation-states which the Western world regards most commonly as its direct political progenitors (Greece and Rome), it is possible to identify distinctive historical and sociological features that help us to trace the evolution of political knowledge, associated principles of conduct and behaviour, and systems of governance to the present day.

158

POLITICS

In today's world *all* societies have the potential for reciprocal action influencing one another, preferably for the better. Whether or not they choose to do so, or *do* act, but in a negative fashion, is, of course, another matter entirely – and speaks directly to the origins of continuing tensions between nations, ethnicities, religions and cultures. Historically, the capacity for a global awareness of different understandings of self and society, of how people think and act as they do, is relatively recent. This is not to say that there has *never* been an opportunity for dialogue between cultures in antiquity; rather, that certain phenomena characteristic of the modern age – the process of international integration known as globalization; mass movements of people due to war, famine, persecution or natural disaster; and issues of demography, philosophy and identity arising from encroaching multi-culturalism – affected political thought in the ancient world only in exceptional circumstances. It is in this light that the surviving written sources – philosophical and religious texts, legal codes, epic poetry, royal/imperial edicts *and* epigraphy – open a window into what people in antiquity knew about political institutions and the way they operated, the actions of those holding authority, and how this power was vindicated, managed and legitimized by ideological systems, information strategies and narrative traditions. Unsurprisingly, the traces of graffiti surviving from antiquity – whether referring to the ballot used by the Areiopagus to banish the tyrant Peisistratos (*ostraca*, Athenian *agora*. mid-sixth century BCE); or to the restoration of a temple to socio-political harmony (Concord) by the consul L. Opimius, responsible for the murder of the people's tribune Gaius Gracchus and 3,000 others (temple façade, Roman Forum, 121 BCE); or even to the wildfire rumours attributing to the emperor Nero his mother Agrippina's murder – contribute remarkable insights into our understanding of these political relationships.

Egypt

As we have already seen (Chapter 5), Egyptian religion actively supported the earliest-known paradigm of a divine order surpassing the range of ordinary physical human experience. Gods and goddesses were seen as omnipotent, omnipresent forces; they exercised control over the cosmos and the intellectual thought of Egyptians, possibly more than of any other people. The people themselves believed that they had been created, and the state founded, by the god.

In Egypt the king was more explicitly recognized as equal in status and capacity with the gods than in any other culture. He embodied in the flesh Horus and Osiris, the son of the supreme god Ra himself. He was superior to all other human beings by virtue of his divine nature – the incarnation of Egypt's religious as well as political order. The relationship of the pharaoh to those who were subordinate to his divinely sanctioned authority, therefore,

159

constituted a spiritual connection. Since the great god Ptah pervaded all categories and levels of existence, by the same token the pharaoh was thought to possess an authentic link to the life-force (*ka*) of every person. Venerated as "greatest god", or the "perfect god", epigraphic and papyrological sources record the widespread belief that the pharaoh was conceived when Amun desired a royal wife, "the god's wife" (G5.1–3). As the extant texts confirm, the pharaoh wielded authority even over the realm of the dead as Osiris and "deceased father" (Chapter 6). He was acknowledged as the repository of the power of divine "utterance"; what he said, in other words, came to be (G6.7).

Egyptian political thought derived its conceptual force from this relationship between religion and the country's civil (theocratic) government. To some extent as a result, it represents the most radical expression in recorded history of absolute monarchy. While other Egyptians could expect fair and reasonable treatment under the legal conventions of the state, there was no indication that the pharaoh could expect to face any kind of judgement, even after death, most probably on the grounds that a god could perpetrate nothing in contravention to accepted codes of principle or behaviour. The priestly functionaries, who officiated over temple cult practices, acted on behalf of the pharaoh, and they were accordingly designated by him to perform this role. The temples' resulting wealth formed part of the estate owned and controlled by the ruler.

Etched on a rocky outcrop along a secondary channel of the Wâdi Hammâmât is a hieroglyphic graffito displaying the *serekh* (rectangular panel enclosing a royal name) of the pharaoh Narmer, the ruler identified conventionally as the founder of dynastic Egypt (*c.*3100–3050 BCE)[1] While no secure inferences can be applied to this isolated text, its historical context – a major route from Thebes to the Red Sea (and eventually to the Silk Road leading to Asia) and a significant source of stone for building projects along the Nile – indicates that Narmer had given official permission for exploration of the region to evaluate Wâdi Hammâmât's resources and strategic location. This graffito confirms Narmer's reputation as the authoritative figure under which the north and south of Egypt united – a role preserved on a decorative palette made of schist, found among the material remains of the temple of Horus at Hierakonpolis (modern al-Kom al-Ahmar), which lies 20 km north of Edfu in southern (Upper) Egypt (Figure 8.1).

Another rock graffito found at Gebel Tjauti reveals the extent to which the political unification of ancient Egypt under a single ruler relied on military action.[2] Comprising both images and text, this large incised scene depicts a stork lifting up a snake, a hieroglyphic cluster signifying the idea of "victory", and the figure of a man bearing weapons dragging a bound captive by a rope. Dating to a period at least a century prior to the production of the Narmer palette, this graphic message provides a unique historical record of the territorial contestations that pre-dated eventual consolidation of Egypt as an integrated political entity. Even more interesting is the fact that one of the

POLITICS

Figure 8.1 Narmer palette, Hierakonpolis (al-Kom al-Ahmar), Egypt (Dynasty 1, c.3100–3050 BCE) (Egyptian Museum, Cairo/JE 32169 – CG 14716; http://en.wikipedia.org/wiki/File:Narmer_Palette.jpg, via Wikimedia Commons).

figures in the graffito is shown with a falcon above his head. This represents the earliest attestation of the use of the Horus title (without the *serekh*) – one of five names which came to signify an Egyptian ruler. In this case, the individual to which the title refers would appear to be the individual known as Scorpion – identified in portraits on two fragmentary mace heads and thought to be the owner of a tomb in Abydos (B50). Recording a strategic action between military forces of competing pre-dynastic groups, the Gebel Tjauti graffito testifies to the pivotal nature of the event in the decades prior to Egyptian unification.

Two additional graffiti found at Gebel Tjauti and Wadi el-Hôl speak about similar military actions in periods of political consolidation under pharaonic rule. Scratched in hieratic near the formal stela whose author gave Gebel Tjauti its name (Chapter 2), the first inscription reads:

G8.1   "The assault troops of the Son of Re Intef."[3]

While the identification is uncertain, it is possible that the "Son of Re Intef" to which this text refers is Sehertawy Intef I, nomarch (provincial governor) of Thebes who rebelled against Herakleopolitan control in the aftermath of civil unrest during the First Intermediate Period and declared himself king.

161

GRAFFITI IN ANTIQUITY

Though Intef is recorded as the second ruler of Dynasty XI (*c.*2134–2118 BCE), he – unlike his father, Montuhotep I, also nomarch of Thebes – was the first whose name was written in a cartouche. The political history of the early Middle Kingdom is murky at best, but we do know that Intef I intended to wrest control of the throne of Upper and Lower Egypt from the nomarch of Hierakonpolis (Ankhtifi), which pitted the Theban usurper against not only Ankhtifi but the powerful rulers of Herakleopolis Magna. In any event, Intef I's campaign resulted in limited political gain. Over the course of his rule, he managed to extend Theban control to Denderah, Koptos and three of the nomes of Hierakonpolis. Preserved in official hieroglyphic texts dating to the New Kingdom, Intef I's name and titles – "Count and Hereditary Prince", "Count of the Great Lord of the Theban Nome", "Great Prince of the South" – confirm that he failed in his ambition to reunify Egypt under his leadership. What the hieratic inscription at Gebel Tjauti (G8.1) may record is an early stage in Intef I's expansionist plans. That the Theban nomarch's troops etched their victory statement close by the stela advertising Tjauti's achievement in building the Alamat Tal road strongly suggests completion of the first stage in Intef I's unification campaign – namely, acquisition of strategic routes, thereby securing passage of military forces north to engage the Hierakonpolitan opposition. Additionally, the intentional proximity of the troops' graffito declaration and the former nomarch's building stela expresses by association transfer of control of the site from Gebtu (Tjauti's nome) to Thebes.

A second graffito – incised onto a section of limestone cliff at Wadi el-Hôl (Chapter 3) – charts the course of similar political upheaval in the final decades of the Middle Kingdom.

G8.2   "The be[ginning …] of the scribe of Hou, Ankh: '(Oh) all people great and small, and all the ar[my], behold – a man is in the City, [whose ki]nd [?] is unknown. … he … might bring up [?] … his … without his being thrown down … [as] he desired. The foreigner is wont to f[all] [because of] his pron[ouncement]s, one who slays as he desires while traversing [th]is [?] gebel, the gebel … his … his tongue [?] … by himself. He does not like the people who are loyal to that his enemy. A true [?] s-man [is he], one intelligent for the officials [?] … amongst the multitude [of enemies], he being haughty because of what has happened, he spending the night hungry until day breaks, and he sees heaven like a flame. His joy is the completion of the watch.'"[4]

Written in eloquent hieratic, this long inscription describes the military actions of an otherwise unknown individual possessing political authority – an *s*-man (or leader) – in "the City" (i.e. Thebes). According to the fragmentary

POLITICS

text, which has survived later (ancient) attempts at erasure, the anonymous ruler would appear to have been the strategic and tactical overseer of initiatives aiming to defend the mountainous region bordering Thebes (the "gebel") against incursions from foreign "enemies". Addressed to "the great and small people" (an inclusive reference to the socio-political constituency of the region) and "the army" (namely, the military officials under the ruler's command), the opening line establishes the supreme position occupied by the subject of the graffito. The status of the unnamed *s*-man may further be inferred in accordance with the principles of Egyptian political rule. In this instance, the graffito represents the divine qualities of "utterance" – by reference to the leader's "pronouncements", which possess the ability to cause "the foreigner" to "fall" – and "absolute power" – "one who slays as he desires". That "his joy is in the completion of the watch" indicates that his leadership resulted in effective protection of the territory under his jurisdiction.

Like the earlier Gebel Tjauti graffito, this inscription illuminates a tumultuous period of Egyptian political history. Toward the end of the Middle Kingdom, and leading into the politically dis-integrated Second Intermediate Period, the Western desert of the southern Nile valley (the Thebaid) experienced foreign attacks from tribal affiliations of mixed Semitic and West Asian heritage – known collectively as the Hyksos – and allied Kerman people from Lower Nubia. It may well be that the Wadi el-Hôl graffito captures a single moment in that struggle for political ascendancy. In this regard, it is interesting to speculate that the qualities exhibited by the text – the carefully framed orthography, the allusions to other literary texts, and the grammatical and syntactical standard of the hieratic – identify this graffito as "the only attested rock-cut literary graffito of pharaonic date in the whole of Egypt".[5] If this interpretation is correct, then it is possible to suggest that this non-official inscription was intended to perform a similar role to formal epigraphic texts in great temples extolling the virtues of the incumbent pharaoh. According to the tenets of Egyptian religious and political ideology, it was the king's exclusive privilege not only to smother open resistance to the established government and its ruler and to protect Egypt from harm or danger, but also to extend the country's territorial limits. Here, we may well have evidence for the display of an informal hymn to the divine ruler: elaborating his abilities and achievements in relation to the socio-political hierarchy of the Thebaid; celebrating his victory over foreign enemies; and confirming his efficacy as the region's military and political leader.

Expressing political thought in written form inevitably entailed reference to the pharaoh. Articulating the ideology of royal rule, naturally, was regarded as of utmost significance to the Egyptian state, both for the promotion of particular political messages and for administering society. The surviving literary and epigraphic sources recognize that political stability – and consequently the essentials of daily life – relied on categorical acceptance of the fact that the pharaoh and his office conformed to religious beliefs and the rule of law.

163

GRAFFITI IN ANTIQUITY

As we have seen, early dynastic graffiti from Wâdi Hammâmât and Gebel Tjauti represented the nature of kingship. However, it was only subsequent to the disintegration of the Old Kingdom and during the century of confusion that followed – the First Intermediate Period (c.2181–2055 BCE) – that social and political principles corresponding to the equivalent of contemporary governmental policy were formulated. The graffito incised by Intef I's troops at Gebel Tjauti (G8.1) reflects the outliers of this phenomenon. During a historical period when the absence of a strong pharaoh most clearly precipitated catastrophic social collapse, engaging in a process whereby such doctrines were transmitted in a coherent fashion made perfect sense. Effective, persuasive speech and writing now became increasingly important in moulding popular attitudes. In essence, rhetoric renewed the reputation of the king and instilled popular submission to royal rule. Inscriptions, therefore, served as a medium of mass communication to elucidate and vindicate the political institution of absolute monarchy.

A variety of graffiti dating to the Middle and New Kingdom testifies to the significant building programmes undertaken by Egyptian rulers. Across the broad sweep of dynastic history, thousands of non-official inscriptions preserving the names and titles of pharaohs – as well as references to the state officials acting on their behalf – cover the limestone cliffs and rocky outcrops of quarries and mines throughout the country. Associated with sites dedicated to the extraction of materials for infrastructure schemes along the Nile valley, these non-official records of state activity delineate in hieroglyphic and hieratic script the hierarchical nature of the Egyptian constitution (pharaonic name), the religious belief system on which it was based (the king's titles), and, by implication, the success of the official programme of rhetorical instruction comprising the testimony of formal epigraphic texts in every temple, civic building and military outpost. To cite a single example of this widespread phenomenon:

G8.3 Names of Dynasty XII rulers and state officials.

(Aswân, Dynasty XII)

The plethora of names and titles of kings and state functionaries testifies to the high level of stone-quarrying activity at Aswân, a frontier town just above the First Cataract looking south from Egypt to Nubia. Moreover, we can infer from the indications of status and occupation conveyed by the markings of individual inscribers that the Egyptian state sanctioned movements of military and civilian officials from Egypt through the First Cataract to and from official appointments in Lower Nubia. Here, as elsewhere along the Nile valley and in the resource-rich desert regions, graffiti bear witness to the institutionalized nature of ancient Egypt's political system and of its ideological foundation – an absolute monarchy authorized by god.

One inscription provides a fragmentary record of the machine of state and its progress across Egypt in service to an otherwise unidentified political

164

POLITICS

action. Written in red ink on a section of the Gebel Tjauti rock shelf devoted – as we have seen – to non-official inscriptions of various types, the partially preserved graffito reads:

G8.4   "Regnal year 11, third month of the Shemu season, day 15 [?], when his majesty came to the Southern City in order to bring about many ..."[6]

That this graffito – and many others found at Gebel Tjauti – was written in red ink indicates the presence of scribes. Travelling with their palettes, the tools of their profession, these individuals will have acted in a variety of bureaucratic capacities on behalf of the king as he journeyed along the Theban desert road. Wishing his message to stand out from the numerous inscriptions incised into the rock, the unknown state official responsible for this graffito (G8.4) took the time to register a royal visit to Thebes – and, we can only assume from the little that remains, his part in the expedition. Dating broadly to the Middle Kingdom – or, on the basis of other graffiti in the vicinity, possibly to the final thirty years of the Second Intermediate Period, Dynasty XVII (c.1580–1550 BCE) – the graffito traces the progress of an unnamed ruler to "the Southern City" (Thebes). While the direction in which the pharaoh – and, we should infer, his accompanying entourage – was travelling cannot be determined, it will be (a) (south) from the royal residence in Memphis or (north) from spending time with the army in the garrison at Abydos (if a Middle Kingdom date is correct), or (b) returning to Thebes after visiting the Abydos garrison or the Gebel Qarn el-Gir outpost (to the north) or Aswan (to the south) (if the text dates to Dynasty XVII). If the inscription refers to a visit to Abydos or Gebel Qarn el-Gir, it is possible that what the king "came to bring about" related to the acquisition of recruits. Regardless of the detail, this fragmentary note inked on Gebel Tjauti limestone forms part of a large corpus of non-official messages charting the history of kingship, statecraft, civil planning and military enterprise that comprised the ideological and practical underpinning of ancient Egyptian politics under pharaonic rule.

Almost four hundred years later, a final inscription – dating to the tumultuous final years of Dynasty XIX (c. the last decade of the twelfth century BCE) – sheds astounding light on the fate of a political powerbroker who fell from favour in radical circumstances.

G8.5   "Year 5 III Shemu the 27th. On this day, the scribe of the tomb Paser came announcing, 'Pharaoh [Siptah] – LPH – has killed the great enemy, Bay'."[7]

A non-indigenous Egyptian of Syrian origin, Ramesse Khamenteru rose to a position of significance under Seti II (c.1200–1194 BCE), taking up the office

165

of Overseer of the Seal (i.e. treasurer, or chancellor). Chancellor Bay, as he is familiarly known, came into his own after the death of Seti II: his close relationship to the incumbent pharaoh Merenptah Siptah (1197–1191 BCE) is reflected in official inscriptions displayed on several of the young king's monuments; his inclusion in the cult of the mortuary temple of Siptah; and the permission granted to him to construct his own tomb in the Valley of the Kings (KV13) in close proximity to those of Siptah and Queen Twosret. However, at some point in Year 4 of Siptah's rule, something happened which marked out Bay as an enemy of the state. Whatever that event may have entailed – possibly a conspiracy, but equally likely the threat he posed to members of the ruling dynasty whose ambition to occupy the throne of the Two Lands was threatened by Bay's prominence in Siptah's inner circle – he disappears from the public record at some point in time prior to Siptah's fifth year as pharaoh.

Found at Deir el-Medina and comprising two inscribed potsherd fragments belonging to a single *ostracon* (O. IFAO 1864) – reused at some later point to list items priced for exchange (two pigs, a plank of wood, a roll of papyrus), given by one person to another – the inscription above (G8.5) explicitly reports Chancellor Bay's execution in Year 5 III Shemu the 27th. Given the proximity in time of Siptah's death (also in Year 5 of his reign), it is reasonable to link Bay's removal from his position in power as a preemptive strike by Queen Twosret, who acceded to the throne in the same year. Almost certainly, the existence of this *ostracon* in Deir el-Medina reflects an official pronouncement halting any further work on the tomb of the now-disgraced former Overseer of the Seal.[8] We do know that his tomb was used in Dynasty XX by a son of Ramesses IX (Mentuherhepshef).

Greece

Unlike Egypt, the Greeks were mariners, divided into small groups; and, while the institution of divine kingship can be located in particular places, it lacked political and social power. When the Greeks emerged from migratory patterns of tribal behaviour and attitudes, they formed communities called *poleis* (sing. *polis*: citizen-state) – distinctive zones of habitation under the jurisdiction of an organized collective or sanctioned leader. Ancient Greece comprised over a thousand distinct political communities stretching from the Atlantic Ocean to the Black Sea, especially on the coastal fringes of the Mediterranean and Eurasia. Geography played a significant role in the socio-political configuration of the Greek world. Archipelagoes, valleys and inlets – the multiplicity of Aegean and S. Italian islands and the mountains, bays and estuaries characterizing the mainland – enabled comparatively small territorial groups to stay free from outside control, and to exchange information and resources with one other through the mechanisms of barter, a common language and cultural discourse. In contrast to Egypt, supreme authority remained with the separate *poleis*. The classical Greek world, from at least the time of Homer onwards, was a widely distributed yet culturally cohesive entity.

The first settled *poleis* function according to the principles underpinning a warrior society – namely, an exclusively male fellowship on which the broader collective's continuing existence and liberty depended. In Homer's epic poems *Iliad and Odyssey* – generally thought to have been first composed *c.*750–700 BCE, but portraying a society from an earlier historical period – we find people already organized in regional groups called *poleis* or *dēmos* (lit. "people"), comprising in general terms a military commander with individual autonomy, his kinship group, those regarded as his adherents or supporters, and various others. In contrast to almost every existing or developing ancient community based on shared customs, laws and organizations, these Homeric (and, of course, later archaic and classical) communities were close-knit territorial affiliations, sufficiently self-contained for all individuals belonging to the group to gather in a single location – specifically, the *agora*, both a centre of commercial exchange and a place where the *demos* could meet for a common purpose. Importantly, within the *polis* there was no particular representative of religious authority. Understood in abstract terms, the ancient Greek citizen-state represented an impersonal construct, separate from any single person or hereditary rule, a medium for the exchange of ideas and the promulgation of actions rather than a structure delegating orders, making decisions and enforcing obedience.

In this light, most scholarship would agree that the history of Western political thought began in ancient Greece. Such a view exists not only because a repertoire of modern terms for particular kinds of political structure – like "democracy" and "oligarchy"; even the word "politics" – may be traced back to the Greeks. It is also because the Greeks discussed politics and political ideas and actions methodically within a sophisticated, coherent and comprehensive view of the world and human life. The ancient Greeks accepted that it was possible to explain the nuanced interrelationships between people and institutions within a social context and then question what particular function, if any, the divine or fortune might possess according to this view. As a consequence, they formulated a variety of interpretations which still constitute today modes of understanding why people act in a certain way in specific social contexts, and whether or not these contexts should be regarded as organic or constructed. By scrutinizing, elucidating and discussing critically the ways and means by which they resolved issues as a community and then complied with collective determinations, they developed political ideas that advocated a set of principles on which efficiently organized societies should be based. In this way, they established rational tenets to manage the complexities of social conduct and to warrant a range of social and political structures according to which they lived. Today, when we speak about a methodical and carefully reasoned understanding of the natural world, of principles of human conduct and the psychological and ethical dynamic that exists between personal interest and its relation to the interests of others within a shared community of ideas and actions, we may not all reach similar conclusions on these matters any more than did the Greeks, but we are coming to an understanding of what it means to be part of a political system using a conceptual vocabulary developed to a high degree in ancient Greece.

Very simply, the Greeks construed politics as a series of mechanisms by which certain cultural concepts such as freedom, equality and justice – ideas which we might not necessarily recognize as compatible with modern definitions of the same terms – could be achieved through reasoned discussion followed by logical patterns of behaviour. In this context, various forms of communication guaranteed that these notions of shared action, legal and moral entitlement and freedom within a civilized social context came to be associated with the sphere of politics – in the Greek world, a domain that was, in all respects, restricted to male soldier-citizens of the *polis*.

One of the most fascinating (and obscure) political institutions in the ancient Greek world – the Athenian practice of ostracism – provides the most exemplary indication of the relationship between official political activity and popular epigraphic discourse. During the course of the fifth century BCE, the Athenians employed ostracism to send certain political figures into exile for ten years. These individuals – including the "hero" of the Persian Wars, Themistocles, and the historian of the Peloponnesian Wars, Thucydides – retained control of their property in Attika, and at the end of the period of exile could return. According to the literary evidence, the people took a preliminary vote in order to decide whether to hold an ostracism, and a quorum was required for an ostracism to take place; the practice could occur only once in any given year.[9] The name of the procedure (*ostrakismos*) was derived from the use of potsherds (*ostraca*) as ballots.[10] When it was resolved by the requisite quorum to hold an ostracism, an area of the central market-place (*agora*) was fenced off – either with planks, boards or ropes – as a means of ensuring that all voters went through the official entrances. The entrances numbered ten, one for each of the voting tribes of Athens. The members of the *polis* council (the Boule) and the nine archons (holders of the highest political offices) presided over the ostracism, presumably to identify the voters as citizens and make certain that they voted only once. A fragment from the works of Philochorus records that citizen voters "entered by tribes and deposited their *ostraca*, inscription-side down".[11] When everyone eligible to vote had deposited his *ostracon*, the ballots were collected and counted. The individual whose name appeared most frequently would be ostracized from the Athenian *polis*.

Ostraca Athenian citizens deposited in the course of these political activities during the fifth century BCE have been found in considerable numbers, particularly in excavations in the market-place (*agora*) and Potters' Quarter (Ceramicus) of Athens – over 1,100 in the *agora* and approximately 8,500 in the Ceramicus.[12] These include the following examples:

POLITICS

G8.6 "[Alcibi]ades, son of C[leinias, of Skamb]o<n>i<d>ai."

G8.7 "Alcibiades, son of Cleinias."

G8.8 "Aristeides, ~~son of Lysi ...~~, ~~of Alopeke~~, son of Lysimachus."

G8.9 "Hyperbolus, son of Antiphanes."

G8.10 "Cimon, son of Miltiades."

G8.11 "[Me]gac[les, son of Hip]pocar[tes]."

G8.12 "Pericles, son of Xanthippus."

G8.13 "For Themistocles, son of Neocles, of Phrearrioi."

G8.14 "For [Thucy]dides, [son of Mele]sias."

G8.15 "This *ostracon* says that Xanthippus, son of Ariphron, does most wrong of the accursed leaders [or: that the accursed Xanthippus wrongs the *prytaneion* ('the state')]."

G8.16 "Vengeance on Hippocrates."

The selection of scratched – and, in one instance, painted (G8.9) – texts testifies to the historical development of male citizen power associated with the Athenian democratic revolution. This political reconstitution under Cleisthenes in 508/7 BCE saw Athenian citizens come to embody a community characterized by principles of equality before the law, freedom of speech and government by the people. With respect to the thousands of graffiti inscribed on potsherds, the close relationship between political power and the power to impose exile – not to mention the need for popular involvement in politics to resolve conflict among the various elites in Athens vying for influence and authority – explains why ostracism came to represent such an important mechanism for popular intervention in political strife.

There was clearly no-one exempt from the threat of exile. Many of the most accomplished statesmen, military commanders, and political figures from the fifth century BCE were ostracized:

- Alcibiades, son of Cleinias, an important Athenian politician, orator and general, who played a significant role in the second half of the conflict between Athens and Sparta in the later fifth century BCE (G8.6, 7).
- Aristides, son of Lysimachus, given the epithet "the Just", and identified

169

as "the best and most honourable man in Athens" by the historian Herodotus (G8.8).[13]

- Cimon, son of Miltiades – the renowned victor of the battle at Marathon which saw the first invasion of the Persians thwarted; played a key role in creating the powerful Athenian maritime empire in the aftermath of the failed second Persian invasion (G8.10).[14]
- Megacles, son of Hippocrates, a leading figure of the Alcmeonid family, members of which were widely believed to have been complicit in an act of treachery in the aftermath of the battle at Marathon which resulted in the Persian attack on an unguarded Athens (G8.11).
- Pericles, son of Xanthippus, the leading political figure during the period between the Persian and Peloponnesian Wars (c.461–429 BCE); acclaimed "the first citizen of Athens" by Thucydides (G8.12).[15]
- Themistocles, son of Neocles, the most prominent politician in Athens in the years leading up to the second Persian invasion; an advocate of naval power whose initiatives in this regard proved crucial in the battles of Artemisium and Salamis (G8.13).[16]
- Thucydides, son of Melesias, Athenian general during the conflict between Athens, Sparta, and the Greek states allied on either side, and the author of the *History of the Peloponnesian War* (G8.14).[17]

In addition to the historical value of these *ostraca* inscriptions, we can also learn a little about the extent to which citizen participation in democratic institutions like ostracism cut across social strata. In this respect, it is interesting to compare the epigraphic testimony provided by the graffiti with a well-known anecdote from the literary tradition.[18] Writing about the politician Aristides (G8.8), Plutarch tells a story designed to exemplify his subject's high moral standards, but which incidentally supposes that indigent, uneducated rural workers could travel to Athens to take part in the political process of ostracism. According to the biographer, at the time of Aristides' ostracism in 482 BCE, an illiterate farmer handed a sherd of pottery to Aristides, whom he did not know on sight, having never encountered the politician before that moment. The farmer asked Aristides to inscribe the *ostracon* with his own name. When Aristides asked the farmer what he (Aristides) had done to him (the farmer), he replied: "Nothing. I don't even know the man, but I'm tired of hearing him everywhere called 'the Just.'" Aristides did not reply to this extraordinary remark; instead, he inscribed his own name on the *ostracon*, and returned it to the farmer. Although other politicians may not have behaved as ethically as Plutarch alleges Aristides to have been here, the story does demonstrate that even illiterate citizens might engage actively in a democratic political institution like ostracism by negotiating with literate citizens to mark their voting sherds for them.

The evidence of the Athenian *ostraca* confirms Plutarch's casual allusion to the custom of allography, where a person wrote someone else's words (or

POLITICS

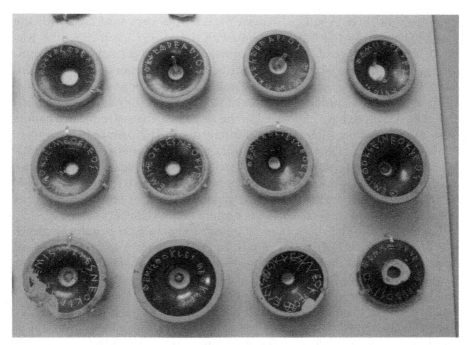

Figure 8.2 *Ostraca* with the name Themistocles, recovered from a well, northern slope of the Acropolis (Ancient Agora Museum, Athens; photo by Xocolatl, via Wikimedia Commons).

Figure 8.3 *Ostracon* with the name Megacles, Potters' Quarter (Ceramicus), Athens (Ancient Agora Museum, Athens; photo by Giovanni Dall'Orto, via Wikimedia Commons).

GRAFFITI IN ANTIQUITY

signature) on their behalf. A deposit of 190 potsherds inscribed with the name Themistocles (G8.13) – and one with the name Cimon (G8.10) – was discovered at the base of a well on the northern slope of the Athenian acropolis (Figure 8.2).[19] The larger find of sherds – inscribed in only a few different hands – suggests that supporters of a political faction opposed to Themistocles had produced a number of *ostraca* inscribed with the name of the politician they sought to have ostracized in the assembly. These pre-incised ballots were most probably intended for participants in the ostracism who were either illiterate or at least found writing a significant challenge. Finding insufficient voters who favoured their political standpoint, the anti-Themistocles partisans most likely dumped the additional *ostraca* down the nearest repository for unwanted materials – in this instance, a well close by the *agora*, later unearthed by modern archaeologists digging in the vicinity.

Intriguingly, of the more than 4,000 *ostraca* naming a certain Megacles (G8.11; cf. Figure 8.3), one Ceramicus sherd also displays an adeptly incised drawing of a horse and rider. The graffito sketch neatly supports the most frequent allegations levelled against Megacles – his elevated social standing, and particularly his pretentious display of affluence and self-indulgent way of life. Five other *ostraca* describe the Alcmeonid politician as "keeping horses" (*hippotrophos*), traditionally an elite occupation, and an indicator of significant material prosperity. These, of course, provide precisely the context necessary to explain the significance of the *ostracon* drawing. Other ballots referring to Megacles' predisposition for cold, hard coinage (*philarguros*) – perhaps implying a susceptibility to bribery in public office – and his status as someone who committed adultery (*moichos*) – an explicit slight against his personal propriety – register the extent to which the process of ostracism could pit popular power against public misconduct, perceived or otherwise. Similarly, a graffito targeting Xanthippus, son of Ariphron (G8.15) – an elegiac couplet incorporating highly loaded language ("accursed") – combines an accusation against improper civic behaviour with a suggestion of religious impropriety – the act of treachery after Marathon noted above.

Although a single example only of the relationship between participatory political action and popular inscribing practices, the evidence of the Athenian *ostraca* highlights the degree to which the ancient Greeks (during the classical period) accommodated experiences of (limited) equality and self-government. In viewing the names and accompanying messages incised and (occasionally) painted on the utilitarian "note-paper" of the ancient Mediterranean – potsherds – the modern student of Greek political history can glimpse a world which developed a viable alternative to monarchic rule. Characterized by a degree of political equality and participation in some ways unimaginable in our age of "illiberal" democracy, the writers and copyists of Athenian *ostraca* encapsulate the ability – in the case of ostracism, within prescribed boundaries (literally) – to express personal opinions in political contexts. Of course, we cannot blind ourselves to the radical socio-political

172

POLITICS

and cultural differences underlying Greek *demokratia*: slavery, gender inequity, and embedded distinctions of class and social condition; the inextricable links between religion, war and public finances; using private property for the public good; and so on. What the Athenian *ostraca* represent is a community which sought strategies for achieving consensus in a large society – a way of conducting public affairs by discussion and voting, explicitly related to marking practices that inscribed what a political community in antiquity could be.

Rome

Founded as a city-state in the middle of the eighth century BCE (*c.*753 BCE), Rome expelled its (Etruscan) kings in the last decade of the fifth century (509 BCE), and was governed, broadly speaking, by an executive council and a range of popular assemblies until the middle of the first century (48 BCE). From 31 BCE onwards it was governed by a single ruler. The history of Roman political thought falls, therefore, into two distinct phases, though with a considerable degree of ideological and structural exchange.

The Roman term for state was *res publica*: "public affairs", "the public sphere", "public space" – in short, the political community. It was, said Cicero, *res populi*, "the people's affair".[20] In simple terms, the concept encompassed everyone's business – a far broader idea than modern expressions of "the state". *Res publica* signified collaborative government based on a body of established precedents or fundamental principles. In consequence, any form of monarchical rule – especially framed in terms of absolute authority (*regnum*) – was incompatible with the notion of *res publica*. But the concept did not always imply "republic" according to modern definitions of the term. Under the principate – the form of government which grew out of the social, political and military crises in the last decades of the first century BCE – there was still a *res publica*. In essence, the Romans came to think of their state as better than all other forms of political system: a "common fatherland" (*patria communis*),[21] providing a context for civic discourse that accommodated all members of Roman society. Accordingly, the Romans may be seen to have elaborated the idea of the state more than any other ancient people; and, to this extent, they should be considered responsible for transmitting the notion to Europe and the West.

The Romans understood the need for differentiating – at least in principle – what we would understand as "public" and "private" spheres of activity. The Latin term for the latter was *res priuata*: "private things", or "accounts". But, as we have seen, the *res publica* – "things held in common" – came to mean the Roman state. The closest modern term that approaches this idea in English is "commonwealth". As the Romans articulated this system of government, the political process was public and open, so that in the period prior to the inception of imperial rule under a single leader – *princeps* (first

173

GRAFFITI IN ANTIQUITY

citizen), *imperator* (military leader), Augustus (the honorary title of Roman emperors, meaning "revered one") – Rome was administered by people who only held office for one year. Ideally, there was an annual turnover of government. In this government, people who held offices of power, the magistracies, would always hold that power equally with colleagues, so that no one person would become more powerful over another. There would always be someone with equal power to another. Under this system the people who would hold power were elected to their office – and this is the public aspect of the *res publica*.

A fragmentary piece of papyrus shines a fascinating light on an aspect of the process of government under the *res publica*. Found in a paper dump used by the inhabitants of Oxyrhynchus – a city in Upper Egypt located about 160 km south-southwest of Cairo – the papyrus scrap in question is an excerpt from a summary of one of the lost books of Livy's *History of Rome*. The fragment deals with the history of the secret ballot – a familiar feature of modern liberal democracy, but something which had an enormous impact on the dynamics of the *res publica*, of politicking in republican Rome, and the politics of public life. The introduction of the secret ballot for voting in elections and voting on laws was a major landmark in the history of the republic. We know from other literary sources *who* introduced the procedure – a certain Aulus Gabinius – but until the discovery of this piece of papyrus we did not know *when*. What the summarizer of Livy's historical account tells us is that in the year 139 BCE Aulus Gabinius introduced *suffragium per ta[bellam]* – that is, suffrage, or the capacity to vote, "by tablet". In other words, from the later second century BCE the Roman people began to vote for laws or to elect men to offices of power in the government by writing on tablets.

The literary tradition provides numerous insights into the circumstances and procedures by which citizens elected officials at Rome and elsewhere in the Mediterranean under Roman rule. For our purposes, an extraordinary collection of painted messages on the exterior facades of private residences, commercial premises and workplaces at Pompeii speaks directly to the continuation of this practice into the imperial period – at least in a small harbour town under the shadow of Vesuvius.

G8.17   "All the mule-drivers [*muliones*], in agreement with Agathus Vaius, [ask you to elect] Gaius Cuspius Pansa as *aedile*."

(*CIL* IV.97)

G8.18   "The onion-sellers [*caeparii*] ask [you to elect] Gaius Iulius Polybius as *duovir*." (*CIL* IV.99)

G8.19   "Phoebus, as well as his customers [*emptores*], asks [you to elect] Marcus Holconius Priscus [and] Gaius Gavius Rufus as *duoviri*." (*CIL* IV.103)

174

POLITICS

G8.20   "Fabius Eupor, first among the ex-slaves [*libertini*], [asks you
to elect] Cuspius Pansa as *aedile*."   (*CIL* IV.117)

G8.21   "All the fruit-vendors [*pomarii*], in agreement with Helvius
Vestalis, ask [you to elect] Marcus Holconius Priscus, *duovir*
for administering justice."   (*CIL* IV.202)

G8.22   "I ask that you elect Gaius Iulius Polybius as *aedile*. He bakes
good bread."   (*CIL* IV.429 = *ILS* 6412a)

G8.23   "All the worshippers of Isis [*Isiaci*] ask [that you elect] Gnaeus
Helvius Sabinus as *aedile*."   (*CIL* IV. 787)

G8.24   "All the Pompeians [ask you to] elect Paquius Proculus as
duovir for administering justice. He is worthy of the state."
              (*CIL* IV.1122)

Hundreds of these electoral notices (*programmata*) survived the devastating
eruption of Vesuvius in 79 CE. Painted on walls throughout Pompeii, they
may tentatively be regarded as corresponding to contemporary campaign
posters, billboards and television advertisements – or, most recently, the
viral programmes promoted via smart-phone technology and social media
(Facebook, Twitter, Instagram and the like). What should be immediately
obvious to even the casual reader is the extent to which these painted messages reveal the interests and frequently the identities of Pompeii's inhabitants, often quite reasonably associated with the properties on which the
graffiti appear. Some, it would seem, were painted to persuade a prospec-
tive voter, which others appear to have been posted simply because there
was space available. All, however, were displayed to be seen and, due to their
formulaic expression, are readily translated and interpreted. In its most
straightforward configuration, this pattern often starts with the candidate's
name – sometimes simply his initials – together with the magisterial position for which he was nominated (e.g. *aedile, duovir*). A verb or phrase followed on – "I ask" (*rogo*), "I ask that you elect" (*oro vos faciatis*, abbreviated
as OVF) – indicating the purpose of the message and drawing attention to
the person whose election was sought. Both individuals – Agathus Vaius
(G8.17), Phoebus (G8.19), Fabius Eupor (G8.20), Helvius Vestalis (G8.21)
– and groups – mule-drivers (G8.17), onion-sellers (G8.18), customers
(G8.19), ex-slaves (G8.20), fruit-vendors (G8.21), worshippers of Isis (G8.23;
cf. G5.12)[22] – putting forward candidates for certain roles (*rogatores*) sometimes added their names. Occasionally particular items supporting the candidate's election – for example, "he bakes good bread" (G8.22), or "worthy of
the state" (*dignum rei publicae*) (G8.24) – were appended.

175

GRAFFITI IN ANTIQUITY

G8.25 "Macerio and all the sleepers [*dormientēs*] ask [that you elect] Vatia as *aedile.*" (*CIL* IV.575)

G8.26 "The petty thieves [*furunculi*] ask [that you elect] Vatia as *aedile.*" (*CIL* IV.576)

G8.27 "All the late-drinkers [*sēribibī*] ask that you elect M. Cerrinius Vatia as *aedile.* Florus wrote this with Fructus." (*CIL* IV.581)

Painted on the walls of buildings along the Via degli Augustali – a back street adjoining the Forum at Pompeii – three election notices (G8.25–7) register the inventiveness of individuals who might be described as the equivalent of political humorists – in this instance, expressing disapproval at the proposal to elect a certain Marcus Cerrinius Vatia to the aedileship. Such graffiti constitute examples of the type of "dirty" or negative advertising campaign not unfamiliar to us today. As we have seen, various professional interest groups in Pompeii often posted notices showing their support for political candidates – but the *furunculi*, *dormientēs* and *sēribibī* must be understood as imaginative caricatures, meant to suggest that all dishonest or unscrupulous persons eligible to vote supported Vatia. All three notices may have been posted by the same individual(s). Florus and Fructus apparently autographed one of the *programmata* (G8.27), but these men can be identified from other graffiti to have been campaigners well-disposed towards Vatia. It is possible, therefore, that their names may have been included here to lend some validation to recommendations in fact poking fun at the candidates registered in the graffiti.

G8.28 "Caprasia, along with Nymphio, asks that you elect Aulus Vettius Firmus as *aedile.* He is worthy. Together with the neighbours, they ask that you elect." (*CIL* IV.171 = *ILS* 6431a)

G8.29 "Appuleia, along with Mustius the fuller, her neighbour, and Narcissus, asks that you elect Pupius *duovir* for administering justice." (*CIL* IV.3527 = *ILS* 6408a)

G8.30 "Statia and Petronia ask that you elect Marcus Casellius and Lucius Albuvius as *aediles.* Citizens like these – in the colony, in perpetuity." (*CIL* IV.3678 = *ILS* 6414)

G8.31 "Maria asks that you elect Gnaeus Helvius Sabinus as *aedile.*" (*CIL* IV.7866)

G8.32 "Asellina asks that you elect Ceius Secundus as *duovir* for administering justice." (*CIL* IV.7873)

POLITICS

G8.33 "Birius, along with Biria, asks [that you elect] Helvius Sabinus
as *aedile.*" (*CIL* IV.9885)

Like ancient Greece, indeed the world of antiquity in general, the franchise
was an exclusively male preserve. However, what the Pompeian *programmata* reveal is a female constituency cognizant of both the electoral process
and the candidates. Over 50 painted notices testify to the active participation of women in the recommendation of candidates for official positions on
Pompeii's *decurio* (local council). The selection of graffiti above (G8.28–33)
show women announcing publicly their choice of candidate – on their own
(G8.31–2), with another woman (G8.30), or in the company of a male supporter (G8.28–9, 33). By inference, it is clear that these women possessed
the money necessary – or shared the costs required – to post the notices.
Comparing these painted messages with those commissioned by male *rogatores*, it is also apparent that women's reasons for recommending certain
individuals for elected office conformed in large part with those expressed
by men – kinship, patronage, neighbourhood ties, economic interest or religious affiliation. While there is no evidence to suggest that women actually
voted in the annual elections at Pompeii, the surviving graffiti point convincingly to the public capacity that women displayed in matters relating to each
year's campaign.

G8.34 "In accordance with the opinion of Suedius Clemens the
sacred judge and with the agreement of the *ordo* on account
of his merits, Sabinus the usher, with applause, elects and
asks that you elect Marcus Epidius Sabinus – defender of the
colony and worthy of the state – *duovir* for administering justice. He is worthy." (*CIL* IV.768)

G8.35 "With the encouragement of his neighbours, Suedius
Clemens, most sacred judge, elects and asks that you elect
Marcus Epidius Sabinus, a worthy young man, *duovir* for
administering justice." (*CIL* IV.1059)

G8.36 "The holy *ordo* elects and asks that you elect Marcus Epidius
Sabinus, most worthy young man, *duovir* for administering
justice. Greetings to Clemens, the holy judge." (*CIL* IV.7579)

These three related *programmata* (G8.34–6) allow us to piece together elements of the radical political transition from late republic to early empire.
The Roman constitution was an informal construct, based on customary
practice and not officially articulated in any formal manner. Under the republic, the Roman state comprised the senate and people of Rome – *Senatus
Populusque Romanus* (SPQR). The senate was composed of former executive

177

GRAFFITI IN ANTIQUITY

and judicial officials (*magistratus*) and their descendants (the "patriciate"). The senate possessed collective prestige (*auctoritas*) – based on a received tradition of principled conduct and ethical decision-making – and the power to assess and initiate civil process and foreign policy. According to accepted practice, magistrates acted only on the senate's recommendations concerning prudent future action. Polybius – the second-century BCE Greek historian of the Hellenistic period (264–146 BCE) whose major work (*Histories*) charts the rise of Rome in the Mediterranean world – tried to elucidate "how and by what kind of constitution almost the whole world" had fallen under the ambit of Roman control "in less than fifty-three years".[23] He selected as pivotal to his explanation the amalgamation of facets of each of the three so-called "good" constitutions: monarchy (rule by one man, inherited by right of birth), aristocracy (rule by the best, determined by social condition, inherited status, education, and so on), and democracy (rule by the people, usually meaning the sub-elite). He proposed that at Rome "each of the parts can, if it wants, counteract or cooperate with the others".[24] As a result, the *res publica* – at least ideally – possessed a series of checks and balances. By tradition, and until the late republic in practice, the senate held preponderant power, so that checks tended to be stressed by supporters of the people. On the other hand, Cicero believed that "without dissensions among the nobles, the kings could not have been driven out", nor the guarantees of personal liberty for the people introduced.[25] This was later seized upon by Machiavelli, and widely used in support of constitutional government with checks and balances, and of political parties, in modern Europe.[26]

What the Pompeian graffiti recommending election of Marcus Epidius Sabinus (G8.34–6) draw out – if only partially – is how this weft and weave of political forces – single rule, rule of the elite and popular rule – played out in a small Roman colony during the first century CE. According to an official inscription set up at Pompeii, the person identified in the graffiti as Suedius Clemens was "a tribune" acting "in accordance with the authority of the emperor Vespasian Caesar Augustus".[27] The formal epigraphic text relates that Clemens "restored to the government (*res publica*) of the Pompeians public lands taken over by private individuals" – depredations which will have occurred in the aftermath of the tumultuous political upheavals after the death of the emperor Nero and the so-called Year of the Four Emperors (68–9 CE). While performing the duties assigned to him by Vespasian, it would seem that he participated in Pompeii's political affairs – at least to the extent of lending his name and title (*iudex*) to the electoral campaign of M. Epidius Sabinus. That the local council (*ordo decurionum*) aligned itself with Clemens in supporting Sabinus' candidacy[28] reflects the importance of imperial favour – in this case, by association with Vespasian's chosen official – in the working out of local politics, albeit the popular election of representatives to the *ordo*.

The testimony to political expression in the epigraphic environment of Pompeii's annual elections may be compared with another collection of

178

POLITICS

non-official inscriptions found in the guardhouse (*excubitorium*) of the seventh cohort serving the fourteenth Augustan region, on the western side of the river Tiber (the Transtiberim).[29] These constitute a dense series of graffiti on the plaster of a series of service rooms in the smaller garrison of the permanent detachment of the cohort, constructed at the end of the second century CE over a private house.[30] Dating to the period 214–45 CE, this rich collection of epigraphic material records the names of the guards (*vigiles*); their fears, their superstitions; their labours, carried out with few and rudimentary aids; and, in a number of cases, the nature of imperial politics in the early third century CE.

Inscriptions of the seventh cohort of *vigiles* nearly all deal with the duty of the *sebac(i)arius*. The word may be derived from *sebaceus* or *sebum*, meaning tallow, and has something to do with tallow-candles or lamps. It is thus manifestly a duty performed at night. Scratched in Latin or Greek into the walls located to the left of the main entrance of the *excubitorium* or of the spaces immediately beyond, these graffiti were inscribed either as free-standing texts or occasionally framed within decorative frames (*tabulae ansatae*). The following provides a useful illustration of the inscribing habit of the *cohors* VII *vigilum*:

G8.37 "Furius Victor, *sebaciaria*, from the seventh *cohors* of *vigiles*, the Severan Felix, made [this] during the month of February [in the year] when Severus Alexander was consul for the third time and Cassius Dio was consul for the second time [229 CE]. Everything is safe. In the tenth year [of Severus Alexander's reign] [the traditional *vota decennalia*], [the emperor distributed] a *congiarium* of ten *aurei*." (*CIL* VI.2998)

Like the Pompeian *programmata*, this graffito exemplifies an epigraphic formula adopted by every member of the seventh cohort who inscribed a statement of service on the walls of their workplace. Here the pattern is fivefold: a consular date; the name and century (military division) of the inscriber; the essential fact, which, in the context of the *excubitorium*, identified the graffito writer as one who "acted as a night watchman" (*sebaciaria fecit*); the month; and a final comment.

What is initially striking about this inscription is the fact that the Roman emperor under which Furius Victor served – Severus Alexander (208–35 CE) – is identified as "consul for the third time", and shares the collegial office with a certain Cassius Dio. The consulship was the supreme office of power during the republic; in the imperial age, it evolved into a position of honour with a variety of attendant duties – for example, supervising certain criminal trials and presiding over the annual games and festivals at Rome. The graffito confirms that the prestige of the office continued – the official Roman calendar maintained the system of identifying each year in relation to the

179

foundation of Rome *and* by which consuls held office. However, that the position was shared with the most powerful man in the Mediterranean world – the emperor, who retained full control over nominations for the office and of the election returns – implies that Cassius Dio's consulship will have entailed little influence. In passing, it is fascinating to note that the Cassius Dio whom the inscription records as sharing the consulship with Severus Alexander is the author of the famous *Roman History* in eighty volumes.

It is also interesting that the final item in Furius Victor's graffito refers to a generous distribution by the incumbent emperor of monetary relief (*congiarium*) to the soldiers living and working out of the Transtiberim way-station. In the early republic, the *congius* was the usual measure of oil or wine which was, on certain occasions, distributed among the people.[31] The Roman rhetorician Quintilian (*c.*35–*c.*100 CE) tells us that a *congiarium* came to refer to liberal donations to the people, in general, whether consisting of oil, wine, corn or – in relation to the seventh cohort – money. Donations made to the soldiers were called *donativa*, though, as this inscription confirms, they were sometimes also termed *congiaria*.[32] In the case of the *congiarium* registered in the graffito above, the donative received by Furius Victor and his fellow *vigiles* – ten *aurei* (gold coins which, in the third century CE, were introduced in a variety of fractions and multiples) – related to Severus Alexander's *vota decennalia*. Celebrated with games every ten years by Roman emperors, this festival owed its origin to the fact that the first emperor Augustus refused supreme power when it was offered to him in perpetuity. Instead, he would only consent to accept it for ten years and, when the original period expired, for another decade, and so on until his death in 14 CE. This Augustan tradition was subsequently preserved by the festival of the Decennalia, solemnized by later emperors every tenth year of their rule – a political façade in all respects but appearance, since Severus Alexander and his fellow emperors received supreme political power (*imperium*) for life, and not for the limited period of ten years. Ironically, items relating to the nature of the festival – and what it implies for the office of the consulship – can be found in the pages of Dio's historical narrative.[33]

Graffiti at Pompeii demonstrate that leaders other than Severus Alexander distributed largesse – not only to those constituencies who, like the Transtiberim *vigiles* or the military more generally, fulfilled their social obligations or performed duties as required by the state; but to citizens in need or communities under distress. Note, too, how the following inscriptions reflect the extent to which such beneficence attracted plaudits from the local population and, in the process, garnered popular – some might say, political – support.

G8.38 "Poppaea sent as gifts to most holy Venus a beryl and a drop-shaped pearl; a large display pearl was included."

(*AE* 1985: 283)

POLITICS

G8.39 "When Caesar [= Nero] came to most holy Venus – when your heavenly feet carried you, Augustus – there were thousands of thousands of gold pieces." *(AE* 1985: 284)

G8.40 "Good fortune to the judgements of Augustus [= Nero]. Puteoli, Antium, Tegianum, Pompeii – these are true colonies." *(CIL* IV.3525 = *ILS* 6444)

G8.41 "Good fortune to the judgements of Augustus [= Nero], father of his country, and of Poppaea Augusta." *(CIL* IV.3726 = *ILS* 234)

The first two graffiti (G8.38–39) were incised on the walls of a large house (IX.13.1–3) that, prior to the eruption of Vesuvius, was still in the process of renovation. The residence and associated shop required restoration as the result of a major earthquake in 62 CE left a swathe of damage across Pompeii. The woman named in the first inscription (G8.38) is almost certainly Poppaea Sabina, mistress and eventually wife of the emperor Nero (until her death in 65 CE). Evidence provided by legal documents from the neighbouring town of Herculaneum as well as a range of epigraphic testimony at Pompeii strongly suggests Poppaea's Pompeian origins. Given the date of Poppaea's marriage to Nero (62 CE) and the content in the second graffito (G8.39), it is most likely that the generous gifts described in both – Poppaea's gift of expensive jewellery and Nero's distribution of gold coins – may be linked to the period when Pompeii required financial support after the earthquake of 62. Mention of Venus in both inscriptions should be understood as a reference to the divine guardian of the city, but the focus of their generosity must remain uncertain. Poppaea and Nero either sought to lend a helping hand to the Roman colony as a whole, or they intended that the Temple of Venus was restored to its proper state as the formal sacred space of Pompeii's patroness.

The second pair of inscriptions (G8.40–41) – two of eight graffiti found at Pompeii relating to similar issues – celebrate what are described as the *iudicia* ("judgement") of Nero individually, and he and Poppaea together. Although the specific details of these "judgements" remain unclear – the Latin term *iudicia* embraces anything from judicial processes of one kind or another (investigation, trial or sentencing) to discerning personal opinions – it is obvious that Poppaea and Nero's actions were political in nature. In the first instance (G8.40), the emperor is singled out for praise. Identified by his imperial title (Augustus), Nero's "judgements" would appear to relate in some way to the determination of colonial status. This connection is confirmed by the historian Tacitus, who names a number of sites where veteran settlements took place under Nero's initiative.[34] These settlements include three of the four sites named in the graffito – Puteoli, another harbour town on the Bay of Naples; Antium, Nero's birthplace; and Tegianum in southern Italy. It may

181

be that the author of the graffito wishes to thank Nero for conferring similar status on Pompeii. The second graffito (G8.41) expresses gratitude jointly to the emperor and his wife. Nero is identified not only as Augustus but also by the designation *pater patriae* ("father of his country"), a title conferred officially first on Cicero in 63 BCE, then Julius Caesar in 45 or 44 BCE, and memorably on Augustus in 2 BCE. The latter ascription constitutes the climax of Augustus' autobiographical inscription, the *Res Gestae et impensae divi Augusti* ("Achievements and Expenses of the Deified Augustus"). Inextricably linked to this title was the idea of a hero who would protect the state with the kind of authority and beneficence that a "father" (*pater*) extended over his dependants. According to the Pompeian graffito, Nero and his wife – notably Poppaea *Augusta* – rendered some form of *iudicia* which elicited a wish of "good fortune" on whatever decisions were reached. If, again, we consider the timing of the actions described in the inscription (63–5 CE), then some draw a connection to the lifting of a senatorial ban on gladiatorial combat in Pompeii's amphitheatre (Chapter 10). In any event, the implications suggested by both pairs of graffiti – relating to bequests and judgements – underline how graffiti capture snapshots of episodes arising from the discourse of Roman political thought and, in some cases, popular responses to particular leaders or those associated with them, or to the results of their actions.

Returning to the Transtiberim *excubitorium*, Furius Victor's graffito – and the ninety-six other messages scratched on the walls of this place – encapsulates the dedication to duty of the individuals serving as fire-fighters and law-enforcers in early third-century CE imperial Rome. As a statement incised on the surface of a wall in a shared workplace, the modern reader may be tempted to categorize this as an ephemeral inscription: that is, an informal text-mark with a limited life-span; distinct, therefore, from the formal legal, commemorative and dedicatory epigraphy inscribed within the context of the monumental intra- and extra-mural urban fabric. But it is clear that Furius Victor and his fellow *vigiles* intended their messages on the walls of the *excubitorium* – declarations of loyalty, piety and collegiality – to last. Over the course of a generation (roughly thirty years), this community of soldiers inscribed on the walls of their work-station a strictly regimented, explicitly codified sequence of micro-plaques – very much akin to the inscribed notices attached to statue-bases and funerary memorials. Moving through this building, the resident or visitor would not fail to register the declarations of identity (expressed in relation to occupation and relationship to their fellow *vigiles*), desire (associated closely to the nature of their service) and dependency (linked inextricably to the emperor and the state). As in the case of the Pompeian *rogatores*, Furius and the other members of the *cohors* VII *vigilum* articulate indelibly the socio-political nature of their community in the shared spaces of their working environment and living area.

Speaking to the nature of the *res publica* in the age of the emperors – in particular, how the non-elite understood their place in relation to issues of

182

POLITICS

social obligation, duty to the state, and imperial authority – a second graffito from the Transtiberim way-station completes this overview of political expression in non-official inscriptions from the Roman world.

G8.42   "I, Vettius Florentinus, acted as night-watchman [*sebaciarius*] in the month of June. I continue to give thanks to the *genius* of the *excubitorium* and [my] colleagues for all time."

(*CIL* VI.3010)

A certain Vettius Florentinus, self-identified as a *sebaciarius*, gives thanks to the *genius* of the *excubitorium*. This declaration of gratitude identifies in physical and conceptual terms the extent to which the essential fabric of the workplace shared by Florentinus and his companions mattered. Here in the Transtiberim, it is not only the emperor whose patronage is recognized with due thanksgiving: Florentinus' graffito gives expression to the collective male spirit of the *cohors VII vigilum* – comprising, we must assume, the spiritual part of each individual, or at the very least, the personification of their natural appetites and desires. In a very real sense, just as Furius Victor's reference to the *vota decennalia* reflected the role of the emperor as provider and protector of the Transtiberim cohort, Florentinus' identification of the *genius excubitori* may be compared to a spirit of place existing in his lifetime that united and watched over those dedicated to service of emperor, city and state.

If we integrate this data with the material already inferred or confirmed, the Transtiberim *cohortes vigilum* should be regarded as a composite, multi-status quasi-military unit with specialist training, domiciled in a specific place, closely associated by affinity of occupation and social condition, acting in the interests of an established multi-status community on the margins of megalopolitan Rome, and subject to the control of one man (the emperor).

FINAL THOUGHTS

The unification of prehistoric Nile communities into a stratified Egyptian state and intimations of political disintegration; the operation of radical democracy in a classical Greek *polis*; the principles of exchange and allegiance under imperial Roman rule – to whatever extent the record of sanctioned history or formal inscription reports facets of ancient political theory or practice, graffiti texts afford us the chance to confirm, clarify or occasionally contest the official consensus. While the wielders of power almost always control the formulation of canonical truth in matters pertaining to the instigation and maintenance of political order, the ephemeral record of non-official markings capture expressions of practical action and private opinion by those belonging to the populations of the disenfranchised and dispossessed as much as the contented and self-interested.

183

CHAPTER 9

SPORT

Kalamodryus (wrestling scene).	(*SEG* 53.811bis)
Epictetos, *oplomachus.*	(*SEG* 52.1845)
Aktia. (wreath) Lucius. Damalis. Hesychius.	(*SEG* 35.1374)

DEFINING THE BOUNDARIES

At first glance it seems easy enough to describe what sport means. The *Oxford English Dictionary* defines sport in the modern world as "any activity involving physical exertion and skill in which an individual or team competes against another or others for entertainment". Any number of "competitive physical activities" corresponding to the parameters of this definition spring immediately to mind – from athletic pursuits relating to running, jumping and throwing to ball games of every kind and water sports like diving and swimming. Regardless of the precise combination of physical effort or proficiency, *all* modern sporting activities involve a contest of some kind between two or more participants. While the nature of the competition may be casual or organized, pitting one individual or team against another is integral to the identification of the activity as a sport. Similarly, if it provides the participants and/or others watching with amusement or enjoyment, the activity is transformed from a recreational pastime to a sporting event. Establishing customary guidelines or formal rules – governing the competitive display of physical athleticism or dexterity and affording a fair basis for consistent adjudication of the eventual winner of the contest – completes the set of requisites designating a sporting activity.

Determining what constituted sport in the ancient world is a more difficult task. First and foremost, there is no single word in the vocabularies of ancient

Egyptian, Greek or Latin which corresponds precisely with the modern definition of the term. Such a lacuna is explained by the fact that the English word "sport" has been part of modern parlance only since the eighteenth century. This is not to say that sport did not exist in the past – far from it. What it *does* mean is that the modern student of antiquity must broaden the conceptual boundaries by which she or he thinks about sport so as to encompass activities which demonstrate *elements* we would recognize as related to sporting endeavour – namely, physical effort and/or skill; competition; and entertainment – but allowing for the possibility that the ancients thought differently about these ideas and practices.

So, for example, we might note that, unlike today, activities in the ancient world exhibiting qualities relating to the modern definition of "sport" were often associated with religious festivals or cult practice of one kind or another. A second characteristic of pre-modern "sport" that distinguishes it – at least ideally – from contemporary activities concerns the fact that participation as a competitor – or, in some instances, as a spectator – depended very much on certain personal traits: for example, citizenship, ethnicity, social condition, even gender. Engaging in what we might describe as "sport" in the pre-modern world required that participants be available in the first place. Leisure time, as we understand it today, was not at all a fact of life for anyone who occupied the sub-elite strata in ancient society – rural or city labourers dependent on work for their livelihood; the unemployed poor or disenfranchised homeless; and, sadly, the larger proportion of many ancient Mediterranean cultures who were enslaved. In this regard, only the wealthy could afford to equip themselves appropriately for particular activities. We must also bear in mind the existence in the past of sharp divisions defined in relation to birthplace, kinship group, political allegiance and cultural heritage. Finally, female participation in officially sanctioned civic contexts was very narrowly defined – in most historical periods, confined to matters relating to marriage, reproduction and inheritance, or religious beliefs and practices. A final quality defining modern sport largely absent from antiquity – some might say, a good thing – was the construct of bureaucratic governance at local, regional or international levels.

By the same token, ancient sporting activities can display similar qualities to their modern counterparts. Like uniquely national or regional competitions (Australian Rules football, American baseball, European handball) or global sports (soccer – in Europe, football – cycling and tennis), a number of ancient pastimes developed a range of roles, strategies and patterns of placement and movement particular to the activity – for example, Egyptian board games like casting sticks, competitive pursuits like bird-netting or ritual activities like acrobatics; Greek athletics or Minoan bull-leaping; Roman chariot racing or gladiatorial combat. A second feature of ancient sport which finds similar expression in modern competitive activity is the phenomenon of record-keeping – namely, the compilation of statistical information relating to individual and team achievements in a variety of contested arenas.

Last of all, but certainly not least, is the quality of *difference* itself. Just as a number of competitive, non-physical activities claim recognition in the twenty-first century as sports – for example, card games (blackjack, bridge, poker); strategy board games (chess, Monopoly, Scrabble); video-games (played on a variety of digital platforms like Microsoft's Xbox 360, Nintendo's Wii and Sony's Playstation) – any number of activities in ancient times follow the same lead – pastimes lacking a competitive component, for instance, or recreations without the need for physical fitness or agility. As the epigraph to this chapter reflects, we should expect to encounter a miscellany of references to ancient contests and their participants: a label identifying a certain Kalamodryas (a famous wrestler from Kyzikos), on a wall painting depicting athletic events at a late second-century/early first-century BCE celebration of the Compitalia games (Delos); a graffito identifying a certain Epictetos as an *oplomachus* (a gladiator armed to resemble a Greek hoplite), written in a gladiatorial scene painted on a second-century CE tomb wall (Kyrene, North Africa); an inscription commemorating the winners at late imperial religious games (Aktia) honouring the god Apollo (Hierapolis, Phyrgia). That the ancients adopted a flexible approach to the classification of sporting activities is understandable. After all, if no single term existed to impose a universal definition of "sport", then it is likely that we should accommodate a variety of activities which would otherwise be found wanting in reference to the modern sense of the word.

Egypt

As noted above, there is no escaping the fact that – despite the existence of the word *swtwt* (technically, "walk"; but which might be loosely translated as "sport") – the ancient Egyptians had no specific term, and hence more than likely no concept, corresponding to the *modern* notion of sports. Wrestling, stick-fighting and archery appear to have been mainly exercises associated with military training; while royal runs – where the pharaoh ran around ritual boundary markers as part of a festival celebrating his continued rule – or the king hitting a ball with a stick were entirely ritual activities.

Involving a complex range of technical skills and rules of engagement, wrestling is a sporting activity very well attested in official and private contexts. The non-official funerary images from the Old Kindgom tomb of Khnumhotep and Niankhkhnum (Figure 9.1) and the Middle Kingdom tomb of Baquet III stand (literally) in sharp relief to the stylized representations under the audience window looking onto the first courtyard of the Temple of Rameses III. Two points, however, are clear: (1) the sporting activities which may be distinguished by the collective term "wrestling" were part of the traditional pattern of socio-cultural practice in all periods of Egyptian history under the pharaohs; (2) depictions of these activities cross over boundaries of

Figure 9.1 Wrestlers: wall painting, tomb of Khnumhotep and Niankhkhnum (Dynasty V, *c.* twenty-fifth century BCE), Saqqara, Egypt (newspaper clipping, *Hufvudstadsbladet*, Helsinki, Finland, published 22 January 1972, via Wikimedia Commons).

representation, permeating civic, religious and funerary spaces both in state-sanctioned and private contexts.

A distinctive sketch inked on a limestone flake performs the same role for stick-fighting as the Old and Middle Kingdom tomb paintings do for wrestling. Most likely drawn by one of the professional artists living in the village of Deir el-Medina (Chapter 3), this non-official depiction of an explicitly competitive sport suggests that the activity had widespread appeal in the New Kingdom and provides a point of comparison with the formally carved figural reliefs at Medinet Habu.

As noted above, the historical record tells us that Egyptian pharaohs participated in a jubilee festival celebrating the continuation of their rule. Known as the *hb-sd* festival, this event was naturally of considerable importance both in a religious and political sense. Traditionally, a pharaoh's first jubilee occurred in the thirtieth year of his reign; and then every two or three years thereafter. Not many pharaohs ruled long enough to celebrate this festival – unless, of course, they modified the rules to accommodate a *hb-sd* before the customary thirty-year mark. An ebony label from the tomb of the pharaoh Den depicts this extremely significant event as part of a private decorative motif which would have been seen by a select number of the king's closest entourage. Though difficult to determine whether the label was intended for more than its eventual funerary context, what is striking is the explicit associations of physical exertion and political power encapsulated in the juxtaposition of the enthroned and running images of the king.

Acrobatics appear to have been closely associated with cult and upper-class entertainment. A processional scene – carved on stone blocks from a wall of the Dynasty XVIII queen Hatshepsut's ceremonial Red Chapel at Karnak – portrays the agile movements of acrobatic women in a manner attested in numerous temple reliefs. The feats of physical skill exhibited in scenes like this are often depicted in association with dance movements of various kinds – and invariably in conjunction with religious festivals. As the

Figure 9.2 Acrobatic dancer (Dynasty XIX, c.1292–1186 BCE), Deir el-Medina, Egypt (Museum of Ancient Egypt, Turin/7052; via Wikipedia Commons).

Red Chapel relief indicates, the Egyptian activity displays qualities similar to those featured in the modern sport – enhanced balance, coordination and agility, requiring strength and flexibility, a developed posture and confident body movement. However, the contexts in which these exercises of skill and movement took place – in the main, processions commemorating the mythological narratives of the state pantheon (Amun-Re, Osiris, Min) – reflect the extent to which the cultural perspective underlying the activity diverges from acrobatics in today's world.

A startlingly beautiful image of a female acrobat provides evidence for the expression of this cultural difference in non-official contexts (Figure 9.2). Sketched in vibrant colour on a flake of chalk found at Deir el-Medina, the artist has captured what appears to be a forward body-flip at a moment midway through the action. Wearing a short black skirt and circular earrings of gold, the female performer demonstrates agility, poise and confidence in executing this element in what we can infer would have been a well-practiced routine. The *ostracon* drawing exhibits exceptional artistic quality, which implies that it was the first draft of a larger composition intended eventually for the wall of a royal tomb. But the final destination of the image – as part of a funerary scene in the burial place of a divine ruler or his immediate family – should not take away from the fact that the artist was clearly familiar with the technicalities of acrobatic performance. What this fragmentary non-official drawing allows us to glimpse is the context which must have formed the basis for the artist's attention to aesthetic *and* technical details – namely, regular attendance at public religious ceremonies. As part of the broader population of Theban residents and visitors to the city, the artist – and, no doubt, his professional colleagues, as well as their families – will have participated in the constellation of activities associated with temple festivals like those dedicated to Amun-Re (Opet, the Beautiful Feast of the Valley). It is not difficult to imagine that acrobatic performances – in the course of ritual processions bearing images of the gods in transit – will have been both much anticipated and enjoyed by all who attended.

If the definition of sporting activity is broadened to include competitive board-games, then one of the most popular pastimes of this kind was *senet* (*snt*) – also known as the "game of thirty" – and a variant form known as "twenty squares". Meaning "to pass" or "to go by", *senet* required two players to negotiate a field of dangerous zones on a board divided into thirty (or twenty) spaces. The evidence for this game – and by association for the cultural practice associated with the activity – is varied, stretches across all periods of Egyptian history *and* reflects the participation of all social strata.

The quality of the Akhmim *senet* board and equipment drawer suggests that its owners belonged to a class which could afford crafted objects of this kind. Informal inscribing practices, however, permitted all echelons of Egyptian society to participate in this activity. A rectangular field of thirty squares scratched into a baked pottery disc confirms the universal appeal of this competitive pastime. Certainly, the Tell Dafana "platter" demonstrates how pervasive a cultural phenomenon such game-play was. The object also attests the extent to which incising a simple grid-pattern in fired clay provided access to such a popular pastime for Egyptians unable to commission or purchase a manufactured version of the board.

All of this reminds us that – in what follows – it is important to remember that what we might classify according to our own cultural standards as sports may have been perceived very differently by the ancient Egyptians.

It should be clear to this point that there is a wealth of data concerning ancient Egyptian sports – sports practiced by Egyptian kings; sports practiced by other Egyptians; the nature of competition in Egyptian sports; ball games, board games and children's play; acrobatics; and hunting. This vivid cultural record allows us to distinguish which sports were restricted to the king or the upper classes and which were played by ordinary people; which were associated with men and with women; which were played by children and by adults; and the social contexts in which games were played. It is also

GRAFFITI IN ANTIQUITY

possible to trace changes in each sport over the three millennia of Egyptian history under pharaonic rule.

In other words, we can learn a great deal from the inscribed and painted images (on temple and tomb walls, and *stelae*), epigraphic and papyrological texts, and material evidence (equipment, sculptures, miniatures) that survive into the modern age. For instance, it is almost certain that the ancient Egyptians did not erect buildings specifically for sporting events. Additionally, for religious reasons, kings could not join in competitive sports, although they might attempt to outperform their predecessors. That said, we should recall the *caveat* that sport in antiquity did not permeate all levels of society on an equal basis. In ancient Egypt, sport seems to have been mainly for the ruling classes, a symbol of their power. As a result, our access to cultural expressions pertaining to sport in pharaonic society is at the mercy of the chroniclers and artists who had more interest in documenting the sports and recreations of kings and their functionaries than in the general population.

The most famous inscription portraying the relationship between sporting ability and pharaonic authority is the Sphinx stela of Amenhotep II. Found in a temple under the shadow of the Dynasty IV sphinx monument at Giza, this round-topped stone slab preserves a formal encomium to Amenhotep II. A large part of the surviving text relates the young king's achievements across a variety of physical endeavours. Written in honour of the Dynasty XVIII pharaoh, the stela represents the extent to which athletic prowess and physical dexterity helped to define the superiority of Egyptian royalty:

> Now then his majesty appeared as king, as a beautiful youth who was well developed and had completed eighteen years upon his thighs in strength. He was one who knew all the works of Mont [god of war]; he had no equal on the field of battle. He was one who knew horses; there was no-one like him in this numerous army. Not one among them could draw his bow; he could not be approached in running.[1]

It is clear that the young Amenhotep II – at least as he is idealized here – followed a robust regimen of physical training, incorporating what we today would recognize as a high-intensity exercise programme that resulted in the acquisition of elite equestrian and athletic skills.

In relation to Amenhotep II's biographical profile formulated in the Sphinx stela, an *ostracon* drawing in ink of a lion-hunting scene demonstrates the fundamental principle of conceptual correspondence by which non-official images can confirm what in state-sanctioned inscribed texts could be viewed with a more sceptical eye. Here the king is shown in the final stages of a ritual hunt. His right hand is raised in the traditional smiting pose; the depiction of the weapon he holds – almost certainly a mace – has not survived. In his left hand he wields a spear, which he can be seen thrusting downward into the

190

left flank of the lion. Already wounded – a fact indicated by the arrow shafts piercing the right front paw and back – the lion also fends off the attack of the king's canine companion. This informal visual composition embodies a similar message to the Sphinx stela inscription: namely, that the king must fulfil his duty of care to the Egyptian people. In the same way that the monumental text articulates young prince Amenhotep II's military prowess, the *ostracon*'s depiction of a successful lion-hunt – the archetype of animals like the hippopotamus and crocodile which regularly threatened the safety of the Nile's inhabitants – establishes his role as protector of Egypt, reinforcing belief in pharaoh's qualities of courage and strength, not to mention confirming his ability to master single-handedly this most majestic of creatures. More than this, however, the nuanced details of physical form and movement capture something of the danger and excitement of what must have been a striking and well-known activity.

Following the introductory lines of the stela's narrative section, we learn that "Strong of arms, untiring when he took the oar, [Amenhotep II] rowed at the stern of his falcon-boat as the stroke-oar for two hundred men".[2] While there is very little by way of surviving evidence for the sport of rowing in ancient Egypt, an *ostracon* from Deir el-Medina provides informal confirmation that Amenhotep II's ability to row would not have been at all unique – even though his level of skill most evidently was. Dating to the later New Kingdom period, the fragmentary piece of painted stone depicts a young boy on a small boat, steering the craft with a long wooden oar. Although nothing like the "falcon-boat" which the young Amenhotep II steered as helmsman, the *ostracon* drawing corresponds to numerous representations in tomb paintings and temple reliefs of fishing and transport vessels plying the waters of the Nile.

The Sphinx stela continues: "when he was still a youth, he loved his horses and rejoiced in them. He was stout-hearted in working them, learning their natures, skilled in training them, understanding their ways."[3] Driving chariots and riding horses were very much the privileged activities of the aristocratic elite not only in New Kingdom Egypt but across the ancient Mediterranean. Introduced during the Second Intermediate Period, references to the specifically military applications of two-wheeled chariot technology in association with equestrian training can be found in a range of textual and graphic sources. The expertise and unstinting effort Amenhotep II displays in the Sphinx stela corresponds to the ideal of pharaonic rule as suited only to individuals embodying the epitome of human accomplishment – and Amenhotep II, who "knew horses" better than anyone in "his numerous army", certainly fit the bill in this regard.

Another limestone flake from Deir el-Medina confirms the fact that equestrian activity of one kind or another was not limited strictly to the echelons of pharaonic power. Even if the painted image has suffered the depredations of exposure over three millennia, it should be relatively clear that the man riding the horse is *not* a king. In fact, as a number of similar depictions displayed in non-royal tombs attest, this *ostracon* drawing captures something of the behavioural awareness and physical control over equine behaviour that Amenhotep II displayed without in any way limiting the extent of his accomplishment to members of the royal family. By the same token, only those who could afford to own a horse would have been in a position to appreciate the nature of the animal, afford to sustain it and provide it with living space, and – over time – acquire mastery over it.

Perhaps the most indelible section of the Sphinx stela's narrative in praise of Amenhotep's extraordinary physical feats relates to his ability with the bow:

> He drew three hundred strong bows, comparing the workmanship of the men who had crafted them, so as to tell the unskilled from the skilled. He also came to do the following which is brought to your attention. Entering his northern garden, he found erected for him four targets of Asiatic copper, of one palm in thickness, with a distance of twenty cubits between one post and the next. Then his majesty appeared on the chariot like Mont in his might. He drew his bow while holding four arrows together in his fist. Thus he rode northward shooting at them, like Mont in his panoply, each arrow coming out at the back of its target while he attacked the next post. It was a deed never yet done, never yet heard reported.[4]

While this might appear nothing more than the official bluster of an over-zealous public relations functionary – and the style and tone of the prose narration certainly echoes *and* foreshadows similar paeans in praise of the god-like abilities of the incumbent king – a painted relief in a private tomb suggests that there might have been an element of truth underneath the hyperbole. On a wall in Theban Tomb 109, Min – major of This and the oases – is shown demonstrating the pulling of the bow to a young prince Amenhotep II. This idiosyncratic portrait records for posterity the role of a trusted functionary as an instructor in the discipline of archery. More than this, it indicates the importance of acquiring such a skill as preparation for male children destined to fulfil the duties of Egyptian royalty. If we combine the testimony of Min's wall painting to the fact that Amenhotep II's physical remains are of a tall man for his time (1.8 m), physically robust and strongly built,[5] it is possible to suggest that the Sphinx stela's apparent exaggerations may be less extensive than at first supposed. Certainly, the role of what we would consider a sporting activity is clearly defined: on the one hand, as integral to the formal propaganda machine underpinning New Kingdom royalty; on the other, as both an informal corroboration of the prestige attributed to the deceased Min by association with the young prince's training *and* a reflection of the place of physical activity in Egyptian society more generally.

After all, if Amenhotep II's ability with a bow approached the level he displays in the stela, then we can only imagine how skilful his tutor was, and the extent, therefore, to which archery constituted a regular part of the educational "curriculum" for elite male children in ancient Egypt.

An earlier inscription adds swimming to the list of sporting skills – in Amenhotep II's case, rowing, archery and horse-riding – at which important Egyptian leaders excelled.

> I was a favorite of the king, a confidant of his princes, his [exalted ones] before Middle Egypt. He caused that I should rule as a child of a cubit [in height]; he advanced my seat as a [youth]. He had me instructed in swimming along with the royal children. I was one correct of [speech], free from [opposition] to his lord, who brought him up as a child. Siut was satisfied with my administration; Heracleopolis praised god for me. Middle Egypt and the Northland (Delta) said: "It is the instruction of a king."[6]

Recorded in the form of an autobiographical funerary inscription, these words belong to a certain Kheti, who belonged to a family of nomarchs based at Siut (Sauty) – capital of the thirteenth nome of Upper Egypt – and ruled during the late First Intermediate Period. It should be clear from the excerpted text above that Kheti was probably closer to the royal family than many other nomarchs, who had become independent of the central power to a large extent during the century-long interregnum between the end of the Old and the beginning of the Middle Kingdom. As the inscription confirms, Kheti inherited his position but was confirmed by the king. Identifying swimming as a physical skill taught to "royal children" *and* the offspring of elite families – in this instance, those families who possessed an established relationship with the dynastic rulers – the deceased nomarch's autobiography may be compared with the depiction of Amenhotep II's instruction at the hands of his tutor Min. In other words, while the activity is most definitely recorded in relation to the highest stratum of Egyptian society, in neither case is there any suggestion that the ability to swim was limited to the elite class. In fact, that the otherwise unknown king "had [Kheti] instructed in swimming along with the royal children" does not require us to imagine a specialist functionary charged with the duty. Indeed, it seems more than reasonable to envisage that nearly all Egyptians – living on the Nile or one of the canals branching from the river – knew how to swim for purely practical reasons.

An *ostracon* most probably sketched at Deir el-Medina enhances the likelihood of this supposition. The drawing depicts a young girl, naked, caught in the act of diving from a river bank into water. She is shown stretching out her arms, reaching for a waterfowl in her left hand and a pair of fish in her right. Clearly decorative in nature, the sketch – dating to Dynasty XX (now in the Museum of Ancient Egypt, Turin) – strongly suggests that Egyptians other than the king, his immediate family, and close retainers possessed the ability to swim.

Text-based graffiti expressing ideas relating to sport in pharaonic Egypt are almost non-existent. However, a repertoire of informal drawings in paint or ink from the workers' village at Deir el-Medina – and related archaeological objects of various kinds – offer visual corroboration of the existence of sporting activities, as well as their ancillary practices. As defined according to the criteria outlined at the beginning of the chapter, these non-official markings in paint, ink and worked materials imply a socially inclusive and culturally diverse understanding of and participation in competitive and non-competitive physical and intellectual pursuits over the course of three millennia of Egyptian history.

Greece

When the concepts of sport and recreation are mentioned in relation to ancient Greece, it is natural to think first and foremost of the Olympic Games. In the modern age, the Olympic Games are global gatherings featuring a variety of competitive summer and winter sports. Regarded as the world's leading sporting competition with over 200 countries taking part, the Olympic Games are currently held biennially – winter and summer Games convened alternately every two years. What must be understood from the outset, however, is that, although the modern Olympics possess a number of features in common with the original events, the ancient Olympic Games – and other athletic festivals (e.g. the Isthmian, Nemean and Pythian Games) – were for the most part religious in nature. Scholarship agrees in general terms that competitive sport in ancient Greece may be seen as equivalent to a sacrifice or oblation satisfying in qualitative terms to gods and heroes. The larger the number of people able to participate in this joint enterprise, the greater was the honour done to gods and heroes and the greater was the contest itself. In this respect, the Greek word for "contest" (*agōn*) originally meant a gathering of people.

Like the ancient Egyptians, then, archaic and classical Greeks placed a culturally divergent emphasis on the significance of sporting activity. Similarly, they did not possess a word which referred strictly to the concept of sport. Instead, the Greeks used the term *athlos*, generally translated as "contest", from which was derived the word *athlētēs* ("athlete"). It is only in the modern Greek that we find the term *athlētismos*, which means both "athletics" and "sport". As a result, when we consider the evidence for formal and informal ideas and practices relating to the conceptualization of sport in *ancient* Greece, it is essential to accommodate the etymological force of the original terminology. *Athlos*, for example, could refer to *any* task requiring vitality,

194

exertion and tenacity. The epic poetry of Homer deploys the term in relation to demonstrations of physical ability or struggle; and the later lyric poety of Pindar refers to persons who competed physically in contests (*athlētēs*). It is only in the fifth century BCE that we begin to see references to the concept of athletics as pertaining to an identifiable group associated with physical training and competition for prizes. In a sense, the contexts in which the term *athlos* appears may be connected directly with social development and cultural advances: in fact, with human life in general. The prize awarded for success in such endeavours – the *epathlon* – was regarded as recompense for an individual's service, effort or achievement, the high point and fulfilment of the *athlos*. Just like the examples of Egyptian sporting activity under pharaonic rule, the nature of competitive sport at festivals and games appears to reflect, in part, the evolution of ancient Greek society since the games were inextricably linked with those collective celebrations held to demonstrate respect to the gods and honour to heroes.

References to sporting activity in ancient Greece may be found in literature (history and poetry), epigraphic testimonia (commemorative, funerary and votive monuments), *and* – as in our survey of pharaonic Egypt – visual depictions of athletic scenes. While it should be noted that regional variations in sporting activity of this kind existed across the Greek Mediterranean, our most secure and plentiful source of information derives from classical Athens. To this end, the following will introduce Athenian examples as a starting-point for elucidating non-official expressions of sport and recreation.

Literary evidence includes what the fourth-century BCE philosopher Aristotle tells us about one of the most important state festivals held at Athens, the Panathenaea.[7] This essentially religious celebration was a national gathering of select male competitors from the main Greek *poleis* of the age – as well as a significant quota of resident and visiting spectators. It comprised not only activities that we would recognize as contests of physical skill – the *gymnikos agon* ("naked competition") or competitive athletic events; and the *hippodromia* ("horse course") or horse- and chariot-racing. According to Aristotle, the Panathenaic Games also featured a religious procession. This procession was so central to the civic function of the festival that its various elements eventually came to comprise the subject of the decorative frieze running in a continuous line around the exterior wall of the Parthenon. In addition, there was a *mousikos agon* ("musical competition") – never part of the Olympic Games, nor originally of the Nemean Games, but integral to the Pythian and Nemean Games. This contest consisted of events like *kithara* (lyre) singing and *aulos* (double-pipe or flute) playing or singing. While the most recent incarnation of the Olympic Games incorporate dramatic and musical presentations as part of the opening and closing ceremonies, these are never part of actual competition – pointing again to the significant conceptual differences underpinning traditional understanding and practical expressions of *athlos* in Greek culture.

In relation to the Pananthenaea, an important public inscription exemplifies official recognition of sport and recreation in classical Athens and confirms the fundamental differences noted above. Dating to the first half of the fifth century BCE, this inscription (*IG* II² 2311) is a record of prizes awarded in the Panathenaic Games. Although fragmentary – and as a result omitting reference to a number of sporting categories – the inscribed list preserves details of the gold crowns (1st place), subsidiary money prizes, *amphorae* of olive oil and animal gifts (bulls) for events including *kithara*-singers, *aulos*-singers and –players, boy and men competitors in running (*stade, pentathlon* – see below), wrestling (*pale, pyx, pankration*), equestrian contests (two-horse and processional chariot), spear-throwing and Pyrrhic dancing. A fragmentary text from the sixth-century BCE poet and philosopher Xenophanes corroborates the detail in the inscription, referring in turn to "the footraces or the *pentathlon* or the *pale* or the painful *pyx* or ... the dreadful struggle which men call the *pankration* ... and ... the horse races."[8]

Perhaps the most ubiquitous evidence in the category of visual evidence pertains to what are mentioned in the fourth-century BCE inscription above – Panathenaic *amphorae*. Large, narrow-necked, two-handled ceramic vessels containing valuable quantities of domestically produced sacred oil (approximately 38 litres), these *amphorae* were awarded as prizes in the Panathenaea. Using the black-figure technique, professional artists working in the leading pottery workshops of the later sixth and fifth centuries BCE depicted the state goddess of the city (Athena) on what we should regard as the "front" of the vessel; and, on the other side (the "back"), a scene portraying the event for which the prize was won (Figure 9.3) – in this instance, a snapshot of one of

Figure 9.3 Athletes running: Panathenaic *amphora* (*c.*500 BCE) (Department of Greek, Etruscan and Roman Antiquities, Louvre/G65; photo by Jastrow, Campana Collection, 1861, via Wikimedia Commons).

SPORT

three possible running events (*stade*, 200 m; *diaulos*, 400 m; *dolichos*, long distance) According to some estimates, this type of painted vessel constitutes almost a quarter of *all* Greek vases that have survived into the modern age.

Unfortunately, there is no equivalent in the world of Greek antiquity to the workman's village of Deir el-Medina. As a result, few images of activities pertaining to sport in classical Greece produced in draft form survive. However, it is possible to survey popular ideas relating to physical training and competitive struggle by way of non-official, mass-produced or commissioned ceramic decoration.

For example, a scene on the equivalent of an ancient Greek wine cooler (a *psykter*) depicts athletes and their instructors exercising in a *gymnasium* (a training facility for competitors in public games). Distinguished by its bulbous body set on a high, narrow foot, this object – dating to the penultimate decade of the sixth century BCE – would have been filled with wine and then placed into a *krater* full of cold water or ice. The context in which this vessel was used – and where its decorative scene, which follows its subject matter in a continuous line around the vessel, will have been viewed – is known as the *symposium*. A key social institution of the Hellenic world, the *symposium* was a private affair held to celebrate the introduction of young men into elite Greek society, but also victories in athletic and poetic contests. On the face of the *psykter* visible in the photograph, a young man – text on the vessel identifies him as Batrachos – readies himself to throw a javelin. To his right, an *aulos*-player (Smikythos) accompanies the physical exercises of another youth (Dorotheos, not pictured), who lifts weights as part of his regimen as a broad-jumper. We know what kind of event he is preparing for because a longer inscription informs the viewer: "he is going to jump." To Batrachos' left is Dorotheos' bearded trainer (Alketes), carrying a pair of measuring sticks and raising his hand in approval.

Produced for an aristocratic household, this specialist vessel displays a scene involving organized physical activity integral to sporting performance in Athenian festival space. Its elite setting – the *symposium*, with its poetic, musical and competitive elements – echoes the cultural context in which the broad-jumper, javelin-thrower and *aulos*-player would seek to achieve victory. This non-official representation of the Attic *athlos* – its participants, its training staff and its accessories – reveals how closely aligned sport and culture were in classical Greek society.

A drinking cup from the northern Italian city of Vulci – a town in the region of Etruria – confirms the relationship between sport and the festival life of ancient Greek communities. Dating to the final decade of the sixth century BCE, the upper rim of this privately-owned *kylix* is divided into two complementary scenes in red-figure style. On one side of the circular frieze (the lower scene as shown), three athletes are shown. One figure (centre) holds a discus above his head, another (to the right) folds his clothing and the third (left) gestures to his companions (fellow competitors?). The *diskos* was one

197

of five events that comprised the contest called the *pentathlon*; the others were the long jump, javelin, running (most likely the *stade*) and wrestling. Perhaps the three young athletes shown in this scene were preparing for – or, given the triumphant gesture of the central figure, had just completed – the *diskos* component of the larger contest. The other side of the cup displays three young men (the same three as shown below?) mixing wine in a large vessel known as a *krater*. Given the context in which this scene will have been viewed and for which it was almost certainly produced, we can situate the young men at a drinking-party. The celebratory connotation of both scenes reflects popular associations of sport and recreation with the idea of freedom (from civic duty and personal responsibility) and the feeling of enjoyment (as part of a satisfying shared experience).

In addition to these highly crafted representations of competitive sporting activity in the classical period, a range of graffiti texts and drawings inscribed by athletes and spectators living in Hellenistic and Graeco-Roman times survive to the present day.

G9.1   "I win. *Telestas*"[9]

G9.2   "Akrotatos is beautiful *to the one who wrote it.*"[10]

G9.3   "Epikrates is beautiful."[11]

These messages – and many others like them – were scratched by athletes on stone blocks at the entrance and on each side of a tunnel leading into the Stadium at Nemea, an ancient Greek city in the north-eastern region of the Peloponnese. Nemea was the site of an important sanctuary dedicated to Zeus, in whose honour the Nemean Games were held. Founded in the early sixth century (573 BCE), this festival was held every two years, alternating with the Isthmian Games. Before the Roman period, they took place in the summer of whichever year no Olympic or Pythian Games were held. Located 400m south-east of the Temple of Zeus, the Stadium tunnel can be dated to the late fourth century (320 BCE).[12]

We know that these brief statements were composed and incised by individuals participating in the Stadium's roster of events because the tunnel on which the graffiti appear could only be entered from the room (*apodyterium*) which served as a dressing and waiting area for athletes and judges preparing for competition in the arena. Well preserved for its entire length of 36.35m, the vaulted tunnel is constructed of a sandy, relatively soft limestone. It was originally smoothly finished, and still preserves traces of stucco. All in all, the surfaces of the tunnel vault provided an excellent canvas on which to scratch graffiti.[13]

The first graffito (G9.1) comprises the verb *nikō* ("I win"), followed, in a different hand (in italics), by the name Telestas. The Telestas identified here may well have been the same Telestas mentioned by the "travel writer" Pausanias, who – as part of his description of the sanctuary of Olympia – recorded in detail the many statues portraying victors of sporting events (both men and horses) at the Olympic Games. The relevant section of Pausanias' *Description of Greece* reads as follows: "Next to the statue of Nicasylus is a small bronze horse, which Crocon of Eretria dedicated when he won a crown with a race-horse. Near the horse is Telestas of Messene, who won the boys' boxing-match. The artist who represented Telestas was Silanion."[14] Though uncertain – and the dating depends in large part on the career of Silanion, the sculptor of Telestas' statue – it is probable that the athlete (or, since he would now have been older, the judge) whose name is scratched in the entranceway to the Nemean Stadium was the same Telestas who won the boxing event at Olympia in the boy's category in the later fourth century BCE (*c.*340 BCE).

The second graffito (G9.2) is another amalgam of two writers. The initial element of the statement – *Akrotatos kalos* ("Akrotatos is beautiful") – is fol-lowed, again in a different hand, by *tou grapsantos* ("to the one who wrote it"). Dating to the early Hellenistic period, it is fascinating to speculate that the Akrotatos named here was the Spartan king who ruled *c.*265–262 BCE. Described in two works by the famous biographer Plutarch (*c.*46–120 CE), Pausanias (again), and the third-century BCE historical writer Phylarchus, the royal Akrotatos was well-known for his physical beauty, his prowess on the battlefield and his strong inclination towards Persian luxuries.[15] These liter-ary attestations correspond favourably with the pithy graffito on the Stadium tunnel at Nemea. In particular, Plutarch tells us that, following his victory in the field against his uncle's (and Pyrrhos') forces, Akrotatos returned through Sparta "covered with blood and gore flushed with victory, and he appeared taller and more beautiful to the Spartan women". The use of the compara-tive ("taller", "more beautiful") implies that the Spartan ruler had, prior to his departure, already appeared tall and beautiful to the women. The presence of such a person as a young athlete writing his name on the wall of the Nemea tunnel is entirely plausible – and confirms the close relationship between ath-letic performance and the underlying concept of *athlos* (achievement), mark-ing the individual in question as a person of exceptional quality and a justified recipient of civic accolades.

Dozens of Nemean graffiti follow this formula – a personal name, accom-panied by the adjective *kalos* ("beautiful", "fair"). On the southern wall of the tunnel closer to the eastern end is another graffito (G9.3) which conforms to this pattern. Scratched in neat, legible strokes, the statement "Epikrates is beautiful" should not be seen solely as an imitative gesture lacking any-thing more than a copyist's attention to detail. With respect to the otherwise unknown Epikrates, the athlete or judge who made his mark here is cer-tainly reiterating the force of similar messages along the length of the tunnel. However, his graffito belongs to a much wider informal epigraphic tradition. The so-called *kalos* inscription is found in abundance on Attic vases *and* as

GRAFFITI IN ANTIQUITY

graffiti, particularly during the classical period but also at other times and in other places across the ancient Mediterranean. Most frequently the subject of the inscription is a young male, though sometimes girls or women find themselves described as *kale*. A finely crafted red-figure *kylix* dating to the end of the sixth century BCE epitomizes this epigraphic type. The interior of the drinking cup depicts a young boy holding a discus. Other accessories associated with athletic activity – a digging tool (pick) used to prepare the landing area for long-jumpers (lower left); weights (dumbbells) used to maintain equilibrium during the jump (upper right) – are also shown. The inscription running around the right edge of the scene reads *Kleomelos kalos* ("Kleomelos is beautiful").

While the purpose of inscriptions of this kind remains obscure, the context of the *symposium* – in which the vases or other ceramic types (like the Kleomelos *kylix*) were almost always used and viewed – would suggest a rationale in some way associated with the aristocratic ethos of classical and Hellenistic Greece. Interestingly, the proportion of graffiti in the Stadium tunnel which emulates this *kalos*-formula would appear to tap into a cult of celebrity which finds at its focus athletic prowess and performance. Epikrates may not be known to us. However, given the fact that writers of antiquity preserve the memory of other names attested here (Telestas, Akrotatos), Epikrates and the other individuals whose physical appearance is commemorated here (e.g. Polyxenos, Andreas, Timostratos) will undoubtedly have been familiar to those who walked along this tunnel into the festival space at Nemea dedicated to Zeus. That these inscriptions express admiration for individuals other than the person waiting to run onto the stadium track supports this contention. Moreover, this is not an isolated example of *kalos*-graffiti or similar markings of fame. We will see the same phenomenon in graffiti relating to sport and recreation from the Roman world – as well as to observations of a sexual nature in Greek *and* Roman contexts (Chapter 11).

An extraordinary series of carefully inscribed graphic representations from the city of Perge – located in the Greek East and dating to the Roman period – reflect the historical continuity and cultural popularity of a particular athletic contest originating in Greek antiquity, not to mention the quality and prominence of non-official inscribing practices in the heart of an ancient civic space. Settled in the early Bronze Age, Perge's Greek heritage extends through the archaic, classical and Hellenistic periods into Roman domination of the Mediterranean from the late second century BCE until the beginning of the fifth century CE. Incised into a column of the northern colonnade of the *agora* at Perge, eleven images record the particularity of knowledge and intensity of enthusiasm which the local population displayed in relation to a pastime originally included in the roster of Olympic events in the middle of the seventh century BCE (648 BCE) – the *pankration*.

The *pankration* was a physically arduous combination of boxing (*pygmē*) and wrestling (*palē*). Blows with the fist were allowed, as well as strikes with

200

the lower extremities. This event was always a hybrid sporting contest. The fifth-century BCE comic playwright Aristophanes tells us that "you can belabour your foes with blows from your fist – or something else"; and the lyric poet Pindar praises the memory of a practitioner of this fighting style who was "once victorious over all that lived around him, battering them with his inescapable hands".[16] The visceral appeal of the contest was undoubtedly amplified by the fact that the fighters did not wrap their hands with the *himantes* (leather straps) used as protection for the knuckles and hands in traditional boxing matches. Boxing in Greek antiquity can, of course, be traced back to the sixteenth century BCE, where two young boys wearing gloves of some kind are depicted trading blows in a wall-painting found on the island of Thera (Santorini).

In relation to *pankration*, a sixth/fifth-century BCE *skyphos* painting depicts a spectator (left) urging on the combatants and a "rod-bearer" (*alytarch*) who enforced the rules of the engagement (right).[17] The fighters (*pankratiasts*) are clearly young adult males, but we know that there were two age groups in ancient competitions since the Olympic games of the late third century BCE – boys and men.

The Perge graffiti drawings portray a variety of the techniques employed by *pankratiasts* to strike each other as well as to grapple their opponent to the ground to secure a submission. In addition to a plethora of striking, locking, choking and throwing techniques, the inscriptions show a straight kick to the stomach – a common move depicted many times in vase-paintings – and an effective upper-cut lifting the opponent's head sharply back – a more traditional boxing exchange. Sheltered under the portico that borders the northern side of the *agora*, these images were clearly visible to residents and visitors to the city moving from the open area contained within the colonnaded walkways on all sides to frequent the shop-fronts just beyond. The fact that the drawings occupy such a prominent location in one of Perge's primary civic spaces points to the city's enduring fascination with this particular athletic contest, the centrality of *pankration* in the popular imagination of the community – at least in the middle of the third century CE (256/7 CE) when these inscriptions were first scratched into the column stones – and the tolerance of local authorities to inscribing practices of this kind.

To conclude, passing reference should be made to the games which adults and children played in Greek antiquity. Literary evidence is scarce, but what survives indicates that games were popular among all social classes and age groups in a range of locations – at home, on streets, in market-places and exercise-grounds, thermal baths and taverns. Depictions are more common, and here we can note the complementary contexts in which representations of games and sporting activities were situated. Most frequently shown in painted scenes of the *symposium* is the *kottabos* game.

In *kottabos*, the dregs or drops of wine were flicked from the drinking cup at a target set in the middle of the room (Figure 9.4). Pride was taken, not

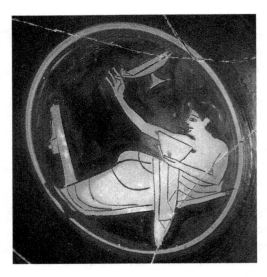

Figure 9.4 Man playing *kottabos*: Attic red-figure *kylix* (*c*.510 BCE), Athens, Greece (Ancient Agora Museum, Athens; photo by Μαρούας, CC BY-SA 3.0, http://creativecommons.org/licenses/by-sa/3.0, or CC-BY-2.5, http://creativecommons.org/licenses/by/2.5, via Wikimedia Commons).

only in hitting the object, which usually was a small metal disk balanced on a lamp stand, but in the correct form of the throwing motion. A simpler form of the game was to hit a basin without spilling any wine, or the symposiasts could attempt to sink one or more small saucers floating in a basin of water. A more complicated version involved striking a small scale and bringing it into contact with a figure below. There were prizes, perhaps special cakes or kisses from a serving girl or boy, as well as penalties.[18] Athenaeus says that some took as much pride in playing *kottabos* as others did in hurling the javelin.[19]

Embedded in this popular pastime is a distillation of the term *athlos* – as concept and practice – with which we began this survey of sport and recreation in Greek antiquity. The competitive hierarchy by which the achievement of a single symposiast is recognized in relation to the assembled dinner-guests marks the game of *kottabos* as equivalent in broad terms to other endeavours (sporting or otherwise) whose end-point was socially rewarded and culturally valued. The transmission of these socio-cultural markers is represented in a scene painted on one of the slabs of a tomb found in the necropolis of Paestum, a Greek city in southern Italy (the Tomb of the Diver, *c*.470 BCE). Part of a decorative repertoire of images – depicting dancers, musicians, athletes and guests at the *symposium* – painted on the four slabs which comprise the burial place of an otherwise unknown individual living in the fifth century BCE, the scene showing one of the symposiasts throwing the dregs of his wine at a target foregrounds the game amidst associated activities of drinking (left) and male bonding (right). As the variety of vase-paintings, incised texts and graffiti sketches we have considered suggest, so this non-official tomb fresco formulates in visual *and* conceptual terms a competitive activity emblematic of ancient Greek culture as predominantly male and aristocratic – a pastime which was both convivial *and* agonistic, both a privileged entertainment *and*

SPORT

a shared cultural tradition. Whether depicting athletic event, equestrian race, no-holds-barred martial contest or recreational pastime, representations of ancient Greek sport in non-official contexts enhance our understanding of the historical, religio-political and socio-cultural meanings imbued in these activities by men and women living in the ancient Greek world.

Rome

Reference to sport in Roman antiquity pertains to terms with a variety of meanings, such as *otium* – what Cicero referred to as "leisure with dignity"[20] – and *ludi* ("games") – in essence, festivals with a strongly defined religious character. Like the Egyptian and Greek sources we have already considered, Roman literature, art and epigraphy reveal a sporting culture resonating with energy and enthusiasm, if less intensely related to issues of personal status or social prestige. Along with a broad spectrum of recreational pastimes – ball games, board games, horseback riding, hunting and fishing, running, wrestling and boxing – the surviving evidence records competitive activities such as beast hunts, chariot racing and gladiatorial combat. Unlike the Greeks, however, freeborn Roman citizens and ex-slaves generally avoided participation in public competition, nor did they subscribe to the practice of competing naked. In fact, where (as we have seen) sporting achievement (*athlos*) influenced the social standing and reputation of Greek athletes, in Rome physical activity was regarded much more as a constructive or pleasurable use of spare time – particularly for the elite and economically secure sub-elite classes. In general, competitive activity in ancient Rome was – in modern parlance – a "spectator sport".

As a result of this culturally specific propensity to watch rather than participate in organized physical competition, the range of graffiti pertaining to sporting events and recreational activity in the Roman world is proportionally significant in comparison with the Egyptian and Greek sources of evidence. This, of course, is not to say that the extant record is any less fragmentary or lacunose. So, too, a percentage of messages and drawings is similarly oblique to modern interpretation or simply opaque in terms of meaning or sensibility. What we can say is this: the traces of informal inscribing practices which speak directly to us about Roman sport and recreation dissolve the philosophical boundaries associated with types of *otium* based on social status. To be clear, Pliny the Younger distinguished a dichotomy between the actions of different social classes when free from the demands of work and other professional social duties. For the first/second-century CE lawyer, author and statesman – and other writers of his or earlier times – the elite had a responsibility during their moments of leisure to produce something worthwhile for the benefit of the wider community. The lower classes, however, will only ever gravitate to unproductive or "vulgar" amusements.[21] In other words, mass entertainments – what came to be known as spectacles

203

(*spectacula*) of various kinds – were an appropriate pastime for the *populus* (the ordinary people); meaningful leisure activity displaying social responsibility was the purview of the elite *only*. The record of graffiti texts and drawings record another reality entirely: a class-inclusive, common leisure culture which, at least in principle, even included the slave population.

One of the competitive activities which is most readily familiar as a Roman sporting event *and* which also reflects the conceptual tension between idealized perspectives on popular leisure and historical reality is gladiatorial combat (*munera*). What we in the modern age think of as a quintessentially Roman entertainment was, in its earliest form, something else entirely – an Etruscan custom which constituted gladiators fighting at funerals in honour of the deceased. The earliest reference to the Roman adoption of this custom speaks about gladiators appearing at the funeral of a certain Brutus Pera in 264 BCE.[22] By the late republic, the traditional relationship between funerals and *munera* began to disentangle – from 42 BCE on, gladiatorial combats featured at official games (*ludi*); and after the death of Julius Caesar the association of *munera* and *ludi* was officially regulated throughout the empire.[23] Usually staged in amphitheatres, gladiatorial games were adopted enthusiastically throughout Italy, the Roman west *and* the Greek east.

The archaeological record of Pompeii provides crucial insight into the world of gladiators. Even more useful, non-official epigraphic testimony opens a unique window on how combatants made sense of their role in society and what spectators thought about those men who fought in the arena. Inscribed on columns in the peristyle of a building near the city's amphitheatre (V.5.3) is a large number of graffiti which reflect the utility of such markings as sources of information about gladiators at Pompeii.

G9.4   "Chariot fighter [*essedarius*]."

G9.5   "28 July. Florus won at Nuceria. 15 August, won at
Herculaneum."   (*CIL* IV. 4299)

G9.6   "Rusticus Malius: 12 fights, 11 wins. Marcus Terentius: 3
fights, 3 wins."   (*CIL* IV.4302)

G9.7   "Felix, belonging to Cassius [name of his owner/trainer or
training school]. 13 fights, 13 wins. Florus, belonging to
Octavius. 14 fights, 14 wins."   (*CIL* IV.4378)

G9.8   "Girls' 'sigh' – Thracian fighter (*thraex*), Celadus, belonging to
Octavus: 3 fights, 3 wins."   (*CIL* IV.4342 = *ILS* 5142a)

G9.9   "Celadus, Thracian fighter – girls' pride."
        (*CIL* IV.4345 = *ILS* 5142b)

SPORT

G9.10 "Crescens the net fighter (*retiarius*), doctor ... of girls in the
night, in the morning, and at other times."   (*CIL* IV.4353)

G9.11 "Samus, the pseudo-Gallic fighter (*murmillo*): 1 fight, 1 win.
The same horseback-and-sword fighter (*eques*) lives here."
(*CIL* IV.4420)

When these inscriptions were first sighted in excavations of Region V during
the late nineteenth century, it appeared that the texts were written by local
inhabitants of the city who enjoyed events staged at the amphitheatre and
therefore pertained to gladiators fighting in such games. However, after the
discovery of the message which states that Samus, a *murmillo* and *eques*,
"lived" in this building (G9.11), it seems irrefutable that these texts were
scratched by the gladiators themselves. Of course, we should not assume
that this was a residential facility for arena combatants along the same lines
as the *ludus.* Incised on the white plastered wall of what may have been a
dining space, the reference to Samus' situation appears to the left of another
graffito which lists various commodities (wine, cheese, firewood, olive oil,
onions). It could be that Samus spent a good deal of time in this building,
but might have resided elsewhere. If that is the correct interpretation, then
it is perhaps more appropriate to regard the building in which these graffiti
were scratched as the equivalent to the headquarters of a gladiator's guild or
collegium.

Following common inscribing practice, the athletes occupying this place
wrote their messages with a stylus on columns plastered in the so-called Third
Style, suggesting that the inscriptions were made between the age of Augustus and 63 CE. Over 140 graffiti on 24 peristyle columns provide information about gladiator types – esse(darius) (G9.5), tr(aex) (G9.8, 9), mur(millo)
(G9.11), ret(iarius) (G9.10), eq(ues) (G9.11) – and the names either of the
fighters' owners/trainers or of the schools (*ludi*) where they learned the
physical skills and strategies of arena combat according to their individual
style of fighting – Appuleius, Bal(onius), Cassius (G9.7), Clod(ius), Jul(ianus),
Marcus, and so on.

In addition to this valuable historical information, it is interesting to note
that the records of fights and wins – represented as two numbers sepa-
rated by a sign (i.e. -,), >, | or the letter C) standing for *coronae* ("victories",
"wins") – are almost universally equal in denomination; nothing like the more
formal attestations of gladiators' careers on tombstone inscriptions, where
the number of fights is usually greater than the number of wins. One of the
two exceptions is the record of Rusticus Malius (G9.5: XII>XI = 12 fights, 11
wins). The possibility that the men who met in this house and fought in the
amphitheatre at Pompeii – as well as elsewhere in the local region (G9.5) –
wished to maintain a certain reputation among their companion fighters is
confirmed by the acclamations of Celadus the *traex* (G9.8, 9) and Crescens the

205

GRAFFITI IN ANTIQUITY

retiarius (G9.10), amounting almost to the ancient equivalent of Italian *braggadocio*. The implications regarding issues of sexuality and erotic representation suggested by these latter messages will be explored later (Chapter 11).

G9.12 "Faustus, slave of Ithacus, Neronian, at the amphitheatre. Priscus, Neronian, fought 6 previous matches. He won. Herennius, who is freed, fought 18 previous matches. He died." (*CIL* IV.1421)

Graffiti drawings of gladiators have been detected in many areas of Pompeii. Unlike the texts scratched in the House of the Gladiators (V.5.3), a considerable number of graphic markings provide spectator views of activities in the arena. As one of a broad range of possible examples, a scene found in the peristyle of the House of the Labyrinth (VI.9.10) captures the essence of these drawings – more often than not, as in this case (G9.12), with accompanying explanatory text.[24]

Taking image and text together, the inscribing artist has set out for viewing three related moments during the course of a spectacle event at Pompeii's amphitheatre. To the left, we can see what appears to be the president of the games, seated in a ceremonial chair on a raised platform. He is looking out over the combat taking place in the central vignette of the tableau, between Priscus (left) and Herennius (right). We know that Herennius' days are numbered. Although a veteran of the arena, the superscript above the helmet his figure wears indicates his fate by the single letter P – the abbreviation for the Latin term *periit*, meaning "he perished". The fact that Herennius' shield lies on the ground before Priscus – who is identified as V, or *vicit* ("he conquered") – corrobates the *murmillo*'s fate.

Another fighter – a *retiarius*, carrying a trident – is shown leaving the presidential podium. This individual may well be the Faustus whose name is inscribed in large letters above the tableau, forming part of what could be described as the drawing's caption. Given that the type of gladiator called "Neronian" is known to have been trained in the imperial *ludus* at Capua, it is reasonable to identify the *retiarius* descending the platform stairs as Faustus. More likely than not, the implication is that he has just finished an audience with the individual presiding over the games, perhaps after winning in a previous encounter not shown here. In any event, the net fighter's (Faustus') trident points in the direction of a third figure standing to the right of the podium. He is wearing a tunic and brandishing a staff, and is almost certainly the referee or adjudicator of the match currently reaching its climax. To the extreme right of the scene, another arbiter – also wearing a tunic and holding a staff – is shown.

Graffiti of this kind can be found in a variety of locations at Pompeii: the exterior facades of public buildings near the Forum, the religious and theatrical precincts, and the amphitheatre itself; the walls of the public areas

206

– entrance-halls, dining rooms – and private spaces – the bedrooms (*cubicula*) of house-owners and sleeping annexes (*cellae*) of house-slaves, and even the columns of peristyle courtyards – of elite and non-elite domestic residences; and, as we have seen, the walls of gladiators' quarters inside the training schools for combatants and hunters near the amphitheatre.[25]

Although plentiful at Pompeii, the frequency of gladiatorial drawings (with or without textual commentary) in other parts of the Mediterranean attests to the widespread popularity of armed physical combat in the Roman world. Graffiti depicting all manner of activities and accessories to combat – fighter types, different weapons and protective gear worn by combatants, and the variety of wild animals stalked in arena hunts – have been found in locations as far removed as Aphrodisias and Pergamon in the Greek East and Magdalensburg, Dura-Europos and Timgad along the European, Asian and African frontiers; as close by as Herculaneum and Stabia; and as central to imperial power as Rome and Ostia. A recently restored section of the only internal passageway in the Colosseum has yielded graffiti like the example below, showing a heavily armed fighter in close combat with a net fighter (Figure 9.5).

Also found throughout Pompeii, one of the more common types of "painted inscription" – the usual term denoting this category of non-official textual message is *dipinti* – is closely linked with the gladiatorial graffiti: the announcement of games (*edicta munerum*).

Figure 9.5 Heavily armed gladiator and net-fighter, Colosseum, Rome.

GRAFFITI IN ANTIQUITY

G9.13 "Twenty pairs of gladiators belonging to Decimus Lucretius
– Celer wrote [this] – Satrius Valens, perpetual priest of Nero
Caesar, son of Augustus [i.e. Claudius], and twenty pairs of
gladiators belonging to Decimus Lucretius Valens, his son, will
fight at Pompeii on the sixth, fifth, fourth, third and second
days before the Ides of April [i.e. 8, 9, 10, 11 and 12 April].
There will be a regular hunt and awnings. Aemilius Celer wrote
[this] on his own by the moon."   (*CIL* IV.3882 = *ILS* 5145)

These painted notices advertised the giving and organization of forthcoming games in Pompeii's amphitheatre, including the date, the giver, the type of show to be exhibited (gladiatorial combat, wild beast fight, athletic show), and additional attractions for the audience (provision of awning, sprinkling of water) (Figure 9.6). The Lucretii Valentes were a prominent family in Pompeii, and the father and son identified in this *dipinto* (G9.13) gave a number of lavish entertainments in the amphitheatre from 50 CE on.[26] We can know the general timing of these (and subsequent) games from an incidental historical detail implied by the inscription. The father is identified as "perpetual priest" (*flamen perpetuus*) of Nero as Caesar, a position created by the emperor Claudius after Nero's adoption, giving us the *terminus post quem* 50 CE.

Another historical detail can further revise our understanding of when these games might have taken place. Tacitus records a riot taking place in the Pompeian amphitheatre in the year 59 CE.[27] Subsequently, the Roman Senate prohibited gladiatorial shows at Pompeii for a period of ten years. As it is possible that Nero may have relaxed this judgement by 64 CE,[28] we can note that the various games given by the Lucretii Valentes occurred between Nero's adoption by Claudius and his assassination (50–68 CE), excluding those years during which the senatorial ban operated without imperial intervention (60–64 CE).

Interestingly, a graphic image with related text which we encountered earlier (Chapter 2) may provide some indication of how the local population felt

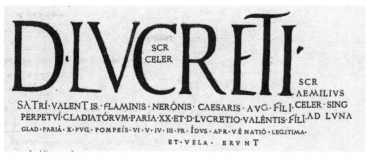

Figure 9.6 Wall poster (*edictum munera*) advertising gladiatorial games and a hunt (*CIL* IV.3884), western side of IX.8, Pompeii, Italy.

208

about the events that transpired in and around the Pompeian amphitheatre in 59 CE.

Inscribed on the exterior wall of VI.ix.6 (the so-called House of the Dioscuri) as a drawing with related text, the graffiti drawing in question depicts a man, probably a gladiator, equipped with a crested helmet and a light oblong shield, wearing a fighter's waistband, and holding a palm in his right hand. To the man's right is a larger palm. The writing below the stairs down which the triumphant gladiator is descending (G2.16, p. 38) makes sense if we read it in relation to the account of the riot in Tacitus. Here we learn that rivalry between inhabitants of the colonies of Nuceria and Pompeii, attending a gladiatorial show (given by a reputed ne'er-do-well, Livineius Regulus), "led to abuse, stone-throwing, and the drawing of weapons". According to Tacitus, the subsequent bloodshed and deadly violence resulted in a general prohibition on any gathering in the amphitheatre and the dissolution of illegal associations. Therefore, the graffitist may be observing, perhaps with more than a casual undertone of bitterness, how the slaughter of Nucerians may have been nothing more than a Pyrrhic victory for the Pompeians. Though the intention is unclear, the image to the left of the victorious gladiator may show an arbiter charged with adjudicating arena contests being joined on the official podium by a visiting dignitary – another echo, perhaps, of the fateful events of 59 CE and their aftermath.

We also learn from the *edictum munera* (G9.13) about the type of entertainment to be exhibited – an extensive gladiatorial programme of combat and a wild beast hunt (*uenatio*). We are also informed about attractions appealing to the audience's desire for comfort in the warmer months: namely, the provision of cloth awnings (*uela*), designed to limit the effects of prolonged exposure to sunlight for the duration of the five-day *munera*.

The degree to which arena entertainments like the April *munera* of the Lucretii Valentes comprised an integral facet of Pompeii's cultural life is also reflected by the existence of professional sign-writers. These are the same individuals responsible for painting the election notices (*programmata*) we considered earlier (Chapter 8). Between the letters C and R of the name LVCRETI in the first line of the advertisement one can see "Celer wrote [this]". To the right of the inscription, one can also read in translation "Aemilius Celer wrote [this] on his own at night [lit. by means of the moon]". Aemilius Celer is known to us from another official *dipinto* – a *programmatum* (on the exterior wall just to the left of IX.6.8) supporting L. Statius Receptus as duovir for administering justice (*iure dicundo*) (*CIL* IV.3775) – and two brief painted inscriptions on the walls of the *insula* in the region adjacent to Receptus' election poster.[29] Celer not only informs us that he is a neighbour (*uicinus*) of the candidate; he also observes in no uncertain terms what will befall anyone who defaces his handiwork – "O you hateful person who erases [this], become ill". The private *dipinti* refer directly to Aemilius Celer, giving his *praenomen* as Publius, and indicating his place of residence (IX.8.7).

GRAFFITI IN ANTIQUITY

Given Celer's claim to local residence in the *programmatum*, these *dipinti* are likely painted by the *scriptor* himself.

Need for the services of individuals who painted posters advertising games (*scriptores*) reflects a developed appetite – locally, of course, but also more broadly, in the various communities of the Vesuvian region – for the latest information regarding forthcoming gladiatorial matches and other activities to be staged in the amphitheatre.

Two related graffiti texts incised on the northern wall of Pompeii's Basilica speak to a sporting activity which is at one and the same time familiar and exotic.

G9.14   "Epaphra is not a *trigon*-scorer."   (*CIL* IV.1926)

G9.15   "Let Amianthus, Epaphra, and Tertius play [ball] – along with Hedystus. Iucundus from Nola is the ball-boy, Citus keeps score. So does Stacus."[30]

The activity to which these texts refer is a ball-game called *trigon* – also the name of the ball. We know from the literary sources that *trigon* required three players, standing in such a manner that they appeared to occupy the corners of a triangle-shaped playing space. We learn most about the game from a letter written by the philosopher and rhetorician Seneca to a certain Lucilius:

> If you want to study, quiet is not nearly as necessary as you might think. Here I am, surrounded by all kinds of noise (my lodgings overlook a bath-house). Conjure up in your imagination all the sounds that make one hate one's ears. I hear the grunts of muscle-men exercising and jerking those heavy weights around; they are working hard, or pretending to. I hear their sharp hissing when they release their pent breath. If there happens to be a lazy fellow content with a simple massage I hear the slap of hand on shoulder; you can tell whether it's hitting a flat or a hollow. If a ball-player comes up and starts calling out his score, I'm done for.
>
> (Seneca, *Letters* 56.1–2)

It is reasonably certain that the game to which Seneca refers is *trigon*. According to the beleaguered intellectual, the playing area is located in the porticoed exercise yard (*palaestra*) of the bath-house adjacent to his apartment building. It is possible that the game of *trigon* featured in the Basilica graffito above (G9.15) may have taken place in the so-called *sphaeristerium* ("ball-court")[31] which has been identified hypothetically in the *palaestra* of the Stabian Baths (VII.1.8).[32] The ball-player (*trigonalis*) whose cries disturb Seneca's contemplation (or perhaps interrupt his afternoon nap) would seem

210

to be counting out his own score. This may have been unusual, however, since the same graffito indicates that a certain Citus was an official counter; and the graffito relating to Epaphra (G9.14) declares that he is *not* the *trigon*-scorer (*pilicrepus*), implying that someone else (in this case, Citus) was.

Usefully, the satirical poet Martial gives a clue to the manner in which the individuals named in the graffiti played this game – under the heading "The Three-Cornered Game": "If you are skilful enough to strike me with rapid left-hand blows, I am yours. You are not sufficiently skilled, so, clown, return the ball" (Martial, *Epigrams* 14.46). It would seem from Martial's observation that striking an opponent was one of the game's objects, as was catching the ball left-handed the mark of a skilled player. Although the rules of the game remain obscure, its popularity is not in doubt. Indeed, the longer graffito suggests that Pompeii hosted a number of *trigon* contests. Certainly, there were sufficient players to warrant at least two teams. Whatever the outcome of the local competition, the game to which the inscribed commentary refers saw Jucundus Nolans as the early aggressor but Amianthus named as the eventual victor.

Graffiti texts and images like these prove extremely useful as indicators of the socio-cultural significance of references to sport and recreation. To round off this survey of graffiti pertaining to arena activity, let us revisit the Palatine Paedagogium – the training school for imperial slaves which we encountered earlier (Chapter 5). The topographical and architectural relationship between the Paedagogium and adjacent Circus Maximus – the largest stadium in the city of Rome and the scene of chariot-racing and other mass entertainments – helps to explain references to chariot racing and gladiatorial combats in the graffiti found on the school's walls (Figure 5.2).[33] On the southern wall of Room 5, a palm was etched; and, on the western wall of Room 6, there survives an outline that resembles the figure of an athlete.[34] Given the proximity of a building described by Dionysius of Halicarnassus as "one of the most beautiful and admirable structures in Rome", which Pliny the Elder estimated was able to seat 250,000 persons, it was likely that the slaves receiving instruction (*paedagogiani*) participated in some fashion in the Circus Games (*ludi circenses*), gladiatorial contests (*munera gladiatoria*) and animal hunts (*venationes*) staged within its monumental spaces.[35] Aside from those in the front row, along a portion of the podium wall reserved for senators, and other seats for the non-senatorial elite (*equites*) who sat behind them, the seats were not segregated as they were in the Colosseum and the theatre.[36] As Ovid and Juvenal elaborate, men and women could sit together.[37] The socially invisible but necessary physical presence of imperial and aristocratic *paedagogiani* accompanying their masters and mistresses to the races, combats, wild animal hunts, athletic events and processions would not have been exceptional.

G9.16   "Victor."

GRAFFITI IN ANTIQUITY

G9.17 "Gordius."

G9.18 "Gordianus [and] Isapeodoros – win!"

Given the very visible and prominent position of the emperor and imperial elite at public spectacles in the Circus, it is not surprising to find twelve citations of the personal name Victor on the Paedagogium walls (G9.16).[38] In the same way that this name connotes a symbolic link between Circus performance and household display, graffiti drawings of palm-bearing horses and combat between gladiators of different types – the net-fighter (*retiarius*) and sword-and-shield fighter (*secutor*) – retain a degree of detail reflecting eye-witness acquaintance with chariot-racing and gladiatorial fighting. To these can be added the following items, all scratched on the north-western wall of Room 8: the bust of a charioteer, with palms and boxes, underneath the name Gordius (G9.17); the names Gordianus and Isapeodoros, followed by an invocation in Greek to win (G9.18); and another image of a gladiator.[39] The drawing and inscription relating to the charioteer may indicate the two-horse chariot-driver (*auriga*) Gordius, favourite of the emperor Elagabalus; certainly the head-gear in the form of a helmet confirm the figure as a chariot-driver in the Circus, and the palm-branches and boxes must represent the charioteer's prizes.[40] The inscription "Gordianus and Isapeodoros – win!" (*Gordianus | Isapeodoros | nika*) appears under the bust of the charioteer identified above as Gordius. It is impossible to determine a clear relationship here, nor is it feasible to identify specifically the named individuals, but the directive to prevail draws out in the graffitist a significant level of engagement with the contest, whether gladiatorial or chariot-racing. With respect to the final image of a gladiator, the figure wears heavy armour, the shield is large and rectangular, and the helmet is characteristic of a *secutor*: that is, without a plume and with a long neck-flap that protects the nape. Perhaps both legs were protected by protectors or greaves (*ocrea*), but these cannot be seen clearly in the facsimile of the drawing. Again, close acquaintance with the minutiae of Circus *spectacula* was essential.

Jonathan Edmundson recently argued that *ludi circenses* and *munera gladiatoria* were occasions for articulating the component elements of the Roman social order.[41] What graffiti that treat these occasions suggest – the texts and images inscribed and painted on the walls of the Palatine Paedagogium and urban façade of Roman Pompeii, as well as the miscellaneous non-official residue throughout the Mediterranean – is that persons occupying a subordinate position in the hierarchy of social relations drew satisfaction from the public performance of individuals of the same class and condition, and took care that their representations preserved in name and figurative detail the identity, status and endeavour of enslaved gladiators and charioteers. By recording events and individuals in this way, the inscribing population – whether slave or freed – commemorated the integrity of slave performances

212

SPORT

in the Circus Maximus that could often result in physical harm or occasionally death. Rather than relegating the performers of public spectacles to the conceptual margins of Roman society, such graffiti dispense with conventional stigmatizing associations to celebrate the duty of gladiators and charioteers and commemorate the dignity adhering to honourable service.

To complete our introduction to expressions of sport and recreation in Roman antiquity, the corpus of graffiti at Pompeii once again comes to our aid. Texts and images scattered throughout the city reveal a number of interests held in common by a cross-section of the Pompeian population. The following inscriptions provide some indication of the more popular diversions. The first type (G9.19) is a better-known example of the diverse graphic games particularly favoured by the ancient Romans.

G9.19   "ROMA | OLIM | MILO | AMOR."   (*CIL* IV.8297)

This is a so-called "magic square", comprising two words – *olim*: once; *amor*: love – and two names – *Roma*: Rome; *Milo*: a male name – that may be read vertically in columns from top to bottom, horizontally in rows from left to right, or in reverse. The meaning is not necessarily coherent – "Rome once Milo love". Pleasure is taken from the recognition, arrangement and alignment of word-patterns.[42]

Another example of this very particular arrangement of words is found not only scratched on Pompeii's walls but elsewhere in the Roman world, including Conimbriga, a Roman colony in the province of Lusitania, Corinium Dobunnorum (modern Cirencester), a fortress town in the province of Britannia, and Dura-Europos.

G9.20   "SATOR | AREPO | TENET | OPERA | ROTAS."   (*CIL* IV.8623)

Readable in four directions – top to bottom, bottom to top, left to right, and right to left – this five-line magic square has been interpreted in any number of imaginative ways. Literally, the text can be translated as "Arepo the sower guides the wheels by his work" (G9.20). If hard pressed, this may suggest an obscure agricultural origin for the word-play. However, it brings us no closer to a secure meaning for the palindrome. Because the letters could be re-arranged to spell the phrase [A(lpha)] PATER NOSTER [O(mega)] – that is, "Our Father, beginning and end" – late nineteenth- and early twentieth-century scholarship associated the SATOR AREPO magic square as an early Christian sign of recognition. The fact that this configuration of letters appears inscribed on visible surfaces in a number of medieval Christian contexts – e.g. the Catholic Cathedral (Duomo) in Siena (thirteenth century CE to the present), the Benedictine Abbey of St. Peter ad Oratorium (seventh to fifteenth centuries CE) – implies that the PATER NOSTER explanation may spring from a retrojected perspective.

GRAFFITI IN ANTIQUITY

In addition to the "magic square" type (in Latin or Greek), Pompeians enjoyed palindromes imitating literary verses. For example:

G9.21   "Roma tibi subito motibus ibit amor."   (*CIL* IV.8297)

What is interesting about the composition of this non-official text is its two-fold nature: the form and meaning of the verse – "Rome, to you love will come suddenly with passion" (G9.21) – conform neatly with expectations of lyric poetry dealing with erotic themes; and reconfiguring the Latin text from right to left, contrary to normal reading practice, produces the same result. In terms of function, this palindromic construction points explicitly to the elegant wit and creative acuity of the person who crafted the mirror-verse in the first place – and the playful taste of the inscriber who copied it and the audience who found it aesthetically pleasing or intellectually diverting. It is impossible, of course, to determine if the latter might also have been responsible for producing the composition.

Other inscriptions exemplify how graffitists in Pompeii sought to combine words and images to produce striking and appealing representations of familiar identities and activities. A graffito comprising three words – identified by the *CIL* editor as [*th*]*alassae fusa optatus* – scratched into the surface of a wall in a private dwelling (*CIL* IV.4225) imitates a sea-going vessel of some kind, with oars, mast and a distinctive bow. In this instance, words and image combine to create a coherent whole. The first word is a Latinized version of a Greek term; the second and third words are adjectives. Though the grammar is poor, when declined and translated, the syntax of the *graffito* could give the meaning, "Of/to the sea, broad and longed-for". Pompeii's geographical proximity to the coastline of the Bay of Naples in ancient times would increase the likelihood of maritime imagery as a natural and recognizable means for expressing identity or sentiment. Another well-known *graffito* (*CIL* IV.4755) incorporates the name of a certain Crescens, whose occupation is registered as "architect", within the picture of a ship.

The inscription illustrated in Figure 9.7 is a four-line Latin poem found near the entrance of a house close to the Nolan Gate. It is a complex graffito, not only rendered in the curving shape of a snake, but conceived so that each line of the poem begins with a sibilant "s". The Latin text reads: "[Ser] pentis lusus si qui sibi forte notauit, | Sepumius iuuenis quos fac(i)t ingenio, | Spectator scaenae siue es studiosus e[q]uorum: | sic habes [lanc]es se[mp]er ubiq[ue pares]." The poem can be translated as follows:

G9.22   "If anyone by chance has noticed the snake game, in which
        young Sepumius has shown his skill, whether you are a specta-
        tor of the theatre or fond of horses, may you always have equal
        balance in any place whatever."   (*CIL* IV.1595)

214

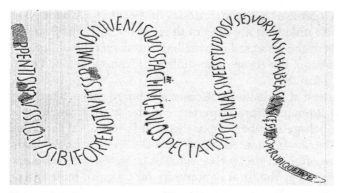

Figure 9.7 Serpent game graffito (*CIL* IV.1595), exterior wall, IV.5 (near the Nolan Gate), Pompeii, Italy.

Sepumius' "skill" would seem to have involved physical prowess of some kind, and may have required a display of virtuosity in completing a circuitous course of competitive activity requiring gymnastic balance. Whatever the nature of the "snake game", Sepumius was clearly its rising star, admired and envied for his ability.

In relation to the "snake game", it is not hard to imagine the exchange of money based on the outcome of Sepumius' physical exertions. Although we cannot identify this activity as anything more than a recreational pastime dependent on the skill of the player(s), the literary record depicts the Romans as a game-playing culture, whether or not hazarding a bet on the outcome was involved. Cicero refers to *alea* or "dice", describing how four dice – each with four flat surfaces and two uneven, rounded sides; the numbers I and VI marked on two opposite sides, III and IV on the other, and II and V missing – were thrown out of a cup onto a table made for the purpose, with a slightly elevated rim to prevent the dice from rolling off. The best throw was called "Venus" or "Venereus", the worst "*canis*".[43]

Other games in which success did not depend on luck, but in large measure on skill, included board-games, two of which are known to have been extremely popular at Rome – XII *scripta* and *latrunculi*.

Like the Egyptian game of *senet*, the board game translated as "game of 12 markings" (*ludus duodecim scriptorium* or XII *scripta*) was a loosely related variant of modern backgammon – though the configuration of the boards used to play both games constitutes the only explicit similarity between Egyptian and Roman pastimes. Characterized by a board arranged in three rows of twelve spaces, each row divided in the centre by a floral design enclosed in a circle, XII *scripta* used three dice and each player began with fifteen pieces. Little more is known about specific game-play. The other well-known Graeco-Roman game – *latrunculi* or *latrones*, the "game of brigands" (*ludus latruculorum*) – appears to have resembled chess or draughts, and is generally

215

accepted to have been a game of military tactics. A first-century CE panegyric in praise of an otherwise unknown member of the Piso family (Laus Pisonis) tells us about the skills of the deceased playing ball (*lusus pilae*) and *latrunculi* – in regard to the latter, the anonymous author provides a detailed outline of the game's main features.

The popularity – indeed ubiquity in some cases – of board games like these as an essential part of Roman cultural experience in the ancient Mediterranean is confirmed by a large number of playing boards inscribed on even, durable surfaces in heavily frequented urban spaces. These game boards (*tabulae lusoriae*) were often set up by civic officials or wealthy benefactors to satisfy a need expressed by the local community for purpose-built entertainment facilities. On game boards which survive in imperial Ephesus, the grid-pattern indicates that XII *scripta* was popular in the Roman East, either incised on dedicated gaming tables cut from marble or etched in the shaded areas between the columns of colonnaded streets or meeting spaces.

When this need was not addressed – either to the extent demanded of the resident population or because leisure activities did not always take priority in determining how best to allocate public funding in certain parts of the Roman world – individuals took on themselves the responsibility of providing for those wishing to do so the means to occupy their leisure time in this manner. Almost a hundred game boards are reported to have been carved on the horizontal surfaces of buildings in the Roman Forum. Many of these still survive as visible reminders of what will have been a hot-spot of gaming practice in the heart of the megalopolitan Roman urban landscape (Figure 9.8).

Figure 9.8 Game board (*tabula lusoria*): Latrones ("game of brigands"), Basilica Julia, Roman Forum, Rome, Italy.

FINAL THOUGHTS

An overview of non-official references to sporting activities and recreational practices in antiquity could only ever touch on the breadth of material which survives into the modern age. Nonetheless, it should be clear that the informal markings considered in this chapter reveal a diversity of social interests and cultural experiences across the ancient world. Reflecting a wide range of physical and intellectual skills, the catalogue of competitive events and non-competitive pastimes finds liberal and enthusiastic expression in the informal texts and images scratched or painted on every available surface from the 1st cataract of pharaonic Egypt to the desert frontier of imperial Dura-Europos. Whether running, jumping or riding a horse; dancing, singing or playing music; throwing a ball, discus or javelin; hunting, fishing or netting birds; playing *senet*, *kottabos* or XII *scripta*; or watching athletic performances, chariot races and gladiator fights – for all classes of population, the celebration of festivals, apart from their religious and political meaning, was a central aspect of leisure activity and provided a regulated context for the pursuit of individual achievement or collective entertainment. While not diminishing the occasions for casual participation in or observation of sport or recreation, graffiti in antiquity situate the impulse to play or compete very much within a calendar of civic events and a variety of public spaces – the stadium or arena; temple or forum; colonnade or thoroughfare; playing area or game board. Howsoever we reconstruct antiquity, one thing is certain: sport was integral to the way the ancients lived and played.

CHAPTER 10

COMMERCE

Toil, little donkey, in the manner in which I have toiled, and it will benefit you. *(Graf. Pal.* I.289)

COMMERCE AND TRADE IN THE ANCIENT MEDITERRANEAN

Economic life in antiquity revolved around the production, storage and transport of food. As a result, pre-modern social structures were in many senses based on agriculture: in particular, the kind of agriculture known as subsistence farming – crop farming and animal husbandry. Geographically distinctive from other areas in the ancient world, the Mediterranean comprised numerous regions suitable for growing crops and raising livestock, located for the most part along the coastal fringes and on suitable stretches of low, flat land. The prevailing weather conditions in the summer months proved beneficial for sea travel. Settled populations of differing sizes and larger towns and cities – for example, Mersa Gawasis (pharaonic Egypt), Baranis (Ptolemaic Egypt); Sidon (Phoenicia), Miletus (Asia Minor), Athens (Greece), Caere (Italy), Carthage (North Africa) – acted as focal points for economic activity. This activity included both the purchase and sale in local or regional contexts of provisions, livestock and associated commodities; and opportunities for trade across territorial boundaries. Colonial outposts and established settlements were also places conducive to the production of material culture on a large scale. Responding to these developing economic conditions, urbanized communities hugging the coastal regions began to construct harbour facilities. With stable crop yields limited to appropriate land on the plains, higher ground was reserved increasingly for livestock and hunting wild animals – legally or otherwise. Forests generating wood used in building and carpentry were located typically in boreal and temperate climes and with a higher incidence of annual rainfall – on the western slopes of mountain ranges and locations close to the coast.

COMMERCE

Although its historical significance was recognized very early on, economic history remains an underdeveloped study in modern scholarship. This state of affairs is due primarily to the nature of the source tradition. In general, the literary record glossed over – or ignored outright – issues which were fundamentally economic in nature.[1] With few exceptions, any technical monographs concentrating on particular aspects of the ancient economy have been lost. On the subjects of agriculture, non-monetary trade and non-reciprocal commodity exchange (gifts; goods plunder in times of war; theft through piracy or robbery), we find references in Homer, Hesiod and Xenophon.[2] Aristotle refers to specialist literature no longer extant and investigates living things, especially animals, central to the theoretical study of nature; Theophrastus speaks authoritatively about plant classification according to their practical uses.[3] Roman writers like Cato, Columella and Varro write about Graeco-Roman agricultural practices; and Varro mentions Greek specialist writers.[4] The Old Testament calls attention to early Phoenician (Sidonian) trading expeditions originating from the twin urban centres of Tyre and Ushu. The Jewish historian Flavius Josephus reconstructs elements of this history of maritime enterprise which arose in the eastern Mediterranean.[5] Mago, a second-century BCE writer from Carthage (a former Phoenician colony), produced an agricultural manual in the Punic language, translated into Latin and Greek and cited frequently in the works of Pliny the Elder and Cicero.

As it currently stands, then, it is most often archaeological data which adds to scholarly knowledge and understanding of commercial activity in the ancient world. That said, what we know about pre-modern trade in the Mediterranean is not limited to the literary and material record. In addition, numismatic sources (coins) *and* the epigraphic record – in particular, non-official inscriptions – shed valuable light on commercial terminology and practice in antiquity. For example, as the epigraph to this chapter and graffiti G10.1–4 below indicate, we can expect to find references to any number of economic agents and commercial transactions: the name and title of a scribe involved with income (grain) flowing into the temple of Amun-Re at Thebes from regional estates (Wadi el-Hôl, Dynasty XVIII); early fifth-century BCE trademarks on Attic neck-*amphorae* (Athens, *c*.500 BCE); early fourth-century BCE redistribution of Greek ceramics by Punic merchants (Spain, 375–350 BCE); an explanatory caption to a visual representation of a donkey turning a grain mill, productive staple of the ancient Mediterranean diet and one of antiquity's most-travelled commodities (Rome, second/third century CE); or the activities of the late imperial merchant and landlord Aurelius Nebouchelos, trader in agricultural products, wool and textiles (Dura-Europos, 235–40 CE).

G10.1   "The grain-accounting scribe of Amun, May."[6]

G10.2   *"6 kotylai ... 7 kotylai."*   (*SEG* 53.79)

219

GRAFFITI IN ANTIQUITY

G10.3   [Graeco-Punic alphanumerical pot-marks.]   (*SEG* 38.1038)

G10.4   "Aurelius Nebouchelos." [Prices for wine, barley, fleece, luxury garments].[7]   (*SEG* 50.1394)

Egypt

Confirmed in the archaeological record since the Neolithic period, commercial activity in North Africa operating between distant places – in other words, economic transactions not involving barter and distribution of property among neighbouring communities based on daily requirements – derived essentially from guaranteeing provision of certain material necessities (metal, building timber) not otherwise able to be obtained locally; and, in addition, on the elite imperative for quality goods, or whatever was needed for manufacturing such products.

Whatever the type and extent of trade in the ancient Egyptian world, durable commodities – bartered, purchased or gifted locally, or imported from other parts of North Africa or Eurasia – came to be understood as the property of individuals, families, communities or institutions. Concomitant with the development of the idea of ownership and all that entailed, methods of identifying the origins and owners of artisanal, commercial and utilitarian merchandise began to evolve. One of the most ubiquitous signifiers of property in pre-dynastic and pharaonic Egypt was the pot-mark.

Interpreted variously as indications of potters, owners, workshops, locations or administrative units, these graphic signs – lacking any phonetic implications, and therefore additional to representative and literate graffiti – were used throughout ancient Egyptian history. A sample of the extant source material reveals early dynastic pottery marks, numbering in the thousands, many incised before the ceramic vessels were fired. For example, bread moulds – easily recognizable in terms of fabric and manufacture – display distinctive pre-firing marks. Extremely common on sites throughout Old Kingdom Egypt, this vessel type has been unearthed in Naqada III (*c.*3200–3000 BCE) sites like Adaima (Upper Egypt) and Tell el-Iswid South (Lower Egypt).[8] Similarly, recent excavations have revealed a large number of pot-marks, incised on bread moulds, trays and several storage jars, identifying a Dynasty IV (*c.*2614–2464 BCE) food production area with bakery that serviced labourers working in a nearby alabaster stone quarry (al-Shaykh Sa'id, Upper Egypt).[9] Current research has amassed a preliminary database of over 3360 individual proto- and early dynastic pot-marks, revealing the degree to which this informal non-textual marking system conveyed meaning and function in relation to objects connected in one way or another with Egyptian commercial life.[10]

Evidence for this non-official inscribing practice appears in all periods of Egyptian history – from a paltry 17 pots among over 18,000 vessels recorded

220

COMMERCE

at the Dynasty XX site of Tell el-Rataba to numerous vessels from Deir el-Medina showing post-firing pot-marks. Intriguingly, many of these marks appear to belong to the same system of marks used by the village workmen in graffiti and administrative *ostraca*. In several respects, *ostraca* with marks may reflect more authentically than the hieratic records – which speak about supplies, the persons responsible for these, and other duties – the lived reality of the necropolis workmen.

Displaying a varying inventory of non-textual signs, these pot-marks inscribed essential economic notions of ownership and production on ceramic vessels. Though unremarkable in any aesthetic or conceptual sense, such marks conveyed meaning in similar ways to later and concurrent linguistic systems (hieroglyphic, hieratic), expressing notions of identity in relation to the production and consumption of commercial activity.

Since the third millennium BCE, Egyptian temples administered the bulk of economic activity, assigning responsibility for the organization of commercial duties and responsibilities to official state functionaries. In Egypt, despite the fact that the concept of alienable private property can be traced to the Old Kingdom at least, the individual with a proprietary claim over all productive farming land was the pharaoh. Throughout the historical period, Egyptian rulers bequeathed or assigned differing parcels of agricultural land and the associated labour to the temples, while preserving authority over institutional operations through their hand-picked officials. An example from New Kingdom times illustrates the extent to which temples were capable of producing large crop quotas and significant quantities of other goods. Recorded in an extensive document commissioned by his son, the so-called Great Harris Papyrus – also known as Papyrus Harris I – tells us that Ramesses III (*c.*1183–1152 BCE) donated to the temple of Amun in Thebes land equivalent to almost two and a half thousand square kilometres and an injection to the workforce of over 80,000 men. Other documentary and archaeological evidence confirms that Egyptian temples could possess estates distributed over a considerable extent, even in regions usurped by military force. These allotments were assigned by royal donation. Temple control of productive land in Egypt could only occur if approved by the pharaoh.

A graffito on a freestanding boulder at Wadi el-Hôl identifies one of the myriad of functionaries engaged in the administration of Egypt's temple economy. Dating to Dynasty XIX and the later years of Ramesses II's kingship (*c.*1233–1213 BCE), the inscription reads:

G10.5   "Made by the second priest of Amun, Roma, vindicated."[11]

Neatly carved into the irregular surface of a hard stone boulder close by the desert road rest area we have already encountered, the graffito belongs most likely to a well-known high priest of Amun, Roma, also called Roy. An official inscription – carved on a granitodorite statue found between the seventh and

221

eighth pylons in the Temple of Karnak – preserves an autobiographical record of Roma-Roy's duties: "Overseer of the [treasury] of Amun, overseer of the granary of Amun, overseer of the priests of all the gods, high priest of Amun."[12]

Another inscription – carved on the left side of a limestone statue found in the same place – reports that "Roy, true of voice ... was the chief overseer of works in Karnak, who gave every instruction to the craftsmen, who assessed knowledge, who was wise in skills."[13] On the right side of the same statue, Roma-Roy adds that he was "strong, vigilant, one effective for his lord, who made monuments in his domain, my heart assessing every work, seeking out what is beneficial for my august god."[14]

Cut expertly into an extremely difficult marking surface, the Wadi el-Hôl graffito confirms Roma-Roy's claims regarding his artisanal skills. Its location on the Western Theban desert road accords well with his administrative responsibilities as, we would expect, the well-travelled supervisor of Ramesses II's extensive temple estates.

Without the Nile river, of course, none of this would have been possible. In fact, Egyptian civilization more generally would not have existed as we know it; nor would it have been possible to stem the encroaching desertification of North Africa. Inhabited since the sixth millennium BCE, but only needing to support a population in the vicinity of hundreds of thousands during the pharaonic period, the habitable regions of the Nile valley included the Delta – apart from the marshes; the Fayum around Lake Moeris; a strip of land along the Nile up to the first cataract at Aswan – never exceeding 25 km in width, but often much narrower; and a few oases in the Western Desert. All in all, ancient Egypt comprised a few tens of thousands square kilometres of irrigated and thus habitable land. It should be clear, therefore, that the temple economy of ancient Egypt depended entirely on the Nile – and when the river failed to rise sufficiently high enough to cover the rich floodplain, or when it rose too much and inundated productive agricultural acreage, it caused economic hardship even during the most prosperous periods.

G10.6 "Year 3, first month of the second season, day 12, under the majesty of the King of Upper and Lower Egypt, Lord of the Two Lands, Usermare-Setepnamon – life, prosperity, health; Son of Re, Lord of the diadems, Osorkon (II) Siese-Meriamon, given life forever. The flood came on, in this whole land; it invaded the two shores as in the beginning. This land was in his power like the sea, there was no dyke of the people to withstand its fury. All the people were like birds upon its ..., the tempest ... his ..., suspended ... like the heavens. All the temples of Thebes were like marshes."[15]

Written in hieratic on an inner wall of the Luxor temple, a graffito records a contemporary account of a destructive inundation early in the rule of the

222

Dynasty XXII pharaoh Osorkon II (872–837 BCE). The inscription (G10.6) reveals the extent to which the Nile breached embankments constructed to prevent this kind of flooding and spread into the temple precinct. The harm this event wrought on the centrally organized and strictly controlled estates of Late Period Thebes – and, we might infer, elsewhere along the course of the Nile – was clearly significant enough for an eyewitness to express in writing his evident dismay. It is instructive to note that the inscriber chose to preserve his concern on the wall of a building integral to the state's institutional maintenance of agricultural production and distribution (the Luxor temple) – *and*, as we have discussed previously (Chapter 5), a monumental representation of the intrinsic relationship between the nominal owner of all productive land (Osorkon II) and those believed to control the rhythms of the Nile's annual cycle (the gods).

A variety of graffiti expresses the fragile nature of Egypt's dependence on the Nile as the source of its continuing economic prosperity during the pharaonic period. For example, a series of hieroglyphic texts inscribed at the Semna Gorge – the narrowest region of the Nile valley, located at the southern frontier of Upper Egypt (Second Cataract) – provides a register of unusually high flood-levels. Royal names recorded in association with each of these uncommon inundations – from Amenemhat III, the sixth ruler of Dynasty XII (*c.*1860–1814 BCE) to Amenemhat VI, seventh ruler of Dynasty XIII (*c.* early eighteenth century BCE) – indicate that this period of severe flooding continued for more than half a decade. The significant number of graffiti pertaining to the reign of Amenemhat III (17 inscriptions) and his successor (3 inscriptions) may be associated with the extraordinary engineering programme conducted during the last years of Dynasty XII and completed in the first decade of Dynasty XIII – namely, construction of a canal (16 km long, 1.5 km wide) and dam linking the Fayuum depression with the Nile. The massive body of water which resulted from this work, Lake Moeris (Qarun), could store almost 13 billion cubic metres of annual flood water. Contemporaneous with Amenemhat III's enormous infrastructure project, the graffiti recording exceptional Nile flood-levels in southern Egypt confirm the river's role as the foundation of the country's economy.

Apart from peaceful commerce, there was a role for organized military expeditions up the Nile from Egypt to Nubia in search of gold or systematic conquest with the aim of securing the required materials in the form of booty and tribute.

G10.7   "The royal acquaintance, Iif."[16]

G10.8   "The assault troops of the son of Re, Antef."[17]

G10.9   "The steward, Sobek."[18]

GRAFFITI IN ANTIQUITY

G10.10 "The chief of the house of recruits – life, stability and dominion; who lives in the praise of the king, the lord, Tem."[19]

G10.11 "[The god's father], beloved of [the god], hereditary prince, overseer of Upper Egypt, Tjauti, [says (?)]: [I] [have] made this for crossing this gebel, which the ruler of another nome had closed, [I] fought with [his] nome. I flew [?] ..."[20]

The inscriptions listed above speak directly to the far-reaching expeditions that traversed the desert regions bordering the Nile valley. Dating to some time prior to Dynasty VI and the end of the Old Kingdom period, the graffito nominating an otherwise unknown official as "royal acquaintance" (G10.7) may simply indicate that the Iif who inscribed the text on the bottom of a narrow rock overhang was in some way connected to the palace. However, given the similarity between the neat hieroglyphic scratches used here and a later Middle Kingdom title, it would appear that Iif was a functionary who assisted in communicating between the state's administrative hierarchy and other officials who supervised control of provincial affairs and lead expeditions. A pair of titles (G10.9–10) confirms the nature of the activity implied by Iif's terse statement. For example, based on comparison with an inscription recording another steward's activities in the desert south of Dakhlah (one of the western desert's seven oases, 350 km from the Nile), which reads "In the year 23 of the Kingdom: the steward Mery, he goes up to search for the oasis-dwellers",[21] Sobek's duties as "steward" (G10.10) would quite possibly have included managing hostile incursions of oasis dwellers that affected adversely trading movements in the western desert. Similarly, the early Middle Kingdom graffito inscribed by Tem (G10.11) attests to an expedition of young soldiers ("recruits"), quite probably dispatched to consolidate pharaonic assets in desert territory outside royal control during the latter years of the First Intermediate Period.

These graffiti may be compared with a significant low-relief inscription cut into the rock to the right of the main concentration of inscriptions at Gebel Tjauti. Previously mentioned (Chapter 2), this unique text (G10.11) – dating to the early Dynasty XI – identifies the newly constructed Alamat Tal road as integral to the existing network of routes operating in the western desert as part of the state's strategic military plan for managing economic and political affairs. The graffito which refers to a military unit operating under the pharaoh Antef I Sehertawy (G10.8) indicates unambiguously how essential to the maintenance of palace control and temple economy the new road was.

As a final illustration of the extent to which graffiti underwrite the economic history of Egypt in antiquity, it is relevant to note the many inscriptions which identify official trade expeditions mounted across the eastern desert to the Red Sea coast. Hieroglyphic and hieratic graffiti dating from Dynasty I to the Late Period confirm the priority of commercial activity in

224

COMMERCE

relation to the formulation of official policy. These include (but are not limited to) the following examples:

G10.12 Inscription of the Horus name of the Dynasty I pharaoh Djet and Hemka, an official.[22]

G10.13 Inscriptions of names and titles of Dynasty V and VI officials Khnum, Sabi abd Idu, supervising turquoise mines in Sinai.[23]

G10.14 Inscriptions of the chief steward of the pharaoh Sankhare Montuhotep III, detailing an expedition to the Red Sea charged with renewing commercial relations with the East African state of Punt.[24]

G10.15 Inscriptions of the name of the Dynasty XVII pharaoh Sobekemsaf II, pertaining to the mining of *bekhen*-stone (used particularly for royal statuary).[25]

G10.16 Inscriptions of the name of Menkheperre, high priest of Amun and *de facto* Theban ruler during Dynasty XXI (*c.*1045–992 BCE), referring either to stone quarrying at Wadi Hammamat or a Red Sea trading expedition.[26]

Greece

Commerce was part of everyday life at all periods in ancient Greece, both in particular areas or local communities and between administrative districts and territories overseas. Economic activity included production, exchange and consumption of essential commodities such as food, artisanal objects or animals; elite goods such as perfume, precious metals and labour-intensive textiles; and, as part of a slave economy, human beings. In the Mycenaean period (*c.*1600–*c.*1100 BCE) Greek commercial networks spanned the entire Mediterranean region, but after *c.*1200 BCE the artefactual sources point to a significant decline in trans-Mediterranean trade. Greek economic interests re-established commercial links outside the mainland during the course of the eighth century BCE, buying and selling agricultural produce, craft-manufactured goods and other essential and desired commodities with Phoenicians, Syrians and Etruscans in thriving communities of exchange like Al-Mīnā (E. Mediterranean) and Pithecusae (Italy).

Although the important trading settlement Al-Mīnā was not itself Greek – there is a strong Phoenician element in the earliest pottery – there can be no doubt that the position of its warehouses at the mouth of the Orontes River provided Greeks with a convenient gateway to the foreign empires beyond.

225

GRAFFITI IN ANTIQUITY

A few enterprising merchants from the large island of Euboea – off the east coast of Boeotia and Attica – and the Cyclades – an extensive archipelago in the Aegean Sea south-east of mainland Greece – must have taken up residence at Al-Mīnā early on. As traditional eastern sources diminished due to political trouble, the emporium at Al-Mīnā in the East was supplemented by enterprising Euboeans with a settlement on the island of Pithecusae, close to the metal-rich regions of Italy already known to the Mycenaeans.

The evidence of non-official inscriptions provides the clearest proof of the presence of Easterners at Pithecusae – specifically, incised marks on an imported *amphora* reused for a burial (Grave 575) of the Late Geometric I period. The *amphora* (numbered 575–1) is of Greek type but it bears three separate Semitic inscriptions. Two of them, identified as Aramaic, define the original function of the *amphora* as a container of "200 [units of liquid]", being "double [the standard quantity]". The physical capacity of the *amphora* has been calculated as 54.826 litres excluding the neck. Like the Egyptian pot-marks we considered earlier, this information is like an ancient customs declaration – one presumably made when the *amphora* was dispatched. It is also very likely that the inscriber had reason to expect that what he was writing would be understood at the intended Western destination – Pithecusae it appears. The signs of these two inscriptions indicate a linguistic area which was closely connected with the development of written Aramaic in North Syria. Ridgway says that, at first sight, it might be tempting to suppose that the *amphora* was inscribed and dispatched to Euboean Pithecusae from Al-Mīnā itself where there were surely Euboean residents – and probably Euboean (or Euboean-trained) potters.[27]

Material testimony for Greek commercial activity comprises in most instances discoveries of pottery like *amphora* 575-1, signifying the existence of buyers and sellers of goods from Greece or closely connected with Greeks. Interestingly enough, pottery did not usually represent the most important good traded; ceramic vessels like *amphorae* served above all as containers for bulk items such as wine or fish sauce. Prestige painted pottery vessels, which were often conveyed in the same shipment as products carried in bulk or high-quality commodities, were of relatively low monetary worth.

You will remember that Pithecusae has produced an example of the very earliest Greek writing, not just in the western Mediterranean but the Greek world at large (Chapter 6). Its eighth century BCE date is partly signalled by the way it was written – from right to left, not left to right. This retrograde, metrical inscription is in several lines and in poetic hexameters which say: "I am Nestor's cup, good to drink from. Whoever drinks this cup empty, at once desire for beautiful-crowned Aphrodite will seize him" (G6.13). Found in a cremation burial (Tomb 168), it is a much more elaborate example than identified elsewhere in the same period. The script itself is revealing. Of all the possible early Greek alphabets, it is written in Chalcidian, which confirms the presence of Euboeans on Pithecusae. As we noted earlier, the similarity in the

226

COMMERCE

graffito to the epics of Homer – the *Iliad* and the *Odyssey* – is what has struck people as remarkable in such an early example of Greek writing. The sort of vessel on which the verse was incised (a *kotyle*) may be dated typologically, and by its associations at Pithecusae, to the last quarter of the eighth century BCE. So this means not only that the inscription is one of the earliest examples of post-Mycenaean writing that have survived from anywhere in the Greek world. Equally significant is the fact that it is the only piece of Greek poetry that has survived in its original form from the period in which it is usually supposed that the Homeric epics themselves were finally written down at the end of a long tradition of oral transmission.

G10.17 "[A potter whose name ends in] -inos made me."

A second graffito on a piece of pottery at Pithecusae is significant too (G10.17). It is the earliest attestation of what becomes a common phrase: "[…]inos made me" (written right to left). It is also accompanied by a piece of painted decoration with clear East Mediterranean connections. This was found at the industrial metal-working site – one of three separate nuclei of human activity discovered on the side of the Mezzavia hill – not in a tomb. The fact that the inscription relates to the identity of the person responsible for manufacturing the vessel attests to the commercial production of prestige ceramics at this site. As we have noted already (Chapter 9), the type of vessel bearing […]inos' personalized "brand" (a *krater*) was commonly used in the context of elite drinking parties (*symposia*). This not only confirms the commercial nature of production but also suggests the likelihood that Pithecusae operated as a nexus of export as well as production.

For the most part, commerce across longer distances in the Greek Mediterranean operated on a strictly limited basis under the ambit of individuals who specialized in mercantile transactions (*émporoi*). These *émporoi* obtained communities from farmers, herdsmen or manufacturers in return for currency of one kind or another; if transacted as part of a barter economy, the exchange would involve goods of equivalent value. The professional merchants would then hand over whatever items were procured to consumers, who in turn paid for them with money or with other goods. Naturally enough, such economic activity placed both parties in potential jeopardy with regard to their respective financial capacity, not to mention the fact that traders were required to frequent many coastal settlements with the necessary harbour facilities in order to sell their merchandise. The literary record represents the ancient Greek trader characteristically as a freeborn person of moderate resources, travelling from one marketplace to another and selling a miscellany of goods in small amounts. This person might retain possession of his own vessel, but most undertook their business in association with ship owners (*naúkleroi*). This picture is in part confirmed from shipwrecks (such as the Giglio and Kyrenia wrecks), whose cargoes consist of a wide variety of different products.

227

A pertinent example of non-official testimony from Pithecusae pertaining to this aspect of economic activity in Greek antiquity also dates to the last quarter of the eighth century BCE. Known as the Shipwreck *krater*, the various fragments of this vase – still lacking its base and stem – were not found actually in a grave but probably represent fragments dropped as the remains from a pyre were being carried to the place of burial.

The *krater* was locally made at Pithecusae, according to the clay, and it is the oldest piece of figured painting so far found on Italian soil. The scene depicts various stages of a shipwreck. If we follow the painted narrative from left to right, the first image recreates the moment when a large maritime craft overturned in the water. A flat-bladed oar used to steer the ship still pivots in its lock fitting, which indicates that the painting captures the catastrophic capsizing of the vessel as it occurred. The sailors are in the water. Some are striving to stay alive, swimming in desperation away from the sinking ship. One of the mariners, far right, appears to float lifelessly. The composition of this sailor's figure – his arms, hanging limply by his side; his feet, facing oddly in the same direction – indicates that he has not survived the ordeal. Slightly to the left of the deceased sailor, a large sea-creature is devouring headfirst an unfortunate victim of the wreck. Below this element of the montage, the image of a suspiciously round fish, standing on its tail, implies the eventual fate of the hapless crew in such dangerous waters. According to Strabo, large aquatic creatures were a feature of the waters around nearby Cumae and there certainly are sharks in the Mediterranean.[28]

The shape of the ship fails to reveal anything useful about its place of origin or previous history. Comparative material from the ancient Greek world of this period is very sparse. It does, nevertheless, resemble fairly closely illustrations of ships on Corinthian ceramic ware. Given that the island of Euboea was renowned for its ships,[29] the Corinthian connection may seem out of place. However, from Pithecusae's geographical perspective, Euboea was on the *far* side of the Greek mainland and, particularly, the notoriously dangerous Cape Malea at the southern end of the Peloponnese. What the type of ship depicted here might indicate is that Corinthians or Corinthian ships provided transport for Euboeans travelling westwards. This would certainly explain why there is so much Corinthian pottery at Pithecusae.

All in all, this non-official painted scene provides a wealth of historical information about the nature of Greek commercial activity in the western Mediterranean during the eighth century BCE. It also reflects in passing how dangerous maritime travel could be and the potential perils faced by those merchants transporting agricultural produce, manufactured goods and human cargo.

Commercial exchange in Greek antiquity occurred in a variety of locations where goods or services were bartered, bought or sold: shops, marketplaces, settlements with harbours where ships loaded or unloaded, even sacred spaces like shrines or sanctuaries. Places set aside for economic activity of

COMMERCE

this kind differed in relative area and importance – from the public open space of a small *polis* to the diversity of social hubs and commercial markets in places like Athens, Miletus, Delos, Alexandria and Rhodes. In such cities there were also specialist marketplaces such as the fish market in Athens.[30] Most coastal cities built trading harbours with appropriate facilities on the quays, such as warehouses and offices for the merchants and the magistrates.

To illustrate this facet of Greek commercial life, let us return briefly to the *agora* at Athens, which we last visited in our discussion of political expression (Chapter 9). Here we are able to discern among the thousands of surviving potsherds a variety of messages, lists and numerical notations which speak directly to the kind of marketplace activity detailed above.

G10.18 Seven horizontal lines. (Early fifth century BCE)

G10.19 Eight vertical lines. (Mid-fifth century BCE)

G10.20 "[Side A] Ten *choes*, two *kotylai*. [Side B] ten *staters*."
(Late fifth century BCE)

G10.21 Four vertical lines + ten horizontal lines.
(Late fifth century BCE)

G10.22 "[Side A] 12 *minas*. [Side B] 20 *minas*."
(Late fifth century BCE)[31]

G10.23 "Kneading trough, long loaves (20+), dishes, platters (middle-sized, 4), little dishes (5+), cups (2+), oil-flask, half-chous [liquid measure] bowl, (?) 10+."
(Late fourth to early third centuries BCE)

G10.24 "... of pine-cones, of buns, of fish or relish, peaches [?], of freight charges [?], of fish or relish, for wine."   (Late Roman)

G10.25 "Aischeas. 5 *staters*. Nikanor."   (Mid-fifth century BCE)

G10.26 "5 (*drachmas*), 1 (*drachma*), 1 (*obol*), ½ (*obol*), ¼ (*obol*)."
(Late fifth century BCE)[32]

According to the finds of informal inscriptions in the Athenian *agora* – incised on a functional vessel or after the broken vessel was discarded – the graffiti conform to a variety of related economic categories:

- marks of volumetric capacity;
- marks of price;

229

- marks of tare and net weight;
- inventories of items; and
- aids to financial calculation.

The first graffito type indicates the capacity of the vessel. In the examples pertaining to this category – the neck of a Chian *amphora* (G10.18), the base of a semi-glazed *krater* (G10.19) – the horizontal or vertical lines incised on the surface of each vessel signify the maximum amount which the container could hold. In both instances, the unit of measure is the *choes* – in order, the Chian (7) or the Athenian (8) *choes*, the final numbers of each indicating the same capacity of 22.9775 litres.

A pair of graffiti, incised on different sides of an *amphora* neck (G10.20), provides both a measure of the vessel's capacity – 10 *choes*, 2 *kotylai* (4.4862 litres) – and an indication of price – 10 *staters* (or 20 *drachmas*). It is almost certain that the price in this instance refers to wine or oil. This is rather than the price of the container itself, which was usually marked in much smaller amounts than that given for the contents of storage vessels. A second example (G10.21) similarly provides the price of the *amphora*'s contents – 14 *staters*.

One of the *agora* graffiti reflects the highly developed nature of commercial measurement in classical Athens (G10.22). The two numerical notations incised on the upper part of a late fifth-century BCE *amphora* identify the metrological quantities corresponding to the vessel's tare weight – that is, the weight of the pot when empty – and net weight. Given these figures, it was a relatively simple calculation to determine the amount of wine or oil (or other liquid, e.g. honey) contained in the vessel.

A number of these informal inscriptions provide details in a fashion which can be described most usefully as lists of items for purchase or stocktaking inventories. The graffiti cited here which conform to this description (G10.23, 24) were found in the vicinity of the building called the Tholos. Named for its circular shape, this temple structure formed part of the complex of civic buildings constituting political assembly in the city (the Bouleuterion). It housed the Prytaneion, the seat of government in Athens. What is interesting to note – in relation to those particular graffiti inscribed on potsherds found nearby – is that the Tholos was a multi-purpose venue, including a dining hall which catered to officials serving on the Athenian council (*boule*). It is possible that the graffiti lists form an inventory of kitchen equipment used for the preparation of food in the Tholos. Implicit in this inference is the fact that the implements for making and serving food must have been manufactured and purchased for use in this way.

The final two examples of Athenian commercial graffiti represent elements of processing and pricing commodities that passed through the Athenian marketplace during the late fifth century BCE. Incised on the foot of a Corinthian *skyphos*, the first graffito (G10.25) comprises the names of two individuals (Aischeas, Nikanor) – or possibly a single person (Aischeas, son

COMMERCE

of Nikanor) – and a numerical notation of weight (5 *staters*). If two people are intended, then Aischeas may be the person to whom the vessel and its contents belongs, and Nikanor, the commercial agent at Athens who certified the transaction pertaining to the *skyphos*. If the latter, then Aischeas son of Nikanor may be either of the individuals inferred above.

Scratched on a fragment of roof tile, the final inscription (G10.26) represents an informal tool for calculating the price of an object. Incised in a horizontal row, each notation stands for a denomination of cost – 5 (*drachmas*), 1 (*drachma*), 1 (*obol*), ½ (*obol*), ¼ (*obol*). Using the tile fragment as an abacus or counting board, the commercial agent could align any number of pebbles under each denomination, then perform the necessary additions or subtractions to arrive relatively simply at an arithmetic sum.

Wine and olive oil were among the important export goods of the archaic and classical periods in Greek history. Strabo tells us about Charaxus, the brother of Sappho, selling wine from Lesbos in Egypt.[33] High profits were also made from trading expeditions to Spain.[34] As early as the beginning of the fifth century BCE, grain imports were acquiring increasing significance for the Greek cities.[35] From the sixth century BCE onwards, wide-beamed ships with large square sails and considerable cargo space were in common use.

As part of this burgeoning maritime economy, Greek merchants also initiated contact with Late Period Egypt, founding settlements in Naucratis. Archaeological evidence indicates that by 660 BCE Greek settlers had established the harbour of Naucratis for the exchange of commodities in the western Delta, not far from the capital Sais. The first of these settlers, however, had not come as colonists as the Greeks colonized many other places, founding cities and instituting Greek laws and governments. A series of graffiti inscribed on the statue of a New Kingdom pharaoh set up in southern Egypt points to the first stage of this unusual – by ancient Greek standards – approach to overseas settlement.

G10.27 "When King Psamtik [= Psammetichos II] came to Elephantine, those who sailed with Psamtik son of Theokles wrote these lines; and they came above Kerkis, as far as the river allowed; and those of foreign tongue Potasimto commanded, and Amasis the Egyptians. Archon son of Amoibochos and Pelekos son of Oudamos wrote us."[36]

Incised on the leg of a colossal statue of Ramesses II at Abu Simbel in Nubia, two graffiti statements and five inscribed signatures preserve information about the participation of non-Egyptian mercenaries in a military action directed by Psamtik (Psammetichos) II. A series of official *stelae* commemorates Psamtik II's victorious campaign into Nubia (593/2 BCE) against the new Kushite ruler, Aspelta. Written by two mercenaries (Archon and Pelekos) on the statue of Ramesses II immediately south of the entrance

231

GRAFFITI IN ANTIQUITY

to the Abu Simbel temple, one of the two graffito statements (G10.27) records that the Egyptian forces were composed of two army corps, one consisting of foreigners – which the appended signatures reveal comprised Jews and Greeks from Rhodes and Caria – and the other Egyptian, respectively under the command of Potasimto and Amasis. According to the graffito, the expeditionary force, which moved along the Nile, did not pass beyond the navigable portion upstream of Kerkis – the region of the Fifth Cataract. The second graffito statement, written by a certain Anaxanor on another statue in the temple precinct, reflects participation in the expedition from a later stage, when Psamtik II joined the army further south and led it into battle.

An unexpected consequence of hiring professional Greek soldiers to defend Saite rulers from dangers to the state arising within Egypt's borders or from neighbouring territories was the growth of foreign trade in Egypt. This led to Psamtik I (664–610 BCE) permitting Greek and other foreign merchants to engage in trading activity with Egypt, particularly in the port city of Naucratis. The later pharaoh Amasis (570–526 BCE), in turn, opened up administrative procedures at Naucratis, allowing it to evolve into a primary nexus of economic exchange in the Mediterranean and, in practical terms, as a Greek colony in Egypt in all but name. Herodotus provides additional understanding into the early history of Naucratis during the Saite Period foreshadowed by the Abu Simbel mercenary graffiti:

> Amasis favoured the Greeks and granted them a number of privileges, of which the chief was the gift of Naucratis as a commercial headquarters for any who wished to settle in the country. He also made grants of land upon which Greek traders, who did not want to live permanently in Egypt, might erect altars and temples.
> (Herodotus, *Histories* 2.178)

Naucratis was a perfect location to set up a commercial port in Egypt – attractive to foreign merchants and Egyptians alike. Situated in the delta region along the Canopic branch of the Nile river, Naucratis accommodated direct access to both the Mediterranean Sea – for mercantile transport and exportation of goods – and the Nile valley – for the distribution of imported commodities through Egypt. As Herodotus records:

> In the old days Naucratis was the only port in Egypt, and anyone who brought a ship into any of the other mouths of the Nile was bound to state on oath that he did so out of necessity and then proceed to the Canopic mouth; should contrary winds prevent him from doing so, he had to carry his freight to Naucratis in barges all around the Delta, which shows the exclusive privilege the port enjoyed. (Herodotus, *Histories* 2.179)

This, in turn, allowed Naucratis to flourish as a vibrant multicultural and economic hub of the Mediterranean and established a lasting cultural dialogue between Greece and Egypt. While the remains of ceramic ware indicate the presence of Greek traders in the delta starting in the late seventh century BCE, the emphasis of early excavators on religious structures at Naucratis rather than commercial and domestic spaces has limited knowledge of the site's mercantile nature. It is fortunate, therefore, that the Abu Simbel graffiti attest to the early history of this symbiotic relationship, fleshing out the Herodotean account of Naucratis' exceptional character.

To conclude this section of our introduction to non-official expressions of commercial activity, consider the variety of graffiti and dipinti in the so-called Terrace House (Hanghaus) 2 – a 4,000 m² insula located in the centre of Roman Ephesus. Exceptionally well preserved, the individual residences comprising this significant urban complex of the imperial period include a number of properties owned by prominent and wealthy Ephesians. Evidence for inscribing practice speaks directly to the use of these residential spaces for the conduct of business activity and the reception of clients and guests. For instance, it is possible to identify the following in two related spaces of a single larger context:

G10.28 List of food items. (House 21: west pillar, north wall)

G10.29 Account. (House 21: central pillar, north wall)

G10.30 Record of delivery. (House 21: east section, north wall)

G10.31 List of expenditures. (House 21: east corner pillar, north wall)

G10.32 List of food items and prices. (House 21: east corner pillar, north wall)

G10.33 List of expenditures. (House 21: east corner pillar, north wall)

G10.34 List of food items. (Room 22: south wall)

G10.35 List of items and prices. (Room 19: north wall)

G10.36 Reference to wine. (House 21: east corner pillar, south wall)

G10.37 Record of delivery. (House 21: west section, north wall)

G10.38 List of expenses. (Room 14c: south door jamb, into Room 14d)[37]

GRAFFITI IN ANTIQUITY

Much of the detail in these informal statements, lists and messages revolves around the products of commercial exchange – references to a type of Italian wine and a belly-shaped bottle with a long neck (G10.28); a person responsible for water supply constructions (G10.29); the name of the person ("Acholios") delivering something to the household (G10.30); a denomination of currency ("bronze drachma") (G10.31); the equivalent of today's "fast food" (*propina*), as well as ingredients and a type of fish (G10.32); and so on. This intriguing collocation of commercial and cultural exchange within residential contexts in the heart of imperial Ephesus captures the essence of ancient Greek socio-economic activity, reflected appropriately by a graffito invoking Hermes, the god of trade, under his epithet Kyllenios:

G10.39 "O Hermes Hyllenios!" (House 21: east corner pillar, north wall)[38]

Rome

Throughout the regal period and over the course of the first two centuries of the republican era, the economy of central Italy relied primarily on agricultural production. Greek, Etruscan and especially Carthaginian merchants plied the waters of the western Mediterranean. The advent of coinage in the third century BCE and increasing intercourse with the Hellenistic economic region changed the basis of commercial activity at Rome. Importantly, between 509 BCE and 279 BCE, Rome and Carthage ratified four treaties formalizing their developing and established economic interests and zones of influence. While these agreements reflected Carthaginian concerns, they also demonstrated Rome's evolving position in the western Mediterranean region.[39]

From the third century BCE, the negotiated reciprocity between Rome and Carthage broke down in no uncertain terms. As a consequence of the resulting first (264–246 BCE) *and* second (218–203/2 BCE) Punic Wars, not only did Rome become a sea power, but Roman merchants followed the legions to Africa in order to profit from the campaigns and the war booty.[40] Already formulated during a lengthy series of internal conflicts between Rome and her Italian neighbours, the Roman–Carthaginian conflicts of the third century BCE entrenched the relationship between Rome's socio-political interests and the favourable exploitation of commercial routes and markets. Carthage's obliteration in 146 BCE saw Rome as the principal economic power in the western Mediterranean.

In this regard, the ubiquity of graffiti drawings depicting ships of various types – oar-driven warships (*naves longae*), transport ships in the Roman fleet (*naves actuariae*), merchant vessels (*naves onerariae*), and other sailing craft – reflects Rome's expanding military ambitions and developing

234

maritime economy. These images were inscribed in a representative catalogue of known centres of mercantile activity under Roman rule – in Italy (Alba Fucens, Boscoreale, Lilybaeum, Ostia, Pompeii, Pozzuoli, Rome, Stabiae, Syracuse, Tarentum) and the West (Cucuron, Saint-Remy-de-Provence); the eastern Mediterranean (Athens, Delos, Dura-Europos, Nymphaion, Pergamon, Samos, Silsile); and North Africa (Alexandria, Elephantine, Sabratha, Utica).

We have already looked more closely at a few of the drawings depicting maritime shipping servicing this expanding network of commercial activity in the Roman Mediterranean (G2.2; Figures 4.2–3). A particularly impressive graffito image capturing the level of detail depicted across the diverse repertoire of extant sea- and river-craft inscriptions can also be found in Chapter 4 (Figure 4.2). Measuring 1.5 × 1.52 m, this spectacular depiction of a merchant vessel named "Europa" is well worth a second look. Occupying a highly visible section of wall surface in the northern area of a house in Pompeii (I.15.3), this drawing is a time-capsule of how the inhabitants of a port like Pompeii expressed their city's relationship to the cosmopolitan mercantile world.

Conforming to the specifications of cargo ships represented in mosaics found at Ostia (e.g. Figure 10.1), the "Europa" was evidently a transport vessel of some kind. The level of technical particularity reflects the knowledge of the inscribing artist – beyond a casual acquaintance with vessels of this kind.

Figure 10.1 Mosaic of cargo vessel, Piazzale delle corporazioni, Ostia, Italy.

235

GRAFFITI IN ANTIQUITY

The drawing shows clearly the keel of the "Europa" and the entire length of the ship's steering oar – even though the underside of the hull and the curved blade of the rudder-pole would normally have been deployed below the surface of the water, and consequently out of sight. Moreover, the intricate system of ropes employed to support the ship's masts (standing rigging) and to control or set the yards and sails is shown in considerable detail. The configuration of sails – a broad square mainsail on a single mast, and a foresail (known as an *artemon*) with its mast projecting over the bow – and lack of oars confirm that the "Europa" was a merchant vessel of the first century CE.

The "Europa" sailed the waters of the Mediterranean during the early years of the imperial period – two centuries which saw the evolution of a new system of Roman government (the Principate) and the prosecution of an empire-wide programme of provincial pacification and cultural appropriation (the *pax Romana*). The resulting *Imperium Romanum* instituted a concomitant escalation of Roman commercial activity. The assurance of safe conduct on long-distance journeys – in particular, previously hazardous shipping routes – and the development of essential structures and facilities – e.g. warehouses, roads, harbours – stimulated economic exchange across the Mediterranean under Roman rule.

G10.40 "[Column 1] Days – of Saturn, of the Sun, of the Moon, of Mars, of Mercury, of Jupiter, of Venus. [Column 2] Markets – Pompeii, Nuceria, Atella, Nola, Cumae, Puteoli, Rome, Capua. [Columns 3–5] List of months and days from 13 [?] October to 12 November. [Columns 6–8] 1–30." (*CIL* IV.8863)

G10.41 "Honeyed red wine from Falernus [Campania]." (*CIL* IV.10309a–e)

G10.42 "[Wine from] Tauromenium [Sicily]." (*CIL* IV.10297–9)

G10.43 "Of Sextus Pompeius Amarantus."[41]

G10.44 "[Wine from the farm of] Fabius at Sorrento [Campania]. When Vespasian was consul for the second time [70 CE]." (*CIL* IV.5521–2)

While transmarine commerce across the Roman empire was significant, it is important to note that the primary driver of economic activity occurred within a local and regional framework. Agricultural and commercial production and exchange fulfilled in large part the common requisites of urban and rural constituencies. The foundation and coordination of numerous city and country markets (*nundinae*)[42] sustained the ongoing traffic in commodities traded by professional merchants. To a degree, such local markets took place

COMMERCE

only seasonally and in conjunction with feast days or court sessions.[43] Prices often varied widely from city to city, especially after harvest failures, which led to rises in grain prices.[44]

Pompeii again provides an insight into the minutiae of the Roman empire's trans-regional commercial revolution as it played out at a local level. In the space identified on the basis of a graffito as a shop selling wine and terra-cotta containers (III.4.1: *taberna vasaria*), inscriptions of numbers with and without words and, importantly, an inventory of markets (*index nundinarius*) speak eloquently of the regional rhythms of commerce in Pompeii, neigh-bouring communities and the wider region (G10.40). Incising clearly visible records of quotidian exchange and a schedule for market transactions in and around the Pompeian colony – and extending north to the capital (Rome) – confirms the ability of the shop-owner and at least a proportion of his or her clientele to calculate in practical terms and plan for the movement and availability of necessary goods and services. Reinforcing patterns of social experience in matters affecting business and the consumption of staple com-modities, this graffito also points to the important role of trade in ensuring the provision of supplies to Roman towns and cities.

We know that Rome's supplies were organized by the collection of grain as a tax (*cura annonae*). Grain was imported from the provinces of Africa and Egypt, transported to the city, stored in large warehouses, and distrib-uted to the population. Oil, wine and the extremely popular fish sauce used as a condiment in ancient cuisine (*garum*) were sourced in large quantities from the Spanish provinces, as well as locally from Italian producers. Incised with details of the contents and the provenance of the product contained in the vessels, Pompeii preserves a range of labelled *amphorae* reflecting com-mercial activity associated with these material goods. For instance, over 70 containers of this kind were found in a small bar and residential storage space located in the south-eastern quarter of Pompeii (I.9.11/12). Certain inscrip-tions identify the presence of prestigious Italian wines from local producers – Falernus (G10.41) and Sorrento (G10.44) – and further afield – Tauromenium in Sicily (G10.42) – as well as the names of the establishment's owner – Sextus Pompeius Amarantus (G10.43) – and one of his suppliers – Fabius (G10.44). Given the quantity of *amphorae* found in the conjoined house and wine-bar, not to mention the quality of wine advertised on the labels, it is interest-ing to speculate about the extent of Amarantus' commercial activity. If we take this information together with the fact a number of the *amphorae* con-form to a type of vessel that we know came from Crete – a major centre of wine production – then it is reasonably safe to suggest that Amarantus not only supplied the needs of his Pompeian clientele, but may well have acted as a commercial agent for regional distribution of sought-after vintages. The ostentatious lifestyle of the Roman upper class and continuing presence of holidaying elite in villas along the coast of the Bay of Naples would undoubt-edly have offered Amarantus a potentially lucrative market.

237

GRAFFITI IN ANTIQUITY

G10.45 "The best *liquamen* of Aulus Umbricius Scaurus." (*CIL* IV.5711)

G10.46 "Scaurus' flower of *garum* made from mackerel, from the workshop of Scaurus, by Martial, imperial freedman."
(*CIL* IV.9406)

The same can be said for another local commodity familiar from literary references as the condiment of choice in Graeco-Roman cuisine.[45] While it might at first sight seem an unappealing concoction, the various types of foodstuff or additive produced from fish – sauce (*garum* or *liquamen*), paste (*allec*), brine (*muria*) – served a broad cross-section of Roman society, representing a market commodity serviced by a Mediterranean-wide production and distribution network. Pompeii formed an important part of this wide-reaching commercial enterprise. Indeed, we read that the town was famous for its *garum*.[46] Here we can refer to a series of mosaics – located in the atrium of a large residential complex belonging to a local producer – which represent at each corner of the central rainwater pool (*impluvium*) the one-handled vessel (*urceus*) used to contain fish sauce. Each of these vessels was inscribed in stone with an indication of the contents, just like the painted inscription (*titulus pictus*) of the original clay jars. Like most inscriptions referring to concepts or subject matter which is familiar to the literate community, the messages on the *urcei* are abbreviated – for example, G(ari) F(los) SCO(mbri), "flower of fish sauce, from mackerel"; LIQUA(men) FLOS, "flower of fish sauce"; and LIQUAMEN OPTIMUM EX OFFICIN(a) A(uli) SCAURI, "the best fish sauce, from the workshop of Aulus Scaurus (Umbricius)". Even though this fish sauce was considered the most expensive, it also was the most commonly labelled. *Amphorae* which once contained the product have been found even in houses belonging to the non-elite population of the town. Whether made only from the blood of the fish and from what type no doubt would determine the exclusivity of the product.

The graffiti cited above (G10.45, 46) represent a sample only of the many non-official references to the fish sauce produced, marketed and trafficked by a certain Aulus Umbricius Scaurus, who exercised a conspicuous influence over local, regional and even overseas markets for *garum* and its derivative products from the mid-first century BCE until the destruction of Pompeii. Over 50 *urcei* have been unearthed in Pompeii and the surrounding area, a significant proportion of which bear inscriptions referring to Scaurus' workshops. That the mosaics mentioned above were found in one of two *atria* of a sprawling three-storey residence occupying a prestigious position along the western perimeter of the town overlooking the sea reflects the owner's (i.e. Scaurus') pride in the product which had obviously brought him such conspicuous wealth.

G10.47 "Ses[tius]" + anchor or nautical hook or trident or five-pointed star or eight-pointed star or Σ or -tius or *caduceus* or palm branch or double-axe.[47]

COMMERCE

Besides trade in agricultural products that streamed out of the entire Mediterranean region to Rome – like the wine and *garum* identified on inscribed containers at Pompeii – graffiti labels similarly record the export of wine from Italy to elsewhere in the Mediterranean. In this regard, the *amphorae* of the Sestii family from Cosa – a Latin colony on the Etrurian coast – attest to the considerable volume of this trade. Finds of pottery marked with the label SES and a pot-mark of some kind (G10.47) – at Cosa (over a thousand), the Athenian *agora* (a few suggestive fragments) and in southern Gaul (another thousand in a sunken transport vessel off the coast of Marseilles) – indicate the "global" nature of the Roman economy during the late republican and imperial periods. If we collate what we know from the archaeological record, then it is clear that mass-produced coarse wares bearing non-official text-and-symbol stamps of the Sestii family corroborate the literary testimony regarding the extent of commercial activity in the Roman world. Certainly the variety of shapes, sizes and ligatures of letters – SES(T) or -TIUS – and the array of associated symbols, devices or logograms – from the anchor to the double-axe – indicate the sheer scale of the enterprise in relation to "worldwide" distribution of commodities in the Sestian containers. Comparison with evidence for labelled contents of pottery vessels at Pompeii – including such commodities as barley, chickpeas, fennel, figs, honey, lentils, nuts, olives and pickling brine[48] – demonstrates how vibrant Roman commerce was.

Perhaps one of the most disturbing aspects of commerce in Graeco-Roman antiquity involves the commodification of human beings in the form of slavery. The literary tradition, documentary evidence and tens of thousands of formal inscriptions testify to the existence of this pernicious social practice across the Mediterranean. While it is outside the remit of this chapter to examine in any detail the system of slavery that formed an inextricable part of the Roman cultural fabric, a specialized form of non-official inscribed text found at Pompeii and Herculaneum provides an indelible portrait of the conceptual and practical connection in Roman minds of the categories of commercial property and human slavery.

Comprising the ancient equivalent of business documents recording contractual agreements, five caches of wooden tablets have been unearthed in the Vesuvian area – one in a house at Pompeii (V.1.26); another in a villa at Murecine, a suburb of Pompeii; and the remaining three in houses in close proximity to each other at Herculaneum (V.13–16, 22; VI.11). Originally coated with wax, these tablets record the commercial activities, respectively, of the Pompeian banker (*argentarius*) Caecilius Jucundus, the Campanian merchants (*mercatores*) Sulpicius Cinnamus and Sulpicius Faustus, and the inhabitants of the three properties in the coastal settlement of Herculaneum.

As an indication of the variety of financial, commercial and legal information contained in these non-official dossiers, here is a tabulation of transactions selected from the Caecilius Jucundus archive:

239

GRAFFITI IN ANTIQUITY

Table 10.1 Selection of receipts relating to transactions brokered by L. Caecilius Jucundus (*CIL* IV.1–155) inscribed on waxed tablets (*tabulae ceratae*) found at Pompeii (V.1.6).

CIL IV	Date	Document
3340.1	May 15 CE	Receipt for sale of a mule at auction by Caecilius Felix
3340.5	May 54 CE	Receipt for auction of goods from the estate of Nasennius Nigidius Vaccula
3340.6	May 54 CE	Receipt for sale at auction of boxwood belonging to C. Julius Onesimus
3340.7	May–June 54 CE	Receipt for sale at auction of slave of L. Junius Aquila
3340.10	January 55 CE	Receipt for 38,079 sesterces from auction for M. Lucretius Lerus
3340.22	November 56 CE	Receipt for proceeds from auction for Histria Ichimas
3340.23	November 56 CE	Receipt for sale of fixtures and fittings at auction by Umbricia Antiochis
3340.24	December 56 CE	Receipt for sale of slave by Umbricia Antiochis
3340.25	December 56 CE	Receipt for goods auctioned for Umbricia Ianuaria
3340.40	December 57 CE	Receipt for auction of goods by Tullia Lampyris

We have already considered how an inscriber would record on waxed tablets (*tabulae ceratae*) the details of transactions itemized above (Chapter 1). What is important to note in this context is the degree to which the buying and selling of material goods, animals and human beings correspond. Receipts for the sales at auction of a mule and the slave of Lucius Junius Aquila are attested in the same language and preserved in the same dossier of transactions. If nothing else, the evidence of non-official textual records like these corroborate the notion propagated in the surviving literature of slaves as human chattel – from Cato the Elder's advice in his second-century BCE agricultural manual to "sell worn-out oxen, blemished cattle, blemished sheep, wool, hides, an old wagon, old tools, an old slave, a sickly slave, and whatever else is superfluous" and Varro's infamous formulation in the later first century BCE of the slave as a "speaking tool" (*instrumentum vocale*) to Livy's incidental remark describing a slave cook as "the most worthless property (*mancipium*)".[49] The Murecine tablets – which refer most frequently over the period of time between 26 and 52 CE to the Sulpicii Faustus and Cinnamus – and the Herculaneum tablets similarly confirm the identification of human being and commercial asset.

By the same token, it is also clear that these documents illustrate the use of slaves and ex-slaves as agents or representatives in commercial activity. For example, the Murecine dossier reveals that Cinnamus was the freedman of Faustus,[50] which adds to the evidence of the tablets that it was common

240

COMMERCE

practice to make use of slaves for the conduct of business. So, too, one of the Herculaneum tablets records the fact that a freeborn landowner, Ulpia Plotina, conducted a number of transactions with Lucius Cominius Primus – most likely the owner of the archive found in V.22 – through Plotina's slaves Venustus and Felix.[51] A single example drawn from the table of documents from the dossier of Caecilius Jucundus demonstrates the degree to which the informal evidence complicates our understanding of the slave economy in Roman antiquity:

G10.48 "[In ink, on the margin of the second tablet]
Acknowledgement of *Nymphius* – slave of [Lucius] Iunius
Aquila. [Pages 2–3] 1,567 [?] sesterces – the sum of money
which is due for payment, as contracted with L. Caecilius
Iucundus, by 13 August next, for the auction of *Ni(m)[ph]ius*,
slave of L. Iunius Aquila, less commission – L. Iunius Aquila
[declared that he has] (received this sum), in cash, from L.
Caecilius Iucundus. Transacted at Pompeii on 29 May [or
28 June], in the consulship of Manlius Acilius and Marcus
Asinius (54 CE). [Page 4, right column (in ink), next to seals,
now missing] Of Sextus Numisius Iucundus, of Lucius Nerius
Hy[ginus?], of [Q.] Caecilius Attalus, of M. Badius Hermes,
of [P.] Paccius Cerinthus, of Aulus Vettius Donatus, of P.
Aefulanus Crysant[us], of C. Nunnidius Sy[n.], of L. Iunius.
[Page 5] I, *Nymphius*, wrote by instruction [and request] of
L. Iunius Aquila that he received from L. Caecilius Iucundus
1,567 [?] sesterces for the auction of *Nymphius*, slave of Iunius
Aquila."   (Emphasis added)

Tablets often were laced together in what we might recognize today as a small booklet. The outer two leaves had wax only on the inside, while the interior leaves were double-sided. As the document above indicates, the second and third "pages" provide a detailed account of the transaction, which was sealed. Page 4 lists in order of social standing witnesses to the contractual arrangement. The last page on which writing was incised records the important elements of the transaction in summary. If a dispute arose at any point after the transaction was concluded, the sealed section of the document could be broken to confirm the nature of the arrangement witnessed by the individuals whose signatures were listed. Vital to our interest here is the name of the individual identified as the slave of L. Junius Aquila (in bold letters). If the document is read through carefully, it becomes clear that the person who is acting as the agent of Junius Aquila in dealing with Caecilius Jucundus – the person who confirms in writing the contractual obligation entailed as a result of the successful transaction – is also the subject of the sale at auction. In other words, Nymphius is the slave purchased by Caecilius Jucundus on

241

behalf of Junius Aquila; *and*, simultaneously, he is acting as Aquila's agent in recording his own purchase. The fact that he was able to do precisely this – that is, he had in some way demonstrated his potential to conduct business, and most certainly had shown that he was literate at a scribal level – will explain why his purchase price was so large. 1,567 sesterces was almost twice the annual income of a veteran soldier.

FINAL THOUGHTS

However one reconstructs the vibrant networks and bustling marketplaces that characterized the ancient world of economic activity, it is safe to say that reimagining these contexts bereft of that information necessary to facilitate even the most basic commercial exchange would constitute a misunderstanding of how business works. And that, of course, is why everything to do with the production, sale and use of goods and services in antiquity displays the marks of manufacture, cost and ownership. Graffiti across the ancient Mediterranean speak eloquently about the ubiquity of a market-driven (literally) economic system, the diversity of labour and enterprise (even in the slave-based cultures of Greece and Rome), and the ability of *all* levels in society to communicate and understand the vocabulary of commercial transaction. It may seem self-evident, but only the evidence of graffiti – be they pot-marks on pre-dynastic Egyptian bread moulds, numerical indicators of capacity, weight and price on archaic and classical Greek potsherds, or the tabulation of brokered goods and services on Roman waxed tablets – confirms the extent to which the urban and rural poor, the businessmen (*and* women) of the working classes, and the elite order shared a common language. Grounded in buying and selling across a spectrum of commodities ranging from the essentials of daily life to the desires of the privileged few, graffiti associated with the world of ancient commerce tell us what we might have guessed but only through the testimony of non-official inscriptions know now to be the case: business in antiquity was booming.

CHAPTER 11

SEXUALITY

If only I might have [a maiden who is both beautiful and tender].
(*SEG* 46.114)

Men on the street would serenade the house and scrawl my doors
black with their love verses.   (Plautus, *The Merchant* 2.3.74)

Aeschrion of Syracuse has a wife named Pippa, whose name the
vicious practices of [the Roman governor] Verres have made a by-
word throughout Sicily. Couplets referring to this woman were
constantly being scribbled over the dais and above the governor's
head.   (Cicero, *Verrine Orations* 2.3.33)

What shall I do for you, little winking eyes?   (*CIL* IV.1780)

SEX, GENDER AND BODY HISTORY IN ANTIQUITY

Strictly speaking, sexuality as we understand it in the twenty-first century
does *not* have conceptual roots in the socio-cultural vocabulary of antiquity. Only since the last decades of the eighteenth century did the notion of
sexuality – derived from the Latin word *sexus*, meaning "(male and female)
gender" – first enter scientific parlance so as to describe the sexual character of animals, plants or single-celled life forms. According to recent definitions of the word, sexuality incorporates biological, mental, emotional and
social facets of the human sexual experience. Current historical research
challenges the view that human sexuality may be formulated as a genetically determined, historically fixed pattern of behaviour. Following modern
anthropology's lead, the findings of socio-cultural and scientific scholarship
propose a behavioural model founded on standards of conduct established

243

and enforced by society. These social norms are historically conditional, and as a result prone to be affected by circumstances or conditions prevailing in society at any given moment in time.[1]

While it would be ludicrous to suggest that sex did not exist in the ancient world, it is clear that patterns of behaviour in antiquity operated according to a different set of conceptual and behavioural principles in relation to notions of sex and gender. In very general terms, it was not at all a historical given in ancient societies that one gender only should constitute the centre of a person's sexual interest or activity. In fact, depending on the conditions connected with or relevant to particular physical or emotional states of mind, both men and women would be perfectly free and often predisposed to engage in intimate behaviour with individuals of the same or the opposite sex.

The surviving source material dealing with ancient sexuality, gender and body history may be divided into the same categories that deal with all other aspects of ancient life. First of all, descriptions of sexual activity in antiquity are preserved in many literary texts. Depending on the category of literary composition, references to sexuality appeared in a variety of guises – broadly speaking, as indirect or tacit observations,[2] graphic comments,[3] or poetic allusions.[4] Naturally enough, the focus of attention diverged considerably. On the one hand, fictional prose narratives might portray the arousal of sexual desire;[5] from another angle, poetry could touch on issues sensitive even in the modern world – for instance, male erectile dysfunction.[6] Of considerable fascination among contemporary audiences (and exerting a similar appeal in the modern age), indulgence in sexual conduct that transgressed traditional normative boundaries engendered vitriolic attention.[7] In classical and post-classical antiquity, such expressions of contempt or ridicule can often be found in descriptions of despots and Roman emperors charged with committing abnormal or unacceptable sexual actions.[8] In this regard, alleged immoderate sexual behaviour displayed by women of the ruling families or the Roman elite became the subject of (often popular) censorious accounts.[9]

Similarly, a spectrum of contexts displaying artistic expressions of ideas and practices associated with ancient notions of sexuality survive into the modern age. It is fortunate – and perhaps, given the nature of the subject matter, to be expected – that the extant remains of ancient art preserve a rich assortment of erotic imagery – reliefs on tombs and temples and drawings on papyrus from pharaonic Egypt; Attic vase paintings dating to the sixth and fifth centuries BCE; images on hand mirrors from the post-classical period; wall paintings, floor mosaics and crafted objects from the Roman period.

Given all that has gone before, it should come as no surprise that the inventory of ancient graffiti texts and drawings pertaining to matters of a sexual nature corresponds to the official record in chronological duration, socio-cultural diversity and thematic range. As the epigraph to this chapter suggests, these might range from a quotation of the sixth-century BCE poet Hipponax on the foot of an Attic *kalyx*-cup (Attica, fifth century BCE) to an

SEXUALITY

off-hand aside in a later comic play referring to the epigraphic response of local men to the sight of a pretty slave-girl (Italy, second century BCE); from the statesman Cicero's caustic observation regarding the corrupt Sicilian governor Verres' adoption of the "royal" practice of polygamy to the affectionate graffito addressed to "little winking eyes" (*oscilli lusci*; Pompeii, first century CE). In navigating what can only be an introduction to non-official representations of sexuality in antiquity, what follows outlines a few general points of reference that should prove useful.

First, on the basis of the literary, documentary and material record, it would appear that the ancients understood male and female sexuality as quintessentially different. This belief was explicitly elaborated in medical, philosophical and scientific works.[10] Second, the tenets which defined and governed a person's sexual conduct can be divided into three sub-categories, relating to one's state-sanctioned social condition – namely, whether an individual was born of enfranchised or freed parents, i.e. free; manumitted; or enslaved – age and gender. Taking age as an example, we find that men and women in antiquity associated distinctive patterns of erotic desire and sexual practice with particular stages in life – young men, for instance, were seen as easily aroused,[11] young women as sexually active;[12] and sexuality in old age was often depicted as unbecoming, improper or simply absurd.[13] Third, ancient writers were less interested in detailed description of the sexual act itself and more so with the degree to which personal character and conduct were affected by sexual desire. Ancient Egyptian love songs examine the emotional impact on men *and* women of erotic impulses.[14] Both Plato and Aristotle advised their readership to curb sexual feelings.[15] In Egyptian and Greek literature alike, sexual relationships between men and women were explored in relation to how particular societies formulated suitable marital arrangements – in most situations, the principles determining the suitability of a marriage centred on guaranteeing legitimate procreation and a prosperous and efficient household.[16] In this regard, treatises from the Imperial period on appropriate marital behaviour represented marriage as a mutual partnership and demanded faithfulness from both partners.[17]

Egypt

We have already encountered reference to non-official image-making dealing with sexual ideas in our discussions of artistic expression (Chapter 4) and magic (Chapter 7). Images of the ithyphallic deity Min and two scenes depicting a mother and child – one painted in black on an *ostracon* from Deir el-Medina; the other, scratched into the stone of a monumental gateway – point to inscribing practices in pharaonic Egypt that incorporate explicitly sexualized or gendered imagery. In this regard, it is almost impossible *not* to allocate biological markers of sex – maleness or femaleness – when

245

representing human beings. Apart from portrayals of biological variation, gender could be designated in Egyptian art by placing human figures indicatively, that is, in terms of perspective, size and colour – which, bearing in mind the degree of generalization underlying this observation, in most instances, can be encapsulated in the formula: male = foreground/large/dark; female = background/small/light. This formative conceptual framework – a pattern of ideas informing practice that underpinned most figural representation in official and informal contexts – can be used to assess the fragmentary remainder of the representative corpus. In other words, what at first may appear to be a non-gendered illustration of male or female figures should instead be regarded as an image which is incomplete or damaged – unfinished in such a way, that is, as to remove the signs of gender (obvious or not) from it. Few material artefacts from ancient Egypt have survived to the modern age in a pristine state. Because of this state of affairs, many representations of people must remain uncertain in relation to intended gender. Some images, however, were not explicitly gendered, often to serve the very practical expedient of being able to represent any gender.

That said, it is possible to uncover instances in the catalogue of non-official Egyptian art and literature – extant *in situ* or in museum collections – where sex, gender and the human (or occasionally animal) body coalesce to generate erotic associations or distinctive sexualized statements. In relation to textual representation, we have looked briefly already at the partially preserved remainder of a love poem in seven verses incised on a piece of New Kingdom pottery (G6.9). It is easy enough to cast a wider net in order to capture a range of exemplary writing. One of the most evocative is the collection of three groups of love songs preserved on a papyrus manuscript in the British Museum (Papyrus Harris 500/BM10060). The artistic merits of this papyrus anthology should not distract from the highly charged erotic undertones of those poetic compositions dealing with affective relationships:

> [Girl] My heart is not yet done with your love, my wolf cub! Your liquor is your lovemaking … [Boy] I will lie down inside, and then I will feign illness. Then my neighbours will enter to see, and then my sister will come with them. She'll put the doctors to shame – for she [alone] will understand my illness.
> (Papyrus Harris 500/BM10060)

In this text, the word translated as "lovemaking" uses a very particular hieroglyphic determinative. In ancient Egyptian script, determinatives are non-phonetic glyphs or signs which provide additional information about the semantic content of words, as well as distinguishing homophones and serving as word dividers in place of punctuation markers. In this instance, the determinative used in regard to the Egyptian term *dd* – a phallus – indicates that the word refers to acts of erotic love, which may encompass a spectrum of possibilities from affectionate caresses to sexual intercourse. Similarly, the term "sister" does not refer to a kinship relationship between the anonymous "Boy" and "Girl". Instead, "brother" and "sister" should be understood as terms of endearment. This affective dimension underscores the significance of the boy's ruse. That he proposes to ensure his beloved visits him by way of a feigned illness might, in fact, represent an authentic malady – namely, love-sickness, over which physicians lack any effective recourse. The erotic sting in the tail of this verse lies in a simple fact: that only his true love – the "girl" of his "dreams" – can ameliorate his suffering.

Comprising two stories ("The Doomed Prince" and "The Capture of Joppa") and a mortuary poem ("The Harper's Song"), in addition to the love song cycle, Papyrus Harris 500 should, of course, be regarded as a literary product of the later New Kingdom period (Dynasties XIX and XX). It may be compared with other literary collections transcribed on papyrus – for example, Papyrus Chester Beatty I, which contains three groups of love songs, "The Tale of Horus and Seth", two hymns to the king, and a short business note. However, instances of transcribing and disseminating erotic literary compositions are not confined to elite papyrus manuscripts. A number of *ostraca* display love songs or phrases typical of such poetry. For example, preserved on a Ramesside *ostracon* from Deir el-Medina, we can read the following:

G11.1 "[Boy] My sister's love is in the ... Her necklace is of flowers; her bones are reeds. Her little seal-ring is [on her finger], her lotus in her hand. I kiss [her] before everyone, that they may see my love. Indeed it is she who captures my heart. When she looks at me, I am refreshed."[18]   (O. Gardiner 304)

Inscribed on a limestone flake dating to the reign of Ramesses III (*c.* 1182–1151 BCE), the similarity of this verse to the literary compositions recorded on Papyrus Harris 500 and Papyrus Chester Beatty I is instructive. In structure, perspective and content, O. Gardiner 304 reflects the same erotic sensibility clearly appreciated by educated Egyptian readers. It is interesting that we find this text carefully "published" – painted on used or recycled stone chips – as part of an "archive" – sherds surviving in contexts of schooling, work and domicile. Recording erotic verse in the same way as the literary miscellanies preserved on papyrus, O. Gardiner 304 and similar *ostraca* pose questions about authorship, reception and transmission of literature in general and erotic compositions in particular. Unfortunately, it is impossible to know the extent of text production or the number of compositions circulating at any period. Nevertheless, we can be certain that there existed an audience for this kind of writing and that love poetry and erotic prose was not only socially approved but actively sought out.

Inscribed with a large collection of poems, the content of 31 surviving fragments of a Deir el-Medina *ostracon* we have already examined in relation to magic (Chapter 6) confirms both the nature of and desire for erotic literature in ancient Egypt. Although most of the hieroglyphic text still visible is profoundly lacunose, it is possible to read about the pleasures of a young woman swimming in the river. She wears a bathing costume, described in sensual terms, and holds a small red fish in her fingers, which can be interpreted as an allusion to the heart of the young man who watches her, enraptured by love. We have already seen how the love of the woman is compared to a magical spell cast on the water in order to protect the young man from the dangers of a river-crossing, namely, a crocodile attack. In the same way that the composer of the O. Gardiner 304 verse describes the boy's heart as ensnared, the young man in the O. CG 25218 song cycle rejoices when he finally embraces his beloved; as the boy is "refreshed", so the young man is described as feeling like an inhabitant of an exotic land, intoxicated by love.

We know how important the belief in an afterlife was to the Egyptians (Chapter 5). In the context of the present discussion, it should be noted that they also believed that the union of male and female was a necessity for the creation of a new being. In contrast, the creation of the world was instigated by the Sun God creating himself in the beginning. According to the eulogy to Amun found on Papyrus Leiden I.350:

> Who began evolution on the first occasion? Amun, who evolved in the beginning, with his emanation unknown – no god evolving prior to him, no other god with him to tell of his appearance, no mother of his for whom his name was made, and no father of his who ejaculated him so as to say "It is I." – Amun, who smelted his egg by himself.[19]

When this first step had been completed he produced two other Gods – Shu, god of the air, and Tefenet, god of humidity – by masturbation. Utterance 257 of the Pyramid Texts, one of the earliest creation legends, describes how the God of creation created the other Gods with his hand; that is, by masturbation: "Atum is he who [once] came into being, who masturbated in On [Heliopolis]. He took his phallus in his grasp that he might create orgasm by means of it, and so were born the twins Shu and Tefenet."[20] Coffin Text, Spell 245, a variant to this account, depicts the god using his mouth and his hand to bring about creation: "Atum spat me out in the spittle of his mouth together with my sister Tefenet."[21]

A number of the several hundred *ostraca* found in houses, chapels and tombs at the worker's village of Deir el-Medina depict what may be categorized as sexualized or erotic behaviour. Some scenes depict semi-naked or naked servant girls, musicians and dancers, but it is unclear if these images expressed erotic undertones in addition to the primary representation – at least, as we might discern such implications today.

248

SEXUALITY

Although, again, it is difficult to ascribe a specific intention to certain images, other drawings may be interpreted more readily as comic or satirical in nature. These sketches show obese, bald men well past their prime having sexual intercourse with young women. Such images appear to play with traditional modes of visual representation, particularly those aesthetic principles associated with formal depictions of men and women in affective contexts. They may also be interpreted without too much difficulty as formulations of sexual activity deliberately exaggerated in terms of the relative ages of the participants, the unexpurgated nature of the content, or the aesthetic parameters of the depictions. Given chronological and cultural differences, determining the purpose of such exaggeration is, of course, elusive. However, it is safe to assert that images like these will have left no room for confusion or doubt in the mind of the viewer but will more than likely not have been construed in literal terms. As a result, we may infer that the artists responsible for these drawings intended a response – or possibly a variety of reactions – keyed to the transgression of traditional pictorial principles and acceptable standards of behaviour. In this regard, the kind of reception most in line with this underlying objective would be amusement of one kind or another: entertainment; laughter; intellectual or emotional pleasure derived from comparison with customary practice, whether based on personal experience or community beliefs.

The explicit content of these pictures is sexualized further by what might be described as the erotic vocabulary of the activity depicted. This sexual coding underpins the manner in which the women are clothed (or not) and positioned in relation to their corpulent senior partners. Wearing heavy wigs and hip girdles, the naked (or semi-naked) women are seen to adopt a receptive or passive attitude in sexual activity. The act of intercourse is depicted almost invariably as penetration from behind, though whether anal or vaginal is unclear. Finally, some of the *ostraca* simply show genital organs, or – as we have seen previously – nursing mothers.

G11.2   "Gentle of skin, gentle of charm."

The scene accompanying the descriptive statement above shows a man and woman having sexual intercourse. Serving as a caption to the scene, the hieroglyphic text – which may refer to the image *in toto* or either of the individuals depicted – qualifies the explicit nature of the artistic representation, incorporating a poetic element reminiscent of literary compositions dealing with erotic themes. Here we can discern the reciprocity of affective and erotic feelings expressed in song cycles concerned with heterosexual relationships. Indeed, while it is highly probable that the artist responsible for this image was male, the inference is by any means an established fact. In addition, the dialogic nature of the literary compositions dealing with erotic themes may reasonably be used to support the contention that the audience for such texts

249

comprised a heterogeneous mix of male *and* female readers and auditors. Following the same logic, it is just as likely that the intended audience *and* readership for a captioned drawing of sexual activity was female as male.

From another angle, there is a second aesthetic on display here which further complicates our reading of the image. In stark contrast to depictions in formal relief sculpture or statuary, the genitalia of the male figure to the right are clearly visible to the viewer. Moreover, given the traditional motifs of formal composition in Egyptian art, it is not strictly possible to differentiate the biological sex of the figure to the left. The inclusion of erect or extended nipples on this figure should not automatically identify the person as female; nor is the absence of male genitalia necessarily problematic. Therefore, although it may be assumed that the penetrated individual is female, this cannot be ascertained with certainty.

In this regard, while homosexuality as a category does not appear to exist in any established sense or as the subject of definitive expression in Egyptian thought, it is interesting to read without further comment another fragmentary verse from the Deir el-Medina "archive" of erotic *ostraca* – a (revised?) version of a love poem in the Papyrus Chester Beatty I anthology involving the relationship between the *persona* or speaker (who may be male), a female friend (and object of affection) and a charioteer called Mehy.

G11.3   "[Boy?] Beer is sweet, when I sit at his side [and my] hands have not been far away. The wind blows as I say in my heart, '... with sweet wine. I am given of [love (?)].' ... My voice is hoarse from saying, 'Mehi – life, prosperity, health!' He is in his fortress. [Boy] The lady sails north while drinking beer. An island is before him ... sail. Cool ... pure gold. We will cast the heel ... We will place [gifts] before Mehi, saying: '... love.' Spend the day."

The sexual acts depicted on the Deir el-Medina *ostraca* correspond remarkably with those found in the famous Turin Erotic Papyrus (Papyrus 5501) – the only surviving Egyptian papyrus displaying explicit sexual activity.[22] Dating to the Ramesside period (1292–1075 BCE), it is thought to have been painted by a professional draughtsman at Thebes in Upper Egypt. That the images were executed with a degree of artistry and on expensive papyrus suggests that the work was intended originally for an elite audience.

Comprising twelve vignettes, what survives of the papyrus depicts two interrelated sequences of physical activity. First, the papyrus shows animals carrying out human tasks; second, a detailed series of scenes reproduce people captured in a startling diversity of sexual positions and actions.

In relation to the initial series of images, fragments of another illustrated papyrus show animals engaged in human activities, including a hippopotamus making beer, a cat waiting on a mouse, a lion making beer and a canine

250

SEXUALITY

carrying grain.[23] Just as we have seen in the case of pictorial *ostraca*, it is uncertain how the papyrus should be interpreted; that is, how it would have been viewed in its contemporary context. The individual "episodes" or "portraits" do not constitute a strictly connected or sequential articulation of successive events, and are therefore not particularly likely to signify a pattern of cognitive associations intended to aid the memory, nor to illustrate the equivalent of a prose narrative, or even to serve as a basis for retelling a coherent story based on the separate images.

Like the pictorial *ostraca* from Deir el-Medina, the Turin Papyrus drawings would appear to function as deliberate exaggerations of activities represented in the traditional contexts of religious or funerary art. By imitating the style, motifs and thematic imagery associated with formal artistic composition – in temple reliefs, tomb paintings and coffin decoration – the images of animals performing human actions subverted generic expectations for comic effect. In the same fashion as the Deir el-Medina workers and their families, the viewers of the animal scenes in the Turin Papyrus will have interpreted the meaning of the images and responded to their intended effect on a primarily visual level.

If this is the case, then we should apply the same reading of comic role-reversal to the latter sequence of sexual vignettes. In relation to the artist's depiction of physical characteristics, the men are shown with unnaturally large genitalia – the enormous phalli define the structural composition of each encounter: in the scene to the far right of the lower register, two servant girls support the hyper-extended length of the male member; the men have balding heads, sport unkempt beards and appear otherwise untidy or dishevelled; and they are both small in stature and of mature age. In contrast, the women are markedly younger than their sexual partners and – uncharacteristically in terms of the traditional Egyptian repertoire of gendered representation – taller; they do not wear clothing of any kind, but display jewellery – bracelets, necklaces – and bodily decoration – lotus-flowers in their hair and girdles around their waists.

In addition to figural depiction, the three scenes – comprising seven individual sexual encounters – include material objects associated with the goddess of love (Hathor) – the *sistrum* (a musical instrument consisting of a fluted handle and U-shaped metal frame, to which were attached small rings or loops of thin metal on mobile crossbars) – and celebration – pottery jars of wine and beer. Various ancillary items – a small chariot, a head-rest, a conical offering table – provide additional opportunity for sexual stimulation. Like the paintings of banquet scenes in private tombs of the New Kingdom period, the visual context within which each sexual act is framed on the Turin Papyrus contains the accoutrements essential to enhance sexual potency and the erotic ambiance.

The illustrations of sexual activity are varied – three of the seven scenes depict *coitus a tergo* (intercourse from the rear). The flexibility and athleticism of the protagonists mirror the energetic displays of male fighters and female dancers found in the traditional repertoire of public art. In one of

251

GRAFFITI IN ANTIQUITY

the scenes – second from the left in the middle register of the reproduction – the male is standing with knees slightly bent, holding the female; she, in turn, clasps her legs around his neck. Interesting from the perspective of later Graeco-Roman sexual discourse, the women are shown to be actively engaged in the performance of sexual congress. In another vignette – first from the left, middle register – the woman seems to ridicule her lover. Physically spent, he has apparently fallen out of bed and is crawling away. According to the text-caption for this visual element, she asks:

G11.4   "Am I doing anything wrong to you?"

One wonders if this suggests male anxiety in relation to explicit female sexuality, mocking the dominant cultural discourse of male preeminence and socio-sexual expertise.

As the textual snippet cited above indicates, at some point a scribe had attempted to augment the imagery of the artist – perhaps the same individual, possibly two composers working in concert to achieve a creative whole. Imagining what the sexual actors in each scene might have been thinking, the scribe incorporated a reconstructed dialogue wherever there was sufficient space. Unfortunately, the damage suffered by the papyrus over the course of time has rendered many of the accompanying text-captions only partially intelligible, leaving the texts that have survived impermeable to satisfactory analysis and interpretation. Nonetheless, in keeping with the effect of imagery pertaining to literary and inscribed love poetry as well as the pictorial *ostraca*, it is plausible to speculate that the Turin Erotic Papyrus performed at the very least a basic purpose common to all genres of erotic expression – the fulfillment of the pleasure principle, whether ironic, satirical, entertaining or enervating. The vignette to the far right of the middle register encapsulates this fundamental intention. The girl is bent over in a position reminiscent of elite funerary decoration, namely, of Nut, the sky goddess, when during the creation of the world she was separated from Geb, the god of earth. The man carries a sack over his shoulder and penetrates her from the rear. Inscribed quickly in the margins, the text-caption articulates enjoyment and delight:

G11.5   "Come behind me with your love. Oh, Sun – you have found
        out my heart. It is agreeable work."

Greece

Looking at the evidence for non-official inscriptions as they pertain to sexual beliefs and practices in Greek antiquity will require a brief survey of what is known about the socio-cultural environment in archaic, classical and

252

post-classical Greece. Whether historically authentic or imaginatively constructed, many culturally specific patterns of sexuality in Greek antiquity – heterosexuality, male and female homosexuality, bisexuality, transsexuality (hermaphroditism), asexuality – may be encountered in the surviving textual and visual record – comedy, forensic speeches, philosophical discourses, poetry and vase paintings.

Regardless of the multiplicity of variant sexualities, one fundamental feature informed *all* erotic preferences and practices – the intrinsic superiority of the adult citizen male. In other words, the principle of socio-sexual predominance applied to all adult men who were eighteen years of age, owned land, were not the property of and therefore subject to another person, and whose parents were also recognized as legitimate inhabitants of a particular *polis* with the same rights and obligations.

As might be imagined, this principle impacted significantly on relationships of every kind in Greek society, including sexual (or sensual) affiliations. This is especially the case if we exclude from consideration as a factor in the choice of affective or sexual partner what until only very recently was perceived as the "natural" or "mainstream" predisposition or orientation in human socio-sexual relationships – namely, heterosexuality. With respect to such relationships, particularly in aristocratic Greek society, adult male citizens regarded themselves – and, at least according to the prevailing view, should have been regarded by others – as superior to females, younger males, slave males, prostitutes of both sexes and even certain members of their own peer group. In simple terms, an ancient Greek adult male citizen could – hypothetically and within limits imposed by factors like personal or familial reputation, social status, or socio-political obligation – establish a relationship based on degrees of physical attraction and/or emotional attachment with an individual who belonged to *any* of these categories of Greek or non-Greek (i.e. foreign) person. Here, of course, it should be clear that, according to this philosophical and socio-cultural perspective, legal, ethical and religious limitations or taboos imposed in the modern age on practices like pederasty, paedophilia, sex slavery, female subjugation, hetero- or homosexual rape, and so on did not apply in the same way in Greek antiquity.

This is an extreme formulation of Greek sexuality as a historical phenomenon. It is intended more than anything else to alert the modern reader to the essential differences in ancient Greek – and, as we shall see, Roman – sexual arrangements. In all of this, what is most important to note relates to the performative roles adopted by or imposed on persons as a result of the principle of superiority – namely, to be dominant or subservient in any relationship; or, as it is more commonly termed with respect to socio-sexual relations, to be active or passive.

With this in mind, let us first consider a number of inscriptions scratched on rocks in the vicinity of a temple of Apollo Carneius (or Delphinios) and a gymnasium located on the Greek island of Thera.[24]

GRAFFITI IN ANTIQUITY

G11.6 "Pheidipidas copulated, Timagoras and Enpheres copulated, Enpylos [was] a fornicator. Enpedocles inscribed this [and] danced by Apollo." (*IG* 12.3.536)

G11.7 "By Delphinius Apollo, here Crimon penetrated the son of Bathycles, brother of ... ." (*IG* 12.3.537a)

G11.8 "Here Crimon fucked Amotion." (*IG* 12.3.538b)

G11.9 "Lacydidas is good." (*IG* 12.3.540(I))

G11.10 "Eumelus is the best dancer." (*IG* 12.3.540(II))

G11.11 "Crimon, first in the Konialos, charmed Simias." (*IG* 12.3.540(III))

G11.12 " ... loves Phanocles." (*IG* 12.3.542)

G11.13 "Barbax both dances well and gave ... ." (*IG* 12.3.543)

G11.14 "Telecrates is a good dancer." (*IG* 12.3.546)

G11.15 "I, ... am beautiful in the eyes of all." (*IG* 12.3.549)

G11.16 "In the presence of Dyman, son of Hermeias, ... always offered ..." (*IG* 12.3.550)

Dating to some point in time from the mid-sixth to the fourth century BCE, these informal messages articulate explicit declarations of male homoerotic attraction (G11.9, 11–12, 15–16), competitive admiration (G11.10, 13–14) and perjorative sexual obscenity (G11.6–8). Given Apollo's association with the initiation of adolescent males (*ephebes*) as citizens and the gymnasium's function as a facility for athletic training and a space for physical contests between initiates, it is not surprising to find graffiti of this kind close by. Nor should we find it unusual for such expressions of affection, rivalry and abuse in the context of intimate same-sex socio-sexual relations.

While it is impossible to determine the age of the inscribing population or those named in particular messages, the repeated references to dancing suggests that the persons engaged in composing and scratching the graffiti texts belonged to an ephebic community. Enpedocles, certainly, qualifies in this respect – "Enpedocles inscribed this [and] danced by Apollo" (G11.6). The allusions to qualitative performance add positively to this speculation – "Lacydidas is good" (G11.9), "Eumelus is the best dancer" (G11.10), "Barbax ... dances well" (G11.13), "Telecrates is a good dancer" (G11.14). The fact

254

that Crimon placed "first in the Konialos" situates the act of dancing squarely in the erotic landscape of archaic Theran ephebic society, since the *konialos* was a lewd, even salacious dance with strong sexual overtones.[25] That said, it is possible to translate the graffito in such a way that "Crimon first delighted Simias with his lascivious dance" – an interpretation which preserves the homoerotic flavour of the message while omitting the agonistic element of a competitive victory.

That certain individuals cast aspersions on sexual activity between young men should not be seen as objecting to the act *per se*. Rather, if we understand that there existed from the archaic period on a general prohibition against sexual activity in sacred spaces, then Enpedocles' use of the word "copulate" (G11.6) in careful conjunction with an identification of place ("here") clearly connote none-too-subtle denigration of the individuals named. Interestingly, the sentiments of those anonymous inscribers in agreement with Enpedocles' denigration of sexual activity (of any kind) so close to the temple of Apollo relate to a serial offender in this regard, Crimon – "*here* Crimon penetrated the son of Bathycles" (G11.7), "*here* Crimon fucked Amotion" (G11.8).

According to the Theran graffiti, then, we may identify historical evidence for pederastic sexual practices in archaic and classical Doric (Spartan) Greek contexts – namely, male homosexual conduct among consenting young adults – in a context which on the one hand explains the concentration of messages dealing with such activity (the temple of Apollo, the gymnasium) and on the other hand confirms strictly held beliefs in relation to limitations to such activity (outside the god's sacred precinct).

G11.17 "Arisemus is beautiful [*kalós*]. Polytime is a cocksucker [*laikástria*]!" (*IG* 1².1402)[26]

G11.18 "The boy is lewd [*mísetos*]." (Mid-seventh century BCE)[27]

G11.19 "Antheme appears beautiful to Aisch ..." (Mid-sixth century BCE)

G11.20 "Titas, the Olympic victor, is wide-arsed [i.e. submits to anal penetration; *katapúgōn*]." (Late sixth century BCE)

G11.21 "Menekrates is beautiful and dear to Lysikles." (Late sixth century BCE)

G11.22 "Hegestratus fucks me." (Early fifth century BCE)

G11.23 "Sosias is wide-arsed. So says the one who wrote this." (Mid-fifth century BCE)

G11.24 "Sydnromachos of the gaping arsehole [*lakkópröktos*] submitted [to me]." (Mid-fifth century BCE)

Dating from the late archaic period to the middle of the classical age (seventh to fourth centuries BCE), graffiti found in the Athenian *agora* and its environs provide a fascinating insight into those facets of sexuality about which men (and possibly women) felt the need to scratch, paint or ink messages on pottery for the interest, entertainment or edification of their contemporaries. Just as the Theran graffiti articulated differing degrees of admiration, affection or invective, so the Athenian inscriptions display a range of sentiments dealing with the expression of sexualized statements – from highly intimate, profoundly favourable remarks (G11.17, 19, 21) to deeply offensive, obscenely explicit vilifications (G11.17–18, 20, 22–4).

We have already met one of the graffiti types listed above. The *kalos*-formula we saw used in wall and pottery inscriptions pertaining to athletic activity (G9.2–3) is also found in a number of the Athenian graffiti (G11.17, 19, 21). In each of the cited examples – and more than ten other instances of *kalos*-names found in the Athenian *agora*[28] – the intention is demonstrably approving. Arisemus (G11.17), Antheme (G11.19) and Menekrates (G11.21) are declared "beautiful" (*kalos*) in the eyes of the inscriber. While the admiring writers of two of the three graffiti catalogued here are certainly or probably male (G11.19, 21), it is not at all certain if the writer of the remaining inscription (G11.17) was male or female – and, importantly, this is also the case in the other examples not listed. This, naturally, has implications for our understanding of male and female participation in relation to informal inscribing practices. Furthermore, the affective relations expressed in the *kalos*-inscriptions encompass a range of sexual relations – male–male (G11.21), male–female (G11.19) and indeterminate (G11.17).

In contrast to the *kalos*-inscriptions, there exists in the surviving record of *agora* graffiti a miscellany of vituperative statements relying on use of obscene or sexually charged terminology. Given the references to pederastic intercourse noted in the Theran graffiti, it should not be surprising to find informal expressions of homo- or heteroerotic activity here at Athens. What is interesting to note is the choice of vocabulary used in many of the abusive inscriptions and the resulting socio-cultural connotations. Terms which are deployed in service to sexualized vituperation include the commonly used "wide-arsed" (*katapúgōn* or *pugaîos*) and the specialist descriptors "cocksucker" (*laikástria*), "lewd" or "abominable" (*mísetos*) and "having a gaping arsehole" (*lakkópröktos*). These words imply a receptive or passive role on the part of the individual named as the recipient of sexual activity performed by another – the inscriber or a putative anonymous or identified other. The graffiti which use these expressions articulate definitively the principle of superiority underpinning Greek cultural relations – possessed by the inscriber, who enacts or embodies the superordinate role of sexual penetrator; most

SEXUALITY

certainly not possessed by the subject of the inscription, on whom the act of penetration (whether oral, anal or vaginal) is performed.

Across this broadly based category of informal communication, it is important to note that a significant proportion of graffiti texts was directed to named persons. Using the vocabulary of sensual affect and sexual activity, such declarations of emotional attachment, indignation and abuse will have resonated with varying effect in a typically Greek socio-cultural context. Seventh/sixth- to fifth/fourth-century BCE Athenian society was grounded very firmly within an ethos of personal, familial and community honour and shame. In consequence, and adding to the impact of explicit sexual language adduced above, broadcasting to the wider local community any remarks likely to alter or destabilize the perceived superiority integral to any person's network of social relations must be – and will have been – seen either as enhancing or diminishing the social reputation of the man or woman named in the message.

G11.25 "Theodosia sucks cock well."[29]

G11.26 "Sosibius, son of Cuntlicker [*Kústholoichos*]."[30]

This active–passive socio-sexual framework helps to explain the discourse of power which permeates a good deal of the most explicit sexual graffiti in Greek antiquity. The first of the listed inscriptions (G11.25) contains the obscene term which may be translated as "cocksucker" (*laikástria*). This graffito also comes from the Athenian *agora* and, like the earlier example (G11.17: Polytime) is applied to a female (Theodosia). The derogatory nature of this epithet is crystal-clear; however, unlike modern usage of the word as a generalized term of abuse – or more particularly in relation to male homosexual acts – *laikástria* appears to have been used in graffiti to indicate the passive recipient of oral penetration. In other words, the word denoted the inferior or subordinate partner in a sexual act, whether between members of the same sex or male and female persons. The second graffito (G11.26) – one of 17 inscriptions (mainly signatures) found at Abu Koueh in the eastern desert of Hellenistic Upper Egypt – adds the imaginary patronymic "Cuntlicker" (*Kústholoichos*) to a frequently attested personal name Sosibius. In the same way that *laikástria* denoted a passive or receptive – and therefore intrinsically inferior – participant in a sexual act, so any person (male or female) identified in ancient literary and sub-literary texts as a performer of oral sex on a female (cunnilingus) was similarly subordinate. This imaginative leap was possible by virtue of the conceptual logic whereby the woman on whom the oral sex was performed was seen as penetrating the mouth of the cunnilingor (*kústholoichos*) – thus preserving the principle of superiority in relation to sexual activity between individuals of the same or different biological sex.

257

We have already considered the use of magic in antiquity (Chapter 6). As part of this discussion, we identified a category of magic employed across the Mediterranean known as the binding spell or curse (*katadesmos, defixio*). As you may recall, one of the texts cited previously (G6.18) – dating to the fourth century BCE – demonstrated how an informal medium of communication like the binding spell could express ideas about erotic relationships in the broader context of ancient magical practice. Another example of this kind of non-official inscription – composed almost eight hundred years later (late third/early fourth century CE) – identifies female homoerotic attraction as part of the spectrum of sexualities existing in Greek antiquity. The following is only a brief part of a much longer text (in all, 62 lines):

G11.27 "By means of this corpse-daemon inflame the heart, the liver, the spirit of Gorgonia, whom Nilogenia bore, with love and affection for Sophia, whom Isara bore. Constrain Gorgonia, whom Nilogenia bore, to cast herself into the bath-house for the sake of Sophia, whom Isara bore; and you, become a bath-woman. Burn, set on fire, inflame her soul, heart, liver, spirit with love for Sophia, whom Isara bore."

Tapered at the beginning and end of the text to form an oval-shaped inscription, this binding spell was found at Hermoupolis Magna in Upper Egypt. Written in Greek script of the later imperial period on a thin sheet of lead, it was commissioned by a woman named Sophia to attract another woman, Gorgonia. The fact that the names of the two women were inserted into the text without appropriate grammatical adjustment – so that the endings of their names in the original Greek would make sense in relation to the sentence structure in which they appeared – reflects the formulaic nature of the magical practice. While this means that the *katadesmos* was incised into the lead tablet by a scribe working from a collection of spells applicable to particular situations, it should also be very clear that the erotic attraction to be effected by the magical text was between two women. It is also interesting to note that the desired location for this compelled homoerotic assignation was the public bath-house. As a space set aside for sanctioned physical exposure and contact between women, the bath-house would seem a logical locus for establishing homoerotic relations. This also explains why the spell envisaged the corpse-daemon – the magical conduit by means of which the attraction will be accomplished – "possessing" the bodily form of a bath-house attendant. Responsible for oiling and washing clients of the bathing establishment, the female slave was the ideal agent for the task.

Like the banquet in the Turin Erotic Papyrus and the gymnasium on Thera, the bath-house would appear to have been another context suitable for evoking a sensual response – albeit in this instance one that relied on magical compulsion. Here, of course, the principle of superiority underlying

SEXUALITY

sexual relations in Graeco-Roman antiquity should not be forgotten. In the excerpted text – and throughout the length of the spell – the vocabulary of domination typical for *katadesmoi* in general is very much part of Sophia's overriding homoerotic imperative with respect to her love-object Gorgonia.

Rome

The object of this final section of Chapter 11 is to find evidence in informal inscriptions of how women and men living in the Mediterranean under Roman rule represented themselves with respect to sexual ideas and practices.[31] This implies an examination of conventionally gendered objects of Graeco-Roman sexual discourse, and its deviant counterparts. As applied throughout *Graffiti in Antiquity*, certain premises underpin this approach:

- the complex intersections of sexual subject positions with class or ethnic status;
- the projection of historical and social contingencies onto the template of Graeco-Roman sexuality; and
- the comprehensive interaction between oral operations (presentation and hearing) and literary operations (reading and writing) in a "manuscript culture with high residual orality" (a process characteristic of a "rhetorical culture" like that of the ancient Mediterranean).[32]

Modern analyses of predominantly literary sources dealing with Roman (and Graeco-Roman) antiquity identify between male–male, female–female and female–male a grid of horizontal social and sexual relationships.[33] This network of connections oscillates among a variety of interpersonal, socially determined valencies. Centred on the idealized subject position of the virile male (*vir*), an individual's position as a member of Graeco-Roman society could be measured from one standpoint against a spectrum of normative descriptions and deviant prescriptions. Normalcies and deviations revolved around the use of anatomical orifices: vagina, anus and mouth. The informal sexual vocabulary recorded by users of the Graeco-Roman linguistic system differentiated between female penetration and the phallic agency of the male penetrator, and representations of male receptivity and the quasi-phallic activity of the female penetrator.

This nexus of socio-linguistic designations is rendered more intricate by a complementary variety of vertical identifiers, *vir*/*homo* (man) and *femina*/ *mulier* (woman). According to recent explorations of these terms in the canonical literature of Republic and Empire,[34] the reader was able to separate *viri* from *homines*. The former category included celebrated men of senatorial rank, upper magistrates, notable *equites*, persons who participated in public life and were politically sound (i.e. the *boni*). It may also range from

259

those who had distinguished themselves in their country's service either in the military or in the provinces and those whom the author wished to flatter. On the other hand, *homines* were almost invariably registered as the *priuati* who had not chosen a senatorial career (e.g. scholars and lawyers), the lower magistrates (particularly tribunes), members of the lower classes, municipals, foreigners (including, with notable exceptions, their aristocracy), freedmen, slaves and any male member of the upper classes whom the author wished to insult.[35]

This explicit differentiation is visibly inscribed in the range of statuses comported by the words *femina* and *mulier*. *Feminae* refer to women of the upper class, and appear synonymous with Roman ideals and standards of behaviour applicable to the idealized female of elite society. In keeping with the *vir/homo* binarism, *mulieres* incorporate those individuals and/or groups who inhabit socio-political or geographical spaces regarded as exemplary of the subordinate (foreign or low-born) antithesis of representative femaleness.[36] Since *vir/homo* and *femina/mulier* are linguistically redundant terms,[37] they may be viewed as appositive epithets, used for various kinds of rhetorical emphasis: exaggeration, invective, exemplification, intensification, and so on.

The epigraphic representation in private Latin inscriptions of this symbolic grammar of male and female identity displays a complementary linguistic field of sexual and social vocabulary. In the majority of recorded instances, men and women are identified in funerary and ritual epigraphy by a range of explicit, qualitative signifiers. The horizontal and vertical relationships of Roman society defined in literary contexts by insertive-receptive and status-specific designations are represented epigraphically primarily in terms of filiation, marital condition, reproductive agency and civic status. Relations of blood, marriage, birth and citizenship inscribe male and female identity.

How does this socio-sexual framework – familiar to us from our brief survey of Greek graffiti – find expression in non-official inscriptions of the Roman world? One of the most compelling yet confronting aspects of inscribed graffiti and painted images at Pompeii is the explicitly sexual content. The three volumes of *CIL* IV contain about 500 graffiti conforming to a specifically erotic taxonomy. Given the challenging nature of some of this material, the following discussion will focus on examples of erotic graffiti displaying a selection of qualitative features. The fact that a significant proportion of graffiti recovered or recorded at Pompeii (15.49% of surviving graffiti, 5.19% of inscriptions in general) reflects a sexualized vocabulary requires consideration.[38]

G11.28 "So may you always flourish, Sabina. May you acquire beauty
and stay a girl for a long time." (*CIL* IV.9171)

G11.29 "Girl, you are beautiful. To you I have been sent by one who is
yours. Farewell." (*CIL* IV.1234)

G11.30 "Love dictates as [or what] I write and Cupid shows me. May I
die if I wish to be a god without you." *(CIL* IV.1928)

The first example of this category of graffiti was inscribed on the tomb of
a certain Septumia, daughter of Lucius, located outside the Vesuvian gate
(G11.28). When restored, the graffitist's composition can be seen to take a
metrical form, that of the elegiac couplet.[39]

This metre, created by the early Greek lyric poets for a variety of themes,
came to be associated with Latin love poetry.[40] It is thus especially suited
to the sentiments expressed in the graffito. The inscriber wanted this message to be seen, and not only by the subject of the expressed desire. Scratching a declaration into the stone façade of a tomb guaranteed a regular and
diverse readership. The memorial's surface was durable, the tomb abutted a
well-travelled pedestrian thoroughfare close to one of the main entrances to
Pompeii, and city-dwellers and visitors capable of reading Latin were used
to reading funerary dedications and official notices as they approached any
urban centre in the Roman Empire. During this historical period, burials
were restricted by law to extra-mural plots, and consequently tombs lined all
roads outside a city's walls. If a person wished to draw the attention of a large
audience to an inscription of any kind, placing it at eye level on a tombstone
facing a main road was the next best thing to the exterior wall of a prominent
building inside the city limits.

While it is not possible to determine the social class of the person who
inscribed this statement, one can note that the individual in question had
acquired some knowledge of Latin love poetry and possessed the ability to
create a personal meaning within the metrical requirements of the literary
form. Another graffito, found on the wall of a private chamber within the so-
called House of Sallust (VI.2.4), displays a similar competence with elegiac
lyricism (G11.29). In this case, the graffitist makes use of a common form of
trochaic verse, the *septenarius*, to express a familiar poetical conceit.[41]

Like the first graffito, this inscription provides us with a snapshot of an
affective relationship. Here, the composer negotiates generically with the
epistolary mode favoured by a number of prominent Latin authors – Horace,
Cicero, Propertius and Ovid. The graffito is an explicit declaration of appreciation, designed to reproduce in style either what may have already been
transmitted in a more private letter written to the object of attraction or an
imitation of the same refashioned in poetic form. Whether the relationship
implied is real or imagined, it should be clear that the apparent simplicity of
an inscribed text like this belies a linguistic sophistication over and beyond
traditional assessments of graffiti as a non-literary product and foregrounds
the range of alternatives and possibilities in the practice of writing by elite
and non-elite Romans during this historical period.

A third example confirms this evaluation (G11.2). It was inscribed on an
interior wall of Pompeii's Basilica (Figure 11.1). As noted in the Introduction

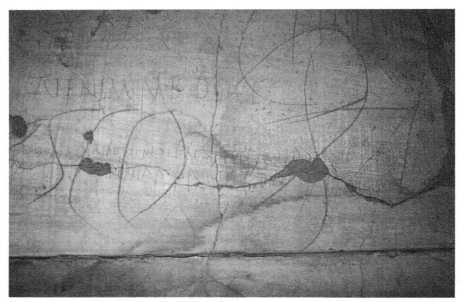

Figure 11.1 Graffito in the Basilica (VII.1), Pompeii, Italy (Archaeological Museum of Naples/NAM 29.4707).

to this book, the building – constructed in pre-Roman times (*c.*120 BCE) – served the administration of justice by appointed officials of the town council, and daily accommodated a variety of commercial transactions conducted by local individuals.[42] Almost two hundred graffiti have been recovered from this single building, testifying to the intensity of activity here and to the acceptance and popularity of graffiti-writing and drawing in Pompeii.[43]

Like the preceding examples, the graffito cited above was composed in the form of an elegiac couplet, and speaks of the writer's desire for a loved one.[44] The inscription resonates with a variety of literary, epistolary and poetic references.[45] It articulates for its intended readership the widespread cultural belief in the relationship between the creative impulse and divine inspiration, and expresses in cognate terms the intensity of feeling consuming the lover.

The comparatively elevated level of theme, tone and style represented by these three inscribed texts can be balanced against a large number of graffiti displaying a limited thematic vocabulary, coarser expression of sentiments and often a simpler grasp of the Latin language. Despite these differences, graffiti of this kind can be found in a variety of public and private spaces in Pompeii, including the Basilica and other buildings in the Forum, a large proportion of the exterior wall surfaces of *insula* dwellings, and the multiplicity of surfaces inside the homes of elite and non-elite residents, including the work- and living-spaces of public and domestic slaves. In other words, just as the composition of verse-graffiti cannot be restricted to members of the elite

SEXUALITY

class, so the phenomenon of writing and drawing sexually suggestive, derogatory or abusive graffiti cannot be confined to the non-elite.

Examples of sexually implicit or explicit graffiti can be identified in a wide variety of locations, including (but not limited to) spatially and socially demarcated contexts like the gladiators' barracks in the Large Palaestra (G11.31–2) and the so-called House of the Gladiators (G11.33–4); Pompeii's many brothels – from the purpose-built *lupanar* located (G11.35–7) to a possible place set aside for sex-work (G11.38); and the Basilica (G11.39–48).

G11.31 "Floronius the fucker [*binetas*], privileged soldier [*miles*] of the seventh legion, was here. Not many women [*mulieres*] came to know him – there were six." (*CIL* IV.8767)

G11.32 "Antiochus stayed here with his girlfriend Cithera." (*CIL* IV.8792b)

G11.33 "Crescens the net-fighter, doctor ... of girls in the night, in the morning, and at other times." (*CIL* IV.4353)

G11.34 "Girls' sigh. Celadus, Thracian fighter [*thraex*]." (*CIL* IV.4397; cf. G9.8–9)

Found in the *ludus* close by Pompeii's amphitheatre (II.7) and a residential complex close to the north-eastern perimeter of the town (V.5.3), these examples (G11.31–4) neatly capture the swaggering *braggadocio* featured in many of the graffiti that detail the sexual prowess of the composer. Moreover, it should be clear that these texts – sometimes with accompanying drawings of phalluses in a variety of sizes – were invariably inscribed by men. In almost every instance – we can ascribe residential status only to Antiochus – the composers were gladiators or persons associated with arena competition or military activity. Scratched on columns and a wall by Floronius, Crescens and Celadus, these declarations of status – privileged soldier, net-fighter, Thracian gladiator – and performance – all but Antiochus boast multiple sexual conquests – conform closely to the model of normative behaviour already identified as integral to socio-sexual relations in the Graeco-Roman world. As outlined, this framework denotes a man (*vir/homo*) as socially dominant, culturally active and physically penetrative, and a woman (*femina/mulier*) as socially subordinate, culturally passive and physically receptive.[46]

G11.35 "I fucked a lot of girls here." (*CIL* IV.2175)

G11.36 "On 15 June, Hermeros fucked here with Phileterus and Caphisus." (*CIL* IV.2185)

263

GRAFFITI IN ANTIQUITY

G11.37 "Sollemnes, you fuck well." (*CIL* IV.2192)

G11.38 "Victor, best wishes to one who has fucked well." (*CIL* IV.2260)

G11.39 "Gaius Valerius Venustus, soldier of the First Praetorian
Cohort, in the century of Rufus, the greatest of fuckers."
(*CIL* IV.2145)

Selected from messages in one of Pompeii's primary brothels (VII.12.18–20) and one of over forty possible residential or single-room spaces set aside for sex-work (VII.12.35), these five graffiti (G11.37–9) express clearly and unequivocally in terms of sexual roles the traditional Graeco-Roman hierarchy of social status. To better understand the clarity of this representation, the graffiti must be viewed in context. In this case, the first three texts were inscribed in relation to a variety of painted scenes illustrating sexual positions, located above the entrances to five spaces set aside for sexual activity inside a public brothel. In all five, the man – alone, or, in one instance, in company with two others – is depicted (or implied) as a penetrator, illustrative of his privileged masculinity and civic prerogatives; the woman – implied, imagined or real – as a passive receptor, indicative of her constrained femininity and civic limitations. The Latin used in the graffiti explicitly – or, in context with other inscriptions nearby – underline this sexualized ideology. The verb of choice denoting vaginal penetration (*futuere*) is used in the active voice in four of the five graffiti, articulating and corroborating the norms of sexual conduct illustrated in the paintings – or, in the case of C. Valerius Venustus, laying out his performative credentials as part of the conventional epigraphic summary of personal identity: tripartite nomenclature (which, implicitly, acknowledges his freed status), civic role and rank (imperial military service under the emperor Nero), and, additionally, sexual stature ("the greatest of fuckers").

In relation to the graffito referring to Victor (G11.38), without context the word used may denote either a person of that name or subsume a general category of sexual agents (a "victor") qualified in competitive terms. However, as nearby graffiti show, Victor appears in a number of messages implying or expanding on his sexual ability – e.g. "Victor fucked well" (*CIL* IV.2218) and, clearly visible at the top of the photograph, "Victor was here with Attinis" (*CIL* IV.2258). All five of the brothel graffiti speak directly to the male clientele of these establishments and to Roman conceptions of sex and gender.

G11.40 "At one time, the Vibii were the most noble at Pompeii. For
that reason, they did not hold the[ir] sceptre in hand like a
penis, as you do habitually in the same manner every day,
holding [your] member in your hand." (*CIL* IV.1939)

SEXUALITY

G11.41 "My life, my delight, let us play for a while: let this bed be a field and let me be a steed for you." (*CIL* IV.1781)

G11.42 "If anyone is looking for tender embraces in this town, no girl waits for letters from a man ..." (*CIL* IV.1796)

G11.43 "Antiochus, slave of Ligatus, *cinaedus*." (*CIL* IV.1802)

G11.44 "Caesius Fidelis loves Meco of Nuceria." (*CIL* IV.1812)

G11.45 "Epaphra, you are smooth [*glaber*]." (*CIL* IV.1816)

G11.46 "Let anyone who loves come [or, perish]; as for Venus, I want to break her ribs with cudgels and maim the goddess's loins. If she can bore through my tender heart, why should I not dash to pieces her head with a cudgel?" (*CIL* IV.1824)

G11.47 "Cosmus, slave of Equitia, is a great *cinaedus* and a cocksucker [*fellator*] with manly calves apart." (*CIL* IV.1825)

G11.48 "Narcissus, the greatest cocksucker." (*CIL* IV.1825a)

G11.49 "Anyone who butt-fucks the 'inflamed' burns his cock." (*CIL* IV.1882)

G11.50 "Lucilia made a profit from [= prostituted] her body." (*CIL* IV.1948)

Inscribed on the interior walls of the Basilica (VII.1), the sample of messages listed above (G11.40–50) illustrates the sheer variety of erotic expression preserved in the non-official record of Pompeii's sexual discourse. The first graffito (G11.40) lies in relatively close proximity to the verse discussed above (G11.30) referring to Cupid's inspiration (Figure 11.2). It is similarly composed in poetic form – in this case, a couplet in trochaic *septenarii*. However, the subject matter (male masturbation) would seem at first glance far less refined. On closer inspection, this three-line graffito neatly skewers the social pretensions of the person to whom the verse refers by contrasting the elite status (*nobilitas*) of the Vibii, one of the most famous families in Pompeii, to the *indignitas* of his socially unacceptable conduct.[47] The composer adeptly vilifies the unnamed (but surely known) local identity in much the same way as the satirical poetry of Horace and Persius treated men's enslavement to money, power, glory and sex.

The remaining examples reflect the spectrum of erotic expression we have come to expect from the inscribing population of Pompeii – and, indeed,

265

Figure 11.2 Graffito in the Basilica (VII.1) (= *CIL* IV.1939), Pompeii, Italy (Archaeological Museum of Naples/NAM 30.4708).

Graeco-Roman antiquity in general. Anonymous detractors scratch slanderous accusations using the explicit terminology of sexual abuse. A certain Antiochus, slave of Ligatus, is labelled a *cinaedus* – a male who submits to anal penetration. Already diminished in the eyes of any who read this graffito (G11.43) by virtue of his servile status, Antiochus – whose name denotes a Greek influence, if not heritage – is identified as sexually receptive and thus doubly inferior in relation to the wider community (of non-passive fellow slaves, freedpersons and freeborn citizens). In terms of the prevailing socio-sexual framework, Antiochus' identity is rendered equivalent to the position and role of women in Roman society. This discursive strategy of reformulating a person's identity is equally visible in the graffiti "assaulting" the reputations of Cosmus, Equitia's slave (G11.47) and Narcissus (G11.48). Like Antiochus, Cosmus and Narcissus are slaves; both are designated as receptive to oral penetration (*fellatores*); Cosmus, additionally, is tagged a *cinaedus*, whose propensity for anal penetration the inscriber emphasizes in terms which contrast the subject's biological sex with his assumed gender role ("with manly calves spread"). One graffitist scratched a general warning about the physical consequences of consorting with persons like Antiochus and Cosmus (G11.47). Referring to the general category of receptive male (or female) sexual partner as "inflamed" is equivalent – in modern terminology – to speaking about persons who had contracted a sexually transmitted disease. Anyone coming in contact with people like Antiochus and Cosmus – and, by implication, Narcissus – would, in effect, "burn his cock".

Two other graffiti cast different types of aspersion at named subjects (G11.45, 50). Epaphra – who may be the same person we encountered as a participant in the *trigon* competition, an event also recorded in the Basilica (Chapter 9) – is described as "smooth" (*glaber*). While the message might simply refer to the fact that Epaphra was bald, it is equally likely that the inscriber wished to foreground his subject's relative youth – denoted by his "hairless" appearance – and, by extension, his status as a "pet" slave or household favourite. We read in the literary sources about long-haired boys (*capillati*) and pets (*deliciae*) who belonged to a category of male slave sex objects. Epaphra may have been – or his designator may have wished him to be seen as – belonging to the latter kind of domestic slave. More will be said about the sexual status of pre-adolescent and adolescent males of servile status in relation to the Palatine Paedagogium graffiti featured shortly.

The second graffito to objectify a person in sexual terms other than penetrative relates to Lucilia (G11.50). Employing commercial terminology, the inscriber designates Lucilia as a person who "made a profit from her body" (i.e. a prostitute). This may or may not have been a statement of fact – but, regardless of the veracity of the claim, the inscription's explicit commodification of Lucilia's physical integrity renders her, by Roman standards, "infamous" (*infamis*). Women and men who prostituted themselves – that is, persons who profited from use of their body for sexual transactions – were considered to be shameful. Most prostitutes were either slaves or former slaves; some

Figure 11.3 Fresco of *coitus a tergo*, corridor, VII.12.18–20 (Lupanar), Pompeii, Italy.

were free by birth. In all cases, they were relegated to the category of person known as *infames* – people lacking in social standing and deprived of most protections accorded to citizens under Roman law. Interestingly enough, persons like Lucilia shared this status with actors and gladiators. Of course, as we have seen, the existence of (male and female) prostitution would not have been intrinsically shocking to any Pompeian reading this message. Roman men of varying social status – and, we must reasonably infer, some Roman women belonging to the same social strata – either claimed their right as members of the possessing class to use their slaves as sex-objects or paid sex-workers for their services (Figure 11.3). The double standard, however, should be glaringly obvious – and hinges, once more, on the principle of superiority.

The remaining examples of Basilica graffiti from the list supplied above (G11.41–2, 44, 46) provide evidence for the sub-literary or prosaic expression of erotic sentiments comprising affection, attachment or emotional conflict. Two of these inscriptions reflect some acquaintance with the popular genre of lyric poetry and its preoccupations with pastoral imagery (G11.40) and epistolary communication (G11.41). In the first example, we find the inscriber representing an erotic assignation in terms which would have been familiar to anyone acquainted with the literary production of a poet like Ovid – or, indeed, with any of the wall paintings in Pompeii portraying scenes just like this. The second inscription playfully debunks the necessity – as the lyric poets would have it – for elite married women or younger unmarried girls to write and receive letters communicating erotic feelings or making practical arrangements for the conduct of extra- or pre-marital affairs. Love, it would seem, was just around the corner in Venusian Pompeii.

The last texts to be considered confirm the range of emotional states expressed by informal inscriptions in the Basilica. While Caesius Fidelis declares matter-of-factly his love for a certain Meco from the neighbouring town of Nuceria (G11.44), the anonymous composer of the verse graffito destroying (literally) the reputation of Pompeii's patron goddess (G11.46) expatiates according to a popular lyric verse form (the *paraclausithyron*) on the profundity of his erotic turmoil and the lengths to which his despair might lead him. We will meet another example of this type of verse in the discussion which follows. Fidelis' statement may appear prosaic in comparison with the poetic embellishments of his lovelorn fellow inscriber. Nevertheless, both graffiti distil the essential ingredients of non-official messages which communicate affective erotic expressions as opposed to the more vulgar, explicit or personally abusive categories of ephemeral text.

To demonstrate the extent to which matters relating to sensual affection exercised the interest of the local inhabitants of Pompeii, consider a final inscription found in the Basilica.

G11.51 Inscriber 1: "If you can, but do not want to, why do you put off joy? Why do you foster hope and tell me continually to come back tomorrow? Therefore, make me die, you who force me to live without you. The reward for the good surely will not be to be put to the rack" (ll. 1–5). Inscriber 2: "What hope has taken away, hope surely returns to the lover" (ll. 6–8). Inscriber 3: "May he who reads this never have to read another thing in future" (ll. 9–10). Inscriber 4: "May he who writes above never be well/safe" (l. 10). Inscriber 5: "You speak truly" (l. 11). Inscriber 6: "Congratulations, Hedys!" (ll. 11–12).

(*CIL* IV.1837)

If not for the inscription preserved in the Archaeological Museum of Naples (Figure 11.4), the English translation above would fail absolutely to convey the spontaneous, energetic quality of the elegiac dialogue and prose addenda inscribed on to the northern wall of the Pompeian Basilica (G11.51). This extended conversation about the nature of love, scratched in a variety of different hands, preserves for us distinct transient patterns of activity associated with graffiti practice in Pompeii. In the opening elegiac couplets and the hexameter that follows, explicit echoes of Ovid, Tibullus and Virgil speak directly to a cultural collaboration between provincial Pompeii and Rome.[48] Engaging as interlocutors within a recognizable literary tradition, the reflections of these inscribers, literary and conversational, resemble the

Figure 11.4 Graffito in the Basilica (VII.1) (= *CIL* IV.1837), Pompeii, Italy (Archaeological Museum of Naples/NAM 10.4700).

269

composite, enduring dispositional states pertaining to matters of the heart (and body) that we have seen expressed throughout this chapter.

The case for the usefulness of Pompeian graffiti as sources of evidence for erotic terminology and the expression of affective relations in Roman antiquity requires little by way of extension. To conclude this survey, consider one final inscribed text and what historical and socio-cultural questions it can suggest to the interested student of the ancient world.

G11.52 "Oh – if only it was permitted to grasp your little arms, clasped around my neck; and bring kisses to your tender lips. Come now, little girl, entrust your sensual delights to the winds. Trust me: slight is men's nature. Often, when desperately in love I keep watch in the middle of the night, you should think on these things with me: 'Many are they whom Fortuna has raised on high; these, suddenly thrown down headlong, she now oppresses. Just as Venus suddenly joined the bodies of lovers, day divides them and ... you [sc. *Fortuna*] will separate those who love ...'" (*CIL* IV.5296)

The graffito above (G11.52; Figure 11.5) is a nine-line verse in cursive script, found on the right-hand side of the entrance to a private dwelling (IX.ix.f), scratched with the large stylus known as the *graphium* into the lime or clay of the house wall.

Readings for this inscription have varied considerably over the last 127 years,[49] and will undoubtedly continue to perplex and stimulate the modern

Figure 11.5 Graffito on entrance wall of IX.9.f (= *CIL* IV.5296), Pompeii, Italy (Archaeological Museum of Naples).

SEXUALITY

interpreter of epigraphic discourse. Associated with the study of the houses and inhabitants of Pompeii, Matteo Della Corte thought that the verse was written by "a cynic without scruple", whom he identified as "a certain Marius".[50] Antonio Varone – currently Pompeii's director of excavations – places the inscription under the rubric "Unrequited Love" (rather than Della Corte's "Bitter Mockery"), and describes it in the following terms: "verses full of consuming melancholy … the lament of a woman who loves another, but at the same time hopes that her fortune may still change and the happy love-affair turn into smoke". He concludes by noting that "the alternating ebb and flow of human fortune can be compared with the subtle and perfidious game of love".[51]

The resonances of this text with the motif of the *paroclausithyron* – discerned in one of the Basilica graffiti above (G11.36) – are evident enough.[52] More pointed, however, is a gendered reading of this self-representation of a woman's lost love: female homoerotic passion.[53] Just as in the case of the late third/early fourth-century CE *katadesmos* from Hermoupolis Magna (G11.27), this is a significant insight, especially in relation to the traditionally sexualized vocabulary of Roman social relationships – that is, active/passive and penetrator/penetrated – previously considered. If this interpretation is accepted, a constellation of possibilities arises, many revolving around questions of transgressive social action and deviant performance.

The critically aware reader might reasonably ask, for instance, when this graffito could have been inscribed to best result: that is, before the cement had hardened, or at some stage subsequent to the building of the house wall. Similarly, in what ways might the content and intention of the verse have been apprehended by the inhabitants of the house – and the composer of the verse need not necessarily be identified with the occupants of the *domus* in question – *and* by those who passed within and by its walls. In this light, a variety of socio-linguistic matters arises, each of considerable importance. Among other questions of interest, what does this inscription tell us about the degrees of discursive competency possessed by the female composer; that is to say, the varying capacities of our love-lorn interlocutor for literacy and the literary? These could include the extent of her vocabulary; her facility with the metrical requisites of the chosen medium of expression, her acquaintance with textual antecedents in the genres of lyric poetry – the wedding ode (*epithalamion*), the lover outside the door (*paroclausithyron*). As well, one might contemplate her level of participation in the inscribing process. Here, should we imagine her manipulating the *stylus* herself, or must we interpose an intermediary inscriber?

As previously noted, the surface context of this lost same-sexed voice – a small house, at odds with the hierarchies of status, education and gender usually associated with the absorption and production of elegiac verse – is now effectively the section of entrance wall conserved in Naples, the *CIL* line drawing and the original note in the annual bulletin of excavation notes

GRAFFITI IN ANTIQUITY

from Pompeii.[54] Contextualizing the different elements of this inscription –
not simply choosing between its material and discursive traces; that is, the
"reality" of *a woman* or *women* (as historical figures), or the "representation"
of *Woman* (as a conceptual category) – affords us a productive initial point
of entry into elucidating potential sites of gender construction and analysis.
The fact that this verse-inscription exists constitutes the beginnings of a constellation of ideas through which regulatory and transgressive discourses of
gender identity, sexual preference and status designation might be engaged.

As a final entry in this overview of sexualized graffiti in the ancient Roman
world, let us return briefly to the Palatine Paedagogium – the training school
for guards and attendants in the imperial palace we first considered in relation to religious expression in non-official inscriptions (Chapter 5).

G11.53 Phallus, ejaculating or urinating.

G11.54 "Saturus Afer" + naked male figure with large phallus.

G11.55 "Peri]genes, a Greek *pedico* [i.e. male who submits to anal
         penetration]."

G11.56 "Felix *pedico.*"

G11.57 "I butt-fuck [*pugizō*] Bassos."

G11.58 "Butt-fucking freely."

G11.59 "Era]*tust* [= (name) Eratosthenes or *eratós* (love-object)]."

As already evinced in relation to contexts designed as or in proximity to
same-sex spaces (the gymnasium, the bath-house), instances of homoerotic
sexual display and activity can be adduced in the Palatine Paedagogium.
These graffiti speak especially to the realities of a slave boy's duty as a *paed-
agogianus* and a basis for interpreting aspects of the school community's
attitudes about this aspect of servile life. Six of the Paedagogium graffiti comprise varieties of language used in Latin and Greek to refer to sexual acts
and four drawings describe male sexual parts and (in two instances) a nude
male figure. The vocabulary in the sexual content of these graffiti is of semantic interest, and the written and graphic representation of sexual organs and
actions can reveal something about the social values of the historical period
in which the graffiti were inscribed.

Drawings of the phallus in the Palatine Paedagogium can be assigned to
contexts that appear to be sexual or excretory in nature, connected with fertility, or representative. An image scratched on the western wall of Room
6 shows a large penis either ejaculating or urinating (G11.53).[55] A phallus

272

on the north-eastern wall of the same room has been added into a drawing which some think may be Mars.[56] A nude male figure was chalked in outline below the inscription of a name: Saturus Afer (G11.54).[57] The male parts are somewhat exaggerated, perhaps alluding to the link between the name Saturus and the priapic demigod of wild places. Two naked male figures scratched on the western wall of Room 6 are well-endowed and could both represent athletes.[58]

The textual residue directly refers to penetrative sexual acts between males. On the western wall of Room 6, to the right of the door, can be read Peri]*genes Graecus pedico* (G11.55).[59] The name Perigenes is uncertain, and could record another person; for example, Diogenes. However, the orthography compares favourably with another instance of the name appearing on the south-western wall of the same room; a third instance, on the same wall, is possible.[60] Another slave, a certain Felix, is identified as a *pedico* on the south-eastern wall of Room 6 (G11.56).[61] The word *pedico* is a nominal correspondent to *pedicare* ("to penetrate anally") and designates a sodomite.[62] Linguistic study of ancient sexual vocabulary indicates that the object of the sexual act relating to the term was usually male, though sometimes female.[63] The character of the word implied a usage which a Latin speaker might feel motivated to avoid. While the individuals who are the subjects of these graffiti possessed Greek and Latin personal names, the fact that Perigenes was identified explicitly as a Greek is inherently interesting. The message attracts additional significance when it is noted that the term *pedico* was most likely derived from Greek words related to homoerotic sexual activity (*paidikóu/tá paidika*). At least in the case of the Perigenes graffito, it is possible to infer that the inscriber wished to indicate a relationship between the act of anal intercourse and the ethnicity of the referent.[64]

In close proximity to the *Felix pedico* graffito is a message in Greek ascribing the same category of sexual congress to a certain Bassos: *Bassou pugizō* (G11.57).[65] The name Bassus appears in six other graffiti: once in Greek, the remaining five times in Latinized form.[66] The late David Bain identified *pugizō* as the commonest word denoting anal intercourse in Greek. Among the items featuring the name Bassos/-us, the subject of the graffiti is identified twice as an inhabitant of one of the various peninsulas and towns known as Cherronesus or Chersonesus,[67] perhaps the Thracian Chersonese, on the north-western side of the Hellespont and once as belonging to Greece.[68] It cannot be verified whether each of these attestations of the name Bassos/-us refers to the same person. There is a weight of probability, however, that there exists some correspondence, in which case these graffiti reflect an attitude among the inscribing population of the Paedagogium that associated and registered the practice of anal intercourse in conjunction with a person of Greek origins.

Another Latin graffito adverting to the same category of sexual activity was inscribed on the south-western wall of Room 15: li]*bente(r) pedicans*

GRAFFITI IN ANTIQUITY

(G11.58).[69] Unlike the collocation of name and ethnic background with the denomination of sexual identity in the preceding item, there are no surviving traces here of letters prior to the expression which would suggest a specific referent. However, on the north-eastern wall of the same room, a graffito written in Greek juxtaposes a term which may allude to a male sexual partner who plays a passive or receptive role (*póthos* = *páthos*) and two personal names (Mydion, Eutyches). Although the reading for *póthos* is tentative, it is possible to infer an allusion to one of the two persons named in terms reminiscent of the Greek vocabulary denoting a darling or love (Greek *tá paidika*; cf. Latin *deliciae*) or a beloved youth (*paidikós*).[70]

There are also two personal names, scratched on the same section of the north-western wall in Room 5, that connote a sexual meaning. Era]*tust*, which can be read as Eratosthenes, may also be Eratus Ti. Cl(audi?), and hence a form of *erastós* (G11.59). The referent may perhaps have been named as a beloved object of his *dominus*.[71] Amatori, which, along with Amatus, is a known family name (*cognomen*), can indicate an enthusiastic admirer, a devoted friend or a lover. The indeterminate nature of these graffiti does not permit any more precise interpretation of meaning or intention on the part of the inscriber.

Unlike the Basilica inscription pertaining to the "smooth" Epaphra (G11.45), in no case is the sexual symbolism of the Paedagogium graffiti related to pedication suggestive. Each instance is direct and uses a language or graphic form which can be classified as obscene in the context of ancient Roman literature and artistic representation. However, as noted in a recent study of *deliciae* in the Roman household, "it is very risky to make judgements about feelings derived from facts which can be ascribed to epigraphic habit".[72] While it is difficult to measure with any precision the degree to which these graffiti may have offended the Palatine slave population, interpreting the context of the sexual images in relation to the literary and iconographic record of sexual attraction to and activity associated with boys and adolescent males – free-born, manumitted or enslaved (including imperial *paedagogiani*) – is illuminating.

Tacitus records that C. Iulius Vestinus Atticus, consul in the year of the Pisonian conspiracy (65 CE), owned a large number of handsome slaveboys, all of the same age, chosen by Vestinus himself.[73] In the same book of the *Annales*, Tacitus describes an occasion on which Sophonius Tigellinus arranged the emperor Nero's male prostitutes – post-pubescent or adolescent young men who were "worn out with age" (*exoleti*) – according to their age and *scientia libidinum* (i.e. sexual speciality).[74] Describing Galba's personal habits, Suetonius collocates the emperor's treatment of his table-slaves when eating and his sexual predilection for "very hard *exoleti*".[75] Lampridius' description of Commodus' excesses within the imperial palace includes a reference to *puberes exoleti* ("mature *exoleti*"). In this instance, while threehundred adolescent males participated in sexual acts while dining and bathing, the writer specifies that they were not slaves, but were taken by force from plebeian and aristocratic families.[76]

274

SEXUALITY

Literary texts that address the relationship between Roman dining parties (*convivia*) and the functions of slave-boys in such contexts are permeated by the assumption that a normal Roman *dominus* will openly seek to have sexual relations with persons of either sex, including the young and adolescent male table-attendants.[77] Seneca the Younger, commenting on the behaviour of the pleasure-seeking Roman elite of his day, refers to the "shameful treatment" (*contumelia*) which unfortunate boys must expect after private dinners. He goes on:

> I shall not mention the troops of *exoleti*, ranked according to nation and colour, which must all have the same smooth skin, and the same amount of youthful down on their cheeks, and the same way of dressing their hair, so that no boy with straight hair may get among the curly-heads."[78]

In another letter expressing his moral reservations about the mistreatment of slaves in elite households, Seneca refers to the wine-server who:

> must dress like a woman and wrestle with his advancing years; he cannot get away from his boyhood; he is dragged back to it; and though he has already acquired a soldier's figure, he is kept beardless by having his hair smoothed away or plucked out by the roots, and he must remain awake throughout the night, dividing his time between his master's drunkenness and his lust; in the chamber he must be a man, at the feast a boy.[79]

FINAL THOUGHTS

Non-official inscriptions and associated textual and visual sources are a rich source of information about ancient Mediterranean ideas and practices pertaining to sexual beliefs and activity – the reproductive economy of origin stories in mythological narratives, the emotional life of affective relations in poetry and prose, the commercial transactions of sex-workers, the explicit expression of heterosexual and homosexual preferences in erotic messages and drawings. This repertoire of informal discourse offers a wide range of evidence for personal identity, the family and society, and socio-sexual life in antiquity. The importance of inscribed writing in the ancient world means that epigraphic texts represent Egyptian, Greek and Roman men and women from a diversity of social backgrounds and cultural traditions. Learning to read the products of this ephemeral epigraphic culture in turn provides a guide to understanding literary representations of social condition and cultural activity in the ancient world.

275

CONCLUSION

GC.1   "There came the scribe Nashuyu to the neighbourhood of the pyramid of Teti, beloved of the god Ptah, and the pyramid of Djoser, discoverer of stoneworking."
(Saqqara, northern Egypt; July 1246 BCE)

GC.2   "200 [units of liquid = 54.826 litres], double [the standard quantity]" + Semitic symbol.
(Pithecusae, Italy; eighth century BCE)

GC.3   "For I shall scrawl the inn's whole frontage for you with phalluses!"   (Catullus, *Carmina* 37.9–10; first century BCE)

GC.4   "So may you forever flourish, Sabina; may you acquire beauty and stay a girl for a long time." (Pompeii, Italy; first century CE)

GC.5   "Good fortune to the judgements of the Augustus [the emperor Nero], father of his country, and of Poppaea, Augusta."   (Pompeii, Italy; 63–8 CE)

GC.6   "ΧΜΓ ['Maria gave birth to Jesus.']."
(Aphrodisias, Turkey; late fourth/early fifth century CE)

If we scratch the various surfaces for what the preceding study of evidence pertaining to non-official inscriptions in antiquity reveals, we discern immediately a threefold network of interconnected phenomena: an extraordinary diversity of mark-making practices throughout the Graeco-Roman Mediterranean; a socio-cultural heterogeneity of participating individuals across a wide-ranging spectrum of urban and rural communities in Egypt, Greece, Italy and elsewhere; and the versatility of informal texts and images

CONCLUSION

as the media of choice for transmitting information, ideas and attitudes. Moreover, although used by producers and consumers of meaning from walks of life, social strata and worlds of thought distant from the modern age in terms of knowledge and understanding, ancient graffiti can still speak as cogently to a twenty-first-century audience – if attuned to the historically contextualized nuances of non-official writing and drawing – as they surely did to their intended constituency.

The proof of this particular conceptual pudding – and an indication of the path which this final chapter will follow – is very much to be found in the digest of exemplary references to graffiti displayed above. Visiting the necropolis of Saqqara during the reign of the New Kingdom pharaoh Ramesses II on the day of the festival of Ptah, the Dynasty XIX scribe Nashuyu inscribed the words contained in the first message (GC.1) in the vicinity of the Middle Kingdom pyramid of the Dynasty XIII pharaoh Userkare Khendjer. The graffito in full reads:

GC.7   "There came the scribe Nashuyu to the neighbourhood of the
        pyramid of Teti, beloved of the god Ptah, and the pyramid
        of Djoser, discoverer of stoneworking. And he said to all the
        gods of the west of Memphis, 'I am in your presence; I am
        your servant.' Year 34 [of the reign of Ramesses II = 1246 BCE],
        fourth month of summer, day 24, the day of the festival of Ptah
        [= July], south of his wall, lord of Saqqara, when he appears at
        eventide. 'Do good, do good, Djoser, discoverer of stonework-
        ing, do good to the scribe Nashuyu.'"

There is much here to interest us: the intentional display of scribal literacy and personal piety within a public landscape of long-standing cultural heritage; the incidental confirmation of a continuing tradition in pharaonic Egypt of pilgrimage to sites of historical and religious significance; and the explicit recognition of non-official inscribing practice as an instrument of human and divine communication. As a highly educated functionary of state, Nashuyu will have been well aware of the historical resonances associated with his visit to the site of the Step Pyramid of the Dynasty III pharaoh Djoser Netjerykhet – the earliest stone structure of its size in Egypt – on the festival day of Ptah – the Memphite patron of craftspeople and inventor of the arts. Emulating the festival god – the god who created the universe from his heart and tongue – Nashuyu inscribed (and possibly intoned) a heartfelt prayer to the long-dead, now-divine Djoser, identified in the graffito by the otherwise unique epithet "Discoverer-of-Stoneworking". If we note – as certainly Nashuyu will have known – that the individual responsible for the design and construction of the monumental complex of funerary buildings associated with the Step Pyramid was a certain Imhotep (Djoser's vizier and architect), then the New Kingdom scribe's graffito holds added significance:

277

as a marker of historical information, recording knowledge of the moment in time when Egypt saw the introduction of a groundbreaking and profoundly influential technological innovation. That Nashuyu attributes this unprecedented technical and logistical achievement to the second ruler of Dynasty III and not his gifted functionary – identified in an official inscription on the pedestal of a statue of Djoser as "Chancellor of the King of Lower Egypt, the first after the King of Upper Egypt, administrator of the Great Palace, hereditary Lord, High Priest of Heliopolis, Imhotep, the builder, the sculptor, the maker of stone vases" – reflects the scribe's wish that his prayer be heard (and acted on) by the divine Djoser, whom he therefore awards the title "Discoverer-of-Stoneworking" in Imhotep's place.

Nashuyu's graffito allows us to glimpse elements of the broader palimpsest of informal mark-making practices in antiquity. Inscribed on the wall of a tomb already many centuries old, the scribe's message – commemorating the physical and spiritual topography of his pilgrimage; assaying the beneficence of the divine Ptah and the deified Djoser, architects of cosmic and temporal order – illustrates how we should understand the ancient paradigm of history: as an integral facet of a culture's individual and collective testimonies. As we found in Chapter 1 of the present study, graffiti like Nashuyu's refract part of the spectrum of intellectual, religious, cultural and political subject matter that we in the modern age articulate as the historical warp and weft of human action and ideas. Like most cultural artefacts, however, non-official inscriptions should not be seen as homogeneous conduits. Indeed, in the same way that – over and beyond the matter-of-fact information about where (the spatial location) and when (the calendrical detail) he made his mark – Nashuyu records religious *and* mythological notions (see Chapters 5 and 7) associated with the purpose and context of his visit, so a variety of ancient graffiti preserve the traces, messages, and memories of the ideas and attitudes as well as the events and places of history.

Found at Pithecusae, an important trading settlement established by Euboean Greeks during the eighth century BCE, the second message (GC.2) – in fact, three inscriptions – was incised on an amphora reused for an infant burial. While the pottery vessel is of Greek typology (Late Geometric I), the inscribed markings are Semitic in origin. The first two, identified as Aramaic, define the original function of the amphora as a container of liquid. The abbreviated designation ("200, double") reveals the utilitarian nature of pot-marks like these: indicators of quantity at the point of shipment, confirming details essential in the outworking of commercial exchange beyond local territorial boundaries. In this instance, we are within our rights to suspect a point of dispatch from a site familiar to Euboean merchants – namely, the emporium of Al-Mīnā, located at the estuary of the Orontes river. A relationship between Euboean Greeks and the local Syrian–Phoenician population is known, and helps to underwrite the discovery of non-official inscriptions in a language (Aramaic) deriving from the linguistic area of northern Syria. It is

278

CONCLUSION

also possible that the amphora came from the island of Rhodes; evidence for the existence of trade in perfumed liquid between Pithecusae and Rhodes is well known. Regardless, it is the fact of commercial activity between eastern and western Mediterannean sites that the first two inscriptions confirm.

Interestingly enough, the *third* inscription on the Pithecusan amphora – a Semitic symbol resembling a triangle – explains the significance of the vessel in relation to its reuse as a burial container and draws out the importance of context when evaluating the significance of graffiti. Given its familiarity in Phoenician and Punic burials around the Mediterranean, the roughly drawn triangular sign – superimposed on the first pot-mark (the numeral "200") – associates a religious meaning to the reused amphora clearly connected to its funerary function. More than this, we may infer from the deliberate overwriting of the third inscription that at least one of the infant's parents performed a non-Greek ritual in relation to the burial. It is likely, therefore, that the parent responsible for the mark was of Semitic origin. Viewed collectively, the triad of non-official inscriptions speaks about patterns of international colonization and trade, the foundation and continuity of ethnically mixed settlements (here, Graeco-Levantine) in the western Mediterranean, and the use by a non-elite inscribing population of figurative text for utilitarian (commercial) and symbolic (religious, funerary) purposes (see Chapters 3, 5 and 10).

The action contemplated by the epigrammatic *persona* of the next item in the catalogue of references to graffiti (GC.3) – in this instance, an excerpt from one of the first-century BCE Roman poet Catullus' shorter verses – may seem at first sight an inscribing practice more familiar in the modern age. Indeed, the latent aggression underpinning the individual threatening to plaster the façade of what he describes as a *salax taberna* ("sleazy tavern") with representations of the clientele's male genitalia (*namque totius uobis | frontem tabernae sopionibus scribam*) reflects precisely the affect of ASB (antisocial behaviour) that is associated with the bulk of graffiti in the twenty-first century. However, we should exert caution before leaping to particular conclusions about ancient mark-making on the basis of what is clearly a polished literary artefact. In other words, it is not appropriate to use Catullus' reference to a threatened act of graffiti vandalism as a means by which to apportion to the inscribers of graffiti in first-century BCE Rome the same pattern of wilful marking, damage and defacement of property which has resulted in the introduction of stringent criminal penalties in the modern age. Rather, Catullus incorporates the *potential* act of non-official mark-making – in this instance, the wholesale overwriting (or over*drawing*) of the façade belonging to a privately owned commercial establishment (the aforementioned *salax taberna*) within view of a public space without the consent of the occupier or person in charge of the premises – for poetic effect. The persona's ill-temper and emotional distress at the loss of his beloved, a certain Lesbia, are directed at the tavern itself: it would seem that Lesbia now frequents the premises in question and is seen in the company of any number of the establishment's

279

unsuitable (in the former lover's view) patrons. Simply put, the threatened display of crudely drawn phalluses is used by Catullus as a means of crystallizing his persona's distraught emotional state. This is not to say that public (or private) surfaces – statues, architectural features, funerary monuments, housefronts – were not vandalized in this fashion; we have encountered a variety of examples which reflect precisely this overstepping of acceptable inscribing practice. Instead, in *Carmen* 47 the persona's intended (though not enacted) overriding of what can be inferred were strict customary boundaries of decorous behaviour in relation to mark-marking activity is sufficient to allow Catullus to convey to his readership the desired metaphorical and emotive frisson.

To demonstrate how the foregoing example provides an explicit reference to graffiti as a familiar element of the urban fabric *and* makes use of non-official mark-making as a literary trope, consider the following literary allusion to official epigraphy and how even the most well known practice might be reinterpreted: "Chloe the murderess inscribed on the tombs of her seven husbands that 'she did it.' What could be plainer?" (Martial, *Epigrams* 9.15; late first century CE).

One of the late first-century/early second-century CE Roman poet Martial's extraordinary output of satirical lyric verse (12 books of epigrams published over the course of almost two decades), the cited couplet confirms the close acquaintance which the poet's readership had with the display of messages in civic contexts.[1] Martial's punch-line – the sevenfold widow's complicity in the deaths of her many husbands – can only be appreciated if one recognizes the epigraphic sub-text. In the original Latin, the poet tells us that Chloe "inscribed" (*inscripsit*) her declaration of guilt: "I did it" (*se fecisse*). That the word *inscripsit* begins the couplet registers the epigraphic landscape as the context essential to drawing out all that Martial wishes us to glean. Funerary inscriptions in ancient Rome almost invariably acknowledge responsibility for the commemoration of the deceased by means of some form of the verb *facere* ("to make", "to do"), usually in the past (perfect) tense and the first or third person: *feci, fecit*. That Chloe, a criminal (*scelerata*) and suspected murderess, declares "I did it" qualifies suggestively what will have been otherwise understood as a typical dedication to a deceased beloved. If we add to this the legal usage of the verb – *feci* carried the semantic force, "I am guilty"[2] – we can see the extent to which Chloe must be seen as responsible for the death of her husbands: what could be plainer (*quod pote simplicius*), indeed?

Both poems advert explicitly to the quality of what might be termed written space as a traditional and familiar medium of communication in antiquity. Whether the method of inscription was official or non-official, it should be clear that a producer of meaning capable of writing or drawing could expect his or her message to be recognized and understood. Graffiti, therefore, should be seen as part of a repertoire of discursive strategies used in the ancient world – analogous, as we noted in Chapter 3, to the spectrum of

280

CONCLUSION

literacies displayed by the variegated communities of men and women comprising Graeco-Roman society. In this regard, it is fascinating to note that Chloe's participation in official epigraphic practice within a funerary context (though not her homicidal propensity) is mirrored in non-official markings recovered in a similar peri-urban space outside the walls of Roman Pompeii.

Excavated outside the Vesuvian Gate at Pompeii, five burial monuments survive into the present age. One of these, an altar tomb belonging to a certain Septumia, bears a marble plaque inscribed with the following commemoration: "To Septumia, daughter of Lucius. Granted by decree of the town councillors: a burial place and 2,000 sesterces for the funeral. Antistia Prima, daughter of Publius, her daughter, built (this monument)" (*AE* 1913.71).

An echo of Chloe's dedicatory inscriptions to her departed husbands may be discerned in Antistia Prima's declaration that she made (i.e. caused to be built or constructed) this tomb to her deceased mother – using the same formula (*Antistia ... fecit*) we have already encountered. What is striking about this funerary context is the fact that an otherwise unknown member of Pompeii's inscribing population scratched the message listed above (GC.4; cf. G11.28). As we found in Chapter 11, this graffito conforms to the category of literary composition known as an elegiac couplet – a metrical unit of lyric poetry used by poets of the late republican and early imperial age (i.e. Cornelius Gallus, Tibullus, Propertius and Ovid). Displaying a level of stylistic development beyond the purely functional, therefore, the aesthetic and rhythmic qualities of the verse form chosen by the otherwise unknown graffitist will have elicited precisely the intellectual and emotional responses implicit to the genre and familiar to a literate reader.

Of course, whoever composed these carefully crafted words did so in the knowledge that the language used and the feelings displayed would be noted – ideally, by the person to and for whom the sentiments were expressed; almost certainly, by those travelling past Septumia's tomb on their way to and from the city. Belonging to one of the cemeteries located outside the northern wall of Pompeii, the tomb – a high podium supporting a column – is one of a limited number of monuments excavated in this location. Situated near the road that enters the city by way of the Vesuvian Gate, its facade offered to anyone interested in sharing a message a prime position for display. Coincidentally, all the tombs identified here belonged to, or were set up by, women: a seat-tomb for Arellia Tertulla; a rectangular monument enclosed by a wall and surmounted with an altar, belonging to C. Vestorius Priscus but paid for by his mother; and our tomb, for Septumia, set up by her daughter. This partially uncovered necropolis represents more than a felicitous collocation of female memorialization. By commemorating the deceased, the dedicator and the remembering community within a socially and architecturally defined spatial context, the formally inscribed capitalized texts displayed on each of the monuments in this cluster of burials confirm the extent to which epigraphic culture permeated antiquity – and, in the same way, the graffito on

Septumia's tomb reflects the degree to which non-official marking practice participated in that culture.

Naturally enough, the identity of the individual who composed this particular message remains indeterminate, as is the case with many of the graffiti inscribed or painted on the durable surfaces of the ancient world. Nonetheless, despite our inability to assign the anonymous marker of Septumia's tomb to a more specific spectrum of socio-economic categories, we can still infer that the individual in question operated within that range of literacy familiar with the form and function – and, it would seem, proficient in imitating the style and effects – of erotic verse written in metrical Latin. The product of someone familiar with popular forms of erotic literature and aware of the function to which such art should be put, this example of non-official inscribing practice corroborates the usefulness of graffiti as a measure of the nexus between degrees of literacy, artistic expression and affective sentiment.

Another Pompeian graffito, found on the wall of a private chamber within the so-called Casa di Sallustio ("House of Sallust") (VI.2.4), displays a similar competence with elegiac lyricism. In this case, the writer makes use of a common form of trochaic verse, the *septenarius*, to express a familiar poetical conceit.

GC.8   "Girl, you are beautiful. To you I have been sent by one who is
        yours. Farewell."   (*CIL* IV.1234)

Like the message to Septumia, this inscription provides us with a snapshot of an affective relationship. Here, the composer negotiates generically with the epistolary mode favoured by a number of prominent Latin authors (Horace, Cicero, Propertius and Ovid). The graffito is an explicit declaration of appreciation, designed to reproduce in style either what may have already been transmitted in a more private letter written to the object of attraction or an imitation of the same refashioned in poetic form. Whether the relationship implied is real or imagined, it should be clear that the apparent simplicity of an inscribed text like this belies a linguistic sophistication over and beyond traditional assessments of graffiti as a non-literary product and foregrounds the range of alternatives and possibilities in the practice of writing by elite and non-elite Romans during this historical period.

Of course, as our preceding surveys of literature and sexuality (Chapters 3 and 11) revealed, the comparatively elevated level of theme, tone and style represented by these inscribed texts (GC.4, 8) can be balanced against a large number of graffiti displaying a limited thematic vocabulary, coarser expression of sentiments, and often a simpler grasp of the indigenous or commonly used language. Regardless of this variation in usage across a spectrum of linguistic or semiotic forms, this type of non-official marking may be identified in a plethora of spatial locations throughout the ancient world – the built environments of urban antiquity (whether cultural, economic, political, or

CONCLUSION

social; civic, commercial, industrial, leisure, ritual, residential) – and used across a range of civil and personal categories (class, wealth, citizenship; religious affiliation, ethnic origin, gender). In simple terms, it is possible neither to allocate varieties of non-official expression to specific spatial coordinates of particular social groups nor to assign kinds of graffiti (ranging from erudite literary compositions to vulgar idiomatic remarks) to specific inscribing communities (whether elite, sub-elite, or otherwise marginalized).

By virtue of their definition as non-official markings produced and consumed along with (and at times outside) the prescribed discourses of the socio-political elite, graffiti can also bring into sharper focus aspects of the historical record – as preserved, that is, in the output of sanctioned literary texts and the formal epigraphic landscape of the urban fabric. Even a cursory review of the formulations of historical theory and representations of political activity encountered previously (Chapters 2 and 8) will have provided sufficient indication of the ways in which graffiti may be used to interrogate and complicate the accepted version of the past. In particular, we can occasionally discern unexpected discrepancies in the stories recounted about well-known personalities and events – individuals, claques or social movements and the actions concomitant on attitudes or beliefs otherwise viewed through the filter of the transmitted historical canon as cut and dried.

A useful test of graffiti's utility as a discriminating analytical instrument in relation to the historical record is the fifth reference to non-official inscribing practice in antiquity (GC.5). To many, Nero is a paradigm of the decadent and tyrannical Roman emperor, corrupted absolutely by his absolute power.[3] Even in his own lifetime, Nero was the object of sensational and hostile anecdotes and these have dominated the tradition about him in one way or another up to the present day. Even the casual student of the ancient world would be familiar with the (erroneous) picture of Nero fiddling while Rome burnt in a metropolis-wide conflagration allegedly initiated at his instigation (July 64 CE).[4]

The problem arises from the fact that there is no major pro-Neronian element in the sources, even though there are some differences between them in the degree to which they dwell on the lurid sensationalism. This situation can be contrasted with the historical portrait of other Roman emperors of the first century CE – the Augustan period, for which we have the fragmentary *Life* by Nicholas of Damascus, for example, or, for Claudius, the documentary evidence of his edicts which provides some balance to the frequent ridicule of him in the literary sources. Even Tiberius is redeemed by the treatment of Velleius Paterculus and to some extent also by comments in Tacitus on the early part of his reign. It is not the case for Nero.

However, the aforementioned graffiti reference – conveying to Nero and his imperial consort Poppaea Sabina a non-official message of congratulations and goodwill – contrasts markedly with the otherwise negative testimony in the literary tradition. Painted on an exterior wall surface between the entrance to a staircase leading to an upper floor and a small dwelling

283

GRAFFITI IN ANTIQUITY

(IX.6.2–3), the *dipinto* (GC.5) is one of eight messages – two in the Basilica, the remainder scattered around Pompeii – acclaiming the "judgements" (*iudicia*) of Nero alone or of the emperor and his wife Poppaea, who was thought to have links with Pompeii and a nearby villa at Oplontis. While it is impossible to confirm the precise nature of the *iudicia* cited in these statements of support and gratitude, the Latin term used implies political interventions of some kind. If we recall our earlier discussion pertaining to a radical civil disturbance centred on Pompeii's amphitheatre (59 CE; see Chapter 3), then it is reasonable to infer that these political interventions may concern the revocation of the edict promulgated by the Roman senate banning gladiatorial games or honorific grants of colonial status to other local communities (Puteoli, Antium and Tegianum).[5]

It is clear from this related sample of non-official inscriptions that such graffiti can shed a different light both on contemporary perceptions and modern reception regarding the characterization of personalities or actions which would otherwise be set in the stone of accepted (i.e. official) tradition. Simply put, the *iudicia* graffiti reflect a localized variation to the otherwise undifferentiated perjorative viewpoint concerning the later years of Nero's rule. By the same token, graffiti can as usefully confirm the prevailing historical sentiment. Here, we may contrast the Pompeian inscriptions with an item from Suetonius' biographical profile of Nero. The excerpt in full reads as follows:

> When he [Nero] had thus aroused the hatred of all, there was no form of insult to which he was not subjected. A curl was placed on the head of his statue with the inscription in Greek: "Now there is a real contest and you must at last surrender." To the neck of another statue a sack was tied and with it the words: "I have done what I could, but you have earned the sack." People wrote on the columns that he had stirred up even the Gauls by his singing.
> (Suetonius, *Nero* 45.1–2)

Here we can identify four graffiti:

GC.9 The drawing of a curl.

GC.10 The Greek inscription "Now there is a real contest and you must at last surrender."

GC.11 The sack with the inscription "I have done what I could, but you have earned the sack."

GC.12 Inscription(s) stating that Nero had stirred up the Gauls by his singing.

284

CONCLUSION

The passage is precisely what we might expect from the bulk of contemporary commentary on Nero's principate following the murder of his mother Agrippina, the death of his *praefectus praetorio* Sextus Afranius Burrus and the dismissal of his tutor Lucius Annaeus Seneca. The graffiti are popular allusions to what we now know were signature affectations of his rule – the "curl" (GC.9), which the defacer of the statue positions on the emperor's head, adverts to the long hair which Nero wore during an extended trip to Greece; the "real contest" (GC.10) is an implicit contrast between the artistic competitions in which the emperor participated, knowing full well his victory was assured, and the impending political challenge he would face, regarded by the inscriber (significantly, writing in the Greek language, a barbed reference to Nero's distinctly un-Roman philhellenism) as a far more telling challenge; the "sack" (GC.11) pertains to the traditional punishment for parricide, the *poena cullei* in which the condemned was sewn into a sack with a dog, a monkey, a snake and a rooster and thrown into a body of water, at one and the same time recalling his mother's murder and invoking his metaphorical destruction of the Roman fatherland (the *patria*); and, finally, the mention of the "Gauls singing" (GC.12) suggests a double pun on the terms *Galli* ("Gauls")/*galli* ("roosters" or "cockerels") and "cantare" ("to sing", "to crow").

What the imperial biographer's item helpfully clarifies is the variety of inscribing practices in use in the first-century CE city of Rome – a range of inscribing strategies and methods of display that we have seen elaborated more widely across the ancient Mediterranean (see, especially, Chapter 1 for the technical apparatus of graffiti practice). The first two messages will most likely have been written or painted on placards affixed or hung from the statues; the last would have been incised or otherwise written in chalk, ink, charcoal or paint on the columns of some structure in a well-frequented urban context (a civic monument, a portico, a public assembly space, even a temple). Moreover, if we draw a comparison with the favourable inscriptions dotted around Pompeii, it makes sense that those sentiments less well-disposed to the emperor will more naturally be expressed in those contexts inhabited by persons who have felt the brunt of ill-conceived policy or indecorous behaviour. That Nero's later years in power will have been perceived in a poor light by men and women privy to inappropriate personal actions or poorly formulated political ideas – words or deeds which could only be regarded as dimishing the reputation or good standing of the Roman state – is only to be expected. A reference in Tacitus' *Annals* illustrates nicely the distinction which we have been able to draw from expressions of opinion about Nero contemporaneously expressed as graffiti – namely, the importance to one's assessment of personal character or political intent of proximity to the heart of historical affairs:

> Antistius, a *praetor* [high public office] whose licentious behaviour during his tribunate I have recalled, scribbled slanderous poems

285

against the *princeps* [the emperor Nero] and publicized them at
a populous party while he was dining at the house of Ostorius
Scapula.   (Tacitus, *Annals* 14.48.1; 62 CE)

Unlike the mark-makers of Pompeii, Antistius – a less than reputable character whose incumbency in an office of state second only to the position of Roman consul reflects (at least as Tacitus sees it) the degree to which Neronian rule should be implicated in a decline in moral standards across the socio-political landscape – is not only aware of the emperor's personal peccadilloes but also his military shortcomings, administrative failings and financial excesses. Nero and Poppaea's *iudicia* may have been feted in Pompeii, but closer to affairs of state the emperor's cachet as Augustus elicited far less admiration. Eventually, Nero became the first emperor officially declared a public enemy (*hostis*) by the Roman senate, and in Pompeii even non-official inscriptions of his name suffer the mutilating excision accorded those condemned as criminals of state (*damnatio memoriae*).

The final attestation of ancient graffiti practice listed at the beginning of this chapter (GC.6) highlights the permeability of official and non-official inscribing practices within the epigraphic environment of late antiquity. The inscription demonstrates the vitality of mark-making as a channel of meaning production, the spectrum of surfaces employed as media of intellectual, ideological, social and cultural communication, and the idiosyncratic strategies of local inscribing populations in articulating ideas, attitudes and feelings consonant with or challenging to the predominant discourse of their respective communities of practice and interest.

Inside an imposing double portico (*stoa*) in front of the Council House (*bouleuterion*) at Aphrodisias, late antique visitors to the city would have found a statue set up at some point in the late fourth or early fifth century CE in honour of a provincial governor (*hegemōn*) named Oecumenius.[6] The stoa in which the statue was placed formed part of the main urban space of Aphrodisias – the North Agora – and therefore constituted a premier site for honorific display. The portrait statue depicts a tall, slim, severe figure, wearing a long cloak (the *chlamys*) adopted as the apparel of late Roman civil administrators during the fourth and fifth centuries CE. The statue holds a scroll in its right hand; a bundle of scrolls lies on the plinth at its left foot. In short, the statue is fashioned to convey the impression of a highly educated imperial official, a person of distinguished rank and function and a model of the age's refined intellectual and aesthetic achievements – an artefact and symbol of the training of the physical and mental faculties which produced a broad enlightened mature outlook harmoniously in concert with refined cultural development. A verse epigram inscribed on the front of the statue base – describing Oecumenius as a *hegemōn*, a person with comprehensive and authoritative knowledge of the law, bilingual in Latin and Greek, and not susceptible to corrupt practices ("pure in mind and in hand") – completes

286

CONCLUSION

the representation of Oecumenius and his political and cultural significance within the context of late antique Aphrodisian society.

What is striking about this statue – and which bears directly on the relationship between official and non-official modes of communication (textual and visual) in antiquity – is an additional inscribed component outside the sanctioned artistic and epigraphic repertoire. Inscribed on top of the statue's head – behind the crown, written from behind and above – are three Greek letters: ΧΜΓ (GC.6). If we take into account particulars of this graffito – the letters were inscribed more expertly than the verse-epigram; they could only be seen from behind the statue, as placement of the statue hard against the wall of the colonnade rendered a visible reading impossible for the intended viewership – it should be clear that the original sculptor was responsible for incising the letters.

What is the significance of this otherwise hidden graffito text? Intriguingly, the chi–mu–gamma symbol can be found inscribed on a variety of surfaces beside this statue – papyri, amphorae, door lintels, tiles, brick stamps. Moreover, depending on the mode of communication – taking the symbol as an acrostic (a series of letters taken in order to form a word or phrase) or an isopsephism (a numerical value corresponding to a word or phrase with an equivalent value) – ΧΜΓ may transmit a range of meanings.[7] Determining the particular phrase which the letters represent – possible interpretations include Χριστὸς ὁ ἐκ Μαρίας γεννηθείς ("Christ, born of Mary"); Χριστὸς Μιχαὴλ Γαβριήλ ("Christ. Michael. Gabriel); χμγ = 643 ("God, help!"); Χριστὸς μάρτυς γεγόνεν (or γεγονώς, γεγώς) ("Christ was made a martyr") – is not, therefore, strictly possible. Of course, while there is no real consensus about the semantic and conceptual force of the letters, it should be clear that scholars *do* agree that ΧΜΓ is a Christian symbol. Importantly for our purposes, then, time, geography and context are significant in attributing a particular meaning. If we are aware that profoundly divisive tensions between adherents of Christian and polytheist cult existed over the course late fourth and fifth centuries,[8] and in light of our preceding discussion of the form and function of ancient graffiti (Chapters 5, 6 and 8), the covert inscription of ΧΜΓ on the statue of a provincial governor in a city riven by religious sentiment takes on added significance – as a private assertion of belief, a personal critique of elite pagan administration, and the codified Christian equivalent (in modern terminology, a "tag") of a magical or apotropaic symbol.

FINAL THOUGHTS

Taking a step back from the observations made in this brief concluding overview of non-official mark-making practices in the ancient Mediterranean world, it should be clear that *Graffiti in Antiquity* has only scratched the surface in relation to the surviving database of primary evidence, the variety

287

of inscribing methods, the range of locations in material and spatial terms used for the incision and display of messages, and the spectrum of artistic, cultural, historical and social meanings permeating graffiti form and function. Given its geographical and chronological breadth, this book has aimed to look at a select few only of the plethora of non-official inscriptions, the historical contexts in which the texts and drawings were inscribed, the location of the inscriptions and the ways in which they were presented. What we can say from all that has gone before is that these verbal and non-verbal texts were produced and consumed within, and relate very much to, the epigraphic environment of a widespread oral-literate culture; within such a landscape, they contribute information about a plurality of spatial locations, historical data, social relations and cultural patterns. They talk about men and women inhabiting the tombs of the dead and the festivals of the living. They use many voices – the language of privileged and aspiring citizens, the declarations of disfranchised, deracinated or otherwise marginalized men and women – and convey their meaning in different ways – memorial portraits of loved ones; symbolic conversations with deities and demi-gods; social histories, commentaries and inventories; statements of fact, affection and abuse; markers of status, economic exchange and property. By looking at the representations of men and women in inscriptions in association with literature about the world that produced inscribed texts, this book has identified multiple expressions of male and female participation in the epigraphic environment of antiquity, its urban fabric and rural manifestations. Graffiti inscriptions (text and image) show men and women engaging directly in cultural activities – individually, inter-personally and communally. In sum, socio-linguistic analysis of material and textual traces from the epigraphic record locates multiple sites of dialogue between male and female composers, inscribers and consumers of meaning, and the traditions, circumstances and conditions of the ancient Mediterranean world.

APPENDIX

WHERE TO FIND ANCIENT GRAFFITI

With few exceptions, no matter where a person lives, works or visits in the modern age, it is more than likely that at some point during the course of any day's activity that person will encounter the phenomenon of graffiti. Given the very mixed attitudes towards writing or drawing on visible surfaces in public locations that exist in our twenty-first-century world – from zero tolerance of actions viewed as anti-social behaviour to community acceptance according to aesthetic or cultural principles – it will still be surprising to many that the ancient world did not proscribe or promote non-official inscribing practices. If nothing else, this book should have illuminated the extent to which men and women in antiquity used informal media to communicate with each other about themselves, their lives, and their ideas and feelings, and how they wished to be seen and remembered by their families, friends and the wider community. Graffiti writing and drawing constituted an integral facet of socio-cultural discourse across space and time in the ancient Mediterranean.

Equally surprising is the fact that visible traces of this very old practice can still be found *in situ*, preserved on display – physically or digitally – in modern museum and institutional collections, and in text-based and photographic archives in print or online. What follows is a very brief sample of the range of locations where the modern student of antiquity can autopsy first-hand extant verbal and non-verbal graffiti from the ancient past or otherwise peruse at leisure in the original language or in translation what others have viewed and recorded for posterity's sake.

This is naturally a survey selection only. Many of the print or digital publications that offer glimpses of this extraordinary ancient phenomenon can also be located by way of individual chapter notes or the bibliographical catalogue of readings in this volume – and, of course, a simple or advanced key word search of the library databases created by any university or research institution with a classics, ancient history or pre-modern archaeology department, or a filtered online search will prove equally useful.

APPENDIX

EGYPT

Museums with online catalogues

Alexandria, Bibliotheca Alexandrina, Antiquities Museum
http://antiquities.bibalex.org/collection/MuseumDatabase.aspx?lang=en#
Search languages: Arabic, English, French

Boston, MA, Museum of Fine Arts
www.mfa.org/collections
Search language: English

Brooklyn, NY, Brooklyn Museum of Art
www.brooklynmuseum.org/opencollection/search/?advanced
Search language: English

Cambridge, Fitzwilliam Museum
www.fitzmuseum.cam.ac.uk/opac/search/searchadvanced.html
Search language: English

Leiden, Rijksmuseum van Oudheden
www.rmo.nl/collectie/zoeken
Search language: Dutch

London, British Museum
www.britishmuseum.org/research/search_the_collection_database.aspx
Search language: English

London, Petrie Museum
http://petriecat.museums.ucl.ac.uk
Search language: English

New Haven, CT, Yale University Art Gallery
http://ecatalogue.art.yale.edu/search.htm
Search language: English

New York, Metropolitan Museum of Art
www.metmuseum.org/collections/search-the-collections
Search language: English

Paris, Musée National du Louvre
http://cartelen.louvre.fr/cartelen/visite?srv=crt_frm_rs&langue=fr&init
   Critere=true
Search languages: French, English

290

APPENDIX

Swansea, Museum of Egyptian Antiquities
www.egyptcentre.org.uk
Search language: English

Toronto, Royal Ontario Museum
http://images.rom.on.ca/public/index.php?function=query&action=select
ed&tbl=aa&sid=&ccid
Search language: English

Graffiti locations

For the adventurous tourist, it is possible to retrace the steps of the intrepid John Coleman Darnell and Deborah Darnell, principal investigators of the University of Chicago's Oriental Institute Western Desert Road Survey. Travelling north from Luxor City or south from the city of Farshut (Qina), there exists a range of tourist expeditions which incorporate travel along the *Luxor-Farshût Road*, which leads to the ancient religious centre of Abydos and to the oases of the Western Desert (Bahariya, Farafra, Dakhla, Kharga, Siwa, Gilf el-Kebir, Gebel el-Uwinat). Ascending the steep cliffs that border the western limits of the Nile Valley, the determined traveller will encounter the sites of Gebel Tjauti (on the Alamat Tal road) and Wadi el-Hôl – as well as lesser-known sites like Gebel Antef, Wadi el-Huôl, Gebel Roma and Gebel Qarn el-Gir – on the high desert plateau. Here it is still possible to examine at each location over forty rock inscriptions dating from the earliest years of pharaonic history to the vestiges of Egyptian hegemony that mark the Third Intermediate Period, and into later Greek and Roman times.

More accessible, but still only for the energetic or longer-term visitor, the *hills of Western Thebes* surrounding the Valley of the Kings and the worker's village of Deir el-Medina provide a good deal of scope for the casual discovery of ancient graffiti. Indeed, the landscape bordering the vast burial grounds of New Kingdom royalty and elite officials – not to mention the tireless artisans, craftsmen, construction workers who cut the cliff-tombs into the rock and carved and painted the texts and images lining the tomb-walls and burial sarcophagi – offers the attentive visitor the chance to view thousands of graffiti scratched, chipped, painted or even inked on visible surfaces.

Careful examination of the walls and columns of the great political, religious and funerary precincts of *New Kingdom Thebes* – notably the Luxor and Karnak temples, the Colossi of Memnon (Amenhotep III), the mortuary temples of Ramesses I (the Ramesseum) and Ramesses III (Medinet Habu) – reveals many drawings and inscriptions. From pictorial representations of kings, gods and animals to messages in hieroglyphic script, demotic, Coptic, Greek, Carian and Arabic, these sites repay close inspection by the patient and keen-eyed.

291

APPENDIX

In addition to the itinerary of site inspections noted above, a journey north to the *Egyptian Museum in Cairo* – which contains the world's most extensive collection of pharaonic antiquities – will provide the interested visitor with access to a dazzling (if cluttered) array of inscribed artefacts dating from prehistoric times through the pharaonic era to the periods of Greek and Roman occupation.

Epigraphic collections

Allen, J. P. 2005. *The Ancient Egyptian Pyramid Texts*. Atlanta, GA: Society of Biblical Literature.

Bréand, G. 2009. "The Corpus of Pre-firing Potmarks from Adaïma (Upper Egypt)". *British Museum Studies in Ancient Egypt and Sudan* 13: 49–72.

Breasted, J. H. 1906a. *Historical Documents. Volume 1: The First to the Seventeenth Dynasties*. Chicago, IL: University of Chicago Press.

Breasted, J. H. 1906b. *Historical Documents. Volume 4: The Twentieth through the Twenty-sixth Dynasties*. Chicago, IL: University of Chicago Press.

Černý, J. 1969–83. *Graffiti de la montagne Thebaine*, 4 vols. Cairo: Le Centre d'Etude et de Documentation sur l'Ancienne Egypte.

Couyat, J., P. Montet. 1912–13. *Les inscriptions hiéroglyphiques et hiératiques du Ouâdi Hammâmât*, 2 vols. Cairo: Institut français d'archéologie orientale du Caire.

Cruz-Uribe, E. 2008. "Graffiti (Figural)". In *UCLA Encyclopedia of Egyptology*, W. Wendrich (ed.). Los Angeles, CA: UCLA. http://escholarship.org/uc/item/7v92z43m (accessed 6 November 2013).

Darnell, J. C. & D. Darnell 2002. *Theban Desert Road Survey in the Egyptian Western Desert. Volume 1: Gebel Tjauti Rock Inscriptions 1–45 and Wadi el-Hôl Rock Inscriptions 1–45*. Chicago, IL: Oriental Institute Press.

Dunbar, J. H. 1941. *The Rock-Pictures of Lower Nubia*. Cairo: Egyptian Government Press.

Fuchs, G. 1989. "Rock Engravings in the Wadi El Barramiya". *African Archaeological Review* 7(1): 127–53.

Huyge, D. 2009. "Rock Art". In *UCLA Encyclopedia of Egyptology*, W. Wendrich (ed.). Los Angeles, CA: UCLA. http://escholarship.org/uc/item/4qx7k7pz (accessed 6 November 2013).

Judd, T. 2009. *Rock Art of the Eastern Desert of Egypt: Contents, Comparisons, Dating and Significance*. Oxford: Archaeopress.

Lichtheim, M. 1976. *Ancient Egyptian Literature: A Book of Readings. Volume II: The New Kingdom*. Berkeley, CA: University of California Press.

Morrow, M. & M. Morrow. 2002. *Desert Rats: Rock Art Topographical Survey in Egypt's Eastern Desert*. London: UCL Press.

Nagel, G. 1938. *La céramique du Nouvel Empire à Deir El Médineh I*. Cairo: Institut français d'archéologie orientale du Caire.

Peden, A. J. 2001. *The Graffiti of Pharaonic Egypt: Scope and Roles of Informal Writings (3100–332 BCE)*. Leiden: Brill.

Posener, G. 1980. *Catalogue des ostraca hiératiques littéraires de Deir el Médineh. Volume III/3: Nos 1607–1675*. Cairo: Institut français d'archéologie orientale du Caire.

Winkler, H. 1938. *Rock-Drawings of Southern Upper Egypt I*. Oxford: Egyptian Exploration Society.

Winkler, H. 1939. *Rock-Drawings of Southern Upper Egypt II*. Oxford: Egyptian Exploration Society.

APPENDIX

GREECE

Museums with online catalogues

Athens, Acropolis Museum
www.theacropolismuseum.gr/en/content/gallery-slopes-acropolis
Search language: English

Athens, National Archaeological Museum of Athens
www.namuseum.gr/collections/index-en.html
Search languages: English, Greek

London, British Museum
www.britishmuseum.org/research/search_the_collection_database.aspx
Search language: English

New York, Metropolitan Museum of Art
www.metmuseum.org/collections/search-the-collections
Search language: English

Paris, Musée National du Louvre
http://cartelen.louvre.fr/cartelen/visite?srv=crt_frm_rs&langue=
fr&initCritere=true
Search languages: French, English

Philadelphia, PA, University of Pennsylvania Museum of Archaeology and
Anthropology
www.penn.museum/collections
Search language: English

St Petersburg, State Hermitage Museum
www.hermitagemuseum.org/fcgi-bin/db2www/browse.mac/
category?selLang=English
Search languages: English, Russian

Graffiti locations

Respectively the hub of commercial, legal, religious and political activity in archaic, classical and post-classical Athens, and the site of an important cemetery from the twelfth century BCE to Roman times, the *Agora* and the *Potter's Quarter* of the city are the locations of three significant museums – the *Ancient Agora Museum*, the *National Archaeological Museum of Athens* and the *Kerameikos Museum*. These buildings house extensive collections of artefacts,

293

APPENDIX

many of which display the fragmentary surfaces on which non-official texts and images were incised and painted – including *ostraca* (the inscribed pottery sherds used as ballots to exile prominent political figures), bronze identification tags (used in selecting Athenian juries), and clay tokens and inscribed lead strips (used in the administration of the Athenian cavalry) – in many cases, in close proximity to where the objects were recovered and are now displayed.

Situated approximately 100 km inland from the coast of modern Turkey, on a plateau south of the Maeander River (modern Büyük Menderes), the site of ancient *Aphrodisias* provides an opportunity to explore many of the typical urban features of the post-classical Graeco-Roman settlement – a theatre, a bouleuterion or odeon, a market, houses and baths, a monumental gateway, and a cult centre (Sebasteion) for worship of the Roman emperor. It is possible to discern the preserved remains of graffiti scratched into wall plaster from the odeon – on display in the *Aphrodisias Museum* – and a number of texts, images and symbols, inscribed on the seats and on the wall of the easternmost recess behind the backstage corridor of the same building.

Whether travelling from Izmir, Kusadasi or Istanbul, the ancient site of *Ephesus* (on the south-western coast of modern Turkey) offers the casual visitor or dedicated graffiti-hunter ample opportunity to view non-official inscriptions at close quarters – whether on the columns of the colonnaded galleries lining the thoroughfare, the mosaics or paving stones of Curetes Street (between the Hercules Gate and the Celsus Library); on many of the marble seats in the Great Theatre (on the slope of Panayir Hill); or on any number of durable surfaces in the extraordinary residences known as the Terrace Houses (on the hill opposite Hadrian's Temple).

A high-end tourist destination in the southern Aegean Sea, the island of modern Santorini (ancient *Thera*) is essentially all that remains of a much larger landmass decimated as the result of a cataclysmic volcanic eruption. Visitors to the archaeological remains of the ancient Greek city – located on the eastern side of Santorini's volcanic caldera – will be able to peruse a number of inscriptions dating to the seventh to sixth centuries BCE, carved into rock surfaces situated mid-way between the temple of Apollo Karneios (or Delphinios) and the sanctuaries of Zeus, Kures, Chiron, Athena, Ge and Artemis. Another sanctuary site that will repay careful attention to the inscribed landscape is the island city of *Delos*, a centre of religious activity and a busy harbour port until the first century BCE. Incised on paving stones, marble statuary bases, portico columns and other architectural features, a range of ephemeral markings dating from the classical period (fifth to fourth centuries BCE) to post-classical Graeco-Roman times (third-first centuries BCE) can be seen as the visitor travels along the Sacred Way from the Maritime Quarter and Theatre District to the Sanctuary of Apollo and the Lion District.

294

APPENDIX

Epigraphic collections

Baur, P. & M. Rostovtzeff (eds) 1929. *The Excavations at Dura-Europos: First Season, Spring 1928.* New Haven, CT: Yale University Press.

Baur, P. & M. Rostovtzeff (eds) 1931. *The Excavations at Dura-Europos: Second Season, 1928–1929.* New Haven, CT: Yale University Press.

Bernand, A. 1972a. *Le Paneion d'El Kanais: les inscriptions grecques.* Leiden: Brill.

Bernand, A. 1972b. *De Koptos à Kosseir.* Leiden: Brill.

Bernard, A. & E. Bernard 1960. *Les Inscriptions Grecques et Latines du Colosse de Memnon.* Cairo: Institute français d'archéologie orientale.

Brenne, S. 2001. *Ostrakismos und Prominenz in Athen. Attische Bürger des 5. Jhs. v. Chr. auf den Ostraka.* Vienna: Holzhausen.

Brenne, S. 2002. "Die Ostraka als Testimonien". In *Ostrakismos-Testimonien I: Die Zeugnisse antiker Autoren der Inschriften und Ostraka über das athenische Scherbengericht aus vorhellenistischer Zeit (487–322 v. Chr.).* Historia Einzelschriften 155, P. Siewert (ed.), 36–166. Stuttgart: Steiner.

Gager, J. G. 1992. *Curse Tablets and Binding Spells from the Ancient World.* Oxford: Oxford University Press.

Lang, M. 1974. *The Athenian Agora XXI: Graffiti and Dipinti.* Princeton, NJ: American School of Classical Studies at Athens.

Lang, M. 1990. *The Athenian Agora XXV: Ostraca.* Princeton, NJ: American School of Classical Studies at Athens.

Langdon, M. K. 1976. *A Sanctuary of Zeus on Mount Hymettos. Hesperia: Supplement XVI.* Princeton, NJ: American School of Classical Studies at Athens.

Langner, M. 2001. *Antike Graffitizeichnungen: Motive, Gestaltung und Bedeutung.* Wiesbaden: L. Reichert.

ROME

Museums with online catalogues

London, British Museum
www.britishmuseum.org/research/search_the_collection_database.aspx
Search language: English

Los Angeles, CA, The J. Paul Getty Museum
www.getty.edu/art
Search language: English

New York, Metropolitan Museum of Art
www.metmuseum.org/collections/search-the-collections
Search language: English

Paris, Musée National du Louvre
http://cartelen.louvre.fr/cartelen/visite?srv=crt_frm_rs&langue=
fr&initCritere=true
Search languages: French, English

APPENDIX

Rome, Musei Capitolini (Capitoline Museums)
http://en.museicapitolini.org
Search languages: English, French, Italian, Spanish

Graffiti locations

The most famous graffiti site in the ancient world is the southern Italian harbour port of *Pompeii*. In concert with neighbouring settlements destroyed as a result of the volcanic eruption of Vesuvius in 78 CE – *Herculaneum, Stabiae* and *Boscoreale* – Pompeii Antica is one of the primary focal points for global research into the phenomenon of graffiti in antiquity. A relatively stress-free train journey from Naples (to the north) or Sorrento (south) – or perhaps by autostrada, ferry or hydrofoil – nothing less than a full day visit to Pompeii will satisfy the avid student of graffiti. From the Suburban Baths adjacent to the Marine Gate at the south-western entrance to the archaeological site, it is possible to identify a multitude of informal inscriptions on stone, mosaic tesserae, wall plaster, columns and seating in the theatres and amphitheatre – especially in the Lupanar or purpose-built brothel (VII.12.18–20), in residential spaces like the Casa di Menandro (I.10.4), and on the north and south walls of the long, narrow corridor running from the Via Stabia behind the Odeon or Covered Theatre to the east entrance of the Large Theatre (VIII.7.20). An essential addendum to a tour of ancient Pompeii is a visit to the *Archaeological Museum of Naples* – one of the foremost collections of antiquities in the modern world, and a treasure-trove of formal and non-official inscriptions.

Little known to modern tourists and rarely visited as a result, the ancient harbour port of *Ostia Antica* – a leisurely half-hour train journey from the centre of Rome – is an archaeological site which in many ways rivals Pompeii for its wealth of surviving material evidence. Given its less-frequented status, the city affords the visitor unparalleled access to a broad range of civic buildings, commercial, religious and entertainment precincts, and domestic spaces still bearing the marks of non-official inscribers. Dating from the early first century CE to the harbour city's zenith in the second century CE, the range and frequency of Ostian graffiti *in situ* provide a complementary perspective on the late-republican and early imperial inscriptions on display at Pompeii. If at all possible, the longer-term traveller should consider a brief side-visit to the nearby cemetery site of *Isola Sacra*, which situates the viewer in a context reflecting how ancient men and women used inscribed text and imagery to produce and consume meaning.

Eminently suited to pedestrian travel, the city of *Rome* – megalopolitan capital and imperial powerhouse *par excellence* in the annals of ancient Mediterranean history – comprises a variety of graffiti experiences on site. For example, the Forum Romanum (Roman Forum) preserves a plethora of

296

APPENDIX

gaming tables incised on the paving stones of the Basilica Julia and Basilica Aemilia; the Amphitheatrum Flavium (Colosseum) displays a number of recently restored pictorial depictions of combatants (human and animal) that prowled the arena for the entertainment of a bloodthirsty populace; and the major and minor Christian and Jewish catacombs represent an extremely important aggregation of evidence for the practice of inscribing informal textual messages and symbolic figural drawings. The visitor will also benefit enormously from careful inspection of museum collections – especially the *Musei Capitolini* and, best of all, the epigraphic museum, which is now part of the *Terme di Diocleziano* (the Diocletian Baths complex). Housing what is undoubtedly the premier collection of Latin epigraphy – from Italian prehistory to the late antique period – there is an eye-watering wealth of informal inscriptions on display pertaining to non-official written and pictorial communication in the Roman world.

Though currently ill-advised due to extremely dangerous civil unrest, a visit to the Hellenistic, Parthian and Roman fortress town of *Dura-Europos* will be worthwhile to anyone with an interest in the use of graffiti as a medium of socio-cultural and religious transmission. In the same way that a variety of Mithraic sanctuaries elsewhere in the Mediterranean world – in London, Rome (the Circus Maximus, the Baths of Caracalla), Ostia, as well as any number in France, Germany, Hungary and Spain – display graffiti which reflect the presence of cult initiates, so the Mithraeum at Dura-Europos features a selection of Greek and Palmyrene textual inscriptions and several accomplished pictorial figures in ink on painted plaster. A full-scale reconstruction of the city's Mithraeum as well as a thematic exhibition of major finds from Dura-Europos can now be seen in *Yale University's Gallery of Fine Arts*.

Graffiti collections

Brandt, O. (ed.) 2008. *Unexpected Voices: The Graffiti in the Cryptoporticus of the Horti Sallustiani*. Stockholm: Swedish Institute at Rome.

Castren, P. & H. Lilius 1970. *Graffiti del Palatino II: Domus Tiberiana*. Helsinki: Akateeminen Kirjakauppa.

Della Corte, M. & P. Ciprotti (eds) 1952–70. *Inscriptiones parietariae Pompeianae Herculanenses Stabianae. Supplementi pars III: Inscriptiones Pompeianae Herculanenses parietariae et vasorum fictilium*. Berlin: De Gruyter.

Ferrua, A. 2001. *Tavole lusorie epigrafiche: catalogo delle schede manoscritte, introduzione e indici a cura di Maria Busia*. Rome: Pontificio istituto di archeologia Cristiana.

Mau, A. (ed.) [1909] 1968. *Inscriptiones parietariae Pompeianae Herculanenses Stabianae. Supplementi pars II. Inscriptiones parietariae et vasorum fictilium*. Berlin: De Gruyter.

Noy, D. 1995. *Jewish Inscriptions of Western Europe. Volume 2: The City of Rome*. Cambridge: Cambridge University Press.

Solin, H. & M. Itkonen-Kaila 1966. *Graffiti del Palatino 1: Paedagogium*. Helsinki: Akateeminen Kirjakauppa.

APPENDIX

Varone, A. 2001. *Erotica Pompeiana: Love Inscriptions on the Walls of Pompeii.* Rome: L'Erma Bretschneider.

Zangemeister, C. (ed.) [1898] 1968. *Inscriptiones parietariae Pompeianae Herculanenses Stabianae. Supplementi pars I: Tabulae ceratae Pompeiis repertae.* Berlin: De Gruyter.

Zangemeister, C. & E. Schoene (eds) 1871. *Inscriptiones parietariae Pompeianae Herculanenses Stabianae.* Berlin: De Gruyter.

NOTES

PREFACE

1. Peden (2001: 31).
2. Shakespeare, *Macbeth* 5.5.26–8.
3. Wagner *et al.* (1999).
4. Frank (1927), Rostovtzeff (1957), Jashemski (1979–93).
5. Woolf (1996: 29).

INTRODUCTION: MODERN APPROACHES TO ANCIENT GRAFFITI

1. Abel & Buckley (1977: 3).
2. Cf. Pliny the Younger, *Letters* 3.21: "I hear that Valerius Martial is dead, and I am much troubled at the news."
3. *Oxford Dictionaries* (www.oxforddictionaries.com): s.v. *graffiti* (World English definition).
4. For example, the Graffiti Prevention Act 2007 (Victoria, Australia); anti-graffiti administrative and penal laws (Titles 10.117, New York City; Title 10.145, New York State); the Criminal Damages Act 1971 (Section 5) and Anti-Social Behaviour Act 2003 (Part 6) (United Kingdom); the Criminal Code Act 1995 (France); the European Council's Rules for Juvenile Offenders 2008 (Rule 45). For the purposes of such legislation, graffiti comprises defacing, writing, scratching or drawing on or property so that the marks can't be removed easily with a dry cloth, and includes stencil art and engraving.
5. The compendium or digest of Roman law compiled by order of the emperor Justinian I in the sixth century CE (*Digest*) defines the term "public place" as applying to such localities, houses, fields, highways and roads as belong to the community at large (*Digest* 9.43.8.3).
6. For a succinct presentation of these relations, see the introductory comments in Elsner (1996).
7. Literature addressing the problematic interactions of gender, orality and literacy is thin on the ground, at least from the standpoint of reconstructing participatory strategies. For efforts to engage with this idea, see (in alphabetical order only) Dewey (1995), Gilleland (1980), Harris (1989), Joshel (1992) and Thomas (1989, 1992).
8. For example, the total of recorded or extant inscriptions at Rome (in *CIL* VI.1–4.3) is 39,340. Discarding fragmentary and extra-regional *addimenta*, this figure falls to 36,602.

299

NOTES

For a fascinating study of epigraphic surfaces which preserve an indisputable indication of slave literacy and the inclination to use it for practical ends, see Gasperini (1971); on the materials used in this region and their effects on the inscriptions, see Susini (1969: esp. 45–8). Of especial interest is the estimation of Gasperini (1971: 174 n. 1) that 30–40 per cent of persons commemorated at Tarentum and in the Salento (where slave labour was abundantly used) were slaves, suggesting that the level of slave literacy was similar to the level in the free population. Harris's offhand remark – "they will always have been a small minority" (Harris 1989: 256 n. 428) – requires no rejoinder.

9. The fourth volume of the *Corpus Inscriptionum Latinarum* (*CIL*) *Inscriptiones Parietariae Pompeianae Herculanenses Stabianae* (i.e. the collection of Latin inscriptions inscribed on the walls of Pompeii, Herculaneum and Stabiae) and the accompanying supplement in three parts.

10. UK Criminal Justice Act (1998).

11. For discussion of the uncertainty over the precise meaning associated with ASB, see, for example, Whitehead *et al.* (2003), Harradine *et al.* (2004), Millie *et al.* (2005a, 2005b), Macdonald (2006).

12. Millie *et al.* (2005a).

13. For example, Abel and Buckley (1977), Castleman (1982), Cooper & Chalfant (1995).

14. For example, Harris (1989), Humphrey (1991), Petrucci (1991), Gordon *et al.* (1993, 1997), Bowman & Woolf (1994).

15. Gigante (1979), Varone (2001).

16. Laurence (1994), Harris (1989).

17. Baird & Taylor (2010).

18. Sears *et al.* (2013), a collection of papers based on a panel session at the 2009 Roman Archaeology Conference (Ann Arbor, Michigan) dealing with the idea of written spaces (incl. the contexts for political and other graffiti) in the ancient world. The author participated in this conference and contributed one of the papers in the collection.

19. Solin (1973).

20. Mouritsen (forthcoming).

21. In the main, two volumes cataloguing graffiti on the Palatine hill: Solin & Itkonen-Kaila (1966), Castren & Lilius (1970); catalogues of Egyptian, Hebrew, Greek and Latin graffiti: Zangemeister ([1898] 1968), Zangemeister & Schoene (1871), Mau ([1909] 1968), Perdrizet & Lefebvre (1919), Della Corte & Ciprotti (1952–70), Bernard (1960), Goodenough (1964), Reisner (1971), Bernand (1972a, 1972b), Solin (1973), Lang (1974, 1990), Posener (1980), Ferrua (2001), Langner (2001), Peden (2001), Darnell & Darnell (2002), Judd (2009). For prosopographical studies of Pompeian graffiti relying on situational context, see Franklin (1978, 1991, 2001); for text-critical and typological studies of Pompeian and other graffiti, see Kruschwitz (2008, 2010); for a political study of Pompeian inscriptions, see Mouritsen & Gradel (1991); for a socio-cultural study of slave graffiti in the city of Rome, see Keegan (2013).

22. The translation is modified from Dillon & Garland (1994: 26).

23. Droysen (1836–43).

1. METHODS, TYPES, CONTEXTS

1. Innis (1951), Poe (2011).

2. Ulbaek (1998).

3. Diringer (1982: 17, 54).

4. Poe (2011).

5. Martinich (1996: i–xi).

6. Accounts of the embedding of text-based languages in the computational processes of

NOTES

reasoners and communicators are relatively well developed, with accounts available for a spectrum of languages ranging from the highly formalized and constrained, such as formal logics, to the highly informal and unconstrained natural languages used in everyday conversations. For discussion of a theory of diagrammatic communication, based upon recent studies of the syntactic, semantic and pragmatic component issues which such a theory must accommodate, see Gurr (1999).

7. Lester (2010: 48). Located in the Ardeche region of southern France, along the bank of the river Ardeche near the Pont-d'Arc, this cave was only discovered as recently as 1994, happened upon by a small team of cavers led by Jean-Marie Chauvet. Chauvet *et al.* (1996) provide a detailed account of the discovery. Recent studies of the French archaeologist Jean Clottes (2002, 2003a, 2003b) offer useful analysis and interpretation. A static photographic overview of the cave system, its natural and archaeological elements, and its artistic ensembles is available at www.culture.gouv.fr/culture/arcnat/chauvet/en. For an immersive 3D cinematic experience of Chauvet Cave, see the extraordinary film *Cave of Forgotten Dreams*, directed by Werner Herzog (2010).

8. Aurignacian is an archaeological culture (i.e. a culture associated with a site that presented material artefacts with features marking them as different from other cultural types). In this case, the name Aurignacian originated from the so-called *type site* of Aurignac in the Haute-Garonne area of France.

9. White (2003: 79–80).

10. From a very early date, as Aristotle (fifth century BCE) attests (*Poetics* 1449a), scenic painting (Greek *skenographia*) was a constituent element of Greek theatrical performance. In the temporary stages recorded as having been built in Rome from about the third century BCE well into the Imperial period, and in Roman permanent stages, *skenographia* employed highly sophisticated perspectival techniques which were designed subtly to modulate between reality and illusion in a variety of ways.

11. Rappenglück (2008b).

12. Rappenglück, in Whitehouse (2000); cf. Clottes (2002).

13. Rappenglück (2008a).

14. Poe (2011).

15. Petroglyphs can still be found in Africa (Tassili n'Ajjer – Algeria; Bidzar – Cameroon; Bambari, Lengo, Bangassou, Bwale – Central African Republic; Niola Doa – Chad; the Niari River valley – Republic of the Congo; Wadi Hammamat, South Sinai – Egypt; Ogooue River valley – Gabon; Akakus, Jebel Uweinat – Libya; Draa River valley – Morocco; Twyfelfontein – Namibia; Dabous Rock – Niger; Driekops Eiland, Karoo, Keiskie – South Africa; Nyambwezi Falls – Zambia); Asia (Aragats, Ughtasar, Urtsadzor – Armenia; Gobustan State Reserve – Azerbaijan; Kau Sai Chau, Po Toi Island, Cheung Chau, Shek Pik, Tung Lung Island, Yin Mountains, Wong Chuk Hang – China; Bhimbetka, Edakkal Caves, Kollur, Ladakh, Perumukkal, Kollur, Unakoti, Usgalimal – India; Awashima shrine, Hikoshima island, Miyajima, Temiya Cave – Japan; Wadi Faynan, Wadi Rum – Jordan; Chumysh River basin, Tamgaly Tas – Kazakhstan; Bangudae – South Korea; Cholpon-Ata, Saimaluu Tash, the Talas valley – Kyrgyzstan; Altai – Mongolia; Pakistan; Rizal – Philippines; Saudi Arabia; Wanshan near Maolin – Taiwan; Cunni Cave, Esatli, Gevaruk Valley, Hakkari Trisin, Kagizman, Latmos, Lena – Turkey; Sapa – Vietnam); Europe (County Durham, Gardom's Edge, Ilkley Moor, Northumberland – England; Hauensuoli – Finland; Vallée des Merveilles – France; Dowth, Knowth, Loughcrew, Newgrange, Tara – Ireland; Valcamonica – Italy; Alta, Møllerstufossen, Tennes – Norway; Côa Valley – Portugal; Galicia – Spain; Kanozero, Petrozavodsk-Lake Onega, Sikachi-Alyan, Tomskaya – Russia; Alvhem, Enköping, Glösa, Himmelstalund, Slagsta, Southwest Skåne, Torhamn – Sweden; Kamyana Mohyla – Ukraine); Latin America and the Caribbean (Cueva de las Manos, Talampaya National Park – Argentina; Ankok National Park, Ayo, Casabari, Quandiriki Caves – Aruba; Costaeo do Santinho, Lagoa Santa, Ivolandia, Serra da

301

NOTES

Capivara National Park, Vale do Catimbau National Park – Brazil; Rincón las Chilcas – Chile; Orongo, Rapa Nui – Easter Island; El Abra – Columbia; Rincon de la Vieja – Costa Rica; Cueva de las Maravillas – Dominican Republic; Boca de Potrerillos, Chiquihuitillos, Coahuiltecan Cueva Ahumada, Cuenca del Rio Victoria, La Proveedora – Mexico; Caguana Indian Park, La Cueva del Indio, La Piedra Escrita, Tibes Indian Park – Puerto Rico; Corantijn Basin – Suriname; Caurita – Trinidad and Tobago; Caicara del Orinoco – Venezuela); North America (Arizona; Arkansas; Nanaimo, Stuart Lake – British Columbia; Nevada; Kejimkujik National Park – Nova Scotia; California; Utah); and Oceania (Arnhem Land-Kakadu National Park, Kuringai-Chase National Park, Mutawintji National Park, Murujuga – Australia).

16. Donaldson (2011).
17. Madsen (1972), Rogers (2009).
18. Diringer (1982: 27). For the hieroglyphic and Greek terms, see Dover (1978: 619) and *LSJ*⁹ s.v. ζραφω.
19. Studies of graffiti in Egypt: Černý (1969–83), Peden (2001); Athens: Lang (1974); Palestine and the Sinai: Stone (1992–4); buildings on the Palatine: Solin & Itkonen-Kaila (1966), Castren & Lilius (1970).
20. Acrophonic means that the symbols for the numerals come from the first letter of the number name.
21. This graffiti is written in the form of the *htp-di-nsw* offering formula usually found on tomb walls or funerary *stelae*.
22. Romer (1982: 157–60). For a brief overview of this graffito (with bibliographical note), see Peden (2001: 73).
23. Lang (1974: 11–15).
24. Langner (2001: 143).
25. For a useful survey of the quantitative problems associated with the phenomenon of literacy, see Harris (1989), Humphrey (1991) and Thomas (1992). The introductory chapters and bibliographies in these works provide an excellent overview of the issues, and a comprehensive entry-point into the continuing debate.
26. Relying mostly, it should be said, on chance information and inference.
27. For the most extensive recent attempt to survey the subject of literacy in the ancient world, see Harris (1989); for reviews, see *L'Année Philologique*, and two collections of responses: Humphrey (1991) and Bowman & Woolf (1994).
28. According to Ovid (*Metamorphoses* 9.521) and Martial (*Epigrams* 14.21), the *stylus* was an iron instrument resembling a pencil in size and shape. It was sharpened to a point at one end, for scratching characters into waxed writing tablets, and flat and circular at the other, for smoothing the wax and erasing what had been written. The *stylus* was also referred to as the *graphium* (Ovid, *Loves* 1.11.23; Suetonius, *Julius Caesar* 82).

2. HISTORY

1. The Egyptian terms meaning "eternity" (*dt* and *nhh*) imply conflicting nuances – possibly continuity and discontinuity (Assmann 1991: 39–46; Servajean 2008). They represent two important factors defining any Egyptian conceptions of their own past.
2. Darnell & Darnell (1996, 1997).
3. Other sites with a similarly long chronological history of recorded use include Wadi Hammamat and Gebel Abu Foda.
4. Examples of *eituns* inscriptions have been found at VI.2.4, VII.7, VI.12.23–5 (House of the Faun), VIII.5/6 (Street of Abundance) and III.4.1–2 (E. end of Street of Abundance).
5. *NSc* 1927, 21, Abb 5.
6. Ancient sources referring to the slave revolt led by Spartacus are: Plutarch, *Crassus*

302

NOTES

8–11; Florus, *Epitome* 2.8.20; Appian, *Civil Wars* 1.111, 116–121; Orosius, *Histories* 5.24.1–8, 18–19.

7. Jacobelli (2003: 75).
8. *CIL* X.852 = *ILS* 5627.
9. *CIL* IV.2993x (Latin): "Good fortune to Decimus Lucretius"; *CIL* IV.2993y (Greek): "Good fortune to Satrius Valens, Augustus Nero".
10. *CIL* IV.1293 = *ILS* 6443a.
11. Relatively unknown, Cluvius Rufus was a Roman senator, governor and historian whose writing and testimony, though now lost, certainly shaped modern understanding of first-century Rome. A contemporary of Caligula, Claudius and Nero, little is known of the extent of his work except that it related to events during the reign of these emperors. Cluvius was one of the primary sources for Tacitus' *Annals* and *Histories*, Suetonius' *Twelve Caesars*, Josephus' *Antiquities of the Jews*, Plutarch's *Parallel Lives* and probably for other later historians as well. Cluvius Rufus is mentioned in: Josephus, *Antiquities of the Jews* 19.1.13; Suetonius, *Nero* 21; Pliny the Younger, *Letters* 9.19; Plutarch, *Otho* 3; Tacitus, *Annals*, 12.20 and 14.2; *Histories*, 1.8, 2.58, 2.65, 3.65, 4.39 and 4.43.
12. For a contextualized reading of this passage, see Hillard (2013: 112–14).
13. Suetonius, *Caesar* 80.3; Plutarch, *Caesar* 62.4, *Brutus* 9.5; Appian, *Civil Wars* 2.112.
14. Tacitus, *Histories* 1.87.
15. *Ibid.*: 2.12.

3. LITERATURE

1. Baines (1983), Baines & Eyre (1983), Lesko (2001).
2. Gallorini (1998).
3. Gardiner & Sethe (1955: 3–5, 17–19, pls. II–IIIA; 5, 20–21, pls. IV–IVa).
4. Janssen (1980).
5. For discussion of the following graffiti (G3.1–2), see Megally (1981); for the translations in English, see Peden (2001: 60).
6. Goody & Watt (1963), Wagner (2010: 161–2).
7. Parry (1971), Lord (1960), Havelock (1982).
8. Thomas (1989, 1992).
9. Langdon (1976: no. 1, 2, 10, 16, 20, 29c, 36, 49).
10. Zeus: Homer, *Iliad* 3.351, 16.233; Aeschylus, *Persians* 762; Apollo: Aristophanes, *Wasps* 524; *Wealth* 748.
11. On the use of *katapugon*, see Milne & von Bothmer (1953).
12. Bernand (1972a).
13. Lichtheim (1976: 52–7).
14. Bernard & Bernard (1960).
15. Johnson & Parker (2011).
16. This was the general term for buildings of this kind in the republican period. The word *amphitheatrum* did not come into regular use until the early imperial period.
17. Horsfall (2003: 25–6).
18. Juvenal, *Satires* 1.7–13.
19. For more on this, see Hillard (2013).
20. The visible parts of the *cryptoporticus* were discovered in 1949–50 in the area of the US Embassy in Rome. For historical and topographical notes on the *Horti Sallustiani* and the Villa Ludovisi (which houses the embassy), see Brandt (2008: 11–35).
21. Hillier & Hanson (1984: 1–2).

NOTES

4. ART AND ARCHITECTURE

1. For a history of rock graffiti in the wadis of the eastern desert, see Winkler (1938, 1939), Dunbar (1941), Fuchs (1989), Morrow & Morrow (2002), Judd (2009).
2. Rohl (2009: 26).
3. On the original Deir el-Medina excavators (Schiaparelli, Moeller and Bruyère), see Bierbrier (1989: 96–7, 140–41, 144), Černý (1969–83).
4. Aphrodisias is closely associated with the goddess of fertility, Aphrodite – an association arising from the proximity of its location to a sanctuary dedicated to a western Anatolian goddess of fertility and war, later assimilated into the guise of the Greek deity.
5. Bier (2008).
6. The Etruscan civilization existed for six and a half centuries, from c.750 BCE to 100 BCE. It began, therefore, when Rome still consisted of only village communities. The flourishing of Etruscan culture was from 700–500 BCE, with the peak of power in the sixth century. Roman conquests began in the early fourth century with the ten-year siege of Veii.
7. Poehler (2006; 2009: 38–121).
8. Verbal graffiti (mules: *CIL* IV.97, 113, 134; porters: *CIL* IV.497) confirm the practice.
9. Strabo, *Geography* 5.4.8.
10. Seneca, *Natural Questions* 6.1.1–3, 10; 6.1.10; 6.27.1–4; 6.31.1–2. This text was written between 62 and 65 CE, the year of the author's suicide.
11. *CIL* IX.846 = *ILS* 6367.
12. Pliny, *Natural History* 14.113, 114.
13. Common usage: *Digest* 7.1.15.6 (Ulpian); 18.1.76 (Paulus). Other terms (*dolia demissa*, *defixa* or *depressa*): Columella 12.18.6; *Digest* 32.93.4 (Scaevola); 33.6.3.1.
14. *Thesaurus Linguae Latinae* s.v. *dolium*.
15. Find-spots of *dolia defossa*: the so-called Magazzino dei dolii (III.14.3), next to the house of Annius, an oil merchant (the location of the *amphora* graffito); the so-called Caseggiato dei dolii (I.4.5), located immediately below the Museum at Ostia; the so-called Magazzino annonario (V.11.5), with over 100 sunken jars, located south of the main east–west road (the Decumanus Maximus) next to the Horrea dell'Artemide; and a building excavated in the late eighteenth century on the Tiber bank near the Horrea dei Mensores.
16. Haselberger (1985, 1995).

5. RELIGION

1. Limme *et al.* (1997).
2. Ritner (2009: 109).
3. For Memnonion and Osireion (Abydos), see Rutherford (2005); for the temple of Mandoulis-Apollo (Talmis), see Mairs (2001); for the mortuary temple of Hatshepsut (Deir el Bahari), see Bataille (1951); for the temple of Isis (Philae), see Festugière (1970); for the Valley of the Kings (Thebes), see Malaise (1987).
4. Demotic is a cursive form of ancient Egyptian script. Written from the middle of the seventh century BCE, demotic was used originally for legal, administrative and commercial purposes, but from the first century BCE and thereafter its use was restricted increasingly to literary and religious expression.
5. Perdrizet & Lefebvre (1919: no. 32).
6. *Ibid.*: no. 390, cf. nos. 414, 426.
7. *Ibid.*: no. 528.
8. *I. Philae. Dem.* 417.1–2.
9. *I. Dak. Dem.* 30.7.

304

NOTES

10. *I. Metr.* 169.
11. Dipylon Jug: *CEG* 432.
12. Henrichs (2003: 44–5).
13. Baur & Rostovtzeff (1929: 38–9, 41; 1931: 126–8).
14. For a general account of *tychē*, see Nilsson (1967–74: 2.200–210).
15. Lehrer (1979: 13).
16. Pliny the Younger, *Letters* 10.96–7.
17. *Graf. Pal.* I.246 (= Solin & Itkonen-Kaila 1966).
18. Tertullian, *Apology* 16, *To the Nations* 1.4; Minutius Felix 9.3, 28.7.
19. Phaedrus, *Fables* 5.7.28, Martial, *Epigrams* 1.3.7, Juvenal, *Satires* 4.118. Cf. Marti (1936: 280–81).
20. *Graf. Pal.* I.246 (= Solin & Itkonen-Kaila 1966).
21. Welborn (2005: 141–2).
22. The sixty known principal Christian catacombs can be found mainly along the Appian Way.
23. Catacombs: Monteverde on the Via Portuensis; in Vigna Randanini; and under Villa Torlonia. *Hypogea*: on the Via Labicana; in Vigna Cimarra; and on the Via Appia Pignatelli.
24. Prudentius, *Hymn* 11.
25. According to the founding tradition, the catacombs in this location were used temporarily as the place of interment for the remains of two Christian martyrs (the apostles Peter and Paul), later transferred to separate basilicas (Peter, on Vatican Hill; Paul, on the road to Ostia). Originally known as the Basilica Apostolorum, the building was dedicated to Sebastian during the ninth century CE.
26. Leon (1926), Noy (1995). Of the 494 inscriptions, 366 (74%) are in Greek, 120 (24.4%) are in Latin, and only 8 inscriptions (1.6%) are in Hebrew or Aramaic. Roughly, then, three-quarters of the inscriptions are in Greek and the remaining quarter in Latin. Of the Latin inscriptions, 12 are written with Greek characters. The sample of graffiti given above (G5.31–3) can be found, transcribed in the original language, in the *CIJ* (*Corpus Inscriptionum Judaicarum*). They are selected from inscriptions located in the largest surviving Jewish catacomb, Vigna Randanini (*CIJ* I.184, 133, 204, 205).

6. MAGIC

1. Graeco-Roman views: Graf (2002). Modern approaches: Hoffman (2002).
2. Exodus 7:8-23.
3. *Shabbat* 104b.
4. Arnobius, *Against the Nations* 1.43.
5. Thessalus of Tralles, *On the Virtues of Plants* 1.13.
6. Pseudo-Cyprian, *Confessions* 12.
7. *Alexander Romance* 1.3.1–2.
8. Lucian, *Philopseudes* 34–6.
9. For detailed discussion of ancient Egyptian magical practice, see Ritner (1993); on Egyptian magic in general, Pinch (1994).
10. Clark (2003: 17–18).
11. Papyrus BM 10188, col. 33/17–18.
12. Edwin Smith Surgical Papyrus (*ibid.*).
13. Sanchez & Meltzer (2010).
14. *Urkunden des aegyptischen Altertums* VI.5.37–53.
15. Demotic Magical Papyrus of Leiden and London, col. 3/20–21, 25–9.
16. Collins (2008).

305

NOTES

17. Faraone & Obbink (1991).
18. Johnson (2004).
19. Dickie (2001).
20. Faraone (1996).
21. Homer, *Iliad* 632–7.
22. Xenophon, *Memorabilia* 3.11.17.
23. *PGM* I.232–47.
24. Demotic Magical Papyrus of Leiden and London, col. 5/24–31.
25. Suetonius, *Augustus* 31.1; Acts of the Apostles 19:19.
26. Gager (1992: 90).
27. *Ibid.*: 50.
28. *Ibid.*: 127–9.
29. *Ibid.*: 188.
30. Strabo, *Geography* 16.785; Pliny, *Natural History* 5.81.
31. Pseudo-Lucian, *Concerning the Goddess Syria*.
32. *ILS* 8753.
33. Gager (1992: 78).
34. *Exodus* 12:23.
35. Pliny the Elder, *Natural History* 12.50.
36. Alciphron, *Letters* 1.15; Heliodorus, *Ethiopian Romance* 3.7; Virgil, *Eclogues* 3.103; cf. Pliny, *Natural History* 7.2.
37. *CIL* IV.7714, 7715.

7. MYTHOLOGY

1. Weeks (1995: 80).
2. Peden (2001: 63 n. 23).
3. The Ennead of Heliopolis: Atum; his children Shu and Tefnut; their children Geb and Nut; and their children, Osiris, Isis, Set and Nephthys.
4. Peden (2001: 99).
5. Staring (2010).
6. West (1982).
7. *CIL* IV.7963: "Fabius Ululitremulus together with Sul(l)a asks that you elect Gaius Cuspius Pansa and Lucius Popidius Secundus, son of Lucius, (to the position of) aediles."
8. There are another thirteen graffiti inscribed on the façade of this building (*CIL* IV.9116, 9125–36).
9. These paintings were removed from the site and survive now in photographic reproductions taken during excavation of the site.
10. *CIL* IV.9885.
11. Virgil, *Aeneid* 3.446.
12. *CIL* IV.10085a, 10086a.

8. POLITICS

1. Peden (2001: 1).
2. Darnell & Darnell (1997: 70–72).
3. Peden (2001: 17).
4. Darnell (1997: 88–90).
5. Peden (2001: 53).

NOTES

6. Darnell & Darnell (2002: 109).
7. Grandet (2000).
8. Callender (2006).
9. Philochoros *FGH* 328 f30; Pollux 8.19–20; Plutarch, *Aristotle* 7.6.
10. *Etymologicum Magnum* , s.v. *exostrakismos*; Photius, s.v. *ostrakismos*.
11. Philochoros *FGH* 328 f30.
12. For the *agora* graffiti, see Lang (1990); for the Ceramicus *ostraca*, see Brenne (2001, 2002).
13. Herodotus, *Histories* 8.79.
14. Plutarch, *Cimon*; Cornelius Nepos, *Lives of Eminent Commanders* 5.
15. Thucydides, *History of the Peloponnesian War* 2.65.
16. Cornelius Nepos, *Lives of Eminent Commanders* 2; Diodorus Siculus, *Historical Library* 11.27, 39–43, 54–8; Herodotus, *Histories* 5.78, 7.142–5, 161, 173, 8.4, 11–22, 50, 62, 71–6, 80–83, 97, 123; Plutarch, *Themistocles*; Thucydides, *History of the Peloponnesian War* 1.90–91, 135–8.
17. For discussion of the listed *ostraca*, see Lang (1990: 32.10, 33.14, 36.34, 64.308, 89.592, 98.651, 116.841, 133, 1051, 134.1065).
18. Plutarch, *Aristides* 7.5–6.
19. Lang (1990: 142–61).
20. Cicero, *Republic* 1.39.
21. Cicero, *Laws* 2.2.5.
22. Other groups with economic or common interests recommending candidates as a collective include bakers (*pistores*), ball players (*pilicrepi*), barbers (*tonsores*), carpenters (*lignarii*), dyers (*infectores*), farmers (*agricolae*), feltmakers (*quactiliari = coactiliari*). fishermen (*piscatores*) and garlic dealers (*aliarii*).
23. Polybius, *Histories* 6.2.3.
24. *Ibid.*: 6.15.1.
25. Cicero, *Orator* 2.198–9.
26. Machiavelli, *Discourses* 1.4.
27. *CIL* X.1018.
28. In addition to the graffiti quoted above (G8.33, G8.35), the council's support for Sabinus is preserved in four other *programmata*: *CIL* IV.7203, 7576, 7584 and 7605.
29. The inscriptions of the *cohors* VII *vigilum* are located in the smaller garrison of the cohort's permanent detachment. For details of the original excavation and epigraphic finds, see *Bullettino dell'Instituto di Corrispondenza Archeologica* (1867: 8–30); *Annali dell'Instituto di Corrispondenza Archeologica* (1874: 111–63); cf. *Bullettino della Commissione Archeologica Comunale di Roma* (1886: 266–9); Lanciani (1898: 549); *CIL* VI.2993–7, 32751.
30. *CIL* VI.2998–3091.
31. Livy, *History of Rome* 25.2.
32. Quintilian, *Institutes of Oratory* 6.3.52. Types of donation: Livy, *History of Rome* 37.57; Pliny the Elder, *Natural History* 14.14, 17, 31.7, 41; Pliny the Younger, *Panegyric* 25; Suetonius, *Augustus* 41, *Tiberius* 20, *Nero* 7; Tacitus, *Annals* 12.41, 13.31. *Congiaria*: Cicero, *Letter to Atticus* 16.8; Curtius Rufus, *History of Alexander* 6.2. For specific detail about the *congiarium* in relation to government in the Roman empire, see Duncan-Jones (1994: 248–50).
33. Cassius Dio, *Roman History* 53.16, 54.12, 58.24, 66.1.
34. Tacitus, *Annals* 13.31; 14.17, 27.

307

NOTES

9. SPORT

1. Lichtheim (1976: 41).
2. *Ibid.*: 41.
3. *Ibid.*: 42.
4. *Ibid.*: 41–2.
5. Amenhotep II's mummified remains can be found in the Cairo Museum (CG 61069).
6. Breasted (1906a: 190).
7. Aristotle, *Constitution of the Athenians* 60.
8. Xenophanes, fr, 2.
9. Miller (2001: 85, 92, 315) (GRAF 2D).
10. *Ibid.*: 85, 330–32 (GRAF 14C) with nn. 639–42, 335–37 (GRAF 16).
11. *Ibid.*: 85, 333, 335 (GRAF 15D).
12. *Ibid.*: 3–11.
13. *Ibid.*: 84–90, 311–66.
14. Pausanias, *Description of Greece* 6.14.4.
15. Plutarch, *Agis* 3.4; *Pyrrhus* 26.8, 28.2–3; Pausanias 3.6.6; Phylarchus *apud* Athenaeus 4.142b.
16. Aristophanes, *Peace* 899–900; Pindar, *Isthmian* 8 (for Cleandros of Aegina).
17. Metropolitan Museum of Art/06.1021.49.
18. Euboulos fr.2 K-A; Plato Comicus fr.46 K-A; Kallimachos fr.2 Pfeiffer; Sophocles fr.537 R; Aristophanes, *Clouds* 1071–3.
19. Athenaeus, *Dinner-table Philosophers* 665d–668f.
20. Cicero, *On Behalf of Sestius* 98.
21. Pliny the Younger, *Letters* 9.6. Cf. Cicero, *On Behalf of Plancius* 66; *On Duty* 3.1; *Republic* 1.33; Sallust, *Catilinarian Conspiracy* 4; Seneca, *Dialogues* 8.3.5.
22. Valerius Maximus, *Memorable Deeds and Sayings* 2.4.7.
23. Games: Cassius Dio, *Roman History* 47.40.6; 54.2.3; Suetonius, *Claudius* 24.2. Regulation: *ILS* 6087; Suetonius, *Tiberius* 34.1.
24. Column drawing, inscribed on the W. Peristyle of VI.9.10 (Casa del Labirinto) at Pompeii. For an illustration, see Langner (2001: table 59.1040).
25. Other examples of *graffiti* depicting gladiatorial scenes and associated details (types of gladiator, names of the fighters, their affiliation, number of fights to date, the outcome of fights, and the reputations of favourite combatants) include *CIL* IV.1421, 1422, 1474, 1481, 1770, 1773, 2508, 4297, 4299, 4342, 4345, 10236a and 10238a.
26. See *CIL* IV.1185, 7992 and 7995.
27. Tacitus, *Annals* 14.17.
28. For the explanation that Nero revoked the prohibition on gladiatorial games in the Pompeian amphitheatre, see Franklin (2001: 123–5); for an alternative hypothesis, see Cooley & Cooley (2004: 64).
29. *CIL* IV.3790: Publius Aemilius Celer; *CIL* IV.3792: Aemilius Celer; *CIL* IV.3794: Aemilius Celer lives here.
30. For the translation of this inscription and related discussion, see Benefiel (2008).
31. Pliny the Younger, *Letters* 2.17.1, 5.6.27; *Digest* 17.1.16.
32. Eschebach (1979: 17, 61, 70).
33. Gladiator, charioteer and animal-hunter inscriptions comprise roughly 40 per cent of surviving graffiti-drawings in the Roman empire For a useful catalogue of these inscriptions, see Langner (1999: table 37-73, fig. 769-1164).
34. *Graf. Pal.* I.58 (palm); 97 (athlete).
35. Dionysius of Halicarnassus, *Roman Antiquities* 3.68; Pliny the Elder, *Natural History* 36.102.
36. Suetonius, *Claudius* 21.3; Tacitus, *Annals* 15.53.

308

NOTES

37. Ovid, *Loves* 3.2; *Art of Love* 1.135–62; Juvenal, *Satires* 11.202.
38. *Graf. Pal.* I.99, 101, 109, 176, 310, 319, 324, 350, 351, 352, 353, 358.
39. *Ibid.*: I.302, 303, 306.
40. Gordius is mentioned in Cass. Dio 79.15.1 in the form Gordios; as well as Lampridius, *Heliogabulus* 6.3, 12.1, 15.2; cf. Stein, *Pauly-Wissowa* 4.1221 and *PIR*² C 1289.
41. Edmondson (1996: 111).
42. For another example of the "magic square" type, see *CIL* IV.8623 (ROTAS–OPERA–TENET–AREPO–SATOR, with a Greek-alpha superscript and -omega subscript), thought by some twentieth-century scholarship to contain a hidden reference to PATER NOSTER and hence a post-Neronian Christian presence in Pompeii. For a brief discussion of "magic square" and palindromic *graffiti* in the Pompeian context, see Cooley and Cooley (2004: 76); for a compilation of all the bibliography to date on the SATOR square, see Sheldon (2003).
43. Cicero, *On Divination* 1.13; cf. Martial, *Epigrams* 14.16; Horace, *Satires* 2.7.17; Propertius, *Elegies* 4.8.45.

10. COMMERCE

1. Plato, *Laws* 677a–682e; Strabo, *Geography* 2.5.26.
2. Homer, *Iliad, Odyssey*; Hesiod, *Works and Days*; Xenophon, *Economics*.
3. Aristotle, *History of Animals*; Theophrastus, *Enquiry into Plants, On the Causes of Plants*.
4. Cato, *On Agriculture* (De Agri Cultura); Columella: *On Agriculture* (De Re Rustica); Varro, *On Agriculture* (Res Rusticae). Specialist Greek writers: Varro, *On Agriculture* 1.1.7–10.
5. Josephus, *Against Apion* 1.18, 21; *Antiquities of the Jews* 8.5.3; 13.2.
6. Darnell & Darnell (2002: 92).
7. Ruffling (2002).
8. Bréand (2009).
9. Vereecken (2011).
10. The International Potmark Workshop, available at www.potmark-egypt.com.
11. Darnell & Darnell (2002: 159).
12. Frood & Baines (2007: 48).
13. *Ibid.*: 52.
14. *Ibid.*: 51.
15. Breasted (1906b: 743).
16. Darnell & Darnell (2002: 26).
17. *Ibid.*: 38.
18. *Ibid.*: 73.
19. *Ibid.*: 123.
20. *Ibid.*: 31.
21. Burkhardt (1997).
22. Weill (1940).
23. Gardiner & Sethe (1955: no. 18, 20, 21).
24. Peden (2001: 21–2).
25. Gasse (1987).
26. Couyat & Montet (1912–13: no. 58, 65–6, 98, 132, 212).
27. Ridgway (1992: 112).
28. Strabo, *Geography* 5.4.4; Ridgway (1992: 59).
29. *Homeric Hymn to Apollo* 218–19: "Soon you came to Iolcus and set foot on Cenaeum in Euboea, famed for ships."

309

NOTES

30. Aristophanes, *Wasps* 790.
31. G10.19–22 = Lang (1956: no. 2, 3, 44, 63, 71).
32. G10.23–26 = Lang (1974: no. B12, B20, E4, E6).
33. Strabo, *Geography* 17.1.33.
34. Herodotus, *Histories* 4.152.
35. *Ibid.*: 7.147.2; Demosthenes, *Orations* 20.30–33.
36. Meiggs and Lewis (1969: no. 7).
37. In order: 136 no. GR 27, 30; 137 no. GR 42; 138 no. GR 50; 138/139 no. GR 51; 139 no. GR 53, 55; 140 no. GR 66; 142 no. GR 96; 143 no. GR 120, 127.
38. 138 no. GR 48.
39. Polybius, *Histories* 3.21–6.
40. *Ibid.*: 1.83.7; 14.7.2.
41. Berry (1997: 122).
42. Cf. Pliny the Younger, *Letters* 5.4; 5.13; 9.39.
43. Dio Chrysostom, *Orations* 35.15.
44. *Ibid.*: 46.10.
45. Pliny the Elder, *Natural History* 31.88, 93–94; Athenaeus, *Dinner-table Philosophers* 2.67c; Isidore of Seville, *Etymologies* 20.3.19–20; Martial, *Epigrams* 13.82, 102; Columella, *On Agriculture* 9.14.3; [Anonymous], *Agricultural Pursuits* (*Geoponica*) 20.46.
46. Pliny the Elder, *Natural History* 31.95.
47. *Amphora* labels from Cosa and the Porta Cosanus.
48. *CIL* IV.5745–60 (barley), 5728–9 (chickpeas), 5371 (fennel), 2568 (figs), 10288 (honey), 6580 (lentils), 5761 (nuts), 5598b (olives), 5721–2 (pickling brine).
49. Cato, *On Agriculture* 2.7; Varro, *On Agriculture* 1.17.1; Livy, *History of Rome* 39.6.7.
50. *TP* (= *Tabulae Pompeianae*) 30 = *AE* 1973.151.
51. *TH* (= *Tabulae Herculanenses*) 7, 8, 52, 54, 90 (Venustus); 43 (Felix).

11. SEXUALITY

1. For useful introductions to ideas and practices pertaining to sexuality and gender in antiquity, see Manniche (2002) for Egypt and Skinner (2013) for the Graeco-Roman world.
2. For example, archaic Greek epic poetry (sexual relations): Homer, *Iliad* 24.675; *Odyssey* 5.154, 10.333–47.
3. For example, classical Greek comedy (explicit sexual vocabulary): Aristophanes, *Assemblywomen* 938–1111; *Wealth* 1067–96; Graeco-Roman prose (temple prostitution in late Ptolemaic Egypt): Strabo, *Geography* 17.1.46.
4. For example, Ramesside Egyptian love poetry: *Papyrus Chester Beatty* I ("The Great Dispenser of Pleasure" cycle); Roman elegiac verse (psychological impact of erotic desire): Propertius 1.1, 2.15.
5. For example, Longus, *Daphnis and Chloe* 1.11–14, 1.23–7, 1.32.
6. For example, Ovid, *Loves* 3.7; cf. Martial, *Epigrams* 11.29, 11.46, 11.81, 12.86.
7. For example, Greek historical prose (female sexualized display in Egyptian religious processions): Diodorus Siculus, *Library of History* 1.85; Herodotus, *Histories* 2.155; Roman satire (sexual activity): Martial, *Epigrams* 11.61, 12.55, 12.75, 12.85.
8. For example, Suetonius, *Caligula* 24, 36; *Nero* 27–9; *Domitian* 22; Tacitus, *Annals* 15.37; *Scriptores Historiae Augustae Commodus* 5.4–11; *Heliogabalus* 5, 8.6, 10.5–7, 26.3–5.
9. For example, Messalina: Tacitus, *Annals* 11.12, 11.34.2; Juvenal, *Satires* 6.116–32; Sabina Poppaea: Tacitus, *Annals* 13.45; Faustina: *Scriptores Historiae Augustae Aurelius* 19.7; Theodora: Procopius, *Secret History* 9.1–28.

NOTES

10. For example, Aristotle, *History of Animals* 539b, 571b, 608a–b; Plutarch, *Morals* 650F–651E.
11. Westcar Papyrus, *Papyrus Berlin* 3033 ("Khufu and the Magicians").
12. Aristotle, *Politics* 1335a.
13. For example, references to the Pappus character in Atellane farces, esp. the (now lost) plays of Pomponius, Novius, Aprissius and Mummius. On the *fabula Atellana*, see Livy, *History of Rome* 7.2; Valerius Maximus, *Deeds and Sayings of Famous Men* 2.4.4; Suetonius, *Nero* 39.3; Juvenal, *Satires* 3.173–6.
14. For example, *Papyrus Harris* 500.
15. Plato *Republic* 389e, 559c; Aristotle, *Nichomachean Ethics* 1118a–b, 1147b 20.
16. For example, *Inscription of Mes* (= *KRI* III, 424); Xenophon, *Economics* 7.18–22; Aristotle, *Nicomachean Ethics* 1162a 16–33.
17. Plutarch, *Morals* ("Conjugal Precepts") 138A–146C; Musonius Rufus, *Sayings* 13.
18. Posener (1980: 91).
19. Papyrus Leiden I.350, Ch. 100 (4.9–11).
20. Faulkner (1969: 198, no. 1248).
21. Faulkner (1973: 77–8, II:4).
22. Omlin (1973).
23. The papyrus showing animals engaged in human activity is currently on display in the British Museum (AN1058479001).
24. Hubbard (2003: 82–3).
25. Hesychius K 3522, s.v. *konisalos*: "a leaping satiric dance of dancers inserting their genitals".
26. Hubbard (2003: 83).
27. G11.18–24 = Lang (1974: no. C1, C3, C5, C7, C8, C18, C23).
28. *Ibid.*: no. C4, C10, C11, C13, C15–17, C19, C21, C28–29, C31.
29. *Ibid.*: no. C33.
30. Bernand (1972b: 52–3, no. 23).
31. For useful overviews of literary and non-literary representations of sexual ideas and practices pertaining specifically to the Roman world, see Clarke (2003) and Richlin (1992).
32. Robbins (1995: 76).
33. For a succinct discussion of the Graeco-Roman sociolinguistic system's propensity to generate normative and monstrous representations of sex/gender, see Parker (1998); for a convincing critique of Parker's grid, see Williams (1999); the same volume also includes a different schematization of the Roman insertive-receptive sexual vocabulary (*ibid.*: 161–2, with 326 n. 4).
34. See especially L'Hoir (1992) and Viden (1993).
35. The late Republican category of the "new man" (*novus homo*) is perhaps the most concrete instance of this phenomenon. On the one hand, individuals like M. Porcius Cato, C. Marius or Cicero rose from outside the senate to the consulship; on the other, each measured the terms of his advancement as part of a self-fashioning regime *per se cognitus* ("known through himself"). In contrast to the *nobilitas* of the "known" men, *novi homines* were required to justify their origins and defend the pattern of their career. Demonstrable moral excellence (*virtus*) and hard work (*industria*) were insufficient; patronage or circumstances determined the registration of a new man's achievement. In these respects, the sociolinguistic resonances of the *vir*(*nobilis*)/(*novus*)*homo* dichotomy stand confirmed. For a particularly apt expression of the rhetorical slipperiness of these denominations, consider Cicero's attack on the lineage and achievements of the son (?) of one of Sulla's "new" senators, the infamous C. Verres, in 2 *Verrines* 5.180ff.
36. For references supporting the *femina*/*mulier* distinction, see L'Hoir (1992: ch. 2).
37. Sexual distinctions can be expressed in Latin (and Greek, for that matter) by substantives (demonstrative and relative pronouns).

NOTES

38. For the only comprehensive study of erotic graffiti at Pompeii, see Varone (2001). That the Archaeological Museum at Naples only recently opened the so-called "secret room" (*camera segretta*) – containing artefacts of a sexual nature recovered from Pompeii and Herculaneum – to the general public indicates how controversial this material remains. For an introductory survey of the Museum's erotic art collection and the general significance of sexual representations in the ancient Roman world, see Grant (1975).

39. In Greek and Latin poetry, the elegiac couplet (or *distichon*) consists of alternating lines of hexameter and pentameter; that is, two dactyls followed by a long syllable and a *caesura* (a dactylic hexameter catalectic), then two more dactyls followed by a long syllable (a double *hemiepes* or first half of a dactylic hexameter).

40. Greek poets used the elegiac metre in public and private contexts (1) in the archaic and classical periods: to exhort their fellow citizens to battle, to express political opinions, to commemorate the dead, and to accompany dedications made at holy places; (2) in the Hellenistic period: to canvass the subject of love, and to articulate a variety of other concerns in narrative form. Quintilian (*Institutes of Oratory* 10.93) informs us that the ancient canon of Latin elegists comprised Cornelius Gallus, Albius Tibullus, Sextus Propertius and Ovid.

41. The trochaic measure consists of a strongly accented syllable followed by a weak (or unstressed) one.

42. The Pompeii Forum Project (http://pompeii.virginia.edu), an interdisciplinary collaborative research venture sponsored by the National Endowment for the Humanities, the University of Virginia and private contributors, provides access to a QuickTime virtual tour of the *basilica*. The URL address for the Project's interactive map of Pompeii is http://hitchcock.itc.virginia.edu/Pompeii/map/Pompeii.html.

43. *CIL* IV records 172 graffiti inscriptions on the interior and exterior walls of the Basilica at Pompeii. These walls have been cut into 32 sections (*tabulae*), presently conserved and stored in the National Archaeological Museum at Naples.

44. If the inscribed text (Figure 11.1) and the Latin transcription here are compared, the practice by Pompeian graffitists of using a combination of vertical strokes to represent certain letters can be seen. In this instance, two vertical strokes (in the words SCRI- *IBENTI*, *PIIRIIAM*, *SINII*, *TII*, *IISSII* and *VIILIM*) indicate the letter "e". Other common abbreviations in Pompeian graffiti are a long vertical and two shorter verticals for "n" (III) and a long vertical and three shorter verticals for "m" (IIII).

45. For example, Plautus, *The Weevil* 1.3.11; Terence, *Hecyra* 5.4.3; Propertius, *Elegies* 3.14.10, 15.40; Cicero, *On Friendship* 23.88, *To Atticus* 12.3; Virgil, *Trifles* 13.3; Horace, *Letters* 1.18.18; Ovid, *Loves* 2.1.38, 3.14.40, *Heroides* 4.13, 20, 29, 31.

46. For a comprehensive introduction to sexuality in republican and imperial Rome, see Skinner (2013: esp. ch. 7–9).

47. For historical details of the Vibii, see Castren (1975: 240–41), with references.

48. Gigante (1979: 26); cf. Varone (2001: 103–4).

49. Antonio Sogliano's original excavation report – in *Notizie degli Scavi di Antichi* (Rome: Accademie di Lincei: 519) – is dated 1888.

50. Della Corte (1960: 73–6).

51. Varone (2001: 100–101). Even the *NSc* report (1888: 519 n. 28) notes that "*e una donna parla*" ("a woman is speaking").

52. The motif of the *paraclausithyron* (the lover before the closed door) is extensively used in classical elegiac love poetry (Propertius, Tibullus, Ovid). See especially Catullus 64.138–44 and 169, the lament in the *epithalamion* (wedding song) of Peleus and Tethys. Cf. also line 8 and Lucretius, *On the Nature of Things* 5.962; line 3 and Juvenal, *Satires* 12.47. Zangemeister (in *CIL* 4 *suppl*: 589) thinks that this graffito is a *cento*, a patchwork conflation of diverse poetic fragments; and cites in support Virgil, *Aeneid* 10.652, Statius, *Silvae* 5.4.14–15, and Apuleius, *Golden Ass* 6.16. The artificiality of this premise would appear self-evident.

312

NOTES

53. Baldi (1982: 166) sees this graffito as recording *"una passione omosessuale femminile"* ("a feminine homosexual passion").
54. Transcription: *CIL* IV *suppl.*: 589. Note: *Notizie degli Scavi di Antichi* (1888: 519).
55. *Graf. Pal.* I.92.
56. Solin & Itkonen-Kaila (1966: 31); *Graf. Pal.* I.134.
57. *Graf. Pal.* I.71.
58. *Ibid.*: I.96, 97.
59. *Ibid.*: I.121.
60. *Ibid.*: I.74, 113.
61. *Ibid.*: I.232.
62. As our discussion of Greek sexual graffiti indicated, *pedico* does not always act as a metonymous substitute for "homosexual". *Pedico/pedicator* may be used to describe men who today would be labeled "homosexual" (or, more specifically, men who play the insertive role in penetrative acts with other males). But the literal meaning, denoting "a man who anally penetrates", can encompass female objects. See, for example, Martial, *Epigrams* 11.78.5–6, 11.99.1–2, 11.104.17–20; cf. *CIL* 10.4483 and the possibly related *CIL* 4.2184, 2194, 2248, which refer to a certain Phoebus as *pedico* and *fututor*. See also the literary equivalent of Phoebus in Martial's portrait of a certain Cantharus: 11.45.
63. Adams (1982: 123).
64. Discussing Roman perceptions of Greece and Greek cultural traditions, Williams (1999: 72) concluded that ancient writers, both Greek and Roman, displayed no preoccupation with pederasty as a distinguishing characteristic of Greek culture. Interestingly, the references to pederastic practices in the Paedagogium graffiti are outside the literary tradition that Williams surveyed.
65. *Graf. Pal.* I.230.
66. *Ibid.*: I.181; 65, 68, 73, 76, 113.
67. Bain (1991: 67).
68. Chersonese: *Graf. Pal.* I.65: *Cherronesita*, 73: *Chersonesita*; Greece: *Graf. Pal.* I.73: *Graecus.*
69. *Graf. Pal.* I.364.
70. For the literary tradition linking *delicia* children to pederastic practices in the imperial household, see Laes (2003: 301–2).
71. *Graf. Pal.* I.11.
72. Laes (2003: 310).
73. Tacitus, *Annals* 15.69.
74. *Ibid.*: 15.37. Cf. Cassius Dio, *Roman History* 62.6.4 (Boudica's reference to Nero's propensity for "sleeping with boys, and boys past their prime at that").
75. Suetonius, *Galba* 22.
76. *Scriptores Historiae Augustae* (Commodus) 7.5.4.
77. On the relationship between sex and slavery in the Roman world, see Williams (1999: 30–38).
78. Seneca, *Letters* 95.24.
79. *Ibid.*: 47.7.

CONCLUSION

1. Messner (1941).
2. For example, Cicero *2 Verrines* 5.6.14, *To Atticus* 4.17.5, *Against Piso* 40, 97; Juvenal *Satires* 6.638–9.
3. For a succinct assessment of historical attitudes to Nero, see Elsner & Masters (1994: 2–8).

NOTES

4. The major accounts of the Great Fire of 64 CE can be found in Tacitus, *Annals* 15.38–44 and Cassius Dio, *Roman History* 62.16–18.
5. Cf. *CIL* IV.528, 670, 671a–b, 820a, 1074, 1612 and 10049.
6. Smith (2002).
7. Nongbri (2011).
8. Roueché (1989: 50–52, 64–6, 85–97, 105), Chaniotis (2002).

ANCIENT REFERENCES

Where texts are quoted, I have supplied my own translation into English from the original work. For easy recognition, titles of all classical references are also translated into English. The inquisitive reader is directed to the following online editions in English of texts cited or translated in this book.

Aeschylus, *Persians*
http://classics.mit.edu/Aeschylus/persians.html

Alciphron, *Letters*
http://www.elfinspell.com/AlciphronIntro.html

Ammianus Marcellinus, *History*
http://penelope.uchicago.edu/Thayer/E/Roman/Texts/Ammian/home.html

Anonymous, *Agricultural Pursuits*
www.ancientlibrary.com/geoponica

Appian, *Civil Wars*
www.perseus.tufts.edu/hopper/text?doc=Perseus%3Atext%3A1999.01.0232

Aristophanes, *Assemblywomen, Peace, Wasps, Wealth*
http://classics.mit.edu/Browse/browse-Aristophanes.html

Aristotle, *Constitution of the Athenians, History of Animals, Nichomachean Ethics, Poetics*
http://classics.mit.edu/Browse/browse-Aristotle.html

Arnobius, *Against the Nations*
http://archive.org/details/thesevenbooksofa00arnouoft

Athenaeus, *Dinner-table Philosophers*
www.attalus.org/old/athenaeus.html

Cassius Dio, *Roman History*
http://penelope.uchicago.edu/Thayer/E/Roman/Texts/Cassius_Dio/home.html

Cato, *On Agriculture*
http://penelope.uchicago.edu/Thayer/E/Roman/Texts/Cato/De_Agricultura/home.html

315

ANCIENT REFERENCES

Cicero, *Against Piso, Laws, Letters to Atticus, On Behalf of Plancius, On Behalf of Sestius, On Divination, On Duty, On Friendship, Orator, Republic, Verrines*
http://classics.mit.edu/Browse/browse-Cicero.html

Columella, *On Agriculture*
http://penelope.uchicago.edu/Thayer/E/Roman/Texts/Columella/home.html

Cornelius Nepos, *Lives of Eminent Commanders*
www.tertullian.org/fathers/nepos.htm

Curtius Rufus, *History of Alexander*
http://penelope.uchicago.edu/Thayer/E/Roman/Texts/Curtius/home.html

Dio Chrysostom, *Orations*
http://penelope.uchicago.edu/Thayer/E/Roman/Texts/Dio_Chrysostom/home.html

Diodorus Siculus, *Historical Library*
http://penelope.uchicago.edu/Thayer/E/Roman/Texts/Diodorus_Siculus/home.html

Dionysius of Halicarnassus, *Roman Antiquities*
http://penelope.uchicago.edu/Thayer/E/Roman/Texts/Dionysius_of_Halicarnassus/home.html

Florus, *Epitome*
http://penelope.uchicago.edu/Thayer/E/Roman/Texts/Florus/Epitome/home.html

Heliodorus, *Ethiopian Romance*
http://archive.org/details/aethiopica00cologoog

Herodotus, *Histories*
http://classics.mit.edu/Herodotus/history.html

Hesiod, *Works and Days*
www.theoi.com/Text/HesiodWorksDays.html

Homer, *Iliad, Odyssey*
http://classics.mit.edu/Homer/iliad.html
http://classics.mit.edu/Homer/odyssey.html

Horace, *Satires*
www.poetryintranslation.com/PITBR/Latin/Horacehome.htm

Isidore of Seville, *Etymologies*
http://penelope.uchicago.edu/thayer/e/roman/texts/isidore/home.html

Josephus, *Against Apion, Antiquities of the Jews*
www.perseus.tufts.edu/hopper/text?doc=Perseus:text:1999.01.0216
www.perseus.tufts.edu/hopper/text?doc=Perseus:text:1999.01.0146

Juvenal, *Satires*
www.princeton.edu/~achaney/tmve/wiki100k/docs/Satires_of_Juvenal.html

Livy, *History of Rome*
www.perseus.tufts.edu/hopper/collection?collection=Perseus%3Acollection%3AGreco-Roman

Longus, *Daphne and Chloe*
www.msu.edu/~tyrrell/daphchlo.htm

ANCIENT REFERENCES

Lucian, *Philopseudes*
www.sacred-texts.com/cla/luc/wl3/wl315.htm

Martial, *Epigrams*
http://archive.org/details/martialepigrams01martiala

Musonius Rufus, *Sayings*
https://sites.google.com/site/thestoiclife/the_teachers/musonius-rufus

Orosius, *Histories*
https://sites.google.com/site/demontortoise2000

Ovid, *Art of Love, Metamorphoses, Heroides, Loves*
www.sacred-texts.com/cla/ovid/lboo
http://classics.mit.edu/Ovid/metam.html

Pausanias, *Description of Greece*
www.theoi.com/Text/Pausanias1A.html

Phaedrus, *Fables*
www.perseus.tufts.edu/hopper/text?doc=Perseus%3Atext%3A1999.02.0119%3Abook%3D1
%3Apoem%3Dprologus

Pindar, *Isthmians*
http://archive.org/details/isthmianodespin00pindgoog

Plato, *Laws, Republic*
http://classics.mit.edu/Browse/browse-Plato.html

Pliny the Elder, *Natural History*
http://penelope.uchicago.edu/Thayer/E/Roman/Texts/Pliny_the_Elder/home.html

Pliny the Younger, *Letters, Panegyric*
www.fordham.edu/halsall/ancient/pliny-letters.asp

Plutarch, *Morals, Parallel Lives* (*Agis, Aristides, Aristotle, Brutus, Caesar, Cimon, Crassus, Pyrrhus, Themistocles, Tiberius Gracchus*)
http://penelope.uchicago.edu/Thayer/E/Roman/Texts/Plutarch/Lives/home.html

Polybius, *Histories*
http://penelope.uchicago.edu/Thayer/E/Roman/Texts/Polybius/home.html

Procopius, *Secret History*
www.fordham.edu/halsall/basis/procop-anec.asp

Propertius, *Elegies*
www.poetryintranslation.com/PITBR/Latin/Prophome.htm

Prudentius, *Hymns*
www.ccel.org/ccel/prudentius/cathimerinon.toc.html

Quintilian, *Institutes of Oratory*
http://penelope.uchicago.edu/Thayer/E/Roman/Texts/Quintilian/Institutio_Oratoria/
home.html

Sallust, *Catilinarian Conspiracy*
http://penelope.uchicago.edu/Thayer/E/Roman/Texts/Sallust/Bellum_Catilinae*.html

Scriptores Historiae Augustae, *Aurelius, Heliogabulus*
http://penelope.uchicago.edu/Thayer/E/Roman/Texts/Historia_Augusta/home.html

ANCIENT REFERENCES

Seneca, *Dialogues, Letters, Natural Questions*
www.stoics.com/seneca_essays_book_1.html

Strabo, *Geography*
http://penelope.uchicago.edu/Thayer/E/Roman/Texts/Strabo/home.html

Suetonius, *Twelve Caesars (Julius Caesar, Augustus, Tiberius, Caligula, Claudius, Nero, Galba, Otho, Domitian)*
http://penelope.uchicago.edu/Thayer/E/Roman/Texts/Suetonius/12Caesars/home.html

Tacitus, *Annals, Histories*
http://classics.mit.edu/Browse/browse-Tacitus.html

Terence, *Hecyra*
www.perseus.tufts.edu/hopper/text?doc=Perseus%3Atext%3A1999.02.0116%3Aact%3Dprologue%3Ascene%3D1

Tertullian, *Apology, To the Nations*
www.tertullian.org/works/apologeticum.htm
www.tertullian.org/works/ad_nationes.htm

Theophrastus, *Enquiry into Plants, On the Causes of Plants*
http://archive.org/details/enquiryintoplant02theouoft

Thucydides, *History of the Peloponnesian War*
http://classics.mit.edu/Thucydides/pelopwar.html

Varro, *On Agriculture*
http://penelope.uchicago.edu/Thayer/E/Roman/Texts/Varro/de_Re_Rustica/home.html

Virgil, *Aeneid, Eclogues, Trifles*
http://classics.mit.edu/Browse/browse-Virgil.html

Xenophon, *Economics, Memorabilia*
www.perseus.tufts.edu/hopper/collection?collection=Perseus%3Acorpus%3Aperseus%2Cauthor%2CXenophon

BIBLIOGRAPHY

Abel, L. & B. E. Buckley 1977. *Towards a Sociology and Psychology of Graffiti*. Westport, CT: Greenwood Press.

Adams, J. N. 1982. *The Latin Sexual Vocabulary*. London: Duckworth.

Allen, J. P. 2005. *The Ancient Egyptian Pyramid Texts*. Atlanta, GA: Society of Biblical Literature.

Assman, J. 1991. *Stein und Zeit: Mensch und Gesellschaft im Alten Ägypten*. Munich: Wilhelm Fink.

Bain, D. 1991. "Six Greek Verbs of Sexual Congress". *Classical Quarterly* 41: 51–77.

Baines, J. 1983. "Literacy and Ancient Egyptian Society". *Man* 18: 572–99.

Baines, J. & C. Eyre 1983. "Four Notes on Literacy". *Göttinger Miszellen* 61: 65–96.

Baird, J. & C. Taylor (eds) 2010. *Ancient Graffiti in Context*. London: Routledge.

Baldi, A. 1982. *Iscrizioni Pompeiane*. Salerno: Cava de'Tirreni.

Bataille, A. 1951. *Les inscriptions grecque du temple de Hatshepsout à Deir el Bahari*. Cairo: Institute français d'archéologie orientale.

Baur, P. & M. Rostovtzeff (eds) 1929. *The Excavations at Dura-Europos: First Season, Spring 1928*. New Haven, CT: Yale University Press.

Baur, P. & M. Rostovtzeff (eds) 1931. *The Excavations at Dura-Europos: Second Season, 1928–1929*. New Haven, CT: Yale University Press.

Benefiel, R. 2008. "Amianth, a Ball-Game, and Making One's Mark". *Zeitschrift für Papyrologie und Epigraphik* 167: 193–200.

Bernand, A. 1972a. *Le Paneion d'El Kanais: les inscriptions grecques*. Leiden: Brill.

Bernand, A. 1972b. *De Koptos à Kosseir*. Leiden: Brill.

Bernard, A. & E. Bernard 1960. *Les Inscriptions Grecques et Latines du Colosse de Memnon*. Cairo: Institute français d'archéologie orientale.

Berry, J. 1997. "Le condizioni della vita domestica a Pompei nell'anno 79 d.C.: un caso di studio delle case 11 e 12, insula 9, regione 1". *Papers of the British School at Rome* 65: 103–25.

Bier, L. 2008. "The Bouleuterion". In *Aphrodisias Papers 4: New Research on the City and its Monuments*, C. Ratte & R. R. R. Smith (eds), 144–68. Portsmouth, RI: Journal of Roman Archaeology.

Bierbrier, M. 1989. *The Tomb Builders of the Pharaohs*. Cairo: American University in Cairo.

Bowman, A. K. & G. Woolf (eds) 1994. *Literacy and Power in the Ancient World*. Cambridge: Cambridge University Press.

Brandt, O. (ed.) 2008. *Unexpected Voices: The Graffiti in the Cryptoporticus of the Horti Sallustiani*. Stockholm: Swedish Institute at Rome.

Bréand, G. 2009. "The Corpus of Pre-firing Potmarks from Adaïma (Upper Egypt)". *British Museum Studies in Ancient Egypt and Sudan* 13: 49–72.

BIBLIOGRAPHY

Breasted, J. H. 1906a. *Historical Documents. Volume 1: The First to the Seventeenth Dynasties.* Chicago, IL: University of Chicago Press.

Breasted, J. H. 1906b. *Historical Documents. Volume 4: The Twentieth through the Twenty-sixth Dynasties.* Chicago, IL: University of Chicago Press.

Brenne, S. 2001. *Ostrakismos und Prominenz in Athen. Attische Bürger des 5. Jhs. v. Chr. auf den Ostraka.* Vienna: Holzhausen.

Brenne, S. 2002. "Die Ostraka als Testimonien". In *Ostrakismos-Testimonien I: Die Zeugnisse antiker Autoren der Inschriften und Ostraka über das athenische Scherbengericht aus vorhellenistischer Zeit (487–322 v. Chr.)*, Historia Einzelschriften 155, P. Siewert (ed.), 36–166. Stuttgart: Steiner.

Budge, E. A. W. 1978. *An Egyptian Hieroglyphic Dictionary.* New York: Dover.

Burkhardt, G. 1997. "Inscription in the Dakhla Region". *Sahara* 9: 152–3.

Callender, G. 2006. "The Cripple, the Queen and the Man from the North". *KMT* 17(1): 49–63.

Castleman, C. 1982. *Getting Up: Subway Graffiti in New York.* Cambridge, MA: MIT Press.

Castren, P. 1975. *Ordo Populusque Pompeianus: Polity and Society in Roman Pompeii.* Acta Instituti Romani Finlandiae VIII. Rome: Bardi.

Castren, P. & H. Lilius 1970. *Graffiti del Palatino II: Domus Tiberiana.* Helsinki: Akateeminen Kirjakauppa.

Černý, J. 1969–83. *Graffiti de la montagne Thebaine*, 4 vols. Cairo: Le Centre d'Etude et de Documentation sur l'Ancienne Egypte.

Chaniotis, A. 2002. "Zwischen Konfrontation und Interaktion: Christen, Juden und Heiden im spätantiken Aphrodisias". In *Patchwork: Dimensionen multicultureller Gesellschaften*, A. Ackermann & K. E. Müller (eds), 83–128. Bielefeld: Transcript.

Chauvet, J.-M., E. B. Deschamps & C. Hillaire 1996. *Dawn of Art: The Chauvet Cave*, P. G. Bahn (foreword), J. Clottes (epilogue). New York: Harry N. Abrams.

Clark, R. 2003. *The Sacred Magic of Ancient Egypt.* St Paul, MN: Llewellyn Publications.

Clarke, J. R. 2003. *Roman Sex: 100 BC to AD 250.* New York: Harry N. Abrams.

Clottes, J. 2002. *Palaeolithic Cave Art in France.* www.bradshawfoundation.com/clottes/index. php (accessed 13 July 2012).

Clottes, J. 2003a. *Return To Chauvet Cave, Excavating the Birthplace of Art: The First Full Report.* New York: Thames & Hudson.

Clottes, J. 2003b. *Chauvet Cave: The Art of Earliest Times*, P. G. Bahn (trans.). Salt Lake City, UT: University of Utah Press.

Coleman, J. 2000. *A History of Political Thought: From Ancient Greece to Early Christianity.* Oxford: Blackwell.

Collins, D. 2008. *Magic in the Ancient Greek World.* Oxford: Blackwell.

Cooley, A. E. & M. G. L. Cooley 2004. *Pompeii: A Sourcebook.* London: Routledge.

Cooper, M. & H. Chalfant 1995. *Subway Art.* New York: Holt, Rinehart & Winston.

Couyat, J. & P. Montet 1912–13. *Les inscriptions hiéroglyphiques et hiératiques du Ouâdi Hammâmât*, 2 vols. Cairo: Institut français d'archéologie orientale du Caire.

Cumont, F. 1934. "Rapport sur une mission archéologique à Doura-Europos". *Comptes rendus des séances de l'Académie des Inscriptions et Belles-Lettres* 1934: 90–111.

Darnell, J. C. 1997. "A New Middle Egyptian Literary Text from the Wadi el-Hôl". *Journal of the American Research Center in Egypt* 34: 85–100.

Darnell, J. C. & D. Darnell 1996. *The Theban Desert Road Survey 1995–1996.* Chicago, IL: Oriental Institute Press.

Darnell, J. C. & D. Darnell 1997. *The Theban Desert Road Survey 1996–1997.* Chicago, IL: Oriental Institute Press.

Darnell, J. C. & D. Darnell 2002. *Theban Desert Road Survey in the Egyptian Western Desert. Volume 1: Gebel Tjauti Rock Inscriptions 1–45 and Wadi el-Hôl Rock Inscriptions 1–45.* Chicago, IL: Oriental Institute Press.

Decker, W. 1987. *Sport and Games of Ancient Egypt.* New Haven, CT: Yale University Press.

BIBLIOGRAPHY

Della Corte, M. 1960. *Loves and Lovers in Ancient Pompeii: A Pompeian Erotic Anthology*, A. W. Van Buren (ed.). Naples: E. di Mauro.

Della Corte, M. & P. Ciprotti (eds) 1952–70. *Inscriptiones parietariae Pompeianae Herculanenses Stabianae. Supplementi pars III: Inscriptiones Pompeianae Herculanenses parietariae et vasorum fictilium*. Berlin: De Gruyter.

Dewey, J. (ed.) 1995. *Semeia 65: Orality and Textuality in Early Christian Literature*. Atlanta, GA: Society of Biblical Literature.

Dickie, M. W. 2001. *Magic and Magicians in the Greco-Roman World*. London: Routledge.

Dillon, M. P. J. & L. Garland 1994. *Ancient Greece* London: Routledge.

Diringer, D. 1982. *The Book before Printing: Ancient, Medieval, and Oriental*. New York: Dover.

Donaldson, M. 2011. "Understanding the Rocks: Rock Art and the Geology of Murujuga (Burrup Peninsula)". *Rock Art Research* 28(1): 35–44.

Dover, K. J. 1978. *Greek Homosexuality*. London: Duckworth.

Droysen, J. G. 1836–43. *Geschichte des Hellenismus*, 3 vols. Berlin: Bei Friedrich Perthes.

Dunbar, J. H. 1941. *The Rock-Pictures of Lower Nubia*. Cairo: Egyptian Government Press.

Duncan-Jones, R. 1994. *Money and Government in the Roman Empire*. Cambridge: Cambridge University Press.

Edmondson, J. C. 1996. "Dynamic Arenas: Gladiatorial Presentations in the City of Rome and the Construction of Roman Society During the Early Empire". In *Roman Theater and Society*, W. J. Slater (ed.), 69–112. Ann Arbor, MI: University of Michigan Press.

Elsner, J. 1996. "Inventing *Imperium*: Texts and the Propaganda of Monuments in Augustan Rome". In his *Art and Text in Roman Culture*, 32–53. Cambridge: Cambridge University Press.

Elsner, J. & J. Masters (eds) 1994. *Reflections of Nero: Culture, History and Representation*. London: Chapel Hill.

Eschebach, H. 1979. *Die Stabianer Thermen in Pompeji*. Berlin: De Gruyter.

Faraone, C. A. 1996. "Taking the 'Nestor's Cup Inscription' Seriously: Erotic Magic and Conditional Curses in the Earliest Inscribed Hexameters". *Classical Antiquity* 15(1): 77–112.

Faraone, C. A. & D. Obbink 1991. *Magika Hiera: Ancient Greek Magic and Religion*. New York: Oxford University Press.

Faulkner, R. O. 1969. *The Ancient Egyptian Pyramid Texts*. Oxford: Clarendon Press.

Faulkner, R. O. 1973. *The Ancient Egyptian Coffin Texts: Spells 1–354*. Warminster: Aris & Phillips.

Ferrua, A. 2001. *Tavole lusorie epigrafiche: catalogo delle schede manoscritte, introduzione e indici a cura di Maria Busia*. Rome: Pontificio istituto di archeologia Cristiana.

Festugière, A. J. 1970. "Les Proscynemes de Philae". *Revue des Études Grecques* 83: 175–97.

Frank, T. 1927. *An Economic History of Rome*. Baltimore, MD: Johns Hopkins University Press.

Franklin, J. T. 1978. "Notes on Pompeian Prosopography: *Programmatum Scriptores*". *Cronache Pompeiane* 4: 54–74.

Franklin, J. T. 1991. "Literacy and the Parietal Inscriptions of Ancient Pompeii". In *Literacy in the Roman World*, H. Humphrey (ed.), 77–98. Ann Arbor, MI: Journal of Roman Archaeology Publications.

Franklin, J. T. 2001. *Pompeis Difficile Est: Studies in the Political Life of Imperial Pompeii*. Ann Arbor, MI: University of Michigan Press.

Frood, E. & J. Baines. 2007. *Biographical Texts from Ramessid Egypt*. Atlanta, GA: Society of Biblical Literature.

Fuchs, G. 1989. "Rock Engravings in the Wadi El Barramiya". *African Archaeological Review* 7(1): 127–53.

Gager, J. G. 1992. *Curse Tablets and Binding Spells from the Ancient World*. New York: Oxford University Press.

Gallorini, C. 1998. "A Reconstruction of Petrie's Excavation at the Middle Kingdom Settlement of Kahun". In *Lahun Studies*, S. Quirke (ed.), 42–59. Reigate: SIA Publications.

321

BIBLIOGRAPHY

Gardiner, A. H. & K. Sethe 1955. *The Inscriptions of Sinai*, vol. II. London: Egypt Exploration Society.

Gasperini, L. 1971. "Il municipio tarentino: ricerche epigrafiche". In *Terza miscellanea greca e romana*, G. Barbieri *et al.* (eds), 143–209. Rome: Instituto Italiano per la Storia Antica.

Gasse, A. 1987. "Une expédition au Ouâdi Hammâmât sous le règne de Sebekemsaf Ier". *Bulletin de l'Institut français d'archéologie orientale* 87: 207–18.

Gigante, M. 1979. *Civilta delle forme letterarie nell'antica Pompei*. Naples: Bibliopolis.

Gilleland, M. E. 1980. "Female Speech in Greek and Latin". *American Journal of Philology* 101: 180–83.

Goodenough, E. R. 1964. *Jewish Symbols in the Graeco-Roman Period*, vols. IX–XI: *Symbolism in the Dura Synagogue*, Bollingen Series XXXVII, New York: Pantheon Press.

Goody, J. & I. Watt 1963. "The consequences of literacy". *Comparative Studies in Society and History* 5: 304–345.

Gordon, R., J. Reynolds & C. Roueché (eds). 1993. "Roman Inscriptions 1986–90". *Journal of Roman Studies* 83: 13–158.

Gordon, R., M. Beard, J. Reynolds & C. Roueché (eds). 1997. "Roman Inscriptions 1991–95". *Journal of Roman Studies* 87: 203–40.

Graf, F. 2002. "Theories of Magic in Antiquity". In *Magic and Ritual in the Ancient World*, P. Mirecki & M. W. Meyer (eds), 93–104. Leiden: Brill.

Grandet, P. 2000. "L'exécution du chancelier Bay. O. IFAO 1864". *Bulletin de l'Institut français d'archéologie orientale* 100: 339–45.

Grant, M. 1975. *Eros in Pompeii: The Secret Rooms of the National Museum of Naples*. New York: Morrow.

Graves-Brown, C. 2010. *Dancing for Hathor: Women in Ancient Egypt*. London: Continuum.

Gurr, C. A. 1999. "Effective Diagrammatic Communication: Syntactic, Semantic and Pragmatic Issues". *Journal of Visual Languages and Computing* 10: 317–41.

Harradine, S., J. Kodz, F. Lernetti & B. Jones 2004. *Defining and Measuring Antisocial Behaviour*. Home Office Development and Practice Report 26. London: Home Office.

Harris, W. V. 1989. *Ancient Literacy*. Cambridge, MA: Harvard University Press.

Haselberger, L. 1985. "The Construction Plans for the Temple of Apollo at Didyma". *Scientific American* 253(6): 126–32.

Haselberger, L. 1995. "Deciphering a Roman Blueprint". *Scientific American* 272(6): 84–9.

Havelock, E. A. 1982. *The Literate Revolution in Ancient Greece and its Cultural Consequences*. Princeton, NJ: Princeton University Press.

Henrichs, A. 2003. "Writing Religion". In *Written Texts and the Rise of Literate Culture in Ancient Greece*, H. Yunis (ed.), 38–58. Cambridge: Cambridge University Press.

Hillard, T. W. 2013. "Graffiti's Engagement. The Political Graffiti of the Late Roman Republic". In *Written Space in the Latin West 200 BC to AD 300*, G. Sears, P. Keegan & R. Laurence (eds), 105–22. London: Bloomsbury.

Hillier, B. & J. Hanson 1984. *The Social Logic of Space*. Glasgow: Cambridge University Press.

Hoffman, C. A. 2002. "Fiat Magia". In *Magic and Ritual in the Ancient World*, P. Mirecki & M. W. Meyer (eds), 179–196. Leiden: Brill.

Horsfall, N. 2003. *The Culture of the Roman Plebs*. London: Duckworth.

Hubbard, T. K. 2003. *Homosexuality in Greece and Rome: A Sourcebook of Basic Documents*. Berkeley, CA: University of California Press.

Humphrey, H. (ed) 1991. *Literacy in the Roman World*. Ann Arbor, MI: Journal of Roman Archaeology Publications.

Innis, H. A. 1951. *The Bias of Communication*. Toronto: University of Toronto Press.

Jacobelli, L. 2003. *Gladiators at Pompeii*. Roma: L'Erma di Bretschneider.

Janssen, J. J. 1980. "Absence from Work by the Necropolis Workmen of Thebes", *Studien zur altägyptischen Kultur* 8: 141–3.

Jashemski, W. 1979–93. *The Gardens of Pompeii, Herculaneum, and the Villas Destroyed by Vesuvius*, 2 vols. New Rochelle, NY: Caratzas.

Johnson, S. I. 2004. *Religions of the Ancient World: A Guide*. Cambridge, MA: Harvard University Press.

Johnson, W. A. & H. N. Parker 2011. *Ancient Literacies: The Culture of Reading in Greece and Rome*. Oxford: Oxford University Press.

Joshel, S. R. 1992. *Work, Identity and Legal Status at Rome: A Study of the Occupational Inscriptions*. Norman, OK: University of Oklahoma Press.

Judd, T. 2009. *Rock Art of the Eastern Desert of Egypt: Contents, Comparisons, Dating and Significance*. Oxford: Archaeopress.

Keegan, P. 2010. "Blogging Rome: Graffiti as Speech Act and Cultural Discourse". In *Ancient Graffiti in Context*, J. A. Baird & C. Taylor (eds), 165–90. London: Routledge.

Keegan, P. 2013. "Reading the 'Pages' of the *Domus Caesaris*: *Pueri Delicati*, Slave Education, and the Graffiti of the Palatine *Paedagogium*". In *Roman Slavery and Roman Material Culture*, M. George (ed.), 69–98. Cambridge: Cambridge University Press.

Kruschwitz, P. 2008. "Patterns of Text Layout in Pompeian Verse Inscriptions". *Studia Philologica Valentina* 11: 225–64.

Kruschwitz, P. 2010. "*Romanes Eunt Domus*: Linguistic Aspects of the Sub-literary Latin in Pompeian Wall Inscriptions". in *The Language of the Papyri*, T. V. Evans & D. D. Obbink (eds), 156–70. Oxford: Oxford University Press.

Laes, C. 2003. "Desperately Different? *Delicia* Children in the Roman Household". In *Early Christian Families in Context: An Interdisciplinary Dialogue*, D. Balch & C. Osiek (eds), 298–326. Grand Rapids, MI: Wm. B. Eerdmans.

Lang, M. 1956. "Numerical Notation on Greek Vases". *Hesperia* 25: 1–24.

Lang, M. 1974. *The Athenian Agora XXI: Graffiti and Dipinti*. Princeton, NJ: American School of Classical Studies at Athens.

Lang, M. 1990. *The Athenian Agora XXV: Ostraca*. Princeton, NJ: American School of Classical Studies at Athens.

Langdon, M. K. 1976. *A Sanctuary of Zeus on Mount Hymettos*. Hesperia: Supplement XVI. Princeton, NJ: American School of Classical Studies at Athens.

Langner, M. 2001. *Antike Graffitizeichnungen: Motive, Gestaltung und Bedeutung*. Wiesbaden: L. Reichert.

Laurence, R. 1994. *Roman Pompeii: Space and Society*. London: Routledge.

Lehrer, G. 1979. *Ennion: A First Century Glassmaker*. Exhibition catalogue. Tel Aviv: Haaretz Museum.

Leon, H. J. 1926. "The Language of the Greek Inscriptions from the Jewish Catacombs of Rome". *Transactions of the American Philological Association* 58: 210–33.

Lesko. L. 2001. "Literacy". In *The Oxford Encyclopedia of Ancient Egypt*, D. Redford (ed.), 2. 297–9. Oxford: Oxford University Press.

Lester, P. M. 2010. *Visual Communication: Images with Messages*, 5th edn. Belmont, CA: Thomson Wadsworth.

L'Hoir, F. S. 1992. *The Rhetoric of Gender Terms: "Man", "Woman", and the Portrayal of Character in Latin Prose*. Mnemosyne Supplement 120. Leiden: Brill.

Lichtheim, M. 1976. *Ancient Egyptian Literature: A Book of Readings. Volume II: The New Kingdom*. Berkeley, CA: University of California Press.

Limme, L., S. Hendrickx & D. Huyge 1997. "Elkab: Excavations in the Old Kingdom Rock Necropolis". *Egyptian Archaeology* 11: 3–6.

Lord, A. B. 1960. *The Singer of Tales*. Cambridge, MA: Harvard University Press.

Macdonald, S. 2006. "A Suicidal Woman, Roaming Pigs and a Noisy Trampolinist: Refining the ASBO's Definition of 'Anti-social Behaviour'". *Modern Law Review* 69(2): 183–213.

Madsen, J. 1972. "Petroglyphs – a method for 'collecting'". *Curator* 15(1): 62–71.

Mairs, R. 2011. "Acrostich Inscriptions at Kalabasha (Roman Talmis): Cultural Identities and Literary Games". *Chronique d'Égypte* 86: 281–97.

Malaise, M. 1987. "Pèlerinages et pèlerins dans l'Égypte ancienne". In *Histoire des pèlerinages*

BIBLIOGRAPHY

non chrétiens entre magique et sacré: le chemin des dieux, J. Chélini & H. Branthomme (eds), 55–82. Paris: Hachette.

Manniche, L. 2002. *Sexual Life in Ancient Egypt*. London: Kegan Paul.

Martinich, A. P. (ed.) 1996. *The Philosophy of Language*, 3rd edn. Oxford: Oxford University Press.

Mau, A. (ed.) [1909] 1968. *Inscriptiones parietariae Pompeianae Herculanenses Stabianae. Supplementi pars II: Inscriptiones parietariae et vasorum fictilium*. Berlin: De Gruyter.

Megally, M. 1981. "Two Visitors' *Graffiti* from *Abusir*". *Chronique d'Égypte* 56: 218–40.

Meiggs, R. & D. Lewis (eds) 1969. *A Selection of Greek Historical Inscriptions*. Oxford: Oxford University Press.

Meskell, L. 2002. *Private Life in New Kingdom Egypt*. Princeton, NJ: Princeton University Press.

Messner, W. S. 1941. "Martial IX.15". *Classical Journal* 36(4): 226–9.

Miller, S. 2001. *Excavations at Nemea II*. Berkeley, CA: University of California Press.

Millie, A., J. Jacobson, M. Hough & A. Paraskevopoulou (eds) 2005a. *Anti-social Behaviour in London: Setting the Context for the London Anti-social Behaviour Strategy*. London: GLA.

Millie, A., J. Jacobson, E. McDonald & M. Hough. 2005b. *Anti-social Behaviour Strategies: Finding a Balance*. Bristol: Policy Press.

Milne, M. & D. von Bothmer 1953. "Katapugon, katapugana". *Hesperia* 22: 215–24.

Morrow, M. & M. Morrow 2002. *Desert Rats: Rock Art Topographical Survey in Egypt's Eastern Desert*. London: UCL Press.

Mouritsen, H. Forthcoming. "Graffiti in the Insula of the Menander".

Mouritsen, H. & I. Gradel 1991. "Nero in Pompeian Politics: *Edicta Munerum* and Imperial Flaminates in Late Pompeii". *Zeitschrift für Papyrologie und Epigraphik* 87: 145–55.

Nagel, G. 1938. *La céramique du Nouvel Empire à Deir El Médineh I*. Cairo: Institut français d'archéologie orientale du Caire.

Newberry, P. E., G. W. Fraser, F, L. Griffith. 1893. *Beni Hasan*, vol. 1. London: Egypt Exploration Society.

Nilsson, M. P. 1967–74. *A History of Greek Religion*, 3 vols. Oxford: Clarendon Press.

Nongbri, B. 2011. "The Lord's Prayer and ΧΜΓ: Two Christian Papyrus Amulets". *Harvard Theological Review* 104(1): 59–68.

Noy, D. 1995. *Jewish Inscriptions of Western Europe. Volume 2: The City of Rome*. Cambridge: Cambridge University Press.

Omlin J. 1973. *Der Papyrus 55001 und seine satirisch-erotischen Zeichnungen und Inschriften Turin 21*. Berlin: Berlin Akademic Verlag.

Parker, H. N. 1998. "The Teratogenic Grid". In *Roman Sexualities*, J. P. Hallett & M. Skinner (eds), 47–65. London: Routledge.

Parry, A. (ed.) 1971. *The Making of Homeric Verse: The Collected Papers of Milman Parry*. Oxford: Clarendon Press.

Peden, A. J. 2001. *The Graffiti of Pharaonic Egypt: Scope and Roles of Informal Writings (3100–332 BC)*. Leiden: Brill.

Perdrizet, P. & G. Lefebvre 1919. *Les graffites grecs du Memnonion d'Abydos*. Nancy: Berger-Levrault.

Petrucci, A. 1991. "Storia della scrittura e della società". *Anuario de Estudios Medievales* 21: 309–22.

Pinch, G. 1994. *Magic in Ancient Egypt*. London: British Museum Press.

Poe, M. T. 2011. *A History of Communications: Media and Society from the Evolution of Speech to the Internet*. Cambridge: Cambridge University Press.

Poehler, E. E. 2006. "The Circulation of Traffic in Pompeii's *Regio VI*". *Journal of Roman Archaeology* 19: 53–74.

Poehler, E. E. 2009. "The Organization of Pompeii's System of Traffic: An Analysis of the Evidence and its Impact on Infrastructure, Economy and Urbanism of the Ancient City". Unpublished PhD Dissertation, University of Virginia.

324

BIBLIOGRAPHY

Posener, G. 1980. *Catalogue des ostraca hiératiques littéraires de Deir el Médineh. Volume III/3: Nos 1607–1675.* Cairo: Institut français d'archéologie orientale du Caire.

Rappenglück, M. A. 2008a. "Astronomische Ikonographie im Jüngeren Paläolithikum". *Acta Praehistorica et Archaeologica* 40: 179–203.

Rappenglück, M. A. 2008b. "The Pleiades and Hyades as Celestial Spatiotemporal Indicators in the Astronomy of Archaic and Indigenous Cultures". In *Prähistorische Astronomie und Ethnoastronomie*, Nuncius Hamburgensis – Beiträge zur Geschichte der Naturwissenschaft 8, G. Wolfschmidt (ed.), 12–29. Norderstedt bei Hamburg: Books on Demand.

Reisner, R. G. 1971. *Graffiti: Two Thousand Years of Wall Writing.* New York: Cowles Book Company.

Richlin, A. 1992. *The Garden of Priapus: Sexuality and Aggression in Roman Humor*, rev. edn. Oxford: Oxford University Press.

Ridgway, D. 1992. *The First Western Greeks.* Cambridge: Cambridge University Press.

Ritner, R. K. 1993. *The Mechanics of Ancient Egyptian Magical Practice.* Chicago, IL: University of Chicago Press.

Ritner, R. K. 2009. *The Libyan Anarchy: Inscriptions from Egypt's Third Intermediate Period.* Atlanta, GA: Society of Biblical Literature.

Robbins, V. K. 1995. "Oral, Rhetorical, and Literary Cultures: A Response". In *Semeia 65: Orality and Textuality in Early Christian Literature*, J. Dewey (ed.), 75–91. Atlanta, GA: Scholars Press.

Rogers, R. A. 2009. "'Your Guess is as Good as Any': Indeterminacy, Dialogue and Dissemination in Interpretations of Native American Rock Art". *Journal of International and Intercultural Communication* 2(1): 44–65.

Rohl, D. 2009. "Secrets of the Desert". *Heritage of Egypt* 2(3): 18–27.

Romer, J. 1982. *People of the Nile: Everyday Life in Ancient Egypt.* New York: Crown.

Rostovtzeff, M. I. 1957. *The Social and Economic History of the Roman Empire*, 2nd edn, P. M. Fraser (ed.). Oxford: Clarendon Press.

Roueché, C. 1989. *Aphrodisias in Late Antiquity: The Late Roman and Byzantine Inscriptions.* London: Journal of Roman Studies.

Ruffling, K. 2002. "Preise und Wertangaben aus Dura Europos und Emgebung". *Laverna* 13: 24–44.

Rutherford, I. 2000. "The Reader's Voice in a Horoscope from Abydos (Perdrizet and Lefebvre, n. 641)". *Zeitschrift für Papyrologie und Epigraphik* 130: 149–50.

Rutherford, I. 2005. "Pilgrimage in Greco-Roman Egypt: New Perspectives on Graffiti from the Memnonion at Abydos". In *Ancient Perspectives on Egypt*, R. Matthews & C. Roemer (eds), 171–89. London: UCL Press.

Sanchez, G. M. & E. S. Meltzer (eds) 2010. *The Edwin Smith Papyrus.* Atlanta, GA: Lockwood Press.

Sears, G., P. Keegan & R. Laurence (eds) 2013. *Written Space in the Latin West 200 BC to AD 300.* London: Bloomsbury.

Servajean, F. 2008. "Duality". In *UCLA Encyclopedia of Egyptology*, J. Dieleman & W. Wendrich (eds). Los Angeles, CA: UCLA. http://digital2.library.ucla.edu/viewItem.do?ark=21198/zz0013x9jp (accessed 6 November 2013).

Sheldon, R. M. 2003. "The SATOR REBUS: an unsolved cryptogram?". *Cryptologia* 27: 233–75.

Skinner, M. 2013. *Sexuality in Greek and Roman Culture*, 2nd edn. Oxford: Blackwell.

Smith, R. R. R. 2002. "The Statue Monument of Oecumenius: A New Portrait of a Late Antique Governor from Aphrodisias". *Journal of Roman Studies* 92: 134–56.

Solin, H. 1973. "Die herkulanensischen Wandinschriften: ein soziologischer Versuch". *Cronache Ercolanesi* 3: 97–103.

Solin, H. & M. Itkonen-Kaila 1966. *Graffiti del Palatino 1: Paedagogium.* Helsinki: Akateeminen Kirjakauppa.

Staring, N. 2010. "Interpreting Figural Graffiti: Case Studies from a Funerary Context". In *Current Research in Egyptology 2010: Proceedings of the Eleventh Annual Symposium,*

325

BIBLIOGRAPHY

Leiden University, The Netherlands, 5–8 January 2010, M. Horn, J. Kramer, D. Soliman, N. Staring, C. Van Den Hoven & L. Weiß (eds), 145–56. Oxford: Oxbow Books.

Stone, M. E. (ed.) 1992–4. *Rock Inscriptions and Graffiti Project: Catalogue of Inscriptions.* Atlanta, GA: Scholars Press.

Susini, G. 1969. "Problematica dell'epigrafia classica nella regione apula e salentina". *Archivio storico pugliese* 22: 38–48

Thomas, R. 1989. *Oral Tradition and Written Record in Classical Athens.* Cambridge: Cambridge University Press.

Thomas, R. 1992. *Literacy and Orality in Ancient Greece.* Cambridge: Cambridge University Press.

Toivari-Viitala, J. 2001. *Women at Deir el-Medina: A Study of the Status and Roles of the Female Inhabitants in the Workmen's Community during the Ramesside Period.* Leiden: Nederlands Instituut Voor Het Nabije Oosten.

Trigger, B. 1996. "Toshka and Arminna in the New Kingdom". In *Studies in Honor of William Kelly Simpson*, P. Der Manuelian (ed), 801–10. Boston, MA: Museum of Fine Arts.

Ulbaek, I. 1998. "The Origin of Language and Cognition". In *Approaches to the Evolution of Language*, J. R. Hurford & C. Knight (eds), 30–43. Cambridge: Cambridge University Press.

Varone, A. 2001. *Erotica Pompeiana: Love Inscriptions on the Walls of Pompeii.* Rome: L'Erma Bretschneider.

Vereecken, S. 2011. "An Old Kingdom Bakery at Sheikh Said South: Preliminary Report on the Pottery Corpus". In *Old Kingdom: New Perspectives. Egyptian Art and Archaeology 2750–2150 BC*, N. Strudwick & H. Strudwick (eds), 297–304. Oxford: Oxford University Press.

Viden, G. 1993. *Women in Roman Literature: Attitudes of Authors under the Early Empire.* Studia Graeca et Latina Gothoburgensia 57. Gothenburg: Acta Universitatis Gothoburgensis.

Wagner, D. A. 2010. "Literacy". In *Handbook of Cultural Developmental Science*, M. Bornstein (ed.), 161–73. New York: Taylor & Francis.

Wagner, D. A., R. L. Venezky & B. V. Street (eds) 1999. *Literacy: An International Handbook.* Boulder, CO: Westview Press.

Weeks, K. R. 1995. *Ramses II: Das Totenhaus der Söhne.* Munich: Droemer Knaur.

Weill, R. 1940. "Sur un graffito de la 1re dynastie au Ouadi Abad". *Revue d'Égyptologie* 4: 121–2.

Welborn, L. L. 2005. *Paul, the Fool of Christ: A Study of 1 Corinthians 1–4 in the Comic-Philosophic Tradition.* New York: T. & T. Clark International.

West, M. L. 1982. "The Orphics of Olbia". *Zeitschrift für Papyrologie und Epigraphik* 45: 17–29.

White, R. 2003. *Prehistoric Art: The Symbolic Journey of Humankind.* New York: Abrams.

Whitehead, C. M. E., J. E. Stockdale & G. Razzu 2003. *The Economic and Social Costs of Anti-social Behaviour.* London: London School of Economics.

Whitehouse, D. 2000. "Oldest Lunar Calendar Identified". *BBC News Online* (16 October). http://news.bbc.co.uk/2/hi/science/nature/975360.stm (accessed 10 February 2011).

Whitley, D. S. 2006. *Cave Paintings and the Human Spirit: The Origin of Creativity and Belief.* New York: Prometheus Books.

Williams, C. A. 1999. *Roman Homosexuality: Ideologies of Masculinity in Classical Antiquity.* Oxford: Oxford University Press.

Winkler, H. 1938. *Rock-Drawings of Southern Upper Egypt I.* Oxford: Egyptian Exploration Society.

Winkler, H. 1939. *Rock-Drawings of Southern Upper Egypt II.* Oxford: Egyptian Exploration Society.

Woolf, G. 1996. "Monumental Writing and the Expansion of Roman Society in the Empire". *Journal of Roman Studies* 86: 22–39.

Zangemeister, C. (ed.) [1898] 1968. *Inscriptiones parietariae Pompeianae Herculanenses Stabianae. Supplementi pars I. Tabulae ceratae Pompeiis repertae.* Berlin: De Gruyter.

Zangemeister, C. & E. Schoene (eds) 1871. *Inscriptiones parietariae Pompeianae Herculanenses Stabianae.* Berlin: De Gruyter.

INDEX

abecedaria *see* alphabets
Abu Simbel 12, 121, 231–2, 233
Abû Sîr 48–9, 50, 51
abuse 37, 53, 139, 209, 254, 257, 266, 288
Abydos 28, 43, 44, 45, 48, 92–3, 145, 161, 165, 291
Aeneas 39, 151, 152–3
Agora (Athens) 12, 22, 32, 33, 45, 73–4, 77, 84, 159, 167, 168, 172, 229, 239, 256–7, 293
Agrippina the Younger 37, 41, 158, 159, 285
Alamat Tal road 28, 29, 47, 162, 224, 291
alphabets (*abecedaria*) xiv, 6, 12, 22, 51, 52, 53, 226
Ammianus Marcellinus 33, 42–3, 45
amphitheatre (Pompeii) 36, 37–9, 60, 80, 84, 104, 154, 182, 204–10, 263, 284, 296
Amun (Amen-Re) xi, xii, 54, 90, 91, 143, 160, 188, 189, 219, 221, 222, 225, 248
Aphrodisias 6, 74–6, 77, 82, 150, 207, 276, 286, 294
Apollo xii, 12, 52, 54, 83, 92, 93, 98, 137, 146, 147, 154, 155, 186, 253–5, 294
Appian 39, 42
athletics xvi, 185, 194–5
Augustus (Octavian) xi, xii, 12, 14, 34, 83, 127, 180, 182, 205

ball games xvi, 61, 184, 189, 203
Basilica (Pompeii) 2, 47, 60, 210, 261–2, 263, 265–9, 271, 274, 284
Bes 43, 45, 92, 93

board games xvi, 185–6, 189, 213, 215–16
Bouleuterion (Aphrodisias) 74–6, 82, 286, 291
Brutus 40–41

Cassius Dio xi, xii, 39–40, 41, 158, 179–80
cave paintings 18–19, 20, 23
children xiv, 37, 43, 47, 57, 90, 189, 192–3, 201
Christianity 9, 14, 66, 74, 87, 102–3, 107–113, 116–17, 158, 213, 287, 297
Colossi of Memnon 44, 55–8, 112, 291
communication systems 17–18, 23–4
curses (*defixiones, katadesmoi*) xv, 115, 127, 132, 138, 259

dates xiii, 31, 47
dedications xi, xiv, 6, 51–3, 63, 95, 99, 261, 281
Deir el-Medina 10, 50, 71–3, 145, 166, 187–8, 191, 193–4, 247–51, 291
dipinti (painted inscriptions) 22, 39, 207, 209–10, 233
Domitian 36, 42
Dura-Europos 6, 97–101, 150, 156–7, 207, 213, 217, 219, 235, 297

education 2–3, 33, 46, 50, 58, 105, 126, 178, 193, 271
El Kanais 13, 54–5, 57
Ephesus 6, 127, 150, 216, 233–4, 294
Etruscans xv, 34, 40, 77–8, 132, 173, 204, 225, 234

327

INDEX

funerary inscriptions 3, 73, 118, 120, 123–4, 145, 182, 186–9, 193–4, 260–61, 280–81

game boards (*tabulae lusoriae*) 215–16
Gebel Tjauti 28, 29, 31, 160–62, 163–5, 224, 291
gender ix, xiv, xvi, 22, 33, 49, 131, 173, 185, 243–6, 251, 259, 264, 267, 271–2
gladiators xvi, 22, 36, 78, 150, 204–9, 212–13, 263, 268
graffiti 4–15
  and anti-social behaviour 7
  aphorisms 105
  commemorative dedications xi, 13, 52, 55, 67, 95, 98
  congratulations
  contexts 5–7, 25–6
  date statements and day names 44, 48–9, 179, 204, 208, 236, 241, 263
  declarations 103, 108, 263–5
  definitions xii, 1, 4
  dialogues 268–9
  drawings 14, 30, 31, 35, 38, 73–85, 90, 136–7, 145, 150, 157, 186–8, 190–94, 200–201, 272
  geometrical figures 24, 51, 238
  household notices 233
  imprecations 5, 114, 119–23, 125, 127–30, 132–3, 137, 169
  insults 2, 13, 52, 210, 254–7, 265, 272, 276
  invocations 111–12, 126–7, 134, 136, 174–7, 181, 210, 254
  items of information xi, 11, 32–3, 34, 38, 47, 161–2, 179, 222–4, 231
  kalos-inscriptions 198–200, 254–6
  in literature xi, 27, 40–41, 42, 46, 62, 86, 131, 148, 149, 158, 243, 276, 284
  and memory 33, 35–6, 49, 54, 57–8, 61–3, 65, 69, 84, 89–91, 126, 143–5, 200–201, 212–13, 278
  mythological names 91–3, 95, 106, 130, 132, 137, 139, 143–5, 150–51, 154–5, 234
  names and titles 35, 44, 63, 90–91, 164, 169, 174–7, 179, 180–81, 183, 184, 198, 204–12, 219–25, 238, 241, 263–4
  numbers without words 31, 64
  palindromes 213–14
  prayers 44, 47, 48–9, 90, 92–3, 100, 104, 110–11, 143–5

price and quantity statements 219–20, 229, 241, 276
property statements 52, 227, 236, 238, 241
and rural spaces 28–9, 47–8, 68–72, 101, 163–5, 217, 221–4, 257, 276, 288, 291
salutations 2, 13
signatures 13, 231, 241
strokes 64, 229
symbols 48, 52, 74, 95, 112, 134–7, 147, 160–61, 238, 276
thanksgiving 180–81, 183, 198, 276
tools 6, 23–4
types 22, 51–2
and urban spaces 5–6, 16–17, 33–4, 41–2, 61–3, 73–4, 81–2, 216, 233, 261, 280–82, 285–8
verses 46, 57–8, 60, 96, 125, 147, 152, 214, 247, 249–50, 252, 260–61, 265, 270, 276, 282

Hadrian 57–8, 74, 84, 294
Herculaneum 8, 81, 181, 204, 207, 239–41, 296
Herodotus 29–30, 33, 45, 56, 170, 232
history, concept of xiii, xiv, xvi, 4, 9–10, 27, 44–5
  Egyptian 27–8
  Greek 29–30, 33
  Roman 33–4, 36, 39
Homer 11, 51, 52, 58, 125, 146, 152, 153, 167, 195, 219, 227

identity xvii, 69, 75, 88, 89, 91, 96, 99, 103–4, 159, 182, 212, 214, 221, 260, 264–6, 272–5
inventories xiv, 22, 230, 288

Jewish tradition 66, 87, 102–3, 109, 112–13, 116, 133–4, 297
Jupiter 81, 103, 106, 132, 136, 137, 154, 236

Karnak xii, 89–91, 187, 222, 292

literacy xiii, xiv, 3, 6, 8, 22–3, 46–8, 50–51, 54, 59, 62, 66, 71, 95–6, 131, 153, 271, 277, 281
Livy 33, 34, 36, 39, 45, 174, 240
Luxor 47, 55, 70, 89–90, 222–3, 291, 292

Memnonion of Seti I 43, 92

328

mosaics xiv, 30, 59, 155, 235, 238, 244, 294
Mount Hymettos 51–5, 58, 95–7

Narmer 29, 160–61
Nero 27, 36, 37, 41, 116, 158, 159, 178, 181–2, 206, 208, 264, 274, 276, 283–5
numerals xiii, 22, 63, 78, 220, 229–31, 242, 279, 287

obscenity xvi, 54, 254, 256–7, 274
oracles 43–5, 86, 92–3, 147, 155
oral tradition 11, 22, 29, 51, 54, 61, 113, 146, 152, 153, 157, 227, 259, 287
Orphic tradition 146–8, 151
Oscan 6, 34–6, 60
Ostia 14, 81–3, 156, 207, 235, 296–7
ostraca see potsherds

petroglyphs 19–20, 24
pilgrimage 44–5, 48–9, 81, 91–3, 109–11, 113, 143–4, 277–8
Plutarch 42, 61–2, 66, 158, 170, 199
poleis (city-states) 51, 166–67, 195
Poppaea (wife of Nero) 39, 180–82, 276, 283–5
pot-marks 24–5, 95–6, 124–7, 145–51, 166–72, 220–21, 226, 242, 278
potsherds (*ostraca*) 5, 6, 10, 32–3, 47, 50, 72–3, 127, 151, 159, 166–73, 188–93, 221, 245–52, 294
prose xiii, 2, 29, 58, 93, 122, 192, 244, 247, 251, 269, 275

quotations xiv, 244

Ramesses II 12, 47, 90, 143–4, 221–2, 231, 247, 277

reliefs xiv, 97, 99, 155, 187, 191, 244, 251
res publica 41, 42, 173–4, 178, 182

Sallust 33, 39, 66
Saqqara 49, 88, 117, 123, 187, 276–7
scribes 49, 72, 89, 165
ships 22, 30–31, 55, 70, 78–80, 82, 150, 191, 214, 227–8, 231–2, 234–6
social status xiv, 3, 22, 203, 253, 264, 268
Spartacus 35–6
spells xv, 116–34, 137, 142, 248, 258–9
Strabo 56, 79, 228, 231
Suedius Clemens, T. 44, 177–8
Suetonius xi, xii, 27, 39, 42, 127, 274, 284

tabulae lusoriae see game boards
Tacitus 33, 36–7, 39, 43, 44, 45, 61, 131, 181, 208, 209, 274, 283, 285,
Thera (Santorini) 11–12, 201, 294
Thucydides 31–3, 168, 170
Tiberius 56, 131, 283
tomb paintings 72, 77, 187, 191, 251
Trajan xi, xii, 81, 103

votive offerings xv, 5, 50, 53, 55, 95, 99, 101, 148, 156

Wâdi Abu Markab 69–70, 84
Wâdi el-Hôl 48, 50, 51, 54, 161–3, 219, 221–2, 291
wall paintings xiv, 25, 30–31, 35–6, 38, 66, 82–4, 97–100, 137, 153, 186, 192, 201, 244, 268
writing systems 20–21

Zeus 51–4, 94–6, 98, 106, 148, 153, 154, 198, 200, 295